Law, Governance and Technology Series

Issues in Privacy and Data Protection

Issues in Privacy and Data Protection aims at publishing peer reviewed scientific manuscripts that focus upon issues that engage into an analysis or reflexion related to the consequences of scientific and technological developments upon the private sphere, the personal autonomy and the self-construction of humans with data protection and privacy as anchor points. The objective is to publish both disciplinary, multidisciplinary and interdisciplinary works on questions that relate to experiences and phenomena that can or could be covered by legal concepts stemming from the law regarding the protection of privacy and/or the processing of personal data. Since both the development of science and technology, and in particular information technology (ambient intelligence, robotics, artificial intelligence, knowledge discovery, data mining, surveillance, etc.), and the law on privacy and data protection are in constant frenetic mood of change (as is clear from the many legal conflicts and reforms at hand), we have the ambition to reassemble a series of highly contemporary and forward-looking books, wherein cutting edge issues are analytically, conceptually and prospectively presented.

Pier Giorgio Chiara

The Internet of Things and EU Law

Cybersecurity, Privacy and Data Protection Challenges

Springer

Pier Giorgio Chiara
Cirsfid Alma-AI and Law Department
University of Bologna
Bologna, Italy

ISSN 2352-1902 ISSN 2352-1910 (electronic)
Law, Governance and Technology Series
ISSN 2352-1929 ISSN 2352-1937 (electronic)
Issues in Privacy and Data Protection
ISBN 978-3-031-67662-8 ISBN 978-3-031-67663-5 (eBook)
https://doi.org/10.1007/978-3-031-67663-5

This Springer imprint is published by the registered company Springer Nature Switzerland AG
The registered company address is: Gewerbestrasse 11, 6330 Cham, Switzerland

To Carola

Acknowledgements

This book represents the culmination of a long, complex, but gratifying journey. I have had the opportunity to delve into these fascinating topics (at least, to me) during my PhD studies in the Law, Science and Technology Joint Doctorate—Rights of the Internet of Everything, funded under the Marie Skłodowska-Curie Actions (ITN EJD GA No 814177 EU H2020).

Looking back, beyond rhetoric, I could not have supported this endeavour just relying on my forces. I am genuinely grateful to have had as my mentors Prof. Mark Cole, who heartedly welcomed me at the University of Luxembourg where I spent two enriching years; Prof. Raffaella Brighi, who thoughtfully walked me through the most technical aspects of the research and with whom I am proud to continue my professional journey; and Prof. Ugo Pagallo, who, after the master's thesis, agreed to oversee my doctoral research. Each of them contributed in his and her own special way, giving me the freedom I needed to grow professionally and personally.

A special thanks also goes to Prof. Monica Palmirani for her relentless efforts in coordinating the doctoral programme. Finally, I am grateful to Prof. Massimo Durante, for the time he dedicated to me, patiently disentangling philosophical issues I encountered during my studies. And for the many coffees too.

While I cannot name each and every member of the 'law & technology' community, this multidisciplinary research would not have been as stimulating without the opportunity of constantly learning from brilliant experts met at various international conferences all over Europe.

During these years of research, while attempting to build a professional network, I was so lucky to have met wonderful colleagues whom I can now call friends. Isadora, Yannick, Nadia, Max, Richard, Mirko, Biagio, Francesca, Emanuela, the two Jacopo, Francesco, Liuwen, Orhan, Aiste, Daniela, Stephan: I am so glad to have shared a piece of my journey with you. And to Isadora, Olimpia and Yannick in particular, thank you for always being there. Then I could not forget those I met in Luxembourg who proved to be true friends: Pier Giorgio, Claudia, Lorenzo, Emiliano, Rubens, Reka, and Daniel.

A few words to my friends in Turin, and elsewhere, and to my family, mom, dad, Mimi and Monica: even when I was far away, I always felt you were close.

A final, special, thought goes to Carola, for always finding the right words to defuse my anxieties, for your ironic wit that unfailingly helps me put things into the right perspective and for being able to endure even the most daunting moments.

Contents

1 Introduction 1
References 4

2 The Internet of (Unsecure) Things: Threats and Risks 5
2.1 Defining the Internet of Things 5
2.2 The IoT Architecture Taxonomy 7
2.2.1 Device Layer 8
2.2.2 Network Layer 12
2.2.3 Application Platform Layer 13
2.3 The IoT Security Threat Landscape 14
2.3.1 Device Layer Attacks: Threats on 'Things' 16
2.3.2 Network Layer Attacks: Threats on the 'Internet' 17
2.3.3 Application Layer Attacks: Threats on 'Data' 19
2.3.4 The Missing Piece of the Jigsaw: IoT Supply Chain Security Threats 21
2.4 Conclusion 23
References 24

3 Disentangling (Cyber)Security from the Privacy Debate in the IoT 29
3.1 The Concept of Cybersecurity in the IoT Era: Beyond Information Security? 29
3.2 The IoT Paradigm Shift: The Relationship Between Cybersecurity, Privacy & Data Protection and Safety 36
3.2.1 Privacy and Data Protection in the EU: A Brief Background 36
3.2.2 Cybersecurity and Privacy: An Instrumental, or Infraethical, Perspective 40
3.2.3 Cybersecurity as a Public Good 47
3.2.4 Degrees of Separation Between Cybersecurity and Safety in the IoT 52

3.3 Conclusion 56
References 58

4 The EU Legal Frameworks Regulating IoT Cybersecurity 65
4.1 The NIS Directive and the Indirect Link with the IoT 65
4.1.1 Right Responsibility, Wrong Actors? The NIS Directive's Exclusion of Hardware Manufacturers and Software Developers 76
4.2 The Cybersecurity Act and the IoT: Exploring EU Voluntary Cybersecurity Certification Legal Framework 80
4.2.1 The State of IoT Cybersecurity Certification and Standardisation 90
4.3 EU Product Safety Legislation and IoT Cybersecurity 97
4.3.1 The Radio Equipment Directive, the Delegated Regulation 2022/30 and the IoT 99
4.3.2 The General Product Safety Regulation: Cybersecurity, Safety and the IoT 103
4.3.3 Cybersecurity Requirements in the Medical Devices Regulation 108
4.3.4 The Machinery Regulation and IoT Cybersecurity 111
4.3.5 The Right Answer? 115
4.4 The Revision of the NIS Directive: The NIS2 and the IoT 116
4.4.1 The Broader Scope of the NIS2 117
4.4.2 Vulnerabilities Handling and Disclosure 120
4.4.3 Supply Chain Cybersecurity Management Measures 121
4.5 The Cyber Resilience Act 124
4.5.1 The Scope of the CRA 125
4.5.2 Obligations for Economic Operators 128
4.5.3 Essential Cybersecurity Requirements and Conformity Assessment 131
4.5.4 Enforcement Mechanisms: Market Surveillance 133
4.5.5 Interplay with Other Union Policies 136
4.6 Conclusion 140
References 142

5 Privacy and Data Protection Challenges in IoT Data and Metadata Processing 149
5.1 The Interplay Between EU Privacy and Data Protection Legal Frameworks Concerning IoT Data and Metadata Processing 149
5.1.1 Lawfulness: The Challenges of 'Consent' in IoT Systems 155
5.1.2 Lack of Control and Information Asymmetry: IoT and Transparency 160

5.1.3 Lack of Adequate Security Controls: Eschewing the Scenario of an 'Internet of Insecure Things' 167
5.2 The Role of Encryption Vis-à-Vis the Fundamental Rights to Privacy and Data Protection 172
5.2.1 The Quest for Encryption, Beyond Pseudonymisation: A Technical Perspective 172
5.2.2 State-of-the-Art Encryption and Pseudonymisation: Is It Always About Personal Data? 176
5.2.3 Encryption's Inherent Conflict, Amidst Inbuilt Vulnerabilities and Innovative Methods to Uphold Fundamental Rights 181
5.3 Privacy Risks Despite Encryption: IoT Metadata Analysis and the EU Privacy and Data Protection Legal Frameworks 185
5.3.1 Device and User Identification: An Overview of Fingerprinting and Inferencing Techniques 186
5.3.2 'Private Surveillance': EU Legal Frameworks Applicable to IoT Metadata Analysis 188
5.4 Conclusion 193
References 195

6 Holistic Risk Analysis for IoT 203
6.1 Risk Assessment in EU Data Protection and Cybersecurity: Similarities and Divergences 203
6.1.1 The Data Protection Impact Assessment 'Risk to Rights' Approach 203
6.1.2 Information Security Risk Management Frameworks 209
6.1.3 Towards a Holistic, Fundamental Rights-Based DPIA 216
6.2 Holistic Risk Analysis Methodology for IoT 219
6.2.1 The CNIL DPIA Methodology for IoT Devices 219
6.2.2 A Critical Analysis of the CNIL Model: Consistency with the Holistic 'Risk-to-Rights' Approach 223
6.2.3 A Rights-Based Data Protection Impact Assessment Methodology for IoT Devices 229
6.3 Conclusion 237
References 239

7 The Path Ahead 243
References 252

List of Abbreviations

AI	Artificial Intelligence
AIOTI	Alliance for the Internet of Things Innovation
CJEU	Court of Justice of the European Union
CNIL	Commission Nationale Informatique & Libertés
CRA	Cyber Resilience Act
CSA	Cyber Security Act
DPA	Data Protection Authority
DPIA	Data Protection Impact Assessment
ECCS	European Cybersecurity Certification Scheme
ECHR	European Convention on Human Rights
ENISA	European Union Agency for Cybersecurity
ePD	ePrivacy Directive
ePR	ePrivacy Regulation
EU	European Union
GDPR	General Data Protection Regulation
GPSD	General Product Safety Directive
GPSR	General Product Safety Regulation
HLEG	High-Level Expert Group
ICT	Information and Communication Technologies
IoT	Internet of Things
MD	Machinery Directive
MDR	Medical Devices Regulation
MR	Machinery Regulation
MSA	Market Surveillance Authority
NCA	National Competent Authority
NIS	Network and Information System
RED	Radio Equipment Directive

Chapter 1
Introduction

A consensus on the definition of the Internet of Things (IoT) has not yet been reached. Yet, it is unlikely that a comprehensive overview of the huge and growing class of IoT hardware components can be drawn, since they are less standardised than hardware for personal computers. To make things more complex, the IoT brings together devices with limited CPU, memory and processing power, such as pressure sensors that require small, low-cost hardware to be economically competitive, and devices with powerful processors and large memories. As a result, the first class of devices (resource constrained devices) does not have the necessary memory and computing power to run the most up-to-date and robust cryptographic protocols. Thus, research focuses on so-called "lightweight" cryptographic algorithms, which are more suitable for such constrained contexts. Like the IoT, the concept of resource-constrained devices remains vague as few technical taxonomies exist.

In the era of the Internet of Things, *security* and *privacy* are deeply intertwined. Manifold layers of complexity are under scrutiny. In a scenario where IoT devices physically interact with individuals, legal, ethical and technical aspects of the concepts of 'security', 'safety', 'privacy' and 'data protection' shall be considered, since they are intertwined more than ever before.

Thus, IoT resource-constrained devices not only are easy targets for attacks, but also assets to be exploited in order to launch attacks. Against this background, until the 2022 Commission's proposal for a Regulation on horizontal cybersecurity requirements for products with digital elements (i.e., Cyber Resilience Act), existing and proposed horizontal and vertical, or sectorial, EU legislation did not address the cybersecurity challenges raised by IoT devices and related services at the core. Directive (EU) 2016/1148 (NIS Directive)—the first piece of EU-wide legislation on cybersecurity—and its revision, namely Directive (EU) 2022/2555 (NIS2 Directive) do not specifically and comprehensively address the problem of unsecure connected devices. And neither does Regulation (EU) 2019/881 (Cybersecurity Act).

Furthermore, in order to secure the IoT environment, cybersecurity technologies are deployed to uphold individuals' rights to privacy and protection of personal data.

P. G. Chiara, *The Internet of Things and EU Law*, Issues in Privacy and Data Protection 67, https://doi.org/10.1007/978-3-031-67663-5_1

However, a closer look reveals that the enjoyment of these fundamental rights may be paradoxically jeopardised by these technologies, as they increase the attack surface and therefore introduce new vulnerabilities. Structural IoT data and metadata harvesting, processing and sharing triggers and challenges specific aspects of the EU privacy and data protection law, such as the notions of consent, transparency and profiling.

ENISA as early as in 2017 warned that, without a common EU-wide approach to addressing the cybersecurity risk in IoT, or a common multi-stakeholder model, IoT manufacturers and vendors will inevitably take their own approach in implementing cybersecurity, resulting in fragmentation and a lack of or slow embracement of IoT security standards, technical measures and good practices.[1]

Related to that, when considering the relevant shortcomings in the field of EU (IoT) cybersecurity, the lack of interoperable solutions (i.e., technical standards) is a major obstacle that still hinders IoT wide-spread adoption in the Single Market. This problem has been taken into consideration by the EU Commission noting that "a large number of proprietary or semi-closed solutions to address specific problems have emerged, leading to non-interoperable concepts, based on different architectures and protocols. Consequently, the deployment of truly IoT applications, i.e., where information of connectable 'things' can be flexibly aggregated and scaled, has been limited to a set of 'intranets of things—or goods'".[2]

Finally, with regard to the risks that IoT system may pose to fundamental rights, existing Data Protection Impact Assessments (DPIA) methodologies, under Art. 35 of Regulation (EU) 2016/679 (GDPR), are still anchored to a traditional understanding of privacy which does not encompass the full depth of the innovative GDPR's requirement to assess risks to the rights and freedoms of data subjects—going beyond therefore the right to privacy and protection of personal data as per Art. 7 and 8 of the EU Charter of Fundamental Rights.

A holistic IoT risk analysis methodology should encompass the full breadth of 'security and privacy' considerations, therefore eschewing the scenario of an 'Internet-of-insecure-things'. In the words of EU Commission President von der Leyen, at the 2021 State of the Union Address, "if everything is connected, everything can be hacked. Given that resources are scarce, we have to bundle our forces. And we should not just be satisfied to address the cyber threat, but also strive to become a leader in cybersecurity". Cybersecurity has become one of the most urgent issues of our days. Not only it can be a pre-condition for individuals' safety and fundamentals rights, but it is also necessary to uphold the critical infrastructure, the economy and national security.

Against this backdrop, this book aims to shed light, from a legal, ethical and technical perspective, on the manifold (cyber) security & privacy challenges brought about by the IoT. Specifically, one of the keys that the book offers for analysing these issues is normative, namely the extent to which existing EU

[1] ENISA (2017), p. 53.

[2] European Commission (2021), p. 30.

cybersecurity and data protection legislation provide manufacturers of IoT devices with appropriate obligations with regard to 'security and privacy' issues and, at the same time, foster consumers' trust whilst protecting their rights.

The methodology underpinning this book consists of a multidisciplinary critical literature review, integrating legal, philosophical, and technical reflections. The desk research builds on relevant documents, that is, EU Primary law and Secondary law, including legislation, decisions, recommendations and opinions; EU and national court rulings; scientific publications, as well as position papers of consumer and industry associations.

From a legal perspective, the book touches on issues of EU Law; criminal procedural law; administrative law. These different areas of law are addressed through the lens of 'technology law': the unifying principle of technology law is to deal with the adequacy of the regulation that faces a risk posed by a particular technology, through the study and understanding of the latter. In the words of Guihot, "it is the synchronicity of the technology, risk and regulatory response that defines technology law. [. . .] It is the speed of change that new technologies can bring, the systemic nature of the threats and risks that they pose and the depth of impact that those changes have the potential to create that requires such a broad mix of regulatory tools to respond".[3]

Accordingly, the aim underlying this volume is to substantiate the strong statement of the c.a.s.e. collective's manifesto with respect to research in the field of 'security' in Europe: "the goal of a critical intellectual is not only to observe, but also to actively open spaces of discussion and political action, as well as to provide the analytical tools, concepts and categories for possible alternative discourses and practices".[4]

Related to that, following the critical approach of the Frankfurt School' philosophers,[5] this book aims to examine the relevant and applicable law in its dependence on society, that is, the philosophical and technical context where the legal framework lies,[6] to assess the impacts it has on the background it regulates. Including in the analysis (Chap. 3) ethics' toolbox ensures the alignment of security research and development with principles like fundamental rights,[7] such as data protection and privacy, and democracy, "instead of quelling these in the name of security".[8]

Against this backdrop, the major hurdle faced by this analytical effort consisted in doing research in a fast-evolving technical and legal landscape, with particular

---

[3]Guihot (2019), p. 332.

[4]C.A.S.E. Collective (2006), p. 476.

[5]Horkheimer (2002), pp. 188–243; Horkheimer and Adorno (2002).

[6]Walter Benjamin (2004), p. 251: in its critique of violence, Benjamin states that it is "the philosophy of its history – [. . .] because only the idea of its development makes possible a critical, discriminating, and decisive approach to its temporal data". Notwithstanding, the abovementioned quote should not be understood as a methodological commitment to the legal dialectic highlighted by Benjamin in terms of law-making—law-preserving.

[7]Stingelin et al. (2012), p. 3.

[8]Leese et al. (2019), p. 63.

regard to EU cybersecurity legal frameworks. For the latter has been substantially created by EU legislature in the last years of the second decade of this century. And it is still evolving to this day.

'Privacy'—to include also EU data protection law—and 'security'—by which I refer both to traditional information security and cybersecurity paradigms as addressed in Chap. 3—are two issues particularly germane to the IoT sector. A joint discussion of these two broad issues is justified from a twofold point of view. First, technical literature traditionally handles privacy as the flip side of the security coin. Second, from a strictly legal perspective, an artificial distinction between these realms brings detrimental effects given the often deeply interrelated obligations and procedures.[9]

'Risk' is unavoidably the *fil rouge* of this work. Information security's basic components, namely vulnerabilities—threats—risks, are extrapolated and assessed using an interdisciplinary method that takes into account not only the technical aspects of security, but also the legal and philosophical ones.

In other words, vulnerabilities are analysed from a twofold perspective. Chapter 2 delves into IoT devices' vulnerabilities—or weaknesses—from a technical standpoint, whereas Chap. 5 explores them from a legal perspective (in particular, taking into account EU data protection and privacy law).

Taking this into account, a holistic risk analysis methodology is introduced in Chap. 6, with a view to mitigating cybersecurity and data protection risks, including specific IoT threat and vulnerability scenarios.

References

Benjamin W (2004) Walter Benjamin: Selected Writings, 1: 1913-1926. Harvard University Press, Cambridge

C.A.S.E. Collective (2006) Critical approaches to security in Europe: a networked manifesto. Secur Dialogue 37:443–487. https://doi.org/10.1177/0967010606073085

ENISA (2017) Baseline Security Recommendations for IoT in the context of Critical Information Infrastructures

European Commission (2021) Rolling Plan for ICT Standardisation 2021

Guihot M (2019) Coherence in technology law. Law Innov Technol 11(2):311–342

Horkheimer M (2002) Critical theory: selected essays. The Continuum Publishing Company, New York

Horkheimer M, Adorno TW (2002) Dialectic of enlightenment: philosophical fragments. Stanford University Press

Leese M et al (2019) Putting critique to work: ethics in EU security research. Secur Dialogue 50:59–76. https://doi.org/10.1177/0967010618809554

Mantelero A et al (2021) The common EU approach to personal data and cybersecurity regulation. Int J Law Inf Technol 28:4

Stingelin N et al (2012) Roles and functions of ethics advisors/ethics advisory boards in EC-funded projects. https://ec.europa.eu/research/participants/data/ref/h2020/other/hi/ethics-guide-advisors_en.pdf

[9] Mantelero et al. (2021), p. 2.

Chapter 2
The Internet of (Unsecure) Things: Threats and Risks

2.1 Defining the Internet of Things

Although the first defining attempts date back to the late 1990s,[1] it is challenging today to provide an all-encompassing definition of the Internet of Things, widely known by its acronym "IoT", given its technical and structural complexity. Yet, there is a solid consensus around IoT twofold constitutive nature: an enabling global technology and infrastructure connecting the physical and the virtual dimensions.[2,3]

According to ISO/IEC, the IoT is the revolutionary "enabling technology that consists of many supporting technologies",[4] to name a few, information and communication networking technologies (e.g., cloud computing, fog computing, edge computing, 5G), sensing and connecting technologies (e.g., wireless sensor networks, radio-frequency identification (RFID), Bluetooth, GPS), software technologies (e.g., artificial intelligence), and device/hardware technologies.

On a lower level, the IoT is a network of "things", embedded with software intelligence, which are connected to the Internet.[5] Each of these technologies has its own vulnerabilities: the ultimate challenge of IoT security is securing the chain of all those technologies as the security resistance of an IoT application will be judged based on its weakest point which is usually referred to as its Achilles' heel.[6,7]

---

[1] Kevin Ashton "invented" the term "IoT" in a presentation delivered at Procter & Gamble in 1999 concerning the integration of RFID technology in the supply chain of P&G. The definition gained momentum and was resumed by MIT (2001) and later by ITU (2005).

[2] Nativi et al. (2020), p. 10.

[3] Nativi et al. (2020), p. 10.

[4] ISO/IEC (2018).

[5] Rayes and Salam (2019), p. 2.

[6] Bertino (2018), p. 8; Rayes and Salam (2019), p. 235.

[7] Rayes and Salam (2019), p. 235; Bertino (2018), p. 8.

P. G. Chiara, *The Internet of Things and EU Law*, Issues in Privacy and Data Protection 67, https://doi.org/10.1007/978-3-031-67663-5_2

In order to unravel such definition, it is worthwhile decoupling the most generic components which enable this network of "things", as addressed in the next section: sensors, to collect data in the environment nearby; actuators, to act upon said environment; identifiers, to identify data sources; and, software elements, to process data.

Furthermore, it is worth clarifying from the outset the relationship between the IoT and cyber-physical systems (CPS), which integrates computational and physical processes, to dispel any ambiguity which still gives rise to speculation about the scope of these concepts. The U.S. National Institution of Standards and Technology (NIST) defines cyber-physical systems as "smart systems that include engineered interacting networks of physical and computational components".[8] Given the above-mentioned provisional definitions of IoT, it makes sense to conclude that both CPS and IoT can be subsumed under the broader category of digital Information Communication Technologies (ICTs).

Marwedel noted that, "[t]o some extent, it is a matter of preferences whether the linking of physical objects to the cyber-world is called CPS or IoT. Taken together, CPS and IoT include most of the future applications of IT".[9] Such understanding of these concepts is reflected in the words of Denardis, who believes that the term CPS, albeit imperfect, is better suited to describe "this phenomenon of blurring physical and digital domains, simply because IoT, over time, has in popular discourse become synonymous with consumer markets, thereby obfuscating the larger phenomenon of embedded devices in critical sectors including agriculture, defense, transportation, and manufacturing".[10]

For the purpose of this work, the term IoT will be preferred to CPS, as legislative texts and legal doctrine increasingly rely on it when referring to the next generation of embedded and interconnected ICT systems.

The pervasive, or ubiquitous, multi-purpose and multi-device computing brought about by the IoT is indeed leading to a paradigm shift, which is a major evolutionary step in Internet history. "Similar to how the inception of the World Wide Web transformed access to knowledge and spurred entirely new industries, cyber-physical systems are now similarly transformational".[11] Thus, some prefer the term Internet

[8]NIST (2016), p. xiii.

[9]Marwedel (2021), p. 4.

[10]Denardis (2020), pp. 27–28.

[11]Denardis (2020), p. 26: against the background of the contextual heterogeneity of these systems, Denardis proposes a fourfold taxonomy which aims to unveil common technical characteristics: (1) the digitisation of everyday objects, including consumer IoT devices and objects connected in municipalities; (2) the Internet of Self, which includes objects in close proximity to the body, such as wearable technologies and digitally connected medical devices; (3) the industrial Internet of Things or "Fourth Industrial Revolution," a term that captures the cyber-embeddedness of objects in industrial sectors; and (4) emergent cyber-physical systems, which include material objects that are born digital, such as additive manufacturing (also called 3D printing), robotics, and augmented reality.

of Everything (IoE),[12] as it brings together things, processes, people—as end-nodes of this network—and data, both related to the environment and the individuals.[13] Regardless of the various classificatory attempts, the IoT is the next step of the transformation of Internet, as it deals with technologies, processes, people and massive real-life interactions.

> Whether one uses the term "Internet of Everything" or "Internet of things" or "embedded systems" or "cyber-physical systems" or "network of everything" is not as important as acknowledging the very real underlying technological transformation—the fundamental integration of material-world systems and digital systems.[14]

In other words, an ecosystem where everyone and everything is connected. From an epistemological viewpoint, IoT ubiquitous computing renders the physical—virtual dichotomy rather anachronistic, as, in the words of Floridi,

> we no longer live online or offline but onlife, that is, we increasingly live in that special space, or infosphere, that is seamlessly analogue and digital, offline and online. If this seems confusing, perhaps an analogy may help to convey the point. Imagine someone asks whether the water is sweet or salty in the estuary where the river meets the sea. Clearly, that someone has not understood the special nature of the place. Our mature information societies are growing in such a new, liminal place, like mangroves flourishing in brackish water. And in these 'mangrove societies', machine-readable data, new forms of smart agency and onlife interactions are constantly evolving, because our technologies are perfectly fit to take advantage of such a new environment, often as the only real natives.[15]

All in all, a functional, high-level and all-encompassing definition of the 'IoT', clustering the elements described above, could be the one recently provided for in by Regulation (EU) 2023/2854 (Data Act). At recital 14 of the Data Act, the term 'Internet of Things' is used interchangeably with 'connected devices'. Accordingly, these digital technologies are characterised by the fact that "obtain, generate or collect, by means of their components or operating systems, data concerning their performance, use or environment and that are able to communicate those data via an electronic communications service, a physical connection, or on-device access".[16]

2.2 The IoT Architecture Taxonomy

The three-layered architecture of IoT presented below builds on Rayes and Salam's[17] taxonomy: due to its simplified configuration, it appears to be the best in order to provide the clearest possible overview of a reference model for the IoT. A further

---

[12] CISCO (2013).

[13] Iannacci (2018).

[14] Denardis (2020), p. 28.

[15] Floridi (2018), p. 1.

[16] Art. 2(5), Regulation (EU) 2023/2854.

[17] Rayes and Salam (2019).

strength of this taxonomy lies in its extreme flexibility, for it can be combined with other existing IoT model architectures, such as the one of the European Network and Information Security Agency (ENISA),[18] the International Telecommunication Union (ITU),[19] the Alliance for the Internet of Things Innovation (AIOTI),[20] the US National Institute of Standards and Technology (NIST)[21] and International Standardisation Organization (ISO).[22]

These high-level models are composed of several layers of abstraction, from the three layers of AIOTI, through the four of ENISA and ITU, to the five of NIST and the six of ISO/IEC. The three-layer model that follows serves to systematically identify and break down the IoT into its core components in light of the analysis of security threats to these assets of Sect. 2.3.

2.2.1 Device Layer

The first layer of the IoT architecture considers the "things" in IoT. Sensing, actuating and unique identification are the three key requirements for this level.[23] At the onset of IoT data gathering, sensors play a pivotal role. These devices, possibly embedded in other devices, are designed to *sense* the immediate environment.

In other words, they generate a practical output, in the form of an electrical measurement, reacting to a specified measurand, a physical quantity or a property.[24] Accordingly, three different set of issues arise: emission or transduction (with regard to the generation of electromagnetic signals); susceptibility (with regard to possible breakdowns due to unwanted emissions);[25] coupling (with regard to the manner which emissions reach targets, such as devices).[26]

Besides sensors, RFID and video tracking are other two technologies through which the surrounding environment is captured or monitored. RFID technology hinges on radio waves to collect data, through a 'reader', from so-called 'tags'—appointed on objects. Video tracking instead captures video feeds of a particular device for short timeframes.[27]

---

[18] ENISA (2017).

[19] ITU-T (2012).

[20] AIOTI (2018).

[21] Voas (2016).

[22] ISO/IEC (2016).

[23] Rayes and Salam (2019), pp. 67–69.

[24] National Research Council (1995), p. 10.

[25] EU directive 2004/108/EC (previously 89/336/EEC) on EMC defines the rules for the distribution of electric devices within the European Union.

[26] Ben Dhia et al. (2006).

[27] Rayes and Salam (2019), pp. 76–80.

This data collection process involves a phenomenon called transduction: sensing technologies convert signals gathered from the physical world into electrical signals. Any kind of physical input, such as motion, sound, pressure, or temperature, can be sampled, encoded, and represented in binary code for transmission over a network.[28] Once data is captured, actuators convert input data collected at sensor-level to action (e.g., motion).[29,30] In other words, they "acts" on the physical world, "converting an electrical form into tangible manipulation of the physical world".[31]

The IoT ecosystem encompasses a wide spectrum of *things*, from peripherals with high computational power and/or capacities to highly resource-constrained devices. Historically, devices connected to the internet could have been grouped into a homogeneous class, that is, fully capable computers or peripherals with endless sources of power, embedding big and costly hardware. This classification is no longer true within the IoT network, which combines devices with limited CPU, memory and processing power e.g., pressure sensors, and devices with powerful processors, large memory and replenishable sources for energy e.g., smartphones.

In fact, a comprehensive overview of the huge class of embedded systems' hardware components[32] could hardly be drawn since they are far less standardised than hardware for personal computers.[33] The exhibition of significant differences in available execution environments, processing, and storage capabilities would add an extra layer of difficulty. In other words, a structured approach is needed in order to uniformly and transparently deploy application components onto a large number of heterogeneous devices.[34]

An IETF report listed the prominent facets to the constraints on nodes, or devices, often applied in combination. They are constraints on the maximum code complexity (ROM/Flash); constraints on the size of state and buffers (RAM); constraints on the amount of computation feasible in a period of time ("processing power"); constraints on the available power; and constraints on the user interface and accessibility in deployment (ability to set keys, update software, etc.).[35] Whereas constraints in networks may include low achievable bitrate, high packet loss and high variability of packet loss (delivery rate).[36]

IETF RFC 7228 designed a taxonomy[37] of constrained devices based on two dimensions: processing power and memory. It recognises three classes of devices

---

[28]Denardis (2020), pp. 46–47.

[29]Rayes and Salam (2019), p. 82.

[30]id.

[31]Denardis (2020), p. 46.

[32]Marwedel (2018), p. 126.

[33]Pagallo et al. (2017), pp. 74–75.

[34]Vögler et al. (2015), p. 78.

[35]Bormann et al. (2014), p. 5.

[36]ibid, 6.

[37]Even though they both belong to the classification methods process; taxonomies are substantially different from typologies. The former deals with abstract and theoretical framework, built upon

accordingly: class '0' devices are very constrained in that they do not possess the resources required to communicate directly with the Internet in a secure manner; class '1' devices are quite constrained in that they cannot easily talk to other Internet nodes employing a full protocol stack (e.g., HTTP; TLS; etc.) but they are capable enough to use a protocol stack specifically designed for constrained nodes; class '2' devices are less constrained and fundamentally capable of supporting most of the same protocol stacks as used on notebooks or servers.[38]

The involvement of sensors with limited energy and storage inevitably brings several security and privacy considerations in terms of authentication, mobility, wirelessness, embedded use, diversity, and scale. Without dwelling on these issues too extensively at this point, as they are addressed in the following chapters, it is worth bringing forth one major consequence of these constraints regarding network security.

Computational power[39] in IoT systems can be plotted in a scalable fashion, from cloud services to resource-constrained nodes. "Much of the computational power used to aggregate, process and provide data to external utilities, such as other services or humans, resides in the core of the network in the form of cloud platforms. Towards the edge of the network, computational power drops off as we shift from intermediate aggregators, such as smart phones or local base stations, to low powered sensors with restricted memory".[40]

Constrained devices always resort to the cloud—or gateways, fog devices, etc.—for outsourced storage and computation.[41] Nevertheless, they may not have the necessary computational power to embed security software or to implement appropriate technical and organisational measures such as encryption, authentication and pseudonymisation[42] in order to secure communication channels. In particular, encryption is the cornerstone of network security protocols.

A study by HP Fortify reported that 70% of the devices do not encrypt communications to the Internet and local network, while half of the devices' mobile applications perform unencrypted communications to the cloud, Internet or local network.[43] Related to that, Cheruvu et al. suppose that in a constrained scenario, the percentage of security-related computing might be more than half of the overall device's resources, whilst it typically stands at around 15% of the total resources' cost.[44]

"ideal types", whilst the latter categorises constructive and empirical entities. Since the analysis at stake deals with inner mechanisms and components, it seems natural to adopt a taxonomical approach to the problem.

[38] Bormann et al. (2014), pp. 8–9.

[39] Durante (2021).

[40] Hegarty and Haggerty (2020), p. 632.

[41] Zhou et al. (2017), pp. 26–33.

[42] European Union Agency for Fundamental Rights (2018).

[43] Hewlett Packard (2014).

[44] Cheruvu et al. (2020), p. 11.

The need to secure data transfer in IoT networks led to investing particular efforts in setting up lightweight[45] protocols suited to the needs of constrained nodes/ devices. A successful application protocol for IoT devices is the Constrained Application Protocol (CoAP), since it can be used on top of the IPv6 infrastructure[46] through the 6LoWPAN protocol (which enables IPv6 in resource-constrained scenarios), and it can be coupled with Datagram Transport Layer Security (DTLS) to encrypt and authenticate messages.[47]

According to some authors, a decisive cause for such constrained hardware is purely economic: "to allow mass deployment of IoT devices, businesses want the cost per unit to be as inexpensive as possible".[48] Moreover, the limited size and computational power can be affected by other reasons, such as environmental (e.g., meteorological sensors in remote and hard-weather condition areas) or contextual to the system in which they are embedded.[49] In other words, to scale up the spread of affordable and physically feasible Internet technologies, the characteristics of the nodes on which (IoT) networks are built need to be scaled down.

A promising answer to the above-mentioned problems may come from research into chips' architecture. Research published in August 2022 in Nature presented NeuRRAM, a resistive random-access memory (RRAM)-based chip for supporting AI applications on edge devices.[50] "Currently, AI computing is both power hungry and computationally expensive. Most AI applications on edge devices involve moving data from the devices to the cloud, where the AI processes and analyses it. [...] By reducing power consumption needed for AI inference at the edge, this NeuRRAM chip could lead to more robust, smarter and accessible edge devices and smarter manufacturing. It could also lead to better data privacy as the transfer of data from devices to the cloud comes with increased security risks".[51]

In this respect, the announcement of an EU Chips Act[52] will be pivotal to the creation of a European chip ecosystem. This will include production, as well as connecting the EU's research, design and testing capacities.[53]

While awaiting a full-scale deployment of technical solutions such as lightweight encryption or NeuRRAM-like chips, the present is made up of IoT systems with often unsecure constrained hardware. Even though it may sound trivial, as many devices connecting to the IoT are constrained, the networks connecting them will

[45] It means that the algorithm under scrutiny has a small-implementation code.

[46] Sehgal et al. (2012).

[47] Pittoli et al. (2018), p. 121.

[48] Siddiqui et al. (2021), p. 2.

[49] Stapko (2008), p. 85.

[50] Wan et al. (2022).

[51] Patringenaru (2022) https://ucsdnews.ucsd.edu/pressrelease/Nature_bioengineering_2022.

[52] European Commission (2021), p. 4.

[53] See https://ec.europa.eu/info/strategy/priorities-2019-2024/europe-fit-digital-age/european-chips-act_en.

also be constrained.[54] Therefore, from a methodological viewpoint, this book relies on the assumption that IoT systems always involve constrained technologies, which are typically sensors at the device layer regardless of potentially unconstrained technologies connected to these systems. And this brings with it security and privacy issues.

2.2.2 *Network Layer*

The intent here is not to disentangle the architectural intricacies underlying the IoT network layer, as it exceeds the boundaries of this book. Rather, this sub-section is preoccupied with presenting a general overview over main IoT network models and protocols. Since this layer is prone to manifold attacks (e.g., man in the middle, spoofing, sniffing etc.), network security is particularly important to IoT security (see Sect. 2.3.2).

Data are seamlessly and oftentimes unsuspectingly collected, processed and shared in IoT networks. "From sensors to gateways and from gateways to data centres in enterprises, or from sensors to gateways for residential services such as video from home monitoring systems to the homeowner's smartphone while he's in a coffee shop".[55]

At a higher layer of abstraction, the network layer answers the question *how* IoT systems' single components *communicate* within the Internet infrastructure. Accordingly, such communication hinges on the traditional OSI model and the TCP/IP protocol.[56] Whereas IPv4 could provide for 4.3 billion addresses, IPv6 has room for 2128 or 340 trillion trillion trillion addresses. Notably, the ITU does not necessarily consider IP as a *constituent* part of the IoT since its network infrastructure might be realised through "evolving networks, such as next generation networks (NGN)".[57]

For the sake of simplicity, IoT data transmission and processing scenarios are plotted in this network layer section in a scalable fashion. Data might firstly be processed *at the edge* (edge computing): in other words, close to the devices who collected them. Data can then be transmitted to the "fog layer" (fog computing) and finally to the more widely known cloud computing.

Edge computing adopts a distributed approach, for the data processing happens 'at the edge', that is, locally in the 'things' where such information is collected.[58] Importantly, edge computing still resorts to the cloud. However, from a cybersecurity and data protection perspective, the 'edge paradigm' may reduce several risks, as

---

[54] Siddiqui et al. (2021), p. 3.

[55] Rayes and Salam (2019), p. 7.

[56] Alani (2014). The OSI model provides for end-to-end connectivity detailing the procedure for packetising, addressing, transmitting, routing and receiving data at the destination.

[57] ITU-T (2012), p. 4.

[58] van der Mulen (2018).

data would be encrypted locally—if lightweight protocols are in place, as shown above—"and translated into a secure communication protocol before being sent to the data center or storage resources shared in the cloud".[59]

Fog computing is conceptually similar to edge and cloud computing[60] and can be defined as a "layered model for enabling ubiquitous access to a shared continuum of scalable computing resources; [it] facilitates the deployment of distributed, latency-aware applications and services, and consists of fog nodes (physical or virtual), residing between smart end-devices and centralised (cloud) services".[61] In other words, fog computing's architecture employs devices—which can be independent components or could be built on top of existing gateways—to carry out large part of computation (usually, pre-processing), storage and communication activities before forwarding data to the cloud.

Fog computing, therefore, is a layer of computation between the device and the cloud: "[c]loud computing is brought closer to the data sources, the Things[:] *Cloud* becomes *Fog* when it is closer to *Things*, pun intended. [...] Fog augments the Cloud to achieve the required pervasiveness and reliability required by rapid mobility in IoT"[62] .The ever-increasing and ubiquitous IoT data sharing showed the need of augmenting and, at the same time, distributing the infrastructure. Processing and storage functions have been progressively moved closer to the "things".

Albeit fog and cloud domains bear striking similarities—starting from the fact that they are both virtualised environments, they do differ in terms of location, mobility and computing capacity. Firstly, fog devices are located in proximity to the smart objects (unlike the "far" cloud servers), resulting in quicker responses; secondly, as the location of the smart things changes, the respective fog domain's virtual machines must be located on the closest fog devices; thirdly, fog devices have a lower computing power than cloud servers.[63]

2.2.3 *Application Platform Layer*

On a preliminary note, the distinction between the application layer of the TCP/IP model and the IoT application level is substantial and crucial: whilst the former pertains to the IoT Network level, the latter aims to assure abstraction across the numerous devices and sources of data. In other words, its function is to integrate all enabling technologies and constituting components—transcending vertical solutions—into a common, open, and multi-application environment. It allows for the management and control of a range of systems and processes: "the operation of

[59] Poletti (2022), p. 180.

[60] Yi et al. (2015), pp. 37–42.

[61] Iorga et al. (2018), p. 2.

[62] ibid., p. 157.

[63] Ibid., p. 225.

this platform requires a comprehensive and diverse set of requisites to gather relevant data, analyse it, and create actionable insights”.[64]

The key features of this level can be grouped in 4 macro areas: (i) traditional management (e.g., configuring, deploying, performance monitoring, security management); (ii) application management (e.g., software/firmware installation, parching, debugging); (iii) application development (e.g., data management, temporary caching, permanent storage); (iv) application services (e.g., data analytics, subscriptions and notification).[65] Therefore, the “application level” is responsible for monitoring and controlling IoT elements in IoT’s device, network and processing layers.

From a (EU) data protection perspective (Chap. 5), the above reflects one part of the conundrum raised by IoT data sharing and processing, that being the difficult of allocating accountability, and therefore responsibility and liability, to the manifold stakeholders along IoT supply chain (i.e., device and integrated device manufacturers, application developers, software development houses, social platforms, further data recipients, data platforms, and standardisation bodies[66])< in terms of (personal) data processing.

2.3 The IoT Security Threat Landscape

This section highlights the main security threats affecting IoT constrained and unconstrained devices. The goal is to comprehensively identify all security threats. This includes vulnerabilities in both the back-end system, at the device level, and the web service it interacts with. The so-called threat landscape has been classified in relation to the consequences the attack scenarios pose to (i) the IoT system itself (service compromising and sensing domain attacks), (ii) to IoT system’s enabling technologies (cloud and fog computing) or (iii) to the underlying data sharing (packets crafting, packets alteration, traffic analysis). Thus, the horizontal nature of security applies to all the elements of the IoT taxonomy presented above.

Since the aim of this book is to study baseline IoT security and privacy aspects in a horizontal and cross-sectorial fashion, this section will not dwell too extensively on the diverse requirements and challenges that different application domains face. Thus, the health sector has different needs than agriculture or domotic sectors. Related to that, same cybersecurity threats have to be assessed in relation to the different deployment scenarios, for the assets that may be impacted by such threats vary in criticality.

Albeit the security threats under scrutiny are the same as “traditional” IT technologies, previous sections have shown that IoT complex architecture is to several

[64] ibid., p. 181.
[65] Ibid., 182.
[66] Poletti (2022), p. 177.

extents different from conventional networks. Therefore, holistic mitigation techniques that take into account the vulnerabilities of all the IoT layers must be adopted to secure these open architectures.[67]

ENISA, building on its 'horizontal' threat taxonomy, tackled IoT security threats for the first time in 2017. The report groups IoT security threats under 7 macro-areas: (i) nefarious activity/abuse (e.g., DDoS, malware, attacks on privacy, exploit kits, etc.); (ii) eavesdropping/interception (e.g., man-in-the-middle, IoT communication protocol hijacking, network reconnaissance, etc.); (iii) outages (e.g., devices/hardware failures, system failures, network outage, etc.); (iv) damages/loss IT assets (e.g., data leakage); (v) failures/malfunctions (e.g., third party failures, software vulnerabilities); (vi) disasters (e.g., natural/environmental disasters); (vii) physical attacks (e.g., device tampering, sabotage).

According to the different application domain, security threats have different potential impacts. Therefore, the impact of each threat has been determined "by calculating a weighted average of the responses from the interviewees, which were based on a five-step scale that ranged from no importance to crucial importance".[68]

ENISA's sevenfold taxonomy has indeed several strengths. It provides a systematic and comprehensive overview of the threats that can affect all the relevant assets in a IoT ecosystem: IoT devices, other IoT ecosystem devices, platform & backend, applications and services and finally network infrastructure and the information collected and shared *via* communication channels.

Yet, for the purposes of this book, it could be questioned whether the type-threat *attacks on privacy* can be subsumed under the first cluster i.e., nefarious activity/abuse. 'Attacks on privacy' is generically described as a threat affecting "both the privacy of the user and the exposure of network elements to unauthorised personnel".[69] Within the same category, ENISA lists malware, DDOS attacks, modification of information, targeted attacks, counterfeit by malicious devices and exploit kits.

Chapter 3 will argue that cyber and information security requirements would be the 'infrastructure', so to speak, of technical norms, controls and rules that are there to facilitate (or hinder, if not well implemented) the right to privacy and data protection. The GDPR defines a 'personal data breach' as "a breach of security leading to the accidental or unlawful destruction, loss, alteration, unauthorised disclosure of, or access to, personal data transmitted, stored or otherwise processed".[70] Therefore, it can be argued that threats to fundamental rights e.g., privacy and data protection, can result from the combination of, and, as a consequence of, *every* macro-area of the ENISA cybersecurity threat landscape.

Against this backdrop, *attacks on privacy*, if we were to use ENISA's classification, would pertain to a different level of abstraction and it should not be placed within the macro-category *nefarious activity/abuse*. For this reason, the model that

---

[67] Rizvi et al. (2018), p. 164.

[68] ENISA (2017), p. 33.

[69] ibid., p. 34.

[70] Regulation (EU) 2016/679, Art. 4(12).

follows only takes into consideration the threats posed to systems' cybersecurity, whereas privacy and data protection will be addressed later in Chap. 5.

2.3.1 Device Layer Attacks: Threats on 'Things'

Sensor nodes usually use ad hoc network technology to dynamically change the network topology, allowing communication with the outer world. Sensed data is sent to fog devices; albeit a direct connection with fog devices—through wires—is possible, sensor nodes often use wireless communication due to the diversity of the deployment environment. In this scenario, attackers can easily eavesdrop on communication between these nodes. Furthermore, the attacker can directly access the related attributes of the device through physical attacks, and then start a further attack, such as tag cloning and spoofing attacks. For example, RFID technology is widely used in this layer: attackers can destroy communication between the reader and RFID tag, e.g., through RF jamming. In general terms, the attack of the perception layer usually aims at destroying the data collection and communication.[71] This section presents four types of attacks that may occur at either IoT device or network architecture layer, following the IoT taxonomy of Sect. 2.2: jamming, vampire, select-forwarding, sinkhole.

The *jamming* attack causes a disruption in the service by interfering with the legitimate signals exchanged in the connection between the smart objects and the fog device. Because of interference at the connection level, from a classificatory standpoint, it can be also considered as a network layer attack. It can mainly take on two forms: receiver jamming or sender jamming. The former degrades the quality of the received signal: "as a result, the receiving end does not acknowledge the reception of these damaged packets and waits for the sender to retransmit those packets".[72] The latter "prevents the neighbouring objects from transmitting their packets as they sense the wireless channel to be busy and back off waiting for the channel to become idle".[73] Jamming attacks can also be classified according to the different strategies that a malicious agent may follow to attack. The best known being constant, deceptive, reactive and random jamming.

The *vampire* attack takes advantage of the fact that the environment of the device/physical/perception layer is generally restricted in terms of resource and power, as seen above. Therefore, the resource-constrained devices 'sleep' to prolong life. A malicious agent could misbehave to force IoT resource-constrained nodes to consume extra amounts of power so that they run out of battery earlier.[74] In other words, attackers can keep the node in working state, by preventing it from switching to

[71] Chen et al. (2018).

[72] Rayes and Salam (2019), p. 228.

[73] Ibid., p. 228.

[74] Id., p. 230.

sleep, to accelerate the consumption of energy. This particular attack is also known as *denial of sleep*. Other vampire attacks differ to the extent that they use different strategies to drain power e.g., flooding attack, carrousel and stretch attacks.

The *selective-forwarding* attack occurs when the device cannot send its generated data packets directly to the fog layer but has to rely on other devices that lie along the path toward the fog device to deliver those packets. Against this background, the malicious device would not forward a part of the packets received. In a constrained scenario, this attack is likely to be successful if mitigation solutions are not deployed: path redundancy is one of those, where packets are forwarded to neighbouring devices multiple times in order to get to the fog device.

The *sinkhole* attack, in a similar fashion to the *selective-forwarding* attack, operates through a malicious device claiming to have the shortest path to the fog device. In so doing, it attracts all neighbouring devices that do not have the transmission capacity to reach the fog layer. Hence, they forward their packets to that malicious actor and count on that device to deliver their data. As a result, all the communication that stems from the neighbouring nodes flows through this malicious node. Needless to say, if the data packets are not encrypted, the malicious node has the ability to look at the content of all the forwarded packets.[75]

2.3.2 Network Layer Attacks: Threats on the 'Internet'

The focus, now, is on attacks that typically characterise the network level. There are many kinds of networks in the IoT, Internet is just one of them. Different networks use different protocols and are run by different devices, so the attacks on the network also vary. The most common network attack is the Denial of Service (DoS) which can exhaust network resources and affect the availability of network service. This section delves into traditional IT network attacks that can specifically affect IoT devices, such as distributed denial of service (DDoS), man-in-the-middle, replay, sniffing/eavesdropping and key logger.

Distributed Denial of Service (DDoS) attacks perhaps have become the best known and feared threat in the IoT domain, as the magnitude of the impact it could attain is unforeseeable. Several existing research works have investigated these increasing threats.[76] When such an attack is successful, users of a system or service are not able to access the relevant information, services or other resources.

This stage can be accomplished by exhausting the service or overloading the component of the network infrastructure by access requests. Malicious actors increased the number of attacks by targeting more sectors with different motives. While defence mechanisms and strategies are becoming more robust, malicious

[75] Id., p. 233.

[76] Cozzi et al. (2018), p. 161; Antonakakis et al. (2017); Minn Pa et al. (2015).

actors are also advancing their technical skills.[77] In particular, IoT's vulnerability to such cyberattacks shall be observed from a twofold standpoint. On the one hand, 5G connectivity supports localised DDoS, "where an attacker interferes with the connectivity of a specific area covered by a slice through a set of compromised devices"; on the other, resource-constrained devices often lack necessary security techniques and controls to counter these threats.[78]

The *Man-in-the-Middle (MitM)* attack requires the attacker to place himself between two communicating parties and secretly forward messages for them, while the two original parties trust they are communicating securely and without any intermediation. The malicious actor can then monitor and eventually modify the information content. Albeit similar attacking patterns have always existed in the physical dimension long before digitisation, IoT data sharing brought MitM to a whole new level.[79]

A *Replay* attack takes place when a malicious actor eavesdrops on a secure network communication, intercepts it, and then fraudulently delays or resends it to misdirect the receiver into doing what the hacker wants. The added danger of replay attacks is that a hacker doesn't even need advanced skills to decrypt a message after capturing it from the network, as the attack could be successful simply by resending the whole thing.[80]

Sniffing is a popular attack used by malicious parties to capture and analyse network communication information. With sniffing, a malicious actor is able to eavesdrop data from network layers and, as a consequence, to link and steal valuable information.[81]

Lastly, *Key logger* is a piece of hardware or a software programme that captures everything a user types on the keyboard.[82]

Since the IoT taxonomy presented fog and cloud computing within the network layer, it seems appropriate to emphasise relevant cloud and fog domain attacks. The *hidden-channel attack* exploits shared hardware components, such as the cache, among the Virtual Machines (VMs) running on the same server: as a result, data could be leaked across VMs that are hosted by the same server.[83] The *VM migration attack* exploits VM migrations from one server to another, which is useful *per se* when a server needs to go offline for maintenance or for patch installation. The malicious agent either attacks the module which is responsible for managing the migration process by exploiting a bug in the software or attacks the network links over which the VM is moved (*via* a sniffing or a man-in-the-middle attack).[84]

---

[77] ENISA (2020a), p. 2.

[78] ENISA (2021), p. 69. See also ENISA (2023), p. 97.

[79] See https://www.enisa.europa.eu/topics/csirts-in-europe/glossary/man-in-the-middle.

[80] See https://www.kaspersky.com/resource-center/definitions/replay-attack.

[81] ENISA (2019), p. 59.

[82] ENISA (2010), p. 17.

[83] Rayes and Salam (2019), p. 217.

[84] Ibid., pp. 220–221.

The *theft-of-service attack* materialises when a malicious VM deceives the hypervisor by getting assigned more resources than it is supposed to receive. The other VMs—the targets of the attack—then get allocated a smaller share of resources than they should actually obtain, which in turn degrades their performance.[85] The *VM escape attack* exploits, again, a software bug in the hypervisor in order to circumvent VM isolation, which prevents access to VMs data from other VMs hosted by the same server.[86] Finally, *insider attacks* consider the case when cloud data centre administrators unlawfully access and modify data.[87]

Albeit fog and cloud share many similarities, there are several security threats specific to the fog domain. "Unlike cloud data centres which are offered by well-known companies, fog devices are expected to be owned by multiple and lesser-known entities":[88] identity authentication of the fog device and trust are therefore crucial. Secondly, VMs migration, in the fog domain, takes place over the Internet rather than over cloud's internal network: the chance of being exposed to compromised nodes or routers is considerably higher. Finally, due to resource constraints, fog devices are more prone to Dos and DDoS than data centres.[89]

2.3.3 Application Layer Attacks: Threats on 'Data'

Also the last layer of the IoT architecture i.e., application, has its own vulnerabilities and attack vectors. The attacks in the application layer mainly target data, possibly sensitive, of the users by seeking (unauthorised) access. This can be done by stealing credentials, by counterfeiting identity of legitimate users or by exploiting the vulnerabilities of programmes and application (e.g., code injection, buffer overflow). Social engineering[90] techniques are increasingly refined and effective: AI tools facilitate automated personalised attacks using information gathered online.[91] In addition to these attacks, the application layer is also threatened by so-called "viruses", malicious software like malware and Trojans. Accordingly, this section takes into account five attacks. They are: SQL injection, malware, ransomware, masquerading and zero-day.

SQL Injection (SQLi) aims to attack the databases that either store or deliver the required information to web services and applications. SQLi are the most common

[85] Ibid., p. 222.

[86] Id., p. 223.

[87] Rayes and Salam (2019), pp. 223–224.

[88] Ibid., p. 226.

[89] Id.

[90] ENISA defines "social engineering" as all techniques aimed at talking a target into revealing specific information or performing a specific action for illegitimate reasons. See https://www.enisa.europa.eu/topics/csirts-in-europe/glossary/what-is-social-engineering.

[91] ENISA (2020b).

threats against such services, corresponding to two thirds of web application attacks[92] .

Malware is perhaps the most famous cyberattack, which occurs in the form of malicious software. The genus malware includes the types crypto-miners, viruses, ransomware, worms and spyware. Its common objectives are information or identity theft, espionage and service disruption.[93] Although malware detections has globally remained at the same levels as in 2018, the ENISA 2020 report observed a 13% increase in malware targeting businesses in services, education and retail among the worst affected sectors.[94] Interestingly, 2020 represented a "never-seen-before spike in IoT malware"—as reported by ENISA in the 2021 threat landscape—mostly due to unpatched devices.[95]

Ransomware is a type of malware that infects the computer systems of users and manipulates the infected system in such a way, usually by encrypting user's files, that the victim cannot (partially or fully) use it and the data stored on it. In such cases, the ransomware victim may suffer economic losses either by paying the ransom demanded or by paying the cost of recovering from the loss, if they do not comply with the attacker's demands. These attacks are one of the main reasons for the increased interest in this type of insurance over the last 5 years.

At the time of writing, the most known (and critical) types of ransomwares are *Lockergoga*, *Katyusha*, *Jigsaw*, *Pewcrypt*, *Ryuk* and *Dharma*. Whereas the most targeted sectors are States, educational institutions, the health sector and cloud service providers.[96] Recent research shows a higher curve towards IoT ransomware "attacks which is expected to be 5 times higher by 2020 and it will exceed more than 6 trillion dollars as ransom against ransomware attacks [:] every 11 s a ransomware attack will occur around the globe".[97]

In the *masquerading* attacks, one entity illegitimately assumes the identity (e.g., a network identity) of another in order to benefit from it.[98]

Finally, "*Zero-Day*" is cybersecurity jargon for the opportunity to exploit a software vulnerability that is not yet publicly known and, by extension, the vulnerability itself. Attacks against these vulnerabilities are also called "Zero-Days" in the mainstream media.[99] To make things more complex, law enforcement and intelligence agencies, by exploiting zero-days vulnerabilities, can more easily install malware in computer systems for law enforcement purposes,[100] at the price of

---

[92] ENISA (2020c), p. 2.

[93] ENISA (2020d), p. 2.

[94] Ibid., p. 7.

[95] ENISA (2021), p. 85.

[96] ENISA (2020e), pp. 2–13.

[97] Humayun et al. (2021).

[98] ENISA (2018), p. 10.

[99] See https://www.enisa.europa.eu/topics/csirts-in-europe/glossary/zero-day.

[100] Koops and Kosta (2018), p. 898; Ziccardi (2018).

exposing the users of the system in question to attacks by malicious actors.[101] Thus, vulnerability of software is a sensitive issue that intersects the conflicting interests of cybersecurity (and, together, of privacy and personal data protection) and national security, as testified by the recent "Pegasus" scandal.[102]

2.3.4 The Missing Piece of the Jigsaw: IoT Supply Chain Security Threats

The traditional concept of establishing a security perimeter i.e., identifying all the relevant assets to protect and setting up the essential equipment and technologies to prevent outside attacks, becomes an extremely complicated task with the advent of ubiquitous IoT. As shown in previous sections, the IoT architecture disproportionately amplifies the attack surface, and the compelling need to secure the supply chain across the IoT ecosystem would make the identification of a perimeter extremely challenging.

In turn, organisations are increasingly at risk of being attacked and breached through one of their suppliers. "Organisations have many vendors, several of which in turn have multiple large corporate and government clients, therefore mapping this cyber-ecosystem of connections of surfaces will be very difficult, as it may involve these other organisations to divulge sensitive information regarding their relationships with other companies".[103]

Whereas US NIST defines the ICT supply chain as "the integrated set of components (hardware, software, and processes) within the organisational boundary that composes the environment in which a system is developed or manufactured, tested, deployed, maintained, and retired/decommissioned",[104] ENISA considers the specific supply chain reference model for IoT by framing the model into the physical aspect (all the physical objects along the supply chain phases) and the logic aspect (software development and deployment; network-based connections and virtual interactions between IoT objects and the supply chain stakeholders).[105]

There is a clear consensus, both in EU and in the US, that supply chain cybersecurity is vital for a secure IoT. Thus, ENISA and NIST both recognize that IoT supply chain security is an unavoidable step for devices' security; at the same time, it is extremely hard for organisations to verify whether market partners along the supply chain take adequate security measures.[106] The guidelines published by

[101] Stockton and Golabek-Goldman (2013), p. 239.

[102] The Guardian The Pegasus project. In: 2021. https://www.theguardian.com/news/series/pegasus-project.

[103] Omitola and Wills (2018), p. 445.

[104] Boyens et al. (2015), p. 4.

[105] ENISA (2020f), p. 5.

[106] Megas et al. (2021), p. 13.

ENISA address IoT supply chain security by breaking down the different phases of a general IoT supply chain model. This serves to identify the different security threats that can arise from each phase and detail the attack scenarios. It concludes with a list of the good practices and security measures that organisations shall put in place.

As regards the supply chain reference model for IoT, 10 different stages are identified: (1) product design; (2) semiconductor fabrication (hardware); (3) component manufacturing (hardware + software); (4) component assembly & embedded software; (5) device programming (SW); (6) IoT platform development (SW); (7) service provision & end-user operation (HW + SW); (8) technical support & maintenance (HW + SW); (9) distribution and logistics (present in every stage); (10) device recovery & repurpose (HW + SW).[107] This tenfold classification can be further divided into five different phases: conceptual phase (stage 1); development phase (stages 2–6); production phase (stage 9); utilisation phase (stage 7); support phase (stage 8); retirement phase (stage 10).[108]

Coherently with the Agency's IoT threat taxonomy, the threats have been classified under a set of high-level clusters: physical attacks (e.g., sabotage, grey markets, exploitation of inadequate physical enclosures); intellectual property loss (e.g., IP theft, reverse engineering, overproduction and cloning); nefarious activity/abuse (e.g., magnetic field attacks, malware insertion, exploitation of debug interfaces, tampering and counterfeits); legal (e.g., standard and regulation non-compliance); unintentional damage or loss of information (e.g., compromise of network, use of factory authentication settings, undetected software or hardware disruptions, user errors, disruption in cloud services, failure of recovery procedures, etc).[109]

Then, ENISA pulls the threads together by addressing the main security considerations to adopt throughout the 10 previously identified stages of the IoT supply chain and by developing good practices for countering and mitigating the above-mentioned security threats. Specifically, good practices were classified into three clusters: actors, processes and technologies.[110]

All in all, the report drafts a set of operational guidelines where each recommendation enucleates good practices and standards. A key condition for enhancing security is forging better relationships between relevant actors: the suggestion would then be to prioritise working with suppliers that provide cybersecurity guarantees, develop trust models and provide security promises to customers. A further step recommended by ENISA is fostering cybersecurity expertise and raising awareness within the workforce, through constant training that will promote a work culture focused on a risk-based approach. From a more technical point of view,

[107] ENISA (2020f), pp. 12–17.

[108] Ibid., pp. 9–12.

[109] Ibid., pp. 18–23.

[110] Ibid., pp. 24–36.

organisations need to adopt a comprehensive, or *holistic,* approach to security. This entails adopting security by design principles, developing threat models for the supply chain, identifying third-party software, establishing a comprehensive test plan, implementing factory settings using security by default principles and leveraging existing standards and good practices.[111]

Against this backdrop, a real-world example might help the reader to grasp how critical it is in practice and what the implications of supply chain cybersecurity are. On 29 March 2024, the worst supply-chain attack known to date was discovered. For this attack, if successful, would have been much worse than the disastrous and infamous Solarwind attack:[112] the NIST awarded it a score of 10/10.[113] In short, a backdoor was installed on the open source code of the widely used data compression library (Xz) using the 'lzma' algorithm, which allows remote code execution on a secure shell protocol (SSH) server without authentication. In other words, a malicious actor might gain unauthorised access to an entire system remotely.[114]

The Xz library has always been used by many other software applications that need to perform data compression (especially for package management). Among its users is also OpenSSH, the most widely used software for making secure connections between client and server via SSH.

It is therefore obvious how serious the implications of the attack are. This attack is also a paramount example of how fragile our digital environment is. The Xz supply-chain attack thus shows how a small component developed within the open-source community has rapidly become a substantial part of a much more complex system used in a large number of contexts, including professional or IT security-related areas. In other (pessimistic) words, it is hard to believe "this was the only attempt to slip a backdoor into a critical piece of Internet software, either closed source or open source. Given how lucky we were to detect this one, I believe this kind of operation has been successful in the past".[115]

2.4 Conclusion

This Chapter provided a working definition of 'Internet of Things'. In line with the definition provided by the Data Act, the IoT can be generally defined as a network of 'things', embedded with software intelligence, that obtain, generate or collect data

[111] Ibid., pp. 37–40.

[112] Wolff et al. (2021).

[113] NIST, national vulnerability database, CVE-2024-3094 Detail. https://nvd.nist.gov/vuln/detail/CVE-2024-3094.

[114] https://www.redhat.com/en/blog/urgent-security-alert-fedora-41-and-rawhide-users.

[115] Schneier (2024).

concerning their performance, use or environment and that are able to communicate information through publicly available electronic communications services. To unravel this rather broad concept, a three-layered IoT technical architecture taxonomy (device, network and application level) has been proposed, building on the model of Rayes and Salam, being one of the clearest—although not simplistic, comprehensive and flexible in IoT technical literature.

IoT networks 'nodes' are generally constrained in terms of computational power and/or memory, mainly due to market dynamics, i.e. scaling up the spread of affordable and physically feasible Internet technologies. Besides economic reasons, technical and environmental issues also have an impact in terms of 'constraints'. While awaiting the increase on the market of innovative technologies that promise to reduce power consumption needed for AI inference at the edge, this book assumes that IoT systems always involve constrained technologies (typically sensors at the device layer).

Building on the IoT taxonomy, this Chapter further mapped out an IoT threat landscape by linking the specific security attacks to each layer of the model. The ENISA IoT threat taxonomy, combined with the more general ENISA threat landscapes, served as a solid foundation for this technical overview. In particular, the analysis has been supplemented by adding the main takeaways from the ENISA IoT supply chain threat taxonomy: not only does the IoT architecture amplify the attack surface disproportionately, but also the compelling need to secure the supply chain across the IoT ecosystem would make the identification of a perimeter extremely challenging.

Before delving into the EU legal frameworks regulating IoT security and privacy, it is necessary to first address the different nuances of the concepts of 'security', 'cybersecurity', 'information security', 'safety' and 'privacy'.

References

AIOTI (2018) High Level Architecture (HLA) AIOTI WG03-loT Standardisation

Alani M (2014) Guide to OSI and TCP/IP models. Springer International Publishing

Antonakakis M, April T, Bailey M et al (2017) Understanding the Mirai Botnet. In: 26th USENIX Security Symposium. pp 1093–1110

Ben Dhia S, Ramdani M, Sicard E (2006) Electromagnetic compatibility of integrated circuits. Springer US

Bertino E (2018) Security and privacy in the IoT. In: Lecture Notes in Computer Science (including subseries Lecture Notes in Artificial Intelligence and Lecture Notes in Bioinformatics). Springer Verlag, pp 3–10

Bormann C, Ersue M, Keranen A (2014) RFC 7228: Terminology for Constrained-Node Networks

Boyens J et al (2015) Supply Chain Risk Management Practices for Federal Information Systems and Organizations

Chen K, Zhang S, Li Z et al (2018) Internet-of-things security and vulnerabilities: taxonomy, challenges, and practice. J Hardw Syst Secur 2:97–110. https://doi.org/10.1007/s41635-017-0029-7

Cheruvu S, Kumar A, Smith N, Wheeler DM (2020) Demystifying internet of things security. APRESS Open
CISCO (2013) The Internet of Everything - Global Public Sector Economic Analysis
Cozzi E, Graziano M, Fratantonio Y, Balzarotti D (2018) Understanding Linux Malware. Proc - IEEE Symp Secur Priv 161–175. https://doi.org/10.1109/SP.2018.00054
Denardis L (2020) The internet in everything - freedom and security in a world with no off switch, 1st edn. Yale University Press, New Haven & London
Durante M (2021) Computational power: the impact of ICT on law, society and knowledge, Routledge
ENISA (2010) Malicious Software - Train the Trainer Reference Guide
ENISA (2017) Baseline Security Recommendations for IoT in the context of Critical Information Infrastructures
ENISA (2018) Reference Incident Classification Taxonomy Task Force Status and Way Forward
ENISA (2019) Threat Landscape for 5G Networks
ENISA (2020a) Threat Landscape - Distributed Denial of Service
ENISA (2020b) Artificial Intelligence Threat Landscape Report
ENISA (2020c) ENISA Threat Landscape 2020 - Web application attacks
ENISA (2020d) Threat Landscape 2020 - Malware
ENISA (2020e) Threat Landscape 2020 - Ransomware
ENISA (2020f) Guidelines for Securing the Internet of Things - Secure supply chain for IoT
ENISA (2021) Threat Landscape 2021: April 2020 to mid-July 2021
ENISA (2023) Threat Landscape 2023: July 2022 to June 2023
European Commission (2021) State of the Union 2021 - Letter of Intent
European Union Agency for Fundamental Rights (2018) Manuale sul diritto europeo in materia di protezione dei dati. EU publishing office, Luxembourg
Floridi L (2018) Soft ethics and the governance of the digital. Philos Technol 311(31):1–8. https://doi.org/10.1007/S13347-018-0303-9
Hegarty R, Haggerty J (2020) Presence metadata in the internet of things: challenges and opportunities. In: Proceedings of the 6th International Conference on Information Systems Security and Privacy (ICISSP 2020). pp 631–638
Hewlett Packard (2014) HP News - HP Study Reveals 70 Percent of Internet of Things Devices Vulnerable to Attack. https://www8.hp.com/us/en/hp-news/press-release.html?id=1744676
Humayun M, Jhanjhi NZ, Alsayat A, Ponnusamy V (2021) Internet of things and ransomware: evolution, mitigation and prevention. Egypt Inform J 22:105–117. https://doi.org/10.1016/J.EIJ.2020.05.003
Iannacci J (2018) Internet of things (IoT); internet of everything (IoE); tactile internet; 5G – A (not so evanescent) unifying vision empowered by EH-MEMS (energy harvesting MEMS) and RF-MEMS (radio frequency MEMS). Sensors Actuators
Iorga M et al (2018) Fog computing conceptual model. http://nvlpubs.nist.gov/nistpubs/SpecialPublications/NIST.SP.500-325.pdf
ISO/IEC (2016) ISO/IEC 30141:2016 Information Technology-Internet of Things Reference Architecture (IoT RA) CD Stage
ISO/IEC (2018) ISO/IEC 30141:2018 Internet of Things (LoT) — Reference Architecture
ITU-T (2012) Overview of the Internet of Things, vol 6
Koops BJ, Kosta E (2018) Looking for some light through the lens of "cryptowar" history: policy options for law enforcement authorities against "going dark". Comput Law Secur Rev 34:890–900. https://doi.org/10.1016/J.CLSR.2018.06.003
Marwedel P (2018) Embedded system design: embedded systems foundations of cyber-physical systems, and the internet of things. Springer

Marwedel P (2021) Embedded system design: embedded systems foundations of cyber-physical systems, and the internet of things, Fourth. Springer
Megas KN et al (2021) Workshop Summary Report for "Building the Federal Profile for IoT Device Cybersecurity" Virtual Workshop NISTIR 8322
National Research Council (1995) Expanding the vision of sensor materials. National Academies Press
Nativi S, Kotsev A, Scudo P (2020) IoT 2.0 and the INTERNET of TRANSFORMATION (Web of Things and Digital Twins) A multi-facets analysis. Publications Office of the European Union
NIST (2016) Framework for Cyber-Physical Systems Release 1.0
Omitola T, Wills G (2018) Towards mapping the security challenges of the internet of things (IoT) supply chain. Procedia Comput Sci 126:441–450. https://doi.org/10.1016/J.PROCS.2018.07.278
Pa YMP, Suzuki S, Yoshioka K et al (2015) IoTPOT: analysing the rise of IoT compromises. In: WOOT '15
Pagallo U, Durante M, Monteleone S (2017) What is new with the internet of things in privacy and data protection? Four legal challenges on sharing and control in IoT. In: Data protection and privacy: (in)visibilities and infrastructures. Springer, Cham, pp 59–78
Patringenaru I (2022) A new neuromorphic chip for AI on the edge, at a small fraction of the energy and size. In: UC San Diego News Cent
Pittoli P, David P, Noël T (2018) Security architectures in constrained environments: a survey. Ad Hoc Networks 79:112–132. https://doi.org/10.1016/j.adhoc.2018.06.001
Poletti D (2022) IoT and privacy. In: Senigaglia R, Irti C, Bernes A (eds) Privacy and data protection in software services. Springer, pp 175–185
Rayes A, Salam S (2019) Internet of things from hype to reality. Springer
Rizvi S, Kurtz A, Pfeffer J, Rizvi M (2018) Securing the internet of things (IoT): a security taxonomy for IoT. Proc - 17th IEEE Int Conf Trust Secur Priv Comput Commun 12th IEEE Int Conf Big Data Sci Eng Trust 2018, pp 163–168. https://doi.org/10.1109/TrustCom/BigDataSE.2018.00034
Schneier B (2024) Xz Utils Backdoor. Schneier on security (blog). https://www.schneier.com/blog/archives/2024/04/xz-utils-backdoor.html
Sehgal A, Perelman V, Küryla S, Schönwälder J (2012) Management of resource constrained devices in the internet of things. IEEE Commun Mag 50:144–149. https://doi.org/10.1109/MCOM.2012.6384464
Siddiqui F, Beley J, Zeadally S, Braught G (2021) Secure and lightweight communication in heterogeneous IoT environments. Internet of Things 14. https://doi.org/10.1016/j.iot.2019.100093
Stapko T (2008) Practical embedded security: building secure resource-constrained systems. Newnes
Stockton P, Golabek-Goldman M (2013) Curbing the market for cyber weapons. Yale Law Policy Rev 32
The Guardian (2021) The Pegasus Project. Available at: https://www.theguardian.com/news/series/pegasus-project.
van der Mulen R (2018) What edge computing means for infrastructure and operations leaders. https://www.gartner.com/smarterwithgartner/what-edge-computing-means-for-infrastructure-and-operations-leaders
Voas J (2016) NIST Special Publication 800-183 Networks of "Things". https://doi.org/10.6028/NIST.SP.800-183
Vögler M et al (2015) LEONORE - Large-Scale Provisioning of Resource-Constrained IoT Deployment, Proceedings - 9th IEEE International Symposium on Service-Oriented System Engineering
Wan W, Kubendran R, Schaefer C et al (2022) A compute-in-memory chip based on resistive random-access memory. Nature 608:504–512. https://doi.org/10.1038/s41586-022-04992-8
Wolff ED et al (2021) Navigating the solarwinds supply chain attack. Procurement Law 56:3

Yi S, Li C, Li Q (2015) A survey of fog computing: concepts, applications and issues. Proc Int Symp Mob Ad Hoc Netw Comput 2015-June:37–42. https://doi.org/10.1145/2757384.2757397
Zhou J, Cao Z, Dong X, Vasilakos AV (2017) Security and privacy for cloud-based IoT: challenges. IEEE Commun Mag 55:26–33. https://doi.org/10.1109/MCOM.2017.1600363CM
Ziccardi G (2018) The GDPR and the LIBE study on the use of hacking tools by law enforcement agencies. Ital Law J 4

Chapter 3
Disentangling (Cyber)Security from the Privacy Debate in the IoT

3.1 The Concept of Cybersecurity in the IoT Era: Beyond Information Security?

With technological evolution and increasing digitalisation, the paradigms of information and computer security have changed to the point of converging into the concept—broad and transversal to different disciplines—of 'cybersecurity'.[1] In a scenario of complex interaction between information systems, society and the digital connected environment, cybersecurity takes into account a broader perimeter of risks and actors involved: as a result, new elements worthy of protection are identified.[2]

While computer security historically aimed at ensuring that systems operate as designed, information security has developed to deal with an understanding of security aimed at the protection of data and information.[3] The expression 'computer security' (and its evolutions, including 'network security') refers to an original vision of digital security pivoting on the protection of the computer or, more broadly, of the computer system and its related equipment, programmes, infrastructures and data, both processed and transmitted. Subsequently, the rise of the so-called "information society"[4] has led to the emergence of a concept of security that is more oriented towards the protection of information, namely "information security".

The well-known CIA triad[5] (confidentiality, integrity and availability of the system or its components), archetypical of computer security, integrates further information security requirements to restore certainty and trust to digital relationships underpinning the continuous flows of data and information that are

[1] Herrmann and Pridöhl (2020), p. 11.

[2] ENISA (2017), p. 6.

[3] Nieles et al. (2017).

[4] Webster (2014).

[5] The CIA triad constitutes the foundation of several technical standards for computer security. See, among others, Guttman and Roback (1995); UNI/EN ISO 27001.

P. G. Chiara, *The Internet of Things and EU Law*, Issues in Privacy and Data Protection 67, https://doi.org/10.1007/978-3-031-67663-5_3

transformed into knowledge: non-repudiation, authenticity, accountability and verifiability.[6]

From a technical and organisational perspective, computer security measures or controls can be clustered in three macro-areas: prevention, detection and response. The first group includes measures to prevent an incident and protect the system from attacks by designing robust systems that can withstand those attacks. The second includes measures for detecting attacks or threats and ensuring the resilience of systems. The third group hinges on measures that, in response to the harmful event, aim to minimise the damage with the timely reactivation of the system and its functions. Such threefold taxonomy is functional and as such not static. For instance, NIST's Framework abides by a different classification that identifies five concurrent security functions with underlying measures and controls: Identify, Protect, Detect, Respond, Recover.[7]

Each macro-area encompasses a wide range of technical tools and organisational measures: access control, disaster recovery, encryption, hardware and software for perimeter defence, intrusion detection systems and physical security measures, etc.

As said, the more technical concepts of computer and information security were progressively replaced, either by the scientific literature or common jargon, with the term cybersecurity.[8] On the definition of the latter, however, a consensus has not yet been reached. Originally coined in the U.S. to refer to the ability of defending and protecting cyberspace against cyberthreats,[9] the term generally refers to the inevitable expansion of the "perimeter" to be protected in the ever-broader cyberspace.

Limiting the concept of cybersecurity to the protection of networks and information systems alone is misleading and quite anachronistic: in the IoT era, the values and assets to be protected are much more. On the one hand, faced with the challenges of increasing threats and attacks, both in quantitative and qualitative terms, cybersecurity has the objective of protecting the information systems of an organisation (public institution or private company) through the study, development and implementation of strategies, policies and operational plans aimed at preventing computer incidents and, when they occur, coping with and overcoming them.[10] Related to that, cybersecurity strives to ensure that the security properties of organisations, alongside users' assets, are maintained at a high level against relevant risks in the cyber environment. Insofar as security is about protecting organisation's assets from threats posed by attackers exploiting vulnerabilities in the system, drawing up a

[6] NIST (2015), p. 42.

[7] NIST (2018).

[8] Veale and Brown (2020): since 2003, the concept of cybersecurity has been increasingly referred to in both academic and mainstream publications, in fields including software engineering, international relations, crisis management and public security, slowly overtaking more technical terms such as computer security, system security or data security (popular in the 1970s/80s) and information security (popular since the mid-1990s).

[9] Paulsen and Byers (2019).

[10] See the technical standard UNI/EN ISO 104559. See also CEN-CENELEC (2020).

security plan consists of identifying and ranking the assets, identifying the threats and estimating the risks.

On the other hand, thanks also to the IoT, the risk factors in today's hyper-connected digital environment are not only linked to the underlying technological and logical infrastructure. An attack could also infringe people's rights, impair individuals' safety and freedoms, alter the political debate of a nation and, if the critical infrastructure is concerned, have serious consequences for communities, institutions and businesses. Procedures, controls and behaviours, together with technology, are the foundations of cybersecurity. In fact, it is less about adopting the latest technological product, and more about defining procedures (legislative, administrative and organisational rules), setting up control mechanisms and promoting the right individual behaviour to manage the *risk*.[11] Risk cannot be merely reduced to the individual relationship with ICTs. Rather, in certain scenarios, it concerns collective interests and affects public and national security.

Indeed, the increasing wave of cyberattacks has raised awareness about the vulnerability of different actors—individuals, businesses, public bodies, institutions, organisations—to cyber threats. The World Economic Forum's Global Risk Report already ranked cyberattacks among the top ten global risks in 2019, and the data documented by the most recent security reports confirm said evaluation.[12] To make matters worse, a shortage of cybersecurity skilled professionals is well documented.

Moreover, the COVID-19 pandemic has forced less-prepared agents to migrate either their businesses or aspects related to personal life to the cyber dimension, resulting in a weakening of the global level of cybersecurity. Cybercriminals have started to exploit the extreme hardship experienced by some sectors—such as manufacturing and healthcare—by targeting their victims with customised attack vectors.[13] As the "2020 Year in Review" report by European Union Agency for Cybersecurity (ENISA) shows, cybersecurity has been faced with a paradox: it has been both the challenge and the opportunity to facilitate transformation as a confidence-building tool in digital services.[14] This ambivalent character of cybersecurity is a recurring theme of this chapter.

As seen in Chap. 2, drawing a picture of dynamically changing threats is not an easy task. The main reason for the major cyber incidents (such as, theft of

---

[11] The concept of risk permeates the entire discipline of computer security. The risk is the effect of uncertainty on the security objectives of the system and, as such, can be measured in probabilistic terms as the combination of the severity of the consequences of a given dangerous event (impact) and the probability of the event itself happening (ISO 73:2009). The methodologies for the "risk control" are many; basically, the activity consists of several steps that may have different perimeters depending on the reference standard. In particular, ISO 31000 defines two steps: (i) risk assessment, which includes hazard identification, analysis and severity weighting, and (ii) risk treatment, which aims to mitigate the effects of the risk by taking appropriate measures and to verify the residual risk.

[12] World Economic Forum (2021).

[13] EUROPOL (2020).

[14] ENISA (2020a).

information, data and user credentials)[15] is economic. The stolen information is usually sold on the dark web and in turn becomes a tool for other types of attacks, such as financial fraud or espionage and sabotage, aimed at acquiring industrial, commercial or expert information, driving companies out of business and causing reputational and organisational damage. The crime-as-a-service model is increasingly acquiring relevance: criminal organisations structured as companies offer ready-to-use software that does not require any particular computer skills to perpetrate attacks.[16]

However, these threats are part of a bigger picture of concern. A relatively new and problematic dimension is related to cyberwar[17] and information warfare,[18] where conflicts between states are conducted through cyberattacks on various types of information systems, national critical infrastructures and services whose malfunctioning cause disruptions. Politics and social life are directly affected by the spreading of fake news, trolls and manipulated information on the web and amplified by social networks.[19] The control of information through security technologies does not only concern criminal law, but also administrative, private and European law:[20] cybersecurity intersects all these different traditional legal domains.

Moreover, new challenges arise from the malicious use of artificial intelligence (AI). AI offers new and more effective ways of conducting cyberattacks. These systems are able to identify vulnerabilities that may escape human expertise; they facilitate automated personalised, social engineering attacks using information gathered online; they generate images and videos that cannot be distinguished from reality (so-called deep fakes); they create malware which are autonomous in masquerading and selecting their target; or they attack other AI systems by adversely applying the same machine-learning paradigms.[21] On the other hand, AI also offer opportunities in terms "of enhanced capacity to pursue cyber security-related goals as well as to cope with emerging threats".[22]

---

[15] A computer incident is any event of a malicious or negligent nature intended to damage tangible, intangible and human resources of value to the system or organisation. A computer incident therefore means not only 'hacker attacks' or external intrusions, but also inappropriate behaviour by system users, equipment failure, software bugs or natural events and disasters.

[16] Manky (2013).

[17] Lancelot (2020).

[18] Rugge (2018).

[19] Jacobs (2024); Ziccardi (2019). Harmful behaviour such as harassment, hatred, bullying and stalking has a strong potential to damage reputations in the online dimension due to the persistence of information and its potential to go viral. Identity theft, often facilitated by security gaps, can become a tool not only for committing fraud and scams, but also for defamation offences and disseminating confidential content for revenge (revenge porn) or extortion and blackmail (sexstortion) and persecution of vulnerable individuals. See Citron and Franks (2014); Ziccardi (2016).

[20] Cole et al. (2020); Mantelero et al. (2021).

[21] ENISA (2020b).

[22] Bonfanti (2022), p. 70.

The attacks are based on the ever-increasing security gaps in information systems, but they also succeed by exploiting the so-called "human factor". A country's overall level of cybersecurity preparedness depends not only on the level of security of public institutions and private sector organisations, but also on the security knowledge of individual users who can be leveraged as attack vectors on institutions or critical infrastructures.[23] The extent to which an individual is vulnerable largely depends on the risk perception and the degree of technical competence. The risks arising from personal data misuse,[24] with severe consequences to the construction of personal identity,[25] online reputation and exposure to cybercrime,[26] are often overlooked. In this respect, traditional threat models, as seen in Sect. 2.3, and attackers' profiles[27] may be limited.

Against the background of the evolution of the concept of 'digital security', the European Union has been contributing to shape a notion of cybersecurity since early 2000s.[28] In this respect, the year 2013 marked a watershed, as the Commission adopted the first, comprehensive, Cybersecurity Strategy,[29] outlining the EU's vision in this domain, clarifying roles and responsibilities[30] and setting out the policy objectives.[31] Importantly, the Cybersecurity Strategy hinged on the strong and effective protection and promotion of citizens' fundamental rights[32] with a view to making EU's online environment the safest in the world.

[23] The next section addresses the concept of "computer hygiene" which emphasises consumers' responsibilities.

[24] Martoni (2020).

[25] Palmirani and Martoni (2019).

[26] Brighi (2017).

[27] For example, family members or acquaintances are not considered as possible attackers, even though they benefit from easy access to the victim's devices in an abusive context.

[28] Digital information security was initially conceived in terms of ensuring the functioning of public communications networks (Directive 90/387/EC; directive 90/388/EC) and data protection (Directive 95/46/EC; directive 97/66/EC). In 2001, the Commission proposed a European policy approach on network and information system (NIS), with a Communication on Network and Information Security (COM(2001), 298 final), to provide the missing link in a regulatory framework where data protection & telecom, cybercrime and NIS would be interrelated.

[29] European Commission and the High Representative of the Union for Foreign Affairs and Security Policy (2013).

[30] To address cybersecurity in a comprehensive fashion, a multi-stakeholder and multi-level model was designed to span across three key pillars—NIS, law enforcement, and defence—operating within different legal frameworks that would involve both national governments and the EU.

[31] The Strategy articulates five strategic priorities: (i) achieving cyber resilience; (ii) drastically reducing cybercrime; (iii) developing cyber-defence policy and capabilities related to the Common Security and Defence Policy (CSDP); (iv) developing the industrial and technological resources for cybersecurity; (v) establishing a coherent international cyberspace policy for the European Union and promoting core EU values.

[32] European Commission the High Representatitve of the Union for Foreign Affairs and Security Policy (2013), p. 4: emphasis is placed on the relationship with fundamental rights and freedoms as enshrined in the CFR of the EU, which will be addressed in Sect. 2.2: not only cybersecurity "can

For the first time, the term *cybersecurity* entered the official lexicon of EU policy. Thus, a footnote in the introduction of the Strategy specifies that cybersecurity:

> [c]ommonly refers to the safeguards and actions that can be used to protect the cyber domain, both in the civilian and military fields, from those threats that are associated with or that may harm its interdependent networks and information infrastructure. Cyber-security strives to preserve the availability and integrity of the networks and infrastructure and the confidentiality of the information contained therein.[33]

Whereas the first part of the definition tends to be more all-encompassing with regard to the scope of protection of cybersecurity, the second sentence partially narrows it down to the upholding of the so-called CIA (i.e., confidentiality, availability and integrity) triad, the cornerstone of computer and information security. This notwithstanding, the broad set of principles that ought to guide EU cybersecurity policy demonstrates the intention to expand the boundaries of this domain.[34]

In 2017, the Commission adopted a new Cybersecurity Strategy. The catalyst, once again, was the increasing dependence of society and the Internal Market on digital technologies, resulting in an amplified threat landscape and growing incidents. To improve cyber resilience,[35] the Commission insisted on the multi-stakeholder approach already introduced in the 2013 Strategy. For cybersecurity is increasingly portrayed as a common societal challenge. It is not only the digital single market that is under threat, but also and foremost "the very functioning of our democracies, our freedoms and our values".[36] Hence, "multiple levels of public administration, the economy and society"[37] should be involved in this challenge.

In this context, Regulation (EU) 2019/881 (Cybersecurity Act) was adopted to reach two goals identified by the Strategy i.e., reforming ENISA (the EU Agency for cybersecurity) through a permanent mandate and establishing an EU cybersecurity certification framework (see later in Chap. 4). Importantly, the Cybersecurity Act is the first EU legal act to provide a definition of 'cybersecurity', which aligns with the vision of the new Strategy, for it is enriched with new objectives compared to the traditional information security approach of the 2013 Strategy. Accordingly, cybersecurity includes all the "activities necessary to protect network and information systems, the users of these systems and other persons affected by cyberthreats".[38]

---

only be sound and effective if it is based on EU core values", notably "individuals' rights cannot be secured without safe networks and systems".

[33] ibid, p. 3.

[34] Ibid., pp. 3–4.

[35] On the relationship between the concepts of 'cybersecurity' and 'cyber resilience', see Bygrave (2022).

[36] European Commission and the High Representative of the Union for Foreign Affairs and Security Policy (2017), p. 2.

[37] Ibid., p. 4.

[38] Art. 2, Regulation EU 2019/881

The notion was intentionally left as a broad one by the European legislature to encompass a broad range of governance risks without conceptualising it in an unduly limited fashion.[39] In addition, the 2017 Strategy acknowledges that a functional approach to cybersecurity must be not only horizontal but also sectoral. Specific sectors (e.g., financial, transportation, health, energy) address specific problems; hence, the 'general Strategy' has to be complemented by sectoral strategies, and consequently regulatory interventions.[40]

In December 2020, the Commission presented a new Cybersecurity Strategy. Cybersecurity is now firmly part and, to some extent, a precondition of citizens' everyday lives. The ineradicable dependence of all sectors of the economy and society on increasingly interconnected information systems and networks results in cybersecurity being seen as essential "for people to trust, make use of, and benefit from innovations, connectivity, and automation, as well as to safeguard fundamental rights and freedoms, including the rights to privacy and the protection of personal data as well as freedom of expression and information".[41] The 2020 Strategy contains a set of proposals at the regulatory (i.e., NIS2 Directive and Critical Entities Resilience Directive proposals), investment and policy levels for three areas of focus, setting itself in line with previous Strategies: (i) resilience, technological sovereignty and leadership; (ii) development of operational capabilities aimed at prevention, deterrence and response; and, (iii) promotion of a global and open cyberspace. The next chapter provides an in-depth analysis of the EU legal framework regulating IoT cybersecurity.

All in all, in complex environments of interaction between people, devices, software and services, a high degree of cybersecurity calls for a holistic approach that integrates the protection of the many values at stake in new coordinated forms of risk management. This may explain why, unlike more technical terms such as *computer security* and *information security*, there is no shared notion of cybersecurity, let alone defined boundaries at any level i.e., scientific, political and doctrinal.[42] As pointed out by Fuster and Jasmontaite, the resulting evolving and highly fragmented field of cybersecurity is a horizontal problem, "which is in a sense a common denominator of various new technologies connected to the World Wide Web".[43]

The IoT, as repeatedly stressed in this work, is a game-changer. And the cybersecurity field makes no exception. As seen in Chap. 2, the ubiquitous data and metadata sharing of these systems, which play an increasingly important role both in the public and the private dimension, implies a paradigm shift. The security of a

---

[39] Fuster and Jasmontaite (2020), p. 103.

[40] European Commission and the High Representative of the Union for Foreign Affairs and Security Policy (2017), pp. 6–7.

[41] European Commission and the High Representatitve of the Union for Foreign Affairs and Security Policy (2020), p. 4.

[42] Bygrave (2022), p. 31.

[43] Fuster and Jasmontaite (2020), p. 98.

network relies on the security of each of its components. Therefore, the (cyber)-security of IoT devices is not just about them, but *it is influenced by and has a direct impact* on every other device, service, platform and online information resource, be it virtual or physical connected. In the words of Denardis,

> [C]ybersecurity has now become one of the most consequential issues of the modern era, necessary for human safety, privacy, critical infrastructure, and national security, as much as for economic security, democracy, speech rights, and acccss to knowledge. Yet connected physical objects are notoriously insecure. There is a huge chasm between the need for security and the state of security.[44]

In the digital era, a functional definition of security shall necessarily weight the broad notion of cybersecurity, in order to sharpen the focus on the private sphere. Against the background where many cybersecurity objectives coincide with the common interest, the following sections of the chapter aim to cast light on how the interplay between cybersecurity, fundamental rights (i.e., privacy and data protection) and individual safety works against the background of the paradigm shift brought about by IoT devices. In particular, the question is whether and to what extent cybersecurity values and practices *always* facilitate or protect the integrity of individuals (the moral value of individual safety) and the enjoyment of the fundamental rights to privacy and to data protection. In other words, this relates to the quandary of whether "security is, like privacy, a human right or rather a precondition for the legal framework on which effective human rights depend".[45]

3.2 The IoT Paradigm Shift: The Relationship Between Cybersecurity, Privacy & Data Protection and Safety

3.2.1 Privacy and Data Protection in the EU: A Brief Background

The right to privacy—or the right to respect for private life—emerged in international human rights law in the aftermath of World War II. First, in the Universal Declaration of Human Rights (UDHR), adopted in 1948,[46] and soon after in the European Convention on Human Rights (ECHR), adopted in 1950 by the Council of Europe (CoE).[47]

---

[44] Denardis (2020), p. 7.

[45] Hildebrandt (2019), p. 266.

[46] Art. 12 of the Universal Declaration of Human Rights: "no one shall be subjected to arbitrary interference with his privacy, family, home or correspondence, nor to attacks upon his honor and reputation. Everyone has the right to the protection of the law against such interference or attacks".

[47] The Convention is legally binding on the contracting parties. CoE established in France (Strasburg), in 1959, the European Court of Human Rights (ECtHR) to ensure that contracting parties observed the obligations enshrined in the Convention. The ECtHR considers complaints

The ECHR provides that everyone has the right to respect for his or her private and family life, home and correspondence.[48] Albeit Article 8 of the ECHR lays down a general prohibition of interference by a public authority, it is not absolute: interference is permitted if in accordance with the law, pursues legitimate public interests (such as national security and public safety) and is necessary in a democratic society.[49]

As the emergence of information technology in the 1960s and 1970s clearly showed an urgent need for more detailed rules to safeguard individuals' personal data, the Committee of Ministers of the CoE adopted various resolutions on personal data protection, on the basis of Article 8 of the ECHR.[50]

In 1981, the Council of Europe opened a Convention for the protection of individuals for signature, that regarded the automatic processing of personal data (Convention 108). The possibility to sign and ratify the Convention was extended to non-contracting parties of the CoE in order to promote a high data protection standard on a global level.

Convention 108 applies to all data processing carried out by both the private and public sectors, including data processing by the judiciary and law enforcement authorities. Although outside the judicial supervision of the ECtHR, the Strasburg Court has taken Convention 108 into consideration in its case law in determining whether or not there has been an interference with Article 8 of the ECHR.[51]

As regards EU primary law, the Charter of Fundamental Rights of the European Union[52] (hereinafter, the "Charter")[53] became legally binding when the Lisbon Treaty came into force on 1 December 2009. The Charter clearly envisioned these two rights in a separate fashion, making a distinction between the traditional right to respect for one's private and family life (Article 7) and the right to the protection of personal data (Article 8).[54] The right to privacy is indeed closely related to the right to data protection.

---

from individuals, groups, NGOs or legal persons bring forward as violations of the convention. The ECtHR can also examine inter-state cases brought by one or more CoE member states against another member state.

[48] Art. 8(1), ECHR.

[49] Art. 8(2), ECHR.

[50] Union Agency for Fundamental Rights - Council of Europe-European Court of Human Rights - European Data Protection Supervisor (2018), p. 24.

[51] ECtHR, 25 February 1997, (Application No. 22009/93), *Z v. Finland*.

[52] Union Agency for Fundamental Rights - Council of Europe-European Court of Human Rights - European Data Protection Supervisor (2018), p. 28: "[i]t incorporates the whole range of civil, political, economic and social rights of European citizens, by synthesising the constitutional traditions and international obligations common to the Member States. The rights described in the Charter are divided into six sections: dignity, freedoms, equality, solidarity, citizens' rights and justice".

[53] Charter of Fundamental Rights of the European Union, OJ 2012 C 326.

[54] Opinion of AG Sharpston, 27 September 2018, Case C 345/17, *Buivids*, ECLI:EU:C:2018:780, § 61: the case law of the European Court of Human Rights (ECtHR) has substantially included the

These two separate rights aim to protect however similar fundamental values, that is, individuals' *autonomy* and *dignity*. Thus, under these rights persons enjoy a personal 'sphere' where they can freely develop their personality and shape their opinions and ideas.[55] In other words, an essential infrastructure for liberal democratic political systems.[56]

Floridi, who has re-interpreted the informational privacy theory in light of the digital revolution,[57] conceptualises an *anthropo-eccentrical* understanding of human exceptionalism—which, in the history of philosophy, provided for various interpretations of the concept of human dignity—to highlight the right to privacy based on human dignity.[58] Indeed, the European approach puts an emphasis on dignity—as enshrined in Article 1 of the EU Charter of Fundamental Rights—understood as to combine 'intimacy' with 'respect', two core dimensions of privacy, while contributing to defining the position of each person in society.[59]

Yet, human dignity is also central to personal data protection,[60] and more generally to the evolution of this right in many domestic jurisdictions.[61] "One can therefore come to the conclusion that dignity is a universal, fundamental, and inescapable term of reference".[62]

Despite substantial overlaps, these rights have different scopes and rationales.[63] The right to personal data protection comes into play whenever personal data are

---

fundamental right to personal data protection within the scope of Article 8 ECHR, by "treating it as a more specific expression of the right to privacy in respect of the processing of personal data".

[55] Union Agency for Fundamental Rights - Council of Europe-European Court of Human Rights - European Data Protection Supervisor (2018), pp. 20–21.

[56] Cohen (2013), p. 1905.

[57] Floridi (2005), p. 194: a new theoretical paradigm has to put the "essentially informational nature of human beings and of their operations as informational social agents" at the heart of the privacy debate. Each person, *rectius*: each agent, is her information. A breach of one's informational privacy is a form of aggression towards one's personal identity: the ontological interpretation relies on the equalisation of the informational sphere and the personal identity. It follows that informational privacy might be conceived as a function of ontological friction, namely the forces that contrast the flow of information in each environment (or a region of the infosphere). In other words, this friction is the effort that an agent must make in order to gain information about others entity in the same infosphere. This expectation of privacy is well suited to dispose of the "false dichotomy qualifying informational privacy in public or in private contexts".

[58] Floridi (2016).

[59] Rodotà (2004), p. 7.

[60] Article 88 of the General Data Protection Regulation (GDPR) states that rules "shall include suitable and specific measures to safeguard the data subject's human dignity [my italics], legitimate interests and fundamental rights, with particular regard to the transparency of processing, the transfer of personal data within a group of undertakings, or a group of enterprises engaged in a joint economic activity and monitoring systems at the work-place".

[61] Lynskey (2015).

[62] Rodotà (2004), p. 7.

[63] Kokott and Sobotta (2013); Elliott (2019); Lynskey (2014).

processed, whereas the right to privacy concerns situations where a private interest, or the "private life" of an individual, has been compromised.

A more traditional, and ultimately surpassed distinction between privacy and data protection would contrappose a 'classic' right (the right to respect for private life), revolving around a general prohibition on interference, with a more 'modern' one (the right to personal data protection), setting up a model of checks and balances to safeguard individuals when their personal data are processed, as claimed by Advocate General Sharpston in *Volker und Markus Schecke*.[64]

Conversely, several authors build the relationship between the two rights in terms of protecting individuals' "opaqueness" *versus* 'transparent' collection and processing of personal data.[65] Whereas privacy refers to the holistic intertemporal protection of an individual's inner dimensions, (personal) data protection rights, triggered when people begin to allow information to leave that private sphere, aim at demanding the transparency of such processing.[66]

Notwithstanding the soundness of the above-mentioned distinctions, as noted by Fuster and Hijmans, "the two rights are clearly coupled in the relevant case law of the Court of Justice of the European Union (CJEU), where they are not *systematically* distinguished – and where they are occasionally presented in complex interwoven manners".[67] Moreover, "place is no longer a useful proxy to delineate the boundaries of the private sphere".[68]

Accordingly, (informational) privacy would then come closer to data protection provided that the latter does not make "any crucial private/public distinction".[69] In a closer look, this interpretation echoes the 'revolutionary' scope of the right to data protection *à la européenne*, namely the recognition all citizens to have permanent power of *management* over their data, wherever they may be.

The term 'management' is more nuanced when it comes to conceptualizing the problematic concept of 'control' within traditional informational privacy theories.[70]

---

[64] Opinion of AG Sharpston, 17 June 2010, Join cases C-92/09 and C-93/02, Volker und Markus Schecke GbR v. Land Hessen.

[65] Gutwirth and De Hert (2008), p. 271; Pagallo (2017), p. 159.

[66] Chiara (2021), p. 27.

[67] Fuster and Hijmans (2019), p. 4. see also Case C-73/16, *Peter Puškár v Finančné riaditeľstvo Slovenskej republiky, Kriminálny úrad finančnej* správy [2017] ECLI:EU:C:2017:253, §112: "the protection of the fundamental right to respect for private life at the European Union level requires that derogations from the protection of personal data and its limitations be carried out within the limits of what is strictly necessary".

[68] See *ex multis* Koops (2014), p. 7. See also ECtHR, 24 June 2004, (Application no 59320/00) *von Hannover v Germany*: the Strasbourg Court held that in a case concerning the interception of telephone calls on business premises, the applicant "would have had a reasonable expectation of privacy for such calls".

[69] Edwards (2016): the author highlights that in Lindqvist Case C-101/01 and in Rynes Case C-212/13 the Court of Luxembourg acknowledged the "house-hold" processing exemption, that is indeed space-dependent, more as a de minimis principle than a spatial one.

[70] Van Wel and Royakkers (2004), pp. 130–140; Mittelstadt et al. (2016), pp. 9–10; Tene and Polonetsky (2013); Schermer (2011), pp. 45–52.

The accountability principle[71] can thus be seen as a fundamental lever[72] through which individuals can demand controllers to demonstrate compliance with the EU principles and rights related to the processing of personal data.

It is worth noting that this *data management power* is also delegated to independent authorities:[73] protection is no longer merely individualistic but involves a specific public responsibility. Chapter 4 will further address the main legal challenges in terms of EU privacy and data protection legal frameworks brought about by IoT structural data and metadata sharing.

3.2.2 Cybersecurity and Privacy: An Instrumental, or Infraethical, Perspective

The multifaceted relationship between (cyber)security and fundamental rights, such as privacy (and data protection) raises the long-standing question, which long has been a concern for philosophers and legal theorists, about how to reconcile these values. At times, European legal order weighs 'security' and 'privacy' in terms of trade-offs, if pursuing the aims of the former lead to infringe the latter; at other times, EU legal frameworks and courts 'balance' the *clashing* values. But there are also instances where security is instrumental to enjoy fundamental rights.

In the attempt to clarify this conundrum, this section presents an analytical framework to examine the state of affairs of the relationship between cybersecurity, privacy and data protection. A similar approach has been proposed by Porcedda, who analyses the relationship between cybersecurity, privacy and data protection in EU law by designing a conceptual axis represented by five relational nodes. Porcedda identifies three high-level states of relationships, namely (i) clash, (ii) indifference and (iii) complementarity: zero-sum outcomes and balancing exercises identify respectively forms of none and weak clash, whereas convergence and overlap are two options of complementarity (strong and complete, respectively).[74]

The legal-philosophical analysis needs thus to assess the cases where security and fundamental rights are on the same level, and accordingly clashes can occur, and where one is conditional, or instrumental, for the other. To do so, Floridi's theory of infraethics comes to our aid.[75]

In July 2020, the EU Commission presented the "EU Security Strategy 2020-2025". The ultimate goal of this policy document is made clear from the very beginning, that is, protecting individuals, society and the environment. "Security is not only the basis for personal safety, it also protects fundamental rights and

[71] Art. 5(2), Regulation (EU) 2016/679.

[72] Pagallo et al. (2019).

[73] Art. 8(3), Charter of Fundamental Rights of the European Union.

[74] See Porcedda (2023), pp. 22–39.

[75] Floridi (2017).

provides the foundation for confidence and dynamism in our economy, our society and our democracy".[76]

The words of the Commission seemingly offer guidance to interpret the perennial philosophical debate on 'security' in moral theory, namely whether security has itself an ethical dimension (thus, a fundamental good) or, rather, it is a precondition for the legal framework on which effective human rights depend.[77]

Thus, terms such as *basis* and *foundation* suggest that the tension between security, on one side, and safety or fundamental rights (e.g., privacy and data protection), on the other, might not be dealt with as a balance within ethics, or rather moral rights on the same level.[78] Hence, this relationship may be conceived in terms of balancing '*infraethics*' (security as an instrumental value) with ethics (safety or privacy, as fundamental goods).[79]

The concept of 'infraethics' has been coined by Floridi to refer to a "not-yet-ethical framework", that is, a "set of conditions that facilitate or hinder evaluations, decisions, actions, or situations, which are then moral or immoral".[80] In other words, if "ethics governs the axiological evaluation of a state of affairs",[81] "the right sort of infraethics is there to support the right kind of axiology"[82] of values that are morally good—such as fundamental rights or personal safety.

Similarly, in the context of cybersecurity, that is, digital security, the Commission and the High Representative of the Union for Foreign Affairs and Security Policy presented at the end of 2020 the last EU Cybersecurity Strategy 'for the Digital Decade'. Importantly, for the sake of the argument under discussion, improving cybersecurity is considered by the Commission "essential for people to trust, use, and benefit from innovation, connectivity and automation, *and for safeguarding fundamental rights and freedoms, including the rights to privacy and to the protection of personal data, and the freedom of expression and information* [emphasis added]".[83]

There were others that also acknowledged the *instrumental* character of cybersecurity vis-à-vis morally good values.[84] Thus, as Jabri emphasised, "the point at which security is transformed into a universal ethical category is also the point at which it becomes a technology of domination, of the governing over the governed".[85]

---

[76] European Commission (2020a), p. 1.

[77] Pagallo (2013), p. 382.

[78] Chiara (2021), p. 21.

[79] Floridi (2017), p. 394.

[80] ibid., p. 392.

[81] Durante (2017), pp. 176–177.

[82] Floridi (2017), p. 397.

[83] European Commission and the High Representatitve of the Union for Foreign Affairs and Security Policy (2020), p. 4.

[84] Loi and Christen (2020), p. 76; contra see van de Poel (2020).

[85] Jabri (2016), p. 27.

Therefore, we assume that cybersecurity and its technologies, viewed within an infraethical perspective, which is not ethically neutral, may either facilitate or hinder morally good values such as fundamental rights and individual safety.

Before embarking on the intricate conundrum of cybersecurity technologies that may hinder fundamental rights two methodological caveats apply. On the one hand, this section will not dwell too extensively on the limitations of the scope of EU fundamental rights law (i.e., the Charter) and international human rights law (i.e., the ECHR), and the caselaw of the CJEU and the ECtHR respectively, since a more in-depth reflection on the challenges brought by the IoT in terms of balances between EU privacy and data protection legal frameworks and security will be addressed later in Chap. 5. Moreover, it does not follow a moral judgement, as suggested by Floridi, of the circumstances where cybersecurity technologies infringe fundamental rights. Rather, the infraethics, here, is seen through the lens of Hildebrandt's model: when it becomes necessary to weigh *cybersecurity-as-a-fundamental-good* and other fundamental goods, such as privacy, a "bad infraethics" applies trade-offs rather than balances. A balancing act implies that the higher the infringement of fundamental rights, the more effective safeguards must be implemented.[86]

With regard to scenarios where cybersecurity indeed clashes with other fundamental goods (e.g., fundamental rights), it is worth recalling two of the three dimensions of cybersecurity, as outlined in Sect. 2.1. These are 'resilience' and 'response', the 'active face' of digital security. Systems resilience is achieved by deploying so-called detection technologies and controls. These include: (i) procedures for analysing log files; (ii) procedures for monitoring network traffic and possible anomalies on the systems, implemented through sophisticated tools such as Intrusion Detection Systems (IDS) and Security Information and Event Management (SIEM).[87] Conversely, response (to attacks) is mainly based on autonomous and semi-autonomous measures as pre-determined responses for a number of threats. They span from advanced backups, disaster recovery procedures and tools to business continuity plans, relying on distributed network architectures and redundant systems.[88]

These two domains of cybersecurity substantially overlap with the second and the third type of digital security technologies (DTSs) described by Hildebrandt. The former aims to detect and counter threats and vulnerabilities in digital environments, thus including monitoring, filtering and blocking technologies. The latter aims to detect and counter cybercrime, thus concerning the power of law-enforcement agencies to search and seize stored digital data, to collect and intercept digital data in real time.[89]

[86] Hildebrandt (2019), p. 270.

[87] Brighi (2021), p. 140.

[88] Id.

[89] Hildebrandt (2019), p. 263.

Undoubtedly, in such scenarios, cybersecurity technologies pose serious risks of undermining and breaching users' fundamental rights to privacy and data protection, and users' exposure to extra risks, should data confidentiality be breached, and may have a mass-surveillance effect.[90]

In the context of human rights law, Article 8(2) ECHR provides for a general prohibition of State interference with the right to respect for private and family life, *except* when the infringement "is in accordance with the law and is necessary in a democratic society in the interests of national security, public safety or the economic wellbeing of the country, for the prevention of disorder or crime, for the protection of health or morals, or for the protection of the rights and freedoms of others".[91]

The balancing act requires a solid legal justification: the infringing measure has to be (i) in accordance with the law; (ii) necessary in a democratic society; (iii) with a legitimate aim. In the case law of the ECtHR,[92] the lawfulness criterion is interpreted as requiring the national law to be sufficiently clear in its terms (adequately accessible) to give everyone an indication as to the circumstances in which and the conditions on which (sufficiently foreseeable) public authorities are empowered to resort to such infringing measures and contains effective safeguards in order to limit such measures either in scope (time and content) or scale.[93]

Hildebrandt therefore concludes that:

> [a] more effective level of digital security is a necessary but not a sufficient condition for giving up some privacy, also taking into account that the more privacy invasive a DST the higher the threshold should be for allowing it. If security threats and proportionate DSTs meet the threshold of a sufficient condition, a balance must be struck: the higher the infringement of human rights, the more effective safeguards must be implemented. In line with data protection by design and default, human rights law must develop the notion of counter-infringement measures as part of the necessary safeguards under human rights law. Like data protection by design this would be another instance of legal protection by design.[94]

Similarly, in its case-law on surveillance,[95] the CJEU assesses the strength of the safeguards embedded in EU and national law for the rights to privacy and data protection vis-à-vis the monitoring activities of State law enforcement agencies. The EU law, and in particular Article 15(1) of the ePrivacy Directive, authorises Member States to derogate to some of the security and confidentiality requirements set out in the Directive when such restriction constitutes a necessary, appropriate and proportionate measure within a democratic society to safeguard national security (i.e., State security), defence, public security, and the prevention, investigation, detection and

[90] Taddeo (2019), p. 353.

[91] Art. 8(2), ECHR.

[92] ECtHR, 28 November 2002, (Application no. 58442/00), *Lavents v. Latvia*, §135.

[93] European Court of Human Rights (2021), p. 108.

[94] Hildebrandt (2019), p. 270.

[95] Case C-623/17, *Privacy International* [2020] *ECLI*:EU:*C*:2020:790*;* Joined Cases C-511/18, C-512/18 and C-520/18 *La Quadrature du Net and Others* [2020] ECLI:EU:C:2020:791; Joined Cases C-293/12 and C-594/12 *Digital Rights Ireland* [2014] ECLI:EU:C:2014:238; Joined Cases C-203/15 and C-698/15 *Tele2 Sverige and Watson and Others* [2016] ECLI:EU:C:2016:970.

prosecution of criminal offences or of unauthorised use of the electronic communication system.[96]

The understanding of *(cyber)security-as-infraethics,* that is, a good infraethics, is meant as a condition of the possibility for fundamental rights and individual safety, without involving any kind of balancing act. The first dimension of cybersecurity i.e., system robustness, focuses on building solid, reliable systems that can withstand and mitigate attacks. Its 'passive character' is essential for understanding why it is not problematic for fundamental rights.

In the era of IoT ubiquitous hyper-connectedness, system robustness has direct implications on the public interest of information societies, for it benefits all users of the network without possibility of exclusion.[97] It enables critical national infrastructures and services to function, and it allows citizens to rely on, or trust, secure IoT technologies since cybersecurity requirements—framed in terms of system robustness—are "essential component[s] of the protection of individuals with regard to the processing of personal data".[98]

Indeed, this instrumental value of security is also acknowledged by the GDPR, whose broad scope is made clear by Article 1(2).[99] Security is one of the core principles around which the framework of protection is based, as per Article 5(1)(f). Article 32 then lays down a general security obligation for both data controllers and processors to implement technical and organisational measures appropriate to the risk of the processing. In other terms, Article 32 directly implements an infraethical framework to prevent processing in infringement of the Regulation[100] and, indirectly, to uphold fundamental primary goods i.e., rights and freedoms.[101]

As noted by Burton, the CJEU seemingly made an equation between data security principles and the essence of the right to data protection[102] in *Digital Rights*

---

[96] Art. 15(1), Directive 2002/58/EU.

[97] Taddeo (2019), p. 350.

[98] Loideain (2019), p. 11.

[99] Regulation (EU) 2016/679, Article 1(2): the Regulation protects fundamental rights and freedoms of natural persons and in particular their right to the protection of personal data.

[100] Regulation (EU) 2016/679, Recital 83.

[101] Art. 32, Regulation (EU) 2016/679 is indeed the *trait-d'union* between legal and technical aspects of data security: it enforces legal obligations on data controllers to ensure the security of processing, by implementing technical and organisational measures appropriate for the level of the risk of the processing. A preliminary step is therefore to assess the (level of) risk. Risk methodologies (Chap. 5), in our digital era, are also strictly connected with safety (Sect. 2.4): practitioners aim to assess the weaknesses of systems by ranking the impact of the harmful event in connection with the probability of their occurrence. However, a necessary remark acknowledge that while the risks assessment is classically known in IT security, the data protection perspective is very different. GDPR and ISO/IEC risk analysis models differ to the extent that the former safeguards rights and freedoms of individuals, whilst the latter aims to protect corporate assets and are in general focused on risks based on which financial or reputation damage for the company could be expected. This understanding, later addressed in Chap. 5, does not necessarily imply a clash between the two: by securing organisations' assets, individuals can also be protected.

[102] Burton (2020), p. 634.

Ireland.[103] Similarly, in *Z v Finland,* the ECtHR maintained that national law must ensure appropriate (security) safeguards to be consistent with Article 8 ECHR.[104] The EU security strategy acknowledges that cooperation between ENISA, data protection authorities and the European Data Protection Board is of the utmost importance to fulfil the most important long-term need of developing a culture of cybersecurity by design:[105] "security (including cybersecurity) and data protection by design are key elements to be considered under the GDPR and would benefit from a common and ambitious approach throughout the EU".[106] Although the security requirements laid down in Article 32 GDPR apply at the time of processing, whereas the duty under Article 25 apply beforehand when the controller determines the means for processing,[107] these obligations are closely linked. Data protection by design and by default principles dictate to data controllers to implement appropriate technical and organisational measures that integrate the requirements of the Regulation, including data security.[108]

The design of robust systems is achieved by deploying so-called prevention measures or controls, including measures for the control of physical and logical access (such as strong passwords, smart cards, biometrics); the adoption of perimeter defence tools (such as firewalls and proxies); the definition of policies for timely updates; the provision of procedures for the definitive deletion of data and lastly, the promotion of user's awareness through constant trainings.[109]

Against the background of prevention, cryptographic technologies—such as encryption—are widely considered to be technical measures that effectively safeguard and promote fundamental rights such as the right to privacy, data protection and freedom of expression.[110] Hildebrandt, while dwelling on the digital security technologies that afford violations of fundamental rights, lists encryption within the first type of DSTs (i.e., the ones that ensure confidentiality). While the philosopher acknowledges that encryption, in principle, does not infringe fundamental rights, she argues that cryptographic techniques nonetheless generate new vulnerabilities by elaborating on their dependency on trusted parties for key management and certification.[111]

---

[103] *Digital Rights Ireland* (n 94), para. 40: "Nor [...] Article 7 of Directive 2006/24 provides, in relation to data protection and data security, that, without prejudice to the provisions adopted pursuant to Directives 95/ 46 and 2002/ 58, certain principles of data protection and data security must be respected by providers of publicly available electronic communications services or of public communications networks".

[104] ECtHR, 25 February 1997, (Application no. 22009/93), *Z v Finland,* paras. 95–96.

[105] European Commission (2020a), p. 8.

[106] European Commission (2020b), p. 10.

[107] Bygrave (2020), p. 576.

[108] ENISA (2018a), p. 19.

[109] Brighi (2021), p. 140.

[110] Art. 32(1)(a), Regulation (EU) 2016/679; European Commission High Level Group of Scientific Adivisors (2017), p. 31; ENISA (2016), p. 5; Wiewiórowski (2020).

[111] Hildebrandt (2019), p. 262.

It can be argued, however, that these weaknesses can be mitigated *via* technical solutions.[112] As further explored in Chap. 5, to increase trust, while avoiding potential collusions, a decentralised re-keying scheme[113] allows for the data subject to take total control over the generation and management of the decryption keys without relying on a trusted authority:[114] if two or more parties (e.g., Cloud service providers) combine the keys, they cannot decrypt data.[115] Thus, there is much thriving literature confirming that secret sharing algorithms can be successfully applied either to distribute the encryption key among a number of cloud nodes[116] or to divide a data subject's encrypted data into shares to be stored in different cloud service providers.[117]

On the other hand, it is true that *strong* encryption comes at a cost for fundamental rights. Law enforcement and intelligence services have always advocated for the creation of means (i.e., backdoors) that allow them to circumvent security solutions that cryptography provides.[118]

To put a (temporary) halt to this quandary, the European Parliament, within discussions on ePrivacy Regulation amendments, proposed a set of constraints (on Member States attempts of breaking encryption) and facilitations (towards privacy and security of individuals' electronic communications), say, a *good infraethics*,[119] in order "to safeguard the security and integrity of networks and services [and] to forbid Member States from imposing any obligation on encryption providers, providers of electronic communications services or any other organisations (at any level of the supply chain) that would result in the weakening of the security of their networks and services, such as the creation or facilitation of backdoors".[120]

In conclusion, by understanding *cybersecurity-as-a-good-infraethics* in the sole dimension of systems robustness, the powerful statement of Denardis can be seen in a more nuanced view:

> the need for strong cybersecurity is the common denominator of the most consequential public interest concerns of the present era. Privacy depends upon cybersecurity technologies. National security and the functioning of critical societal and industrial infrastructure require strong cybersecurity. Cybersecurity is increasingly connected to the legitimacy of

[112] Chiara (2020).

[113] Egorov et al. (2017).

[114] Ismail et al. (2020), p. 257.

[115] Ibid., p. 253.

[116] D'Souza et al. (2011).

[117] Zhang et al. (2018); Ermakova and Fabian (2013).

[118] Koops and Kosta (2018); Ziccardi (2018).

[119] Chiara (2021), p. 24.

[120] European Parliament, Draft Report by Marju Lauristin (PE606.011v01-00), Respect for private life and the protection of personal data in electronic communications and repealing Directive 2002/58/EC (Regulation on Privacy and Electronic Communications), Amendment 276, Sophia in 't Veld, Angelika Mlinar, Proposal for a regulation Recital 26 a (new).

> democratic elections. Cybersecurity is necessary for human safety. Trust in financial systems and the stability of the global economic system depend upon cybersecurity.[121]

Privacy and, more broadly, fundamental rights therefore depend upon *some* cybersecurity technologies, and not others. As it has been stressed above, by setting the right sort of infraethics i.e., the instrumental values we want to assign to security, the axiological state of affairs will accordingly be determined through balances, thus eschewing trade-offs. The following section attempts a closer investigation of the strand of cybersecurity as an infraethical facilitator of fundamental rights, namely system robustness, through the lens of the public goods doctrine.

3.2.3 Cybersecurity as a Public Good

An initial clarification on the legal-economical conceptual boundaries of "public goods" is advisable here. In economic theory, a good is 'public' when its consumption presents the characteristics of non-rivalry and non-excludability. In the first case, the good can be consumed by several agents simultaneously; in the second case, no member of society can be excluded from its consumption because exclusion would imply an excessive cost.[122] The latter, however, implies the possibility of using the good in question without bearing the costs: this phenomenon is called free riding.

A doctrine characterising cybersecurity as a public good is certainly not a theoretical novelty. For about twenty years, especially in the United States, several scholars have been developing theoretical models aimed at justifying the equation between cybersecurity and public goods, drawing analogies with national defence and with the protection of public health. Some have argued that only the objectives, and not the institutions, of public health—which is undisputedly a public good—can provide solid grounds for a rationale applicable by analogy to cybersecurity. Public health and cybersecurity both aim to achieve a positive outcome for society at large (health or security). This metaphor would mainly have two consequences. First, when balancing collective versus individual interests, the emphasis would be on the collective's. Second, the management of non-secure systems and networks would increasingly be handled by public intervention, through incentives and duties.[123]

This theory combines three approaches: (i) persuasion through education, ideologies and social norms; (ii) monitoring through transparent information gathering and exchange; and (iii) state intervention in the choices of private individuals. Albeit intriguing and—to some extent—intuitive, this metaphor raises a number of theoretical and practical problems. The latter point (iii) in particular highlights the fact that if society wants to treat many, if not all, aspects of cybersecurity as a public

[121] Denardis (2020), p. 218.

[122] Mcnutt (1999), p. 927.

[123] Mulligan and Schneider (2011).

good, then what the public health metaphor demonstrates is that it may be necessary to accept a higher level of coercion on behaviours than what hyper-historical[124] information societies are used to.[125] Moreover, a *tout court* application of the public good doctrine to the field of cybersecurity calls for a careful reflection on how to compensate for the underproduction of cybersecurity goods in a market failure scenario.

Section 3.1 has already pointed out that there is no stable consensus on the conceptual boundaries of "cybersecurity", both from a political and doctrinal standpoint. Yet, it is undisputed that cybersecurity does not consist of a single dimension, let alone a single product, capable of holistically addressing all the different cases of cyberthreats (viruses, malware, ransomware, DDoS, etc.). Rather, it is a mix of various assets, goods and processes. Many cybersecurity products and solutions, such as advanced cryptographic schemes, antivirus software, and intrusion detection systems,[126] are not public goods: they are bought and sold between private sector actors, they are rivals, because their use affects other actors, and excludable, because their owners can restrict their use by others. Therefore, Rosenzweig argues that cybersecurity is a public good only and exclusively in its dimension of information-sharing regarding vulnerabilities and threats,[127] since it is the only domain that is truly non-rival and non-excludable.

Similarly, a theory based on the classical tripartition of information security has been proposed. Taddeo argues that only the first domain—the robustness of the system, and therefore the degree of divergence between the current and the desired behaviour of the system—should be included in the public goods legal framework. Conversely, this doctrine would not be applicable to the remaining areas of cybersecurity, albeit for different reasons. In fact, as Sect. 3.2.2 addressed above, resilience—understood in the dimension of threat detection—imposes a delicate balance between the desired degree of security and fundamental rights, such as the right to privacy and data protection; similarly, facilitating responsiveness may not lead to a global and collective improvement of cybersecurity. On the contrary, it is likely to lead to an intensification of cyberattacks.[128]

The aim of this framework is not to find an economic justification, but rather to lay the groundwork for a theoretical reflection on the need to treat the requirement of robustness of systems as a public good, due to the underlying public interest and crucial role it plays in tech-driven societies. Given the exponential growth of cyberattacks and threats, the non-rival but exclusive approach to this aspect of cybersecurity would continue to prove ineffective.[129] In general, developing robust systems has high costs: security aspects are often conceived in a trade-off with the

---

[124] Floridi (2020), pp. 85–91.

[125] Weber (2017).

[126] Tselios et al. (2019).

[127] Rosenzweig (2011), pp. 7–9; Weiss (2015).

[128] Taddeo (2019), p. 354.

[129] Ibid., p. 350.

final cost of the product. A case in point is the IoT sector, where most of the connected devices are resource-constrained and for this reason more vulnerable to attacks.

A first direct consequence of applying the theory of public goods to cybersecurity would be to compare the externalities arising from the application of this doctrine.

The first negative externality to be analysed is the "diversionary effect": some cybersecurity technologies, such as firewalls, which arguably belong to the dimension of resilience, simply divert attacks from a more impenetrable target to one that is more easily attacked. This means that improving the security of one actor may lead to a lower security state for other systems,[130] rather than increasing the overall level of security. In this context, circumscribing the public goods doctrine to the dimension of robustness alone, and not to cybersecurity *tout court*, would counter this externality, since the very rationale of this theoretical framework lies in the improvement of the overall level of cybersecurity.

A second negative externality is the "externalisation of costs": when software fails to prevent an intrusion or a service provider fails to block a malware attack, there is no mechanism by which these private actors can be held responsible for the costs of these failures. The costs are borne entirely by the end users.[131] The robustness of the system should not necessarily be free of charge for end users. On the other hand, it is essential that its costs do not become a discriminating factor, determining access: through a fair distribution of costs among the various market actors, access to appropriately secure digital technologies should be guaranteed for all users.[132] As a result, systemic, or holistic,[133] approaches would be favoured i.e., focusing on the relationships between different cybersecurity technologies and, above all, on the outcome of these technologies in terms of their impact on the ecosystem in which they operate.[134]

Managing system robustness as a public good also requires collaboration between the private and public sectors in order to ensure a high level of security, through a balanced division of competences and responsibilities. On the one hand, the public will have to establish standards, certification and testing, and supervision procedures, to ensure that a sufficient level of security is maintained to protect and promote the public interest, and that there are remediation and compensation measures when responsibilities are not properly discharged.[135] In this sense, Regulation EU 2019/881 (Cybersecurity Act) defines a European framework of cybersecurity certification schemes, to attest that ICT products, services and processes "comply

---

[130] Rosenzweig (2011), p. 9.

[131] Ibid., p. 10.

[132] Taddeo (2019), p. 351.

[133] In the literature, the so-called "holistic approach" is gaining more and more support, although it has no single interpretation. Floridi and Strait (2020); Raab (2020); Mantelero (2018).

[134] Taddeo (2019), p. 350.

[135] Ibid., p. 351.

with specified security requirements for the purpose of protecting the availability, authenticity, integrity or confidentiality of stored or transmitted or processed data or the functions or services offered by, or accessible via, those products, services and processes throughout their life cycle".[136] On the other hand, the private sector has a responsibility to design robust systems, develop and improve methods to foster the robustness of the services and products it offers, and cooperate with the public sector on controls and testing mechanisms.[137]

In general, the need for structured public-private collaborations is evidenced by the growing number of initiatives and policy statements[138] emphasising the value of public-private partnerships (PPPs) to provide or enhance cybersecurity, especially in the field of critical infrastructure.[139] There are predominantly four areas of intersection, at a higher level of abstraction: (1) the reliable provision of access to the Internet and ICTs infrastructure; (2) the co-regulation of technical aspects of security and data processing; (3) the exchange of information on threats and vulnerability; and (4) mutual assistance in dealing with threats or illegal content in cyberspace.[140]

Against this background of redistribution of responsibilities to all those who may be decisive in obtaining a satisfactory level of system robustness, with a view to protecting a common interest, some responsibilities will necessarily also fall on users, with particular reference to their "computer hygiene".[141] In the words of Denardis, "[t]hose who purchase and install systems have a responsibility to be aware of the product's privacy and security policies, when available, including not only devices but also associated back-end systems and applications, and to take whatever precautions are available".[142]

From a legal point of view, such a conclusion would imply complex considerations on the desirability of different degrees of legal responsibility (e.g., contractual and extra-contractual liability) held by the users. From a comparative perspective, in the United States, in a workshop organised by NIST on the cybersecurity of IoT devices, it emerged that the security of such systems should be a responsibility shared by producers and users.[143] Without dwelling too extensively on the liability issue here, which would go beyond the scope of this work, Article 122 of the Italian

---

[136] Art. 46(2), Regulation EU 2019/881; Bruno (2020).

[137] Taddeo (2019), p. 351.

[138] Ministry of Foreign Affairs of Italy (2021), p. 11: "[I]taly considers public-private cooperation as key to guaranteeing cybersecurity and effective capacity-building".

[139] Martino and Cappelletti (2021); European Commission (2015); ENISA (2018b).

[140] Bossong and Wagner (2018), p. 227.

[141] Taddeo (2019), p. 352.

[142] Denardis (2020), p. 120.

[143] Megas et al. (2021), pp. 9–10: "eighty-two percent of responses to one poll question agreed that the responsibility for securing IoT devices is shared between manufacturer and customer. [...] Customers, then, are responsible for implementing IoT devices in accordance with manufacturer guidance, ensuring devices have connectivity to receive updates, and monitoring devices to ensure continued security".

Consumer Code, in particular its second paragraph, may serve as an adequate legal basis for this responsibility framework.[144]

In less controversial terms, computer "hygiene" could therefore consist of best practices that should become part of the skills of every Internet-user.[145] In the background of these reflections, however, remain the critical issues related to the digital divide,[146] or *Onlife divide*—i.e., an exclusion not only from the mere dimension of connection, but from social life and knowledge more generally[147]—although it has been shown that age is not always a vulnerability factor when it comes to perceiving the importance of such practices.[148]

Such a recalibration of responsibilities, coupled with the need to consider the externalities arising from the production of cybersecurity goods, would facilitate cooperation between public and private actors and information-sharing on systems' vulnerabilities.[149] While the *public-private cooperation* is certainly the best interface through which we can better appreciate cybersecurity as a public good, due to its non-rival and non-exclusive nature,[150] it may be wrong to assume that sharing information about vulnerabilities and threats generates a positive impact for all the stakeholders involved.[151]

Firstly, software vulnerability is a sensitive issue that intersects the conflicting interests of cybersecurity-as-robustness (and privacy and data protection as well) and national security: law enforcement and intelligence agencies, by exploiting so-called zero-days vulnerabilities,[152] can more easily install malware in computer systems for law enforcement purposes,[153] at the price of exposing the users of the system in question to attacks by malicious actors.[154] Therefore, it is easy to understand why Member States are reluctant to give up their prerogatives on vulnerability reporting.[155]

Secondly, companies that are aware of cyber vulnerabilities, or that have been attacked,[156] are reluctant to disclose them for fear of reputational consequences or

[144] Art. 122(2), Codice del Consumo (D. Lgs. 6 September 2005, n. 206): *"[i]l risarcimento non è dovuto quando il danneggiato sia stato consapevole del difetto del prodotto e del pericolo che ne derivava e nondimeno vi si sia volontariamente esposto".*

[145] Pupillo (2018), pp. 6–7.

[146] Sultan (2019).

[147] Floridi and Sideri (2021), p. 2.

[148] Schaffer et al. (2020).

[149] Taddeo (2019), p. 352.

[150] Rosenzweig (2011).

[151] Bossong and Wagner (2018), p. 228.

[152] A security flaw that is not yet known to the developers/producers of a computer system and, a fortiori, to the users of the system itself.

[153] Koops and Kosta (2018), p. 898; Ziccardi (2018).

[154] Stockton and Golabek-Goldman (2015), p. 239.

[155] Fantin (2019).

[156] Of course, this would not apply to the subjects falling within the scope of the EU Directive 2016/1148 (NIS): operators of essential services must notify, without undue delay, the competent NIS

possible liabilities for the event.[157] Indeed, the cost of disclosing an incident or threat is mainly private, as it is borne entirely by the company, while the benefits of better disclosure are pervasive. The imbalance between the costs borne by a company and the collective benefits generates a market failure.

On the one hand, this explains the temptation to move from the instrument of partnership to a more markedly top-down model of governance, consisting of institutionalised processes governing a "duty to notify",[158] albeit in contexts that guarantee confidentiality and reciprocity such as those identified in the computer emergency response teams (CERTs) and computer security incident response teams (CSIRTs).[159] On the other hand, it is clear that a new conceptual approach to cybersecurity is needed to make the behaviour of all market players more compatible with incentives.[160] The doctrine of the public good, in this sense, is an answer to this need.

In conclusion, the resulting theoretical framework is functional to outlining a model consisting of several proxies, or indicators, which can serve as a guide for the legal analysis of this chapter on EU legal frameworks regulating (IoT) cybersecurity. At a high level of abstraction, the *redistribution of responsibilities*, *cooperation* and *information-sharing* are cardinal elements for the doctrine of cybersecurity as a public good. Chapter 4 will assess whether and to what extent the newest legislative texts issued e.g., the NIS 2 Directive and the Cyber Resilience Act proposal, follow these indicators.

3.2.4 Degrees of Separation Between Cybersecurity and Safety in the IoT

The relationship between security and safety, which partly emerged in Sect. 3.2.2, reflects a strand of the distinction between a condition of possibility for the enjoyment of instrumental goods (security-as-infraethics) and fundamental goods (security-as-a-fundamental-good, safety and fundamental rights).

This section casts light on the distinction between the connected concepts of safety and (cyber)security from a twofold perspective: (i) the two concepts are assessed against the background of the paradigm shift brought about by the IoT, which blends the physical and the virtual dimensions; and, (ii) how this distinction matters in relation to the relevant EU regulatory frameworks analysed in the next Chapter.

---

authority (the CSIRT) of incidents with a "significant" impact on the services provided; providers of digital services must instead notify those incidents with a "substantial" impact.

[157] Banca d'Italia (2018), p. 14; Nolan (2015), p. 5.

[158] Bossong and Wagner (2018), p. 228.

[159] Banca d'Italia (2018), pp. 14–15.

[160] Pupillo (2018), p. 7; Denardis (2020), pp. 117–118.

Reflections around safety and security have always been at the centre of the philosophical, political theory and legal debate—from Hobbes[161] and Locke[162] to Waltz,[163] Bobbio[164] and Waldron.[165] According to the "pure safety conception", as Waldron put it, security is a function of individual safety. This make sense: we are more secure against cyberattacks when the probability of such a harmful event is reduced. Without entering Waldron's pure safety process of enrichment, in terms of its breadth and depth, suffice here to say that this theory falls short of addressing collective and—more generally—"collateral" aspects that revolves around safety (e.g., fear, other types of harm rather than death or physical injury, assurance of being *actually* safe, etc.).[166]

Durante contributes to the scholarly debate on the relation between safety and security by acknowledging that whereas "[s]afety is mainly aimed to ensure the integrity of life against the threat of imminent dangers, [s]ecurity is mainly aimed to the protection of the conditions for the enjoyment of goods against the threat of dangers that may be subject of anticipation and calculation".[167] A considerable divergence exists, according to the philosopher, in relation to the temporal sphere. Safety has a precise temporal dimension which is linked to *immediate* relationships, whereas security has an inter-temporal nature which is grounded on *mediated* relationships.

In this respect, Durante's reflection revolves around security as "key policy lever"—due to the progressive conversion of security issues into safety issues (represented as more urgent and impending)—which allows governments to gain greater powers of direction and control with the aim of immunising society against the risks that seem to threaten its integrity.[168]

This notwithstanding, the "removal of a sphere of mediation between the request of fiduciary forms of risk management and their standardized and automated application",[169] which increasingly blurs the distinction between safety and security, is dealt with by the instruments of political theory. Although this critical reconstruction is useful for framing the boundaries of the concepts of safety and security, this section addresses this debate from a different angle.

What is at stake, here, is the alignment of theoretical legal-philosophical analyses of 'safety and security' with technical literature, as this distinction plays a crucial

[161] Hobbes (1996).
[162] Locke (1967).
[163] Waltz (1979).
[164] Bobbio (1987).
[165] Waldron (2006).
[166] Ibid., pp. 461–463.
[167] Durante (2019), p. 372.
[168] Ibid., p. 379.
[169] Id.

normative role in shaping technologies, in particular, having regard to the IoT, through the means of standardisation.[170]

Against this background, several authors argue that the paradigm shift brought by the IoT, by bringing together the physical and cyber dimensions, increasingly leads to addressing traditional notions of security and safety in a more interchangeably or unified way:[171] "in order to refer to different aspects of one and the same dimension as security flaws often turn out to be the flip-side of safety risks and vice versa".[172]

As a matter of fact, e-health (e.g., "smart" pacemakers and insulin pumps, etc.) is a prime example of how (cyber)security is increasingly taking on safety features, as security technologies and controls have to ensure the integrity of life against the threat of imminent dangers. Smart locks[173] and cars[174] are other clear cases where security threats, coming from the exploitation of flaws at design and implementation level, might jeopardize individual safety. Moreover, attacks on national critical infrastructure—from hospitals and water supplies to banks, police departments and transportation—reveal the true magnitude of IoT cyberthreats. Countless injuries, or even deaths, may incur as a result thereof. In late 2021, the Secretary of US Department of Homeland Security Alejandro Mayorkas referred to these new menaces as *killware*.[175]

Among others, Serpanos and Wolf presented a unified safety and security design methodology for IoT based on a holistic threat analysis. In their framework, the threat analysis serves (also) to discern safety issues from security ones: safety threats' analysis is mainly preoccupied with risks at the *application domain*, whilst security's assessment focuses on *systems' architecture* and *module design*.[176]

They further distinguish security from safety properties. The former conceives information in an all-or-nothing fashion; the latter emphasises operation with reduced capability as safety attacks may be limited to certain time window.[177] It therefore appears necessary to recall the above-mentioned temporal and intertemporal connotations associated with safety and security. Albeit within a holistic understanding, they acknowledge that such notions operate at different technical implementation levels.

Traditionally, IT literature considers physical safety as the result of the absence or minimisation of hazards that may harm both life and property; computer security used to focus on the CIA triad, as addressed in Sect. 3.1. Can safety, therefore, be considered as a requisite of cybersecurity? Hildebrandt, thus, points out that *traditional* digital security, that is, computer security, does not necessarily involve safety,

---

170 Vedder (2019), p. 11.

171 Wolf and Serpanos (2020), pp. 35–36.

172 Vedder (2019), p. 21.

173 Ho et al. (2016).

174 Spector and Yadron (2015).

175 Meyer (2021).

176 Wolf and Serpanos (2020), pp. 35–36.

177 Ibid., p. 35.

providing an example in which a cyberattack towards a web platform does not jeopardise anybody's safety.[178]

Yet, the hyper-connectedness of *every* social sphere brought by the IoT shows the dependence of "human safety on encryption, authentication, data integrity, availability, and other dimensions of cybersecurity".[179] In this regard, increased cybersecurity—in its dimension of robustness—*does* imply increased individual safety. And the contrary seems to be no longer true.[180] With the advent of the IoT, safety has become a requirement for cybersecurity, which has the ability to (re-) shape systems' architecture and design, therefore directly influencing safety properties.

At the same time, safety requirements include infrastructure (cyber)security ones: "security is a requirement for safety as well, since data integrity is necessary at least".[181] A similar reasoning can be found in the European Commission Communication on "Building Trust in Human-Centric Artificial Intelligence", according to which emerging digital technologies "should integrate safety and security-by-design mechanisms to ensure that they are verifiably safe at every step, taking at heart the physical and mental safety of all concerned".[182]

All in all, in the IoT era, safety, cybersecurity and privacy can no longer be deemed as separate domains. Instead, they will increasingly interact and affect each other. Therefore, *holistic* approaches[183] for the assessment of 'security & privacy' risks in the IoT will be required. In this respect, Chap. 5 specifically integrates security requirements in a data protection model (data protection impact assessment i.e., DPIA).

A normative distinction between the concepts of safety and security matters vis-à-vis the legal frameworks that regulate each aspect in the IoT context. As addressed in the next chapter, in the EU, product safety legislation aims to ensure the public policy objective of placing products in the single market that meet high health, safety and environmental requirements and that such products can circulate freely throughout the Union. Safety is usually conceived in a broad context, defined in "the code of ethical conduct of robotics engineers"—in the European Parliament resolution of 16 February 2017 with recommendations to the Commission on Civil Law Rules on Robotics—as *physical wellbeing, safety, health and rights.*[184]

Moreover, the concept of safety is linked to the use of the product and the risks—including also cyber risks and risks related to the loss of connectivity of devices—to be addressed to make the product safe.[185] The EU Commission acknowledges that

[178] Hildebrandt (2019), p. 260.
[179] Denardis (2020), p. 184.
[180] Hildebrandt (2019), p. 260.
[181] Serpanos and Wolf (2018), p. 57.
[182] European Commission (2019), p. 5.
[183] Grotto and Schallbruch (2021).
[184] European Parliament (2017), p. 20.
[185] European Commission (2020c), p. 6.

connectivity challenges the traditional understanding of safety, as it may compromise the safety of the product, and indirectly when it can be hacked leading to security threats and affecting the safety of users.[186]

Besides Directive 95/2001/EU (General Product Safety Directive, GPSD) - now repealed by Regulation (EU) 2023/988, which applies to all product categories as *lex generalis* (usually referred to in as "safety net"), the siloed thinking underpinning the rationale of the New Legislative Framework (NLF)[187] results in a sectoral regulatory approach. Therefore, the application of safety essential requirements to IoT devices depends on their classification according to product categories.[188] NLF Regulations and Directives were enacted before IoT hyper-connection. As a result, they risk being outdated when facing new cybersecurity threats that may result in safety harms.[189]

3.3 Conclusion

Security, safety, privacy and data protection are ever more intertwined in the age of IoT: a normative and theoretical reflection on the distinct rationales and scopes underlying these values is therefore needed to steer the legal analysis of the EU legal frameworks that regulate those aspects, as addressed in the following chapters.

---

[186] Ibid., p. 5.

[187] The new legislative framework (NLF) aims to improve the internal market for goods and strengthens the conditions for placing a wide range of products on the market (CE marking), *via* a package of measures which improves market surveillance and boosts the quality of conformity assessments. The NLF consists of (i) Regulation (EC) 765/2008 setting out the requirements for accreditation and the market surveillance of products; (ii) Decision 768/2008 on a common framework for the marketing of products, which includes reference provisions to be incorporated whenever product legislation is revised; and (iii) Regulation (EU) 2019/1020 on market surveillance and compliance of products.

[188] The directives and regulations that Decision 768/2008/EC aligned with, or was based on, the principles of NLF reference provisions are: Toy Safety - Directive 2009/48/EU; Transportable pressure equipment - Directive 2010/35/EU; Restriction of Hazardous Substances in Electrical and Electronic Equipment - Directive 2011/65/EU; Construction products - Regulation (EU) No 305/2011; Pyrotechnic Articles - Directive 2013/29/EU; Recreational craft and personal watercraft - Directive 2013/53/EU; Civil Explosives - Directive 2014/28/EU; Simple Pressure Vessels - Directive 2014/29/EU; Electromagnetic Compatibility - Directive 2014/30/EU; Non-automatic Weighing Instruments - Directive 2014/31/EU; Measuring Instruments - Directive 2014/32/EU; Lifts - Directive 2014/33/EU; ATEX - Directive 2014/34/EU; Radio equipment - Directive 2014/53/EU; Low Voltage - Directive 2014/35/EU; Pressure equipment - Directive 2014/68/EU; Marine Equipment - Directive 2014/90/EU; Cableway installations - Regulation (EU) 2016/424; Personal protective equipment - Regulation (EU) 2016/425; Gas appliances - Regulation (EU) 2016/426; Medical devices - Regulation (EU) 2017/745; In vitro diagnostic medical devices - Regulation (EU) 2017/746; EU fertilising products – Regulation (EU) 2019/1009.

[189] Fosch-Villaronga and Mahler (2021), p. 6.

Cybersecurity has not merely replaced the 'old fashioned' technical concepts of computer and information security. This chapter showed that it represents a new paradigm. Limiting the concept of 'security' in the cyber domain to the protection of networks, information systems and information is too restrictive and ultimately anachronistic. The IoT expands the *perimeter* of the values and assets that need to be protected. Risk factors and threats in today's IoT hyper-connected digital environment go beyond the technological infrastructure of information systems, networks and the underlying information. An attack could also infringe individuals' fundamental rights, impair physical safety and, as much as the critical infrastructure is concerned, have serious consequences for communities, institutions and businesses.

As regards the relationship between cybersecurity and the fundamental right to privacy (understood within the theory of informational privacy, to include personal data protection issues), the chapter has explored two possible perspectives. Cybersecurity as an *instrumental* value to uphold *fundamental* values (e.g., fundamental rights and liberties, physical safety) and cybersecurity as a *fundamental* value *per se*, involving therefore balancing exercises in the event of compression of other fundamental values on the same level. Building on the three dimensions of cybersecurity (i.e., robustness, resilience and response), the analysis concludes that only in the latter two cases does cybersecurity pose risks to privacy. In this respect, bad '*infraethics*' apply trade-offs rather than balances. Privacy is therefore 'facilitated' by *some* cybersecurity technologies and not others.

On the contrary, the first dimension of cybersecurity i.e., systems' robustness, which focuses on building solid, reliable systems that can withstand and mitigate attacks, can be seen within an *instrumental* or *infraethical* horizon. Yet, an attempt has been made in developing a theoretical framework for the application of the public good theory to this sole dimension of cybersecurity. Taking into account the possible externalities that may arise, the resulting model pivots around three pillars, which can be observed in the recent EU legislative developments in EU cybersecurity *acquis*, as addressed in this chapter. These are: redistribution of responsibilities, cooperation between private and public sectors and information-sharing.

Finally, the chapter shed light on the distinction between the concepts of (cyber)-security and safety. The IoT paradigm shift, which brings together the physical and cyber environment, increasingly leads to the addressing of traditional notions of security and safety in a more holistic way. With the advent of the IoT, increased cybersecurity *does* imply increased individual safety. Safety becomes a requirement for cybersecurity, which has the ability to (re-)shape systems' architecture and design, directly influencing safety properties. This reflection would serve as a solid benchmark in critically analysing the EU legal frameworks regulating IoT security & safety in Chap. 4.

References

Banca d'Italia (2018) Sicurezza cibernetica: il contributo della Banca d'Italia e dell'Ivass. https://www.bancaditalia.it/pubblicazioni/tematiche-istituzionali/2018-sicurezza-cibernetica/index.html

Bobbio N (1987) Future of democracy. Wiley Polity

Bonfanti M (2022) Artificial intelligence and the offense-defense balance in cyber security. In: Dunn Cavelty M, Wenger A (eds) Cyber security politics: socio-technological transformations and political fragmentation. Routledge, London

Bossong R, Wagner B (2018) A typology of cybersecurity and public-private partnerships in the context of the European Union. In: Bures O, Carrapico H (eds) Security privatization: how non-security-related private businesses shape security governance. Springer International Publishing, pp 219–247

Brighi R (2017) Cibercrimine e anonimato in Rete. Riflessioni su sicurezza, efficacia investigativa e tutela delle libertà personali. Sicur e Sci Soc 29–43. https://doi.org/10.3280/SISS2017-003004

Brighi R (2021) Cybersecurity. Dimensione pubblica e privata della sicurezza dei dati. In: Casadei T, Pietropaoli S (eds) Diritto e Tecnologie Informatiche - Questioni di Informatica Giuridica, Prospettive Istituzionali e Sfide Sociali. Cedam, Milano, pp 135–147

Bruno B (2020) Cybersecurity tra legislazioni, interessi nazionali e mercato. Federalismi.it 14

Burton C (2020) Article 32 Security of processing. In: Kuner C, Bygrave AL, Docksey C, Drechsler L (eds) The EU General Data Protection Regulation (GDPR): a commentary. Oxford University Press, pp 630–639

Bygrave LA (2020) Article 25 Data protection by design and by default. In: Kuner C, Bygrave AL, Docksey C, Drechsler L (eds) The EU General Data Protection Regulation (GDPR): a commentary. Oxford University Press, pp 571–581

Bygrave LA (2022) Cyber resilience versus cybersecurity as legal aspiration. In: Jančárková T, Visky G, Winther I (eds) 14th International Conference on Cyber Conflict, CYCON. NATO CCDCOE, pp 27–43

CEN-CENELEC Cyber Security Focus Group (2020) Definition of Cybersecurity

Chiara PG (2020) Disentangling encryption from the personalization debate: on the advisability of endorsing the "relativist approach" underpinning the identifiability criterion. Univ Vienna Law Rev 4:168–188

Chiara PG (2021) The balance between security, privacy and data protection in IoT data sharing: a critique to traditional 'Security&Privacy' surveys. Eur Data Prot Law Rev 7:18–30. https://doi.org/10.21552/EDPL/2021/1/6

Citron D, Franks M (2014) Criminalizing revenge porn. Wake For Law Rev 49

Cohen JE (2013) What privacy is for. Harv Law Rev 126:1904–1933

Cole MD, Etteldorf C, Ullrich C (2020) Cross-border dissemination of online content, 1st edn. Nomos Verlagsgesellschaft mbH & Co. KG

D'Souza R, Jao D, Mironov I, Pandey O (2011) Publicly verifiable secret sharing for cloud-based key management. In: Progress in Cryptology – INDOCRYPT 2011. Springer, Berlin, Heidelberg, pp 290–309

Denardis L (2020) The internet in everything - freedom and security in a world with no off switch, 1st edn. Yale University Press, New Haven & London

Durante M (2017) Ethics, law and the politics of information: a guide to the philosophy of Luciano Floridi. Springer, Netherlands, Dordrecht

Durante M (2019) Safety and security in the digital age. trust, algorithms, standards, and risks. In: Berkich D, D'Alfonso MV (eds) On the cognitive, ethical, and scientific dimensions of artificial intelligence. Springer Nature, pp 371–383

Edwards L (2016) Privacy, security and data protection in smart cities: a critical EU law perspective. Eur Data Prot Law Rev 2

Egorov M, Wilkison M, David Nuñez N (2017) NuCypher KMS: decentralized key management system

Elliott D (2019) Data protection is more than privacy. Eur Data Prot Law Rev 5:13–16
ENISA (2016) Opinion Paper on Encryption - Strong Encryption Safeguards Our Digital Identity
ENISA (2017) Overview of cybersecurity and related terminology Foreword by the Executive Director
ENISA (2018a) Recommendations on Shaping Technology According to GDPR Provisions
ENISA (2018b) Public Private Partnerships (PPP) - Cooperative models
ENISA (2020a) The year in review ENISA Threat Landscape - From January 2019 to April 2020
ENISA (2020b) Artificial Intelligence Threat Landscape Report
Ermakova T, Fabian B (2013) Secret sharing for health data in multi-provider clouds. Proc - 2013 IEEE Int Conf Bus Informatics, IEEE CBI 2013, pp 93–100
European Commission (2015) Public consultation on the public-private partnership on cybersecurity and possible accompanying measures
European Commission (2019) COMMUNICATION FROM THE COMMISSION TO THE EUROPEAN PARLIAMENT, THE COUNCIL, THE EUROPEAN ECONOMIC AND SOCIAL COMMITTEE AND THE COMMITTEE OF THE REGIONS Building Trust in Human-Centric Artificial Intelligence COM/2019/168 final
European Commission (2020a) COMMUNICATION FROM THE COMMISSION TO THE EUROPEAN PARLIAMENT, THE EUROPEAN COUNCIL, THE COUNCIL, THE EUROPEAN ECONOMIC AND SOCIAL COMMITTEE AND THE COMMITTEE OF THE REGIONS on the EU Security Union Strategy
European Commission (2020b) COMMUNICATION FROM THE COMMISSION TO THE EUROPEAN PARLIAMENT AND THE COUNCIL Data protection as a pillar of citizens' empowerment and the EU's approach to the digital transition - two years of application of the General Data Protection Regulation COM/2020
European Commission (2020c) REPORT FROM THE COMMISSION TO THE EUROPEAN PARLIAMENT, THE COUNCIL AND THE EUROPEAN ECONOMIC AND SOCIAL COMMITTEE Report on the safety and liability implications of Artificial Intelligence, the Internet of Things and robotics COM/2020/64 final
European Commission and the High Representatitve of the Union for Foreign Affairs and Security Policy (2020) Joint Communication to the European Parliament and the Council: The EU's Cybersecurity Strategy for the Digital Decade
European Commission and the High Representative of the Union for Foreign Affairs and Security Policy (2013) Joint Communication to the European Parliament, the Council, the European Economic and Social Committee and the Committee of the Regions Cybersecurity Strategy of the European Union: An Open, Safe and Secure Cyberspace JOIN(2013) 1 final
European Commission and the High Representative of the Union for Foreign Affairs and Security Policy (2017) Joint Communication to the European Parliament and the Council Resilience, Deterrence and Defence: Building strong cybersecurity for the EU
European Commission High Level Group of Scientific Adivisors (2017) Cybersecurity in the European Digital Single Market
European Court of Human Rights (2021) Guide on Article 8 of the European Convention on Human Rights. Council of Europe
European Parliament (2017) Resolution of 16 February 2017 with recommendations to the Commission on Civil Law Rules on Robotics (2015/2103(INL))
EUROPOL (2020) Internet organised crime threat assessment (IOCTA)
Fantin S (2019) Weighting the EU Cybersecurity Act: progress or missed opportunity?, KU Leuven Citip blog post. https://www.law.kuleuven.be/citip/blog/weighting-the-eu-cybersecurity-act-progress-or-missed-opportunity/
Floridi L (2005) The ontological interpretation of informational privacy. Ethics Inf Technol 7:185–200. https://doi.org/10.1007/s10676-006-0001-7
Floridi L (2016) On human dignity as a foundation for the right to privacy. Philos Technol 29:307–312. https://doi.org/10.1007/S13347-016-0220-8

Floridi L (2017) Infraethics–on the conditions of possibility of morality. Philos Technol 30:391–394. https://doi.org/10.1007/S13347-017-0291-1
Floridi L (2020) Il verde e il blu - Idee ingenue per migliorare la politica. Raffaello Cortina Editore
Floridi L, Sideri M (2021) Piramide Onlife, Corriere Innovazione
Floridi L, Strait A (2020) Ethical foresight analysis: what it is and why it is needed? Minds Mach 30:77–97. https://doi.org/10.1007/S11023-020-09521-Y
Fosch-Villaronga E, Mahler T (2021) Cybersecurity, safety and robots: strengthening the link between cybersecurity and safety in the context of care robots. Comput Law Secur Rev 41. https://doi.org/10.1016/J.CLSR.2021.105528
Fuster GG, Hijmans H (2019) The EU rights to privacy and personal data protection: 20 years in 10 questions - Discussion paper. In: International Workshop 'Exploring the Privacy and Data Protection connection: International Workshop on the Legal Notions of Privacy and Data Protection in EU Law in a Rapidly Changing World'. pp 1–13
Fuster GG, Jasmontaite L (2020) Cybersecurity regulation in the European Union: the digital, the critical and fundamental rights. In: Christen M, Gordijn B, Loi M (eds) The ethics of cybersecurity. Springer, Cham, pp 97–115
Grotto AJ, Schallbruch M (2021) Cybersecurity and the risk governance triangle. Int Cybersecur Law Rev 2:77–92. https://doi.org/10.1365/S43439-021-00016-9
Guttman B, Roback E (1995) An introduction to computer security: the NIST Handbook, Special Publication (NIST SP). Gaithersburg, MD
Gutwirth S, De Hert P (2008) Regulating profiling in a democratic constitutional state. In: Hildebrandt M, Gutwirth S (eds) Profiling the European citizen: cross-disciplinary perspectives. Springer, Netherlands, pp 271–302
Herrmann D, Pridöhl H (2020) Basic concepts and models of cybersecurity. In: Christen M, Gordijn B, Loi M (eds) The ethics of cybersecurity. Springer Science and Business Media B. V., pp 11–44
Hildebrandt M (2019) Digital security and human rights: a plea for counter-infringement measures. In: Susi M (ed) Human rights, digital society and the law, 1st edn. Routledge, London
Ho et al (2016) Smart locks: lessons for securing commodity internet of things devices. Electrical Engineering and Computer Sciences University of California at Berkeley, Technical Report No. UCB/EECS-2016-11. http://www.eecs.berkeley.edu/Pubs/TechRpts/2016/EECS-2016-11.html
Hobbes T (1996) Leviathan [1651]. Cambridge University Press
Ismail T, Touati H, Hajlaoui N, Hamdi H (2020) Hybrid and secure E-health data sharing architecture in multi-clouds environment. In: ICOST 2020: the impact of digital technologies on public health in developed and developing countries. Springer, Cham, pp 249–258
Jabri V (2016) Security: critique, analysis and ethics. In: Nyman J, Burke A (eds) Ethical security studies: a new research agenda. Routledge
Jacobs B (2024) The authenticity crisis. Comput Law Secur Rev 53:105962
Kokott J, Sobotta C (2013) The distinction between privacy and data protection in the jurisprudence of the CJEU and the ECtHR. Int Data Priv Law 3:222–228. https://doi.org/10.1093/idpl/ipt017
Koops B-J (2014) On legal boundaries, technologies, and collapsing dimensions of privacy. Polit e Soc 3:247–264
Koops BJ, Kosta E (2018) Looking for some light through the lens of "cryptowar" history: policy options for law enforcement authorities against "going dark". Comput Law Secur Rev 34:890–900. https://doi.org/10.1016/J.CLSR.2018.06.003
Lancelot JF (2020) Cyber-diplomacy: cyberwarfare and the rules of engagement. J Cyber Secur Technol 4:240–254. https://doi.org/10.1080/23742917.2020.1798155
Locke J (1967) Two treatises of government [1690]. Cambridge University Press
Loi M, Christen M (2020) Ethical frameworks for cybersecurity. In: Christen M, Gordijn B, Loi M (eds) The ethics of cybersecurity. Springer Science and Business Media B.V., pp 73–95
Loideain NN (2019) A port in the data-sharing storm: the GDPR and the internet of things. J Cyber Policy 4:178–196. https://doi.org/10.1080/23738871.2019.1635176

Lynskey O (2014) Deconstructing data protection: the 'added-value' of a right to data protection in the eu legal order. Int Comp Law Q 63:569–597. https://doi.org/10.1017/S0020589314000244

Lynskey O (2015) The foundations of EU data protection law. Oxford University Press

Manky D (2013) Cybercrime as a service: a very modern business. Comput Fraud Secur 2013:9–13. https://doi.org/10.1016/S1361-3723(13)70053-8

Mantclcro A (2018) AI and Big Data: a blueprint for a human rights, social and ethical impact assessment. Comput Law Secur Rev 34:754–772. https://doi.org/10.1016/J.CLSR.2018.05.017

Mantelero A, Vaciago G, Samantha Esposito M, Monte N (2021) The common EU approach to personal data and cybersecurity regulation. Int J Law Inf Technol 28:297–328. https://doi.org/10.1093/IJLIT/EAAA021

Martino L, Cappelletti F (2021) Achieving robust European cybersecurity through public-private partnerships: approaches and developments Content. Eur Lib Forum 4

Martoni M (2020) Datificazione dei nativi digitali e società della classificazione. Prime riflessioni sull'educazione alla cittadinanza digitale. Federalismi.it 1:119–136

Mcnutt P (1999) Public goods and club goods. Encycl law Econ 1:927–951

Megas KN et al (2021) Workshop Summary Report for "Building the Federal Profile for IoT Device Cybersecurity" Virtual Workshop NISTIR 8322. <https://nvlpubs.nist.gov/nistpubs/ir/2021/NIST.IR.8322.pdf>

Meyer J (2021) The next big cyberthreat isn't ransomware. It's killware. And it's just as bad as it sounds. USA Today

Ministry of Foreign Affairs of Italy (2021) Italian Position Paper on "International Law and Cyberspace" <https://www.esteri.it/mae/resource/doc/2021/11/italian_position_paper_on_international_law_and_cyberspace.pdf>

Mittelstadt BD, Allo P, Taddeo M et al (2016) The ethics of algorithms: mapping the debate. Big Data Soc 3:205395171667967. https://doi.org/10.1177/2053951716679679

Mulligan DK, Schneider FB (2011) Doctrine for cybersecurity. Daedalus 140:70–92

Nieles M et al (2017) NIST Special Publication 800-12 Revision 1 - An introduction to information security

NIST (2015) NISTIR 8074 - Supplemental Information for the Interagency Report on Strategic U.S. Government Engagement in International Standardization to Achieve U.S. Objectives for Cybersecurity

NIST (2018) Framework for Improving Critical Infrastructure Cybersecurity

Nolan A (2015) Cybersecurity and information sharing: legal challenges and solutions, Congressional Research Service, 7-5700. https://sgp.fas.org/crs/intel/R43941.pdf

Pagallo U (2013) Online security and the protection of civil rights: a legal overview. Philos Technol 26:381–395. https://doi.org/10.1007/S13347-013-0119-6/METRICS

Pagallo U (2017) The group, the private, and the individual: a new level of data protection? In: Taylor L, Floridi L, van der Sloot B (eds) Group privacy. Springer, pp 159–173

Pagallo U, Casanovas P, Madelin R (2019) The middle-out approach: assessing models of legal governance in data protection, artificial intelligence, and the Web of Data. Theory Pract Legis 7: 1–25. https://doi.org/10.1080/20508840.2019.1664543

Palmirani M, Martoni M (2019) Big data, governance dei dati e nuove vulnerabilità. Not Polit 35:9–22

Paulsen C, Byers R (2019) Glossary of key information security terms, NIST Interagency/Internal Report (NISTIR). National Institute of Standards and Technology, Gaithersburg, MD

Porcedda MG (2023) Cybersecurity, privacy and data protection in EU law: a law, policy and technology analysis. Hart Publishing

Pupillo L (2018) EU cybersecurity and the paradox of progress, CEPS Special publications

Raab CD (2020) Information privacy, impact assessment, and the place of ethics. Comput Law Secur Rev 37:105404. https://doi.org/10.1016/J.CLSR.2020.105404

Rodotà S (2004) Privacy, libertà, dignità - Privacy, Freedom, and Dignity. In: Conclusive Remarks at the 26th International Conference on Privacy and Data Protection

Rosenzweig P (2011) Cybersecurity and public goods the public/private "partnership". Emerg Threat Natl Secur Law - Hoover Institution, Stanford Univ

Rugge F (2018) Mind hacking: la guerra informativa nell'era cyber. Not Polit 34:108–117

Schaffer SM, Schaffer DR, Colson DG (2020) A reverse digital divide: comparing information security behaviors of generation Y and generation Z adults. Int J Cybersecurity Intell Cybercrime 3. https://doi.org/10.52306/03010420GXUV5876

Schermer BW (2011) The limits of privacy in automated profiling and data mining. Comput Law Secur Rev 27:45–52. https://doi.org/10.1016/j.clsr.2010.11.009

Serpanos D, Wolf M (2018) Internet-of-Things (IoT) systems - architectures, algorithms, methodologies. Springer International Publishing

Spector M, Yadron D (2015) Regulators Investigating Fiat Chrysler Cybersecurity Recall. Wall Str. J

Stockton P, Golabek-Goldman M (2015) Curbing the market for cyber weapons. Yale Law Policy Rev 32

Sultan A (2019) Improving cybersecurity awareness in underserved populations. CLTC White Pap Ser Berkeley

Taddeo M (2019) Is cybersecurity a public good? Minds Mach 29:349–354. https://doi.org/10.1007/S11023-019-09507-5

Tene O, Polonetsky J (2013) Big data for all: privacy and user control in the age of analytics. Northwest J Technol Intellect Prop 11:239

Tselios C, Tsolis G, Athanatos M (2019) A comprehensive technical survey of contemporary cybersecurity products and solutions. In: Fournaris A, Athanatos M, Lampropoulos K et al (eds) Computer Security LNCS11981 - ESORICS 2019 International Workshops, IOSec, MSTEC, and FINSEC. Springer, Cham, pp 3–19

Union Agency for Fundamental Rights - Council of Europe-European Court of Human Rights - European Data Protection Supervisor E (2018) Handbook on European data protection law. Publications Office of the European Union, Luxembourg

van de Poel I (2020) Core values and value conflicts in cybersecurity: beyond privacy versus security. In: Christen M, Gordijn B, Loi M (eds) The ethics of cybersecurity. Springer Science and Business Media B.V., pp 45–71

Van Wel L, Royakkers L (2004) Ethical issues in web data mining. Ethics Inf Technol 6:129–140. https://doi.org/10.1023/B:ETIN.0000047476.05912.3D

Veale M, Brown I (2020) Cybersecurity. Internet Policy Rev 9:1–22. https://doi.org/10.14763/2020.4.1533

Vedder A (2019) Safety, security and ethics. In: Vedder A, Schroers J, Ducuing C, Valcke P (eds) Security and law. Intersentia, pp 11–26

Waldron JJ (2006) Safety and security. Neb Law Rev 85:455–506

Waltz KN (1979) Theory of international politics. Addison-Wesley Publishing Company

Weber S (2017) Coercion in cybersecurity: what public health models reveal. J Cybersecur 3:173–183. https://doi.org/10.1093/CYBSEC/TYX005

Webster F (2014) Theories of the information society. Routledge, London

Weiss NE (2015) Legislation to Facilitate Cybersecurity Information Sharing: Economic Analysis

Wiewiórowski W (2020) Keynote: Data protection needs encryption, EDPS 1st Online IPEN Workshop.

Wolf M, Serpanos D (2020) Safe and secure cyber-physical systems and internet-of-things systems. Springer

World Economic Forum (2021) The Global Risks Report 2021

Zhang H, Yu J, Tian C et al (2018) Cloud storage for electronic health records based on secret sharing with verifiable reconstruction outsourcing. IEEE Access 6:40713–40722. https://doi.org/10.1109/ACCESS.2018.2857205

Ziccardi G (2016) L'odio online: violenza verbale e ossessioni in rete. Raffaello Cortina Editore
Ziccardi G (2018) The GDPR and the LIBE study on the use of hacking tools by law enforcement agencies. Ital Law J 4
Ziccardi G (2019) Tecnologie per il potere: come usare i social network in politica. Raffaello Cortina Editore

Chapter 4
The EU Legal Frameworks Regulating IoT Cybersecurity

4.1 The NIS Directive and the Indirect Link with the IoT

The more they play a vital role in our society, the more network and information systems and services are at risk. Their reliability and security are both crucial aspects for upholding the functioning of the market as well as for the protection of the rights and liberties of individuals. Against this backdrop, Directive (EU) 2016/1148 (hereinafter, the Directive)[1] was the first piece of EU-wide legislation on cybersecurity, providing legal measures to boost the overall level of cybersecurity in the Union, and now repealed by Directive (EU) 2022/2555 (NIS2 Directive, see Sect. 4.4).

The Directive lays down measures with a view to achieving a high common level of security of network and information systems (NIS) within the Union as a baseline set of *minimum* cybersecurity standards in order to improve the functioning of the internal market.[2] Accordingly, the Directive has Article 114(1) of the Treaty on the Functioning of the European Union (TFEU) as legal basis.[3] Moreover, the Directive

[1] Directive (EU) 2016/1148 of the European Parliament and of the Council of 6 July 2016 concerning measures for a high common level of security of network and information systems across the Union.

[2] Directive (EU) 2016/1148, article 1(1).

[3] Consolidated version of the Treaty on the Functioning of the European Union *OJ C 326, 26.10.2012*, article 114(1): [T]he European Parliament and the Council shall, acting in accordance with the ordinary legislative procedure and after consulting the Economic and Social Committee, adopt the measures for the approximation of the provisions laid down by law, regulation or administrative action in Member States which have as their object the establishment and functioning of the internal market.

P. G. Chiara, *The Internet of Things and EU Law*, Issues in Privacy and Data Protection 67, https://doi.org/10.1007/978-3-031-67663-5_4

establishes a *lex generalis – lex specialis* relationships with already existing or future EU sector-specific legislation with NIS-related rules.[4]

The responsibility to ensure NIS security lies—besides Member States[5]—with the two macro categories of actors under the scope of the Directive: operators of essential services (OES) and digital service providers (DSP). In particular, the burden of identifying the OESs is placed upon Member States which, pursuant to Article 5 of the Directive, shall determine which entities, having an establishment on their territory, ought to be classified as OESs. These entities are to be sought in those actors whose services' provision depends on network and information systems[6] throughout seven pre-identified sectors[7]—and relative subsectors—deemed as essential for the maintenance of critical societal and economic activities.[8] The significant disruptive effects that an incident would have on the provision of the service is yet a further criterion for the identification of OESs.[9]

To weigh the significance of a "disruptive effective", Member States shall take into account not only several *cross-sectorial factors*—such as the number of users affected, the degree and duration of the impact on economic and societal activities or public safety, the geographic spread, the market share of that entity, the dependency of other sectors on the service provided by that entity, and the importance of the entity for maintaining a sufficient level of the service[10]—but *sector specific factors* as well.[11] Interestingly, the Directive may not apply indiscriminately to every public administration, but only to those that are identified as OESs.[12] Finally, in those cases where an OES offer its services in two or more Member states, those States shall engage in bilateral/multilateral consultations.[13]

Conversely, the threefold classification of DSP, i.e., online marketplaces, online search engines and cloud computer services,[14] covers every entity falling into one of those categories. Consequently, Member States do not have to identify those actors.

[4]Directive (EU) 2016/1148, article 1(7); recital 9.

[5]Within Member states obligations, Article 7 mandates the adoption of a national NIS/cybersecurity strategy, defining the strategic objectives and appropriate policy and regulatory measures; Article 8 imposes on each Member State the duty to designate one or more national competent authorities on the security of NIS and a single point of contact; whereas Article 9 foresees the obligation to designate one or more CSIRTs (which could be established within a competent authority).

[6]Directive (EU) 2016/1148, Article 5(2)(b).

[7]Directive (EU) 2016/1148, Annex II: (i) energy; (ii) transport; (iii) banking; (iv) financial market infrastructures; (v) health sector; (vi) drinking water supply and distribution; (vii) digital infrastructure.

[8]Directive (EU) 2016/1148, Article 5(2)(a); Recital 20.

[9]Directive (EU) 2016/1148, Article 5(2)(c).

[10]Directive (EU) 2016/1148, Article 6(1).

[11]Directive (EU) 2016/1148, Article 6(2), Recital 28: for example, with regard to energy suppliers, "such factors could include the volume or proportion of national power generated".

[12]Directive (EU) 2016/1148, recital 45.

[13]Directive (EU) 2016/1148, article 5().

[14]Directive (EU) 2016/1148, Annex III.

The ratio of this divergence of treatment has to be found in the almost unavoidable reliance on DSPs services by EU businesses and users, including OESs.[15] Moreover, the Directive considered OESs and DSPs *fundamentally* different in that the former have a direct link with physical infrastructure while the latter have a cross-border nature.[16] Hence, the EU legislator wanted to eschew a scenario of a lack of harmonisation vis-à-vis the identification—with the subsequent application of NIS obligations in terms of security measures and incidents reporting—of DSPs by Member States.

The differentiation in treatment of OESs and DSPs does not amount solely to their identification by Member States. As regards security and incidents notification requirements for OESs and DSPs, arguably the core of the Directive (Chapter IV and V respectively), the Directive lays down stricter obligations for operators of essential services than the ones foreseen for digital service providers. The rationale behind this approach was the assumption that the degree of risk for operators of essential services is higher than for digital service providers, resulting in lighter security requirements for digital service providers.[17] As a result, Member States are not allowed to impose any further security or incidents notification requirements on DSPs, other than the ones laid down at Article 16.[18]

The nature of DSPs' operations justified the so-called "light-touch",[19] which is prominent in the enforcement phase. Thus, Member States' competent authorities can only take action on DSPs through *ex-post* supervisory measures, when provided with evidence that a digital service provider does not meet the security and incidents notification requirements.[20] The difference with the corresponding Article 15 is striking: in particular, competent authorities shall have the powers and means to require—at any time—OESs to provide the information necessary to assess the security of their NIS and evidence of the effective implementation of security policies (e.g., results of a security audit).[21]

This lighter regime has received a lot of criticism in literature, given the crucial importance of DSPs (for example, we can refer to ubiquitous cloud service providers) in today's society and economy.[22] There is an unavoidable dependency of our societies on DSPs that is acknowledged by the Directive itself.[23] However, ENISA helps in clarifying that "applying a light touch approach should not prevent a specific authority from being fully able to exercise its supervision authority upon a DSP, should the case require it. For example, applying fewer provisions for DSPs as

[15] Directive (EU) 2016/1148, recital 48.
[16] Directive (EU) 2016/1148, recital 57.
[17] Directive (EU) 2016/1148, recital 49.
[18] Directive (EU) 2016/1148, article 16(10).
[19] Directive (EU) 2016/1148, recital 60.
[20] Directive (EU) 2016/1148, article 17(1).
[21] Directive (EU) 2016/1148, Article 15(2).
[22] Markopoulou et al. (2019).
[23] Directive (EU) 2016/1148, Recital 48.

compared to OES might not be beneficial if certain limits are exceeded".[24] Moreover, the possibility of public administrations to require DSPs to have additional security measures, for the services they use, *via* contractual obligations can be seen as a partial mitigation of the light-touch approach.[25]

As regards the security and incident notifications requirements, Article 14(1) does not give any indication on the nature, appropriateness, and proportionality of technical and organisational measures that OES shall take in managing the risks (involving therefore measures to prevent and minimise the impact of incidents[26]) posed to the security of network and information systems. Rather, security measures and controls are ultimately decided by the OES, following a risk-based approach, as the European legislator opted for a principles-based model of governance, rather than enforcing prescriptive rules.[27]

Notwithstanding the security measures put in place by the OES, if an incident—with a *significant* impact (in terms of the numbers of users affected, the duration and the geographical spread) on the continuity of the essential services provided—occurs, the OES must notify the competent authority or CSIRT[28] without undue delay.[29]

Albeit following the same risk-based approach,[30] Article 16 includes specific elements that DSPs have to take into account when identifying the security measures. These are: (a) the security of systems and facilities; (b) incident handling; (c) business continuity management; (d) monitoring, auditing and testing; (e) compliance with international standards.[31] This specification, absent in the corresponding Article 14, can be attributed to the aforementioned "light-touch": given the softer control and enforcement, the Directive wants to make sure that at least baseline requirements are met.

---

[24] ENISA (2017a), pp. 9–10.

[25] Directive (EU) 2016/1148, Recital 54.

[26] Directive (EU) 2016/1148, Art. 14(2).

[27] Schmitz-Berndt and Cole (2022), p. 8: "[w]hile the national transposition of the NIS Directive repeat the general wording of the Directive, complementary guidance or regulations amending national law define the indefinite legal concepts further".

[28] Directive (EU) 2016/1148, Art. 14(5): "the competent authority or the CSIRT shall inform the other affected Member State(s) if the incident has a significant impact on the continuity of essential services in that Member State".

[29] Directive (EU) 2016/1148, Arts. 14(3), 14(4).

[30] Directive (EU) 2016/1148, Art. 16(2): "Member States shall ensure that digital service providers take measures to prevent and minimise the impact of incidents affecting the security of their network and information systems".

[31] Directive (EU) 2016/1148, Art. 16(1). These elements were further specified by the Commission Implementing Regulation (EU) 2018/151, in article 2.

Like OESs, DSPs must notify the competent authority or CSIRT,[32] without undue delay, of any incident having a *substantial* impact on the services provided.[33] The three parameters that apply for determining the significance of the impact of an incident affecting an OES are added to by two more: (i) the extent of the disruption; and (ii) the extent of the impact on economic and societal activities.[34]

Interestingly, if an OES relies on a service provided by a DSP, which is essential for the maintenance of critical societal and economic activities, and yet an incident affects the DSP, the OES has to notify the NIS authority of the event if it results in a *significant* impact on the continuity of the essential services, leaving the DSP off the hook. However, where an incident has a *substantial* impact on the provision of a digital service, but the impact on the continuity of an OES is not significant, the DSP will have to notify.

Against the background of the NIS Directive's scope, the question arises as to whether and to what extent the Directive addresses IoT security challenges. First, a link between the IoT and the Directive has to be established. The analysis above has clearly shown that the NIS Directive was not conceived to *directly* enhance products' cybersecurity or were the terms "Internet of Things" or "new emerging technologies" mentioned in the legislative act. Yet, Article 4(1)(b) of the Directive defines "network and information systems" as "any device or group of interconnected or related devices, one or more of which, pursuant to a programme, perform automatic processing of digital data".[35] As long as these devices are connected to the Internet, this provision arguably includes IoT systems in the scope of the Directive. It follows that if an OES or a DSP, in the context of the provision of their services (that must be essential to societal and economic activities, as regards OES), relies on the deployment of an IoT system, it *must* take the appropriate and proportionate technical and organisational cybersecurity measures and controls to manage the risks—following the risk-based approach—posed to that particular IoT system or device.

Although the NIS Directive enhanced the overall level of cybersecurity in the Union, critical issues have been raised regarding the standard of protection it enforced. In particular, given its peculiar architecture, with regard to IoT—as presented in Chap. 2, the challenges posed by the differentiation in treatment of OESs and DSPs mentioned above (the "light-touch") are particularly evident.

Let us think of the case of an OES that provides its essential service by making use of IoT systems. For example, a supplier or distributor of drinking water deploys connected sensors that monitor quality levels and actuators that manage the quantity levels of chemicals in the water, to help to maintain the pH stability. Now, almost any IoT device resorts to the cloud for data storage and processing. It follows that a

[32]Directive (EU) 2016/1148, Art. 16(6): "[i]f the incident [...] concerns two or more Member States, the competent authority or the CSIRT shall inform the other affected Member States".

[33]Directive (EU) 2016/1148, Art. 16(3).

[34]Directive (EU) 2016/1148, Art. 16(4).

[35]Directive (EU) 2016/1148, Art. 4(1)(b).

DSP is involved insofar as it provides cloud computing resources and services to such IoT systems.

This leads to two main consequences. First, the overall security of an OES relying on IoT systems will ultimately also depend on the adequacy—in terms of both appropriateness and proportionality—of the technical and organisational cybersecurity measures implemented by the DSP. Nevertheless, the light enforcement granted by the Directive to DSPs, through eventual and *ex post* supervisory measures issued by national competent authorities,[36] might jeopardise the correct provision of services that are essential to societal and economic activities. Second, if an incident, occurring at cloud level, does not meet the quantitative and qualitative thresholds established by the Implementing Regulation (EU) 2018/151,[37] and thus it could not be deemed *substantial* but, at the same time, it has *significant* impact on the continuity of the essential services provided by the OES, then it is the OES that has to notify the event to the NIS authority. In cybersecurity, incident handling procedures and timeframes are crucial.[38] The more time an OES spends on comprehensively understanding the extent of the incident, due to a lawful non-notification of the incident occurring to the DSP, the bigger the impact that will threaten the functioning of the essential service concerned.

In this regard, it has been noted in the literature a risk of legal fragmentation resulting from the potential overlap of cybersecurity and incident reporting duties between the NIS Directive and other existing requirements under different pieces of EU legislation, e.g. the GDPR or the European Electronic Communications Code (EECC). This issue is of particular concern to the stakeholders working within the extremely cross-sectoral IoT market.[39]

Indeed, different sector-specific legal acts already regulate certain sectors of the Digital Single Market in terms of cybersecurity rules related to "network and information systems".[40] In order to avoid legal uncertainty, Article 1(7) of the NIS Directive sets forth a general rule of prevalence of sector-specific EU legal acts over NIS Directive's provisions if they require OESs or DSPs "either to ensure the security of their network and information systems or to notify incidents, provided

[36] Directive (EU) 2016/1148, Art. 17(1).

[37] Commission Implementing Regulation (EU) 2018/151 Article 3 specifies the parameters set out by Directive (EU) 2016/1148 Article 16(4) to be taken into account by the DSP to determine whether the impact of an incident is substantial (e.g., the DSP will be able to estimate the number of affected natural or legal persons with whom a contract for the provision of the service has been concluded or the number of affected users having used the service based on previous traffic data). Whereas Article 4 introduces quantitative thresholds in order to determine whether the impact is substantial: (a) at least 5M user-hours have to be affected by the incident in terms of availability of the service; (b) if the incident has resulted in a loss of integrity, authenticity or confidentiality of stored or transmitted or processed data has to affect more than 100.000 users; (c) the incident has created a risk to public safety, public security or of loss of life; and, (d) the incident caused material damage to at least one user in the Union exceeding 1M euros.

[38] Cfr. for example, with ISO/IEC 27000:2016.

[39] Weber and Studer (2016), p. 726.

[40] Directive (EU) 2016/1148, Recital 9.

that such requirements are *at least equivalent in effect* to the obligations laid down in this Directive, *those* provisions of that sector-specific Union legal act shall apply [emphasis added]".[41]

The obscure phrasing of the article would suggest that, when assessing the applicable regime, cybersecurity measures and cybersecurity incident reporting duties should be evaluated separately. It follows that some sector-specific cybersecurity provisions could not meet the *equivalence* threshold set by the NIS Directive, while some others do (whether in terms of security measures or breach reporting), creating therefore concurrent application. "Concretely, where security requirements of EU sector-specific legislation would apply in lieu of NIS security provisions, remaining NIS notifications obligations would still be applicable, should there not be "at least equivalent" notification obligations in the EU sector-specific legislation".[42] In this respect, Ducuing argues that Recital 9 explicitly takes another view since it rules out[43] NIS Directive's identification process for those OESs to whom "at least equivalent"[44] cybersecurity requirements are already imposed by sector-specific legislation, precluding therefore the application of the NIS Directive altogether.[45]

With specific regard to security incident reporting requirements, the NIS Cooperation Group[46] published a report aiming at investigating existing overlaps and possible synergies between a plethora of EU security incident reporting schemes.[47] Aligning and harmonising cybersecurity incident reporting mitigates the compliance burden for companies (e.g., in terms of costs) and, on the other hand, helps national authorities in (i) saving costs; (ii) improving efficiency; (iii) achieving a better understanding of root causes and cross-sectoral impact; (iv) identifying and correlating cross-sectoral issues and effects; (v) enhancing cross-sectoral collaboration; (vi) exchanging good practices.[48]

Accordingly, seven EU legal acts have been identified. Besides the NIS Directive, the pieces of EU legislation analysed by the report are Directive (EU) 2018/1972

---

[41] Directive (EU) 2016/1148, Article 1(7).

[42] Ducuing (2021), p. 8.

[43] Directive (EU) 2016/1148, Recital 9: "Whenever those Union legal acts contain provisions imposing requirements concerning the security [...] or notifications of incidents [...], Member States should then apply the provisions of such sector-specific Union legal acts, including those relating to jurisdiction, and should not carry out the identification process for operators of essential services as defined by the Directive".

[44] Ducuing (2021), p. 11: as regards the criterion that ought to be applied when assessing the equivalence of the cybersecurity requirements of the legal frameworks under scrutiny, in order to determine whether it should prevail over the NIS Directive, the author contends that the 'level of details' of the sector-specific legislation should consider whether "a legal framework takes into account the specificities of the sector, actors, technologies and more generally ecosystem at stake".

[45] Ibid., p. 8.

[46] Established by Directive (EU) 2016/1148 (art. 11) to support and facilitate strategic cooperation and the exchange of information among Member States and to develop trust and confidence.

[47] NIS Cooperation Group (2020).

[48] Ibid., p. 20.

(hereinafter, the EECC), Directive 2002/58/EC (ePrivacy Directive), Regulation (EU) 2016/679 (GDPR), Regulation (EU) 910/2014 (eIDAS Regulation), Directive (EU) 2015/2366 (PSD2 Directive) and Regulation (EU) 2017/745 (MDR).

Without dwelling on a comparative analysis of the provisions of these legal acts too extensively, it suffices here to cast light on the more specific interface, in terms of security breach reporting duties, between the NIS Directive, on the one hand, and, on the other, the EECC and the GDPR. Thus, the scope of these two legal acts is horizontal vis-à-vis the IoT market, as it is potentially applicable to every IoT deployment scenario. Conversely, the eIDAS Regulation,[49] PSD2 Directive[50] and the Regulation on Medical Devices are too (IoT) sector-specific and therefore exceed the scope of the present work.

Directive (EU) 2018/1972[51] is part of the revision of EU telecommunications legal framework within the Digital Single Market Strategy of the Commission. The rationale behind a European electronic communications code (EECC) is to harmonise, to the extent possible, all electronic communications networks and services, with the exception of content-related matters. Thus, the EECC "does not cover the content of services delivered over electronic communications networks using electronic communications services, such as broadcasting content, financial services and certain information society services".[52]

In this respect, the scope of the EECC shall be considered horizontal, or rather cross-sectorial, vis-à-vis the Internet of Things,[53] regardless therefore of the different IoT sectors or verticals, as the Directive applies to electronic communication networks and services. The former are defined by article 2(1) as "transmission systems [. . .] and, where applicable, switching or routing equipment and other resources [. . .] which permit the *conveyance of signals* by wire, *radio*, optical *or other electromagnetic means*, including satellite networks, fixed (circuit- and packet-switched, including internet) and mobile networks, electricity cable systems, to the extent that they are used for the purpose of transmitting signals" [emphasis added][54]; and

[49] Directive (EU) 2016/1148 Article 1(3) states that NIS Directive's security and notification requirements shall not apply to trusted service providers subject to the requirements of Article 19 of the eIDAS Regulation. Therefore, the prevalence of sector-specific legislation, ie Regulation 910/2014, over the NIS Directive is here operationalised by the Directive itself.

[50] European Commission, 'ANNEX to the COMMUNICATION FROM THE COMMISSION TO THE EUROPEAN PARLIAMENT AND THE COUNCIL Making the Most of NIS—towards the Effective Implementation of Directive (EU) 2016/1148 Concerning Measures for a High Common Level of Security of Network and Info' (2017) 37 <https://eur-lex.europa.eu/resource.html?uri=cellar:d829f91d-9859-11e7-b92d-01aa75ed71a1.0001.02/DOC_4&format=PDF>, the European Commission concludes that "pursuant to Article 1(7) NIS Directive, both security and notification requirements set out in Article 95 and 96 of the PSD 2 should apply instead of the corresponding provisions of Article 14 of the NIS Directive".

[51] DIRECTIVE (EU) 2018/1972 of the European Parliament and of the Council of 11 December 2018 establishing the European Electronic Communications Code.

[52] Directive (EU) 2018/1972, Recital 7.

[53] Hadzovic (2021).

[54] Directive (EU) 2018/1972, Article 2(1).

the latter are defined by article 2(4)(c) as " [also] services consisting wholly or mainly in the *conveyance of signals* such as transmission services used for the provision of machine-to-machine services and for broadcasting" [emphasis added].[55]

The conveyance of (radio) signals is pivotal for underpinning the evolving wireless IoT communications technologies and applications in radio spectrum management.[56] Indeed, the overall aim of the regulatory framework is to cover the use of radio spectrum "by all electronic communications networks, including the emerging self-use of radio spectrum by new types of networks consisting exclusively of autonomous systems of mobile radio equipment that is connected via wireless links without a central management or centralised network operator recitals".[57]

Unsurprisingly, the EECC framework pose several regulatory challenges for the telecom sector that could eventually hinder the deployment of IoT in the EU, in terms of legal certainty, in particular taking into account the scope of the Directive and some definitions (for example, the definition of "conveyance of signals" may prove to be troublesome when it comes to IoT transmissions services that are bundled with other types of services; or the exclusion from the rules related to interpersonal communication services, whereby an IoT service includes interpersonal communication only as an "ancillary feature" to the main service) and lack of harmonisation.[58]

Coming now to the cybersecurity and incident notification requirements under the EECC, Article 40 lays down the legal basis for the security of network and information systems of electronic communication networks and services providers. Similar to the OESs' cybersecurity requirements under the NIS Directive, the providers of public electronic communications networks or of publicly available electronic communications services, having regard to the state of the art, shall take appropriate and proportionate technical and organisational measures, such as encryption, to appropriately manage the risks posed to the security of networks and services.[59] Notwithstanding the cybersecurity risk management, if a security incident *significantly* impacts on the operation of networks or services, the providers have to notify to the competent authorities without undue delay.[60] Interestingly, the notification duties under the EECC goes beyond the provision of article 14 of the

---

[55] Directive (EU) 2018/1972, Article 2(4)(c).

[56] Directive (EU) 2018/1972, Recital 30.

[57] Directive (EU) 2018/1972, Recital 12.

[58] To make things worse, on 4 February 2021, the EU Commission opened infringement procedures against 24 Member States for not transposing the EECC: <https://ec.europa.eu/commission/presscorner/detail/en/IP_21_206>.

[59] Directive (EU) 2018/1972, Article 40(1).

[60] Directive (EU) 2018/1972, Article 40(2). To determine the significance of the incident, the EECC lays down five parameters: (a) the number of users affected by the security incident; (b) the duration of the security incident; (c) the geographical spread of the area affected by the security incident; (d) the extent to which the functioning of the network or service is affected; (e) the extent of impact on economic and societal activities.

NIS Directive to include threats.[61] The alignment and harmonisation assessment between the NIS Directive and the EECC, as regards security and incident notification requirements of specific NIS Directive's OESs like EECC's providers of public electronic communications networks or of publicly available electronic communications services, is carried out by the NIS Directive at article 1(3), whereby a rule of prevalence of articles 13a and 13b of Directive 2002/21/EC—then repealed by the EECC—over the security and notification requirements of the NIS Directive is established.[62]

As far as the NIS Directive and the GDPR are concerned, the potential overlap between these two legal instruments is threefold at least, regarding (i) the risk-based security measures; (ii) the incident notification obligations; and (iii) the processing of personal data under the NIS Directive.[63] This begs the question of to what extent the coexistence of the incident notification obligations arising from the two different regimes, which have different scope (i.e., the security of network and information systems and the protection of natural persons' fundamental rights and freedoms, in particular, with regard to their right to the protection of personal data), may prove to be troublesome for the stakeholders involved (i.e., the national competent authorities, the reporting entities, and finally the individuals concerned).

Under the GDPR, a data controller has the duty to notify a personal data breach, without undue delay[64] and no later than 72 hours after becoming aware of it,[65] to the supervisory authority unless the incident is unlikely to result in a *risk* to the rights and freedoms of individuals[66] and to the data subjects concerned if the breach is likely to result in a *high risk* to their rights and freedoms.[67] Not surprisingly, the GDPR defines a personal data breach as a breach of *security* "leading to the accidental or unlawful destruction, loss, alteration, unauthorised disclosure of, or

---

[61] Directive (EU) 2018/1972, Article 40(3); Gijrath (2021), p. 10.

[62] Directive (EU) 2016/1148, Article 1(3); Schmitz-Berndt and Anheier (2021), p. 104.

[63] Schmitz-Berndt and Cole (2022).

[64] Regulation (EU) 2016/679, Article 33(1): if the notification is not made within 72 h, it shall be accompanied by reasons for the delay.

[65] Regulation (EU) 2016/679, Recital 87: "[t]he fact that the notification was made without undue delay should be established taking into account in particular the nature and gravity of the personal data breach and its consequences and adverse effects for the data subject".

[66] Regulation (EU) 2016/679, Article 33(1). Article 33(3) lays down the minimum information that must inform the notification: (a) the nature of the personal data breach, the categories and number of data subjects and personal data records concerned; (b) the contact details of the data protection officer; (c) the likely consequences that follow the breach; (d) the measures taken or proposed by the controller to address the personal data breach.

[67] Regulation (EU) 2016/679, Article 34(1). Article 34(3) contains an exception to the first paragraph. The notification is not required if (a) the controller has implemented appropriate technical and organisational measures that render the personal data intelligible to unauthorised parties; (b) the controller has taken subsequent measures ensuring that the *high risk* is no longer likely to materialise; (c) the effort to notify would be disproportionate: in such case, there shall be a public communication or similar measure.

access to, personal data transmitted, stored or otherwise processed".[68] Indeed, as stressed in Chap. 3, the fundamental rights to privacy and data protection depend on *some* cybersecurity technologies, as not every security technology should be framed as fundamental rights *infraethical* facilitator.

Provided this logical and technical nexus between cybersecurity measures and personal data protection,[69] it is non-contended that a cybersecurity incident would most of the times involve a personal data breach. Certainly, these incidents shall be distinguished in terms of the affected assets—as cybersecurity incidents may not involve personal data breaches[70]—and the protection regime they would trigger. The same incident in fact would fall under the scope of both the NIS Directive and the GDPR if it *significantly* or *substantially* affects an OES or a DSP and, at the same time, leads "to the accidental or unlawful destruction, loss, alteration, unauthorised disclosure of, or access to, personal data transmitted, stored or otherwise processed". Whether this is the case, "the same incident may be reported to two separate regulators under different reporting schemes and notably with different objectives",[71] even by two different entities, giving rise potentially to conflicts and confusion. As a consequence, different authorities will receive diverging information with regard to a single incident and [. . .] one incident may be treated as if there were separate".[72]

To make things more complex, on a lower level of abstraction, the diverging incident notifications timeline under the NIS and the GDPR may add further problems, as early notifications to the data subjects might jeopardise the cybersecurity operations aiming at minimising or recovering from the breach.[73] On the one hand, recital 86 GDPR acknowledges the need to counter a cyberattack as a justification to delay the communication to the data subject pursuant to Article 34 GDPR; on the other, "the justification is limited to continuing and ongoing data breaches and does not encompass ongoing security incidents as such, [falling] short in an incident which incidentally compromised consumer data but leads to an ongoing attack targeted at other vital systems of the OES or DSP".[74] Therefore, "the mitigation of the impact of a cybersecurity incident in the context of compromised personal data, may thus require the cooperation of the competent NCA (national competent authority) and DPA (data protection authority)".[75]

As already addressed by Chap. 3 in the context of the public good doctrine for cybersecurity, it is becoming increasingly clear that *cooperation*, *coordination*,

[68] Regulation (EU) 2016/679, Article 4(12).

[69] See Case C-340/21 *VB v Natsionalna agentsia za prihodite*, ECLI:EU:C:2023:986, para. 55. The next Chapter will cover this judgement extensively.

[70] Burton (2020), p. 645.

[71] Schmitz-Berndt and Anheier (2021), p. 101.

[72] Ibid., p. 105.

[73] Schmitz-Berndt and Schiffner (2021).

[74] Ibid., pp. 9–10.

[75] Schmitz-Berndt and Anheier (2021), p. 105.

experience and *information-sharing* are crucial elements when facing cyberattacks. A lack of collaboration and information sharing between the authorities under the NIS Directive and GDPR regimes might seriously hamper the rationale underlying the notification requirements of the two legal acts. In this respect, some have argued that it would be appropriate to have a single point of contact for notifications, which may then inform the appropriate authority or authorities of a security incident involving personal data.[76] Against this background, the Commission proposal for a revision of the NIS Directive (Sect. 4.4) explicitly addressed this issue. Recital 56 of the so-called NIS 2.0 Proposal read as follows:

> Essential and important entities are often in a situation where a particular incident, because of its features, needs to be reported to various authorities as a result of notification obligations included in various legal instruments. Such cases create additional burdens and may also lead to uncertainties with regard to the format and procedures of such notifications. In view of this and, for the purposes of simplifying the reporting of security incidents, Member States should establish a single entry point for all notifications required under this Directive and also under other Union law such as Regulation (EU) 2016/679 and Directive 2002/58/EC. ENISA, in cooperation with the Cooperation Group should develop common notification templates by means of guidelines that would simplify and streamline the reporting information requested by Union law and decrease the burdens for companies.[77]

The next section addresses the limited scope of the Directive with regard to the exemption of hardware manufacturers and software developers: taking into special account the IoT domain,[78] the question is whether it is desirable to address operators of essential services or digital service providers when either software or hardware vulnerabilities of IoT systems—which would eventually be part of the "network and information systems" of the NIS actor under scrutiny—are exploited by attackers, and, as a result, a security incident occurs. In other words, why and to what extent OESs (or DSPs) should be considered the best placed actors to draw up and implement the appropriate and proportionate *technical* and *organisational* measures to manage the risks posed to the security of IoT systems they use in their operations?

4.1.1 Right Responsibility, Wrong Actors? The NIS Directive's Exclusion of Hardware Manufacturers and Software Developers

This section addresses yet another key challenge of the EU governance of cybersecurity, that is, "to impose the right obligations on the right actors, through the right instrument".[79] In particular, the exclusion of hardware manufacturers and software

[76] Schmitz-Berndt and Cole (2022), p. 20.

[77] NIS 2.0 Proposal, Recital 56.

[78] Weber and Studer (2016), p. 726.

[79] Fuster and Jasmontaite (2020), p. 109.

developers from the scope of the NIS Directive might enlighten a regulatory failure that negatively impacts the IoT market. Recital 50 of the NIS Directive, albeit not legally binding,[80] explicitly exclude from the scope of the Directive hardware manufacturers and software developers, as (i) they are not OESs nor DSPs; and (ii) the European legislator considered the existing rules on product liability to be sufficient.[81]

The impact of the so-called emerging digital technologies (such as AI or the IoT) on EU product liability rules, notably Directive (EU) 85/374/EEC (Product Liability Directive),[82] has received wide attention by both legal scholars[83] and EU institutions.[84] The question whether the Product Liability Directive could play a role within the allocation of liability, stemming from cybersecurity vulnerabilities, of the variety of actors involved in the IoT chain—such as hardware manufacturer or software developer—would exceed the scope of the book since it would require an analysis of product liability and tort law theories.[85]

Rather, the question worth asking is whether it is fair to hold OES and DSP responsible—and ultimately liable—for cybersecurity incidents that are likely to be beyond their control. This could be the case if intrinsic IoT vulnerabilities that could not be mitigated by the OES in question—either at device (hardware) or network and application (software) level—are successfully exploited by an attacker.

By holding NIS actors responsible for such incidents, rather than directly addressing the actors in charge of security features' design and implementation which will eventually affect OESs' and DSPs' network and information systems, the problem of *insecure* IoT devices is "not addressed at the core".[86] In this respect, the remaining sections of this Chapter address the revision process of EU product safety legislation and recent initiatives undertook by the Commission (in particular,

[80] Klimas (2008).

[81] Directive (EU) 2016/1148, Recital 50.

[82] Council Directive 85/374/EEC of 25 July 1985 on the approximation of the laws, regulations and administrative provisions of the Member States concerning liability for defective products.

[83] See *inter alia* Fairgrieve et al. (2017), van Dam (2013), Tulibacka (2016), Borghetti (2019), Miquel Martìn-Casals (2019), Pagallo (2013), Sartor and Omicini (2016), Weber (2017a), Chiara (2022d).

[84] The European Parliament issued a Resolution calling for updated civil liability rules: European Parliament (2017). The European Commission then published a document to provide a first mapping of liability challenges that occur in the context of emerging digital technologies: European Commission, 'Commission Staff Working Document - Liability for Emerging Digital Technologies - Accompanying the Document: Communication from the Commission to the European Parliament, the European Council, the Council, the European Economic and Social Committee' (2018). Moreover, in March 2018 the EC appointed a group of experts to provide the Commission with expertise on the applicability of the Product Liability Directive to traditional products, new technologies and new societal challenges. The report of November 2019, is the final deliverable of the Expert Group on "Liability and New Technologies": European Commission Expert Group on Liability and New Technologies (2019).

[85] Sterk (2018), Chiara (2020a).

[86] Sterk (2018), p. 32.

the revision of the NIS Directive and the Cyber Resilience Act) with a view to tackling the issue of connected devices cybersecurity.

To make things worse, this exclusion could hinder the efforts to enhance IoT supply chain cybersecurity. The majority of IoT devices is thus comprised of many components from different hardware and software vendors, part of which could even be accounted for by small companies, including start-ups—excluded from the scope of the NIS Directive too.[87] Chapter 2 already showed how the IoT expands the global attack surface disproportionately due to the variety of integrated and interconnected products and manufacturers.

Recent discussions, both in Europe and in the US, find a consensus that IoT supply chain security is crucial: ENISA and the US National Institute of Standards and Technology (NIST) acknowledge that the supply chain represents a challenge and an opportunity. On the one hand, it lays down the foundation for devices' security and, on the other hand it raises concerns since organisations are hardly aware of the security measures adopted by supply chain partners.[88,89] The need to "secure" the entire IoT supply chain is making it much harder for the stakeholders involved in IoT cybersecurity—notably, OESs pursuant to article 14 of the NIS Directive—to fulfil their duties in managing vulnerabilities and risks.

Ironically, the Directive acknowledges the important role played by hardware manufacturers and software developers.[90] Their products (and services) are the backbone of the network and information systems infrastructure of OESs and DSPs.[91] They are thus crucial in enabling OESs and DSPs to enhance the security of their NIS infrastructure.

In fact, hardware manufacturers and software developers of IoT solutions actually maintain a pivotal role during the lifecycle of their devices. IoT devices frequently contact several actors for manifold reasons (e.g., updates, data processing, functionality reports, etc.): there is a large consensus in the literature in considering the manufacturer of the device as a first party, whilst cloud service providers are usually classified as support parties, among the manifold machine communication's destinations.[92]

The central role of manufacturers and developers vis-à-vis the state of systems' cybersecurity has been highlighted by ENISA's gap analyses several times. NIS Directive's goal of managing cybersecurity risks through appropriate and proportionate security measures can only be effectively if pursued *via* the involvement of vendors, "since they are in charge of designing and developing the devices, they are

[87] Directive (EU) 2016/1148, Article 16(11) states that Chapter V i.e., security of the network and information systems of digital service providers, does not apply to micro and small enterprises; European Commission (2020), p. 1.

[88] ENISA (2020a), p. 5; Megas et al. (2021), p. 13.

[89] ENISA (2020a), p. 9.

[90] Directive 2016/1148, recital 50.

[91] Weber and Studer (2016).

[92] Mandalari et al. (2020).

in an ideal position to implement the changes needed – they are able to proficiently and cost-efficiently include new security features or characteristics. [. . .] Through their lifecycle, IoT devices must be able to be patched and updated rapidly to ensure their correct operation and to amend all the vulnerabilities that are continuously being discovered".[93]

Accordingly, the objective of managing the number and severity of IoT vulnerabilities—and risks—should shift the emphasis from deployment of security measures and controls in a later phase by "indirect" actors (i.e., OESs), towards an effective and proactive systems' designing and developing, having therefore 'security in mind'. Several security challenges of the IoT can be addressed by manufactures and developers by establishing a set of secure development guidelines i.e., Software Development Life Cycle principles, such as checking for security vulnerabilities, secure deployment, ensuring continuity of secure development in cases of integrators, continuous delivery etc.[94]

Nevertheless, IoT manufacturers and vendors "usually consider functionality and usability much more important than implementing secure design and programming [:] the main reason for these companies no to dedicate much of their budget to security is the general perception that there is no direct return-on-investment for security, which can be attributed to the economic cost and the difficulty to assess".[95] Thus, a growing number of OES and DSP believe that implementing the NIS Directive has strengthened their detection capabilities and their ability to recover from incidents, while the compliance process required additional budget.[96]

From a legal-economic perspective, the lack of economic[97] incentives eventually hinders the development of secure IoT solutions and leads to market failures. This notwithstanding, regulatory failures play a role as well. The legal *formula* of the NIS Directive placed the burden of the cost of an incident on a party (i.e., the OES) who is unable to reduce the probability of the occurring (security) incident[98] in the same way as the producer/developer. The latter are undoubtedly better placed to adopt cybersecurity measures to manage the risks posed to their products and services than OESs. In accordance with the theoretical framework addressing "cybersecurity as public good" in Chap. 3, increased sharing NIS responsibilities[99] to be borne by IoT vendors would create legal incentives to implement secure design and development.

In the review process of the NIS Directive, different stakeholders have been commented on the Commission's inception impact assessment and roadmap for the

---

[93] ENISA (2017b), p. 56.

[94] ENISA (2019a), p. 7.

[95] ENISA (2017b), p. 55.

[96] ENISA (2021a), pp. 66–67.

[97] Id.

[98] Calabresi (1970).

[99] The reference here is to the duties enshrined in Article 14 of the NIS Directive.

adoption of a new NIS Directive.[100] Against the background of an expanded scope, having particular regard to the inclusion of software vendors, BSA argued that such market sector was already cover "within the Cloud services' inclusion in Annex III, notably through the Software As A Service principle. For the very limited cases where a software would not be delivered or serviced through the cloud (i.e. when embedded), the incident reporting obligations would be irrelevant, as the manufacturer would not have the visibility of the incident affecting that specific piece of software".[101]

It is highly debatable whether the cases of 'embedded software', that is, not cloud-based, are 'limited' in the increasingly evolving market of IoT, robotics and AI. Moreover, even assuming that this is the case, BSA only accounts for security breaches reporting duties (regarding them as irrelevant), completely ignoring security measures requirements. On the contrary, GSMA firmly supports the need to include in the scope of the revised NIS Directive software developers and hardware manufacturers to ensure robust end-to-end security. "Such extension of the NIS Directive would ensure that each actor takes responsibility for their part in a secure and resilient digital value chain. Overall, introducing clear legal requirements (notably security and notification requirements) on these actors will help to achieve a higher level of cybersecurity in the EU".[102]

In conclusion, this section demonstrated that the lack of legal obligations on hardware and software manufacturers and developers in terms of 'products' cybersecurity has a negative impact on OESs. However, addressing this regulatory gap with the legal instrument of the NIS Directive is not the right answer. Thus, the principle-based model of governance of the NIS was not meant to cover product-related requirements, which are already contained in product safety legislation as will be addressed in Sect. 4.4. Rather, it focuses on administrative and organisational aspects (e.g., laying down a procedural framework for the notification of incidents having a significant or substantial impact on the network and information systems of the entities in scope). Against this backdrop, Sect. 4.5 casts light on the recent EC initiative for a Cyber Resilience Act which would directly tackle the problem of unsecure connected devices by setting forth common cybersecurity rules for manufacturers and vendors of products with digital elements.

---

[100] See <https://ec.europa.eu/info/law/better-regulation/have-your-say/initiatives/12475-Cybersecurity-review-of-EU-rules-on-the-security-of-network-and-information-systems_it>.

[101] BSA (2020).

[102] GSMA (2020), p. 12.

4.2 The Cybersecurity Act and the IoT: Exploring EU Voluntary Cybersecurity Certification Legal Framework

The European Commission published in 2017—just after the entry into force of the NIS Directive—its second Cybersecurity Strategy.[103] In order to scale up the EU's cybersecurity preparedness and improve IoT connected devices' robustness and resilience, the Commission proposed a permanent status, alongside a stronger mandate, for the ENISA and the "establishment of an EU cybersecurity certification framework that will ensure the trustworthiness of the billions of devices ("Internet of Things") which drive today's critical infrastructures, such as energy and transport networks, and also new consumer devices, such as connected cars".[104]

Especially in a technical field such as cybersecurity,[105] certifications build up on security technical standards,[106] which are "the most effective tool to introduce technical requirements without overly prescriptive normative provisions that might become outdated as technology evolves".[107] In other words, given that hardware and software manufacturers and developers—and, therefore, 'IoT manufacturers'—are excluded from the scope of the NIS Directive, certifications, albeit voluntary, would be an instrument to achieve policy goals,[108] namely, enhancing the cybersecurity posture of these stakeholders by encouraging them to implement measures at the earliest stages of design and development of their products, services and processes.

The sectors regulated by Directive (EU) 2016/1148 are domains in which cybersecurity certification is critical.[109] ENISA report on 'NIS investments' highlights a strong correlation—which does not necessarily imply causation—between "a very positive self-perception of cybersecurity maturity and the existence of cybersecurity certifications for processes, people and products. Organisations that certify their staff and systems and buy products with cybersecurity certifications are 36.36 % more likely to self- assess their cybersecurity maturity as 'far above industry standards'".[110]

---

[103] European Commission and the High Representative of the Union for Foreign Affairs and Security Policy (2017).

[104] European Commission (2017), p. 1.

[105] The interface between IoT and standards is not limited to the field of cybersecurity. Within Intellectual Property and Competition Law, see *inter alia* Borgogno and Colangelo (2021).

[106] Kohler (2020); ENISA, *Standardisation in Support of the Cybersecurity Certification: Recommendations for European standardisation in relation to the Cybersecurity Act*, 2019; AIOTI, *AIOTI position on the EU Cybersecurity Act Proposal*, 2018.

[107] Digital Europe, "Defining the way forward for IoT security and certification schemes" (2019) white paper, 5, available at: https://www.digitaleurope.org/resources/defining-the-way-forward-for-iot-security-and-certification-schemes/.

[108] Kamara (2021), p. 85.

[109] Regulation (EU) 2019/881, recital 65.

[110] ENISA (2021a), p. 67.

In this respect, this section focuses on the question whether and to what extent the European cybersecurity certification framework, established by Regulation 2019/881 (hereinafter, Cybersecurity Act),[111] addresses legal uncertainty and closes regulatory gaps vis-à-vis IoT security as addressed in the previous section.

Against this backdrop, *cybersecurity law* shall be considered as a privileged interface in which one can better appreciate the paradigm shift in the EU's institutional landscape, from a European Law perspective, elsewhere described as 'agencification'. "EU agencies – like ENISA – are also increasingly authors of standards to be used in implementation of EU law by Member States. These roles of agencies have developed next to and alongside the more 'traditional' approach of regulatory law, which consists of references to 'outside' standards set by private and semi-private standardisation bodies and scientific expertise".[112]

As remarkably put by Busch, "standards are means by which we construct realities [, means] of *partially* ordering people and things so as to produce outcomes desired by someone. As such, they are part of the technical, political, social, economic, and ethical infrastructure that constitutes human societies".[113]

Whereas a broader understanding of the concept of 'standard' underpins this book, that is, standards as means that normatively mediate interactions between individuals,[114] this section is mainly preoccupied with exploring the concept of 'standard' as outlined in Article 2(1) of Regulation (EU) 1025/2012[115] i.e., a technical specification, adopted by a recognised standardisation body, for repeated or continuous application, with which compliance is not compulsory.

As noted by Gonzalez Fuster and Jasmontaite, EU's 'cybersecurity area' "revives itself by both law and inter-area policy measures. Policy measures from various policy areas eventually led to changes and adjustments in various EU legal frameworks and *vice versa*".[116] This book has already given account to the pivotal role played by the first Cybersecurity Strategy (2013) of the Commission in EU cybersecurity legislation: the policy objectives of the first area of strategic intervention ('achieving cyber resilience') were notably achieved through the adoption of the NIS Directive.

---

[111] Regulation (EU) 2019/881 of the European Parliament and of the Council of 17 April 2019 on ENISA (the European Union Agency for Cybersecurity) and on information and communications technology cybersecurity certification and repealing Regulation (EU) No 526/2013 (Cybersecurity Act).

[112] Hofmann (2016), p. 13.

[113] Busch (2011), p. 13.

[114] Durante (2019).

[115] Regulation (EU) No 1025/2012 of the European Parliament and of the Council of 25 October 2012 on European standardisation, amending Council Directives 89/686/EEC and 93/15/EEC and Directives 94/9/EC, 94/25/EC, 95/16/EC, 97/23/EC, 98/34/EC, 2004/22/EC, 2007/23/EC, 2009/23/EC and 2009/105/EC of the European Parliament and of the Council and repealing Council Decision 87/95/EEC and Decision No 1673/2006/EC of the European Parliament and of the Council.

[116] Fuster and Jasmontaite (2020), p. 101.

Similarly, the policy objectives outlined by the 2017 Commission's Cybersecurity Strategy resulted in legislation, that is, the Cybersecurity Act. Interestingly, this is the first EU legal act that provides for a definition of 'cybersecurity', which differs substantially from the previous conceptualisation contained in the 2013 Cybersecurity Strategy: "cybersecurity means the activities necessary to protect network and information systems, *the users of such systems and other persons affected by cyber threats* [emphasis added]".[117]

In 2013, the notion of cybersecurity mainly hinged on threats that could harm the underlying network and information system (NIS) infrastructure. The new understanding of 'cybersecurity' broadens the perimeter, echoing the substance of the considerations contained in Chap. 3, to include not only the users of NIS but *any other persons,* and possibly their (fundamental) rights, that could be impacted by any cyber threats, going thus beyond information security's CIA triad dependency of the 2013 definition.

The Cybersecurity Act has mainly two focal areas. The first, from Article 3 to 45, reshapes ENISA's critical position in defending the digital ecosystem of the Union,[118] whereas the second, from Articles 46 to 65, establishes the European cybersecurity certification legal framework. In face of the changed and rapidly evolving cybersecurity landscape, the Commission deemed it necessary to enhance ENISA's role, with new objectives[119] and tasks.[120] The Agency is also given a permanent mandate[121] and will "act as a reference point for advice and expertise on cybersecurity for Union institutions, bodies, offices and agencies as well as for other relevant Union stakeholders".[122]

The purposes of an European cybersecurity certification framework are twofold: (i) increase trust in ICT products, services and processes that have been certified under European cybersecurity certification schemes (ECCS) and, (ii) avoid the proliferation of national cybersecurity certification schemes thereby reducing the costs for undertakings operating across the digital single market.[123]

---

[117] Regulation (EU) 2019/881, Article 2(1).

[118] Regulation (EU) 2019/881, Recital 19.

[119] Article 4 of Regulation (EU) 2019/881 outlines the main objectives of the Agency, such as assisting Union institutions, bodies, offices, agencies as well as Member States in implementing EU policies on cybersecurity, supporting capacity-building and preparedness across the Union, promoting cooperation, including information-sharing and coordination at Union level, contributing to increasing cybersecurity capabilities and promoting the use of EU cybersecurity certification.

[120] Article 5 of Regulation (EU) 2019/881 mainly refers to 3 strands of actions: *assisting* in the development, review, implementation of Union cybersecurity policy and law; *contributing* to the work of the Cooperation group; *supporting* the development and implementation of cybersecurity policy in Union legislation as well as the regular review of Union policy through an annual report on the state of the implementation of the respective legal framework.

[121] Regulation (EU) 2019/881, Article 68(4).

[122] Regulation (EU) 2019/881, Article 3(1).

[123] Regulation (EU) 2019/881, Recital 69.

The Cybersecurity Act considers that the slow (or none) embracement of the 'security by design' principle hinders IoT cybersecurity.[124] A lack of certification schemes enhances information asymmetries underpinning consumers' insufficient understanding of the overall security of ICT products, processes and services.[125] One the main regulatory driver underpinning the Cybersecurity Act, as said, is that the lack of trust in ICT products, services and processes cybersecurity, due to insufficient information about the security features of such solutions,[126] might prevent the full realisation of a secure Single Market.[127]

Without dwelling on the epistemological meaning of 'trust',[128] we can assume here that 'trust' refers to the (successful) delegation to third parties (whether national cybersecurity certification authorities,[129] conformity assessment bodies[130] or manufacturers themselves[131]) of the conformity evaluation procedure that ICT products, services and processes must undergo in order to be certified.[132]

In other words, consumers trust would be enhanced by a proof of conformity "with specified security requirements for the purpose of protecting the availability, authenticity, integrity or confidentiality of stored or transmitted or processed data or the functions or services offered by, or accessible via, those products, services and processes throughout their life cycle".[133] It follows that the notion of trust in the certification domain is linked to transparency.[134]

Conversely, the risk of fragmentation—despite some efforts made with a view to ensuring mutual recognition of certificates within the Union, such as the Senior Officials Group—Information Systems Security (SOG-IS) Mutual Recognition Agreement (MRA)[135]—is particularly acute for the IoT domain, as testified by the wording of Recital 67 CSA:

> Currently, the cybersecurity certification of ICT products, ICT services and ICT processes is used only to a limited extent. When it exists, it mostly occurs at Member State level or in the framework of industry driven schemes. In that context, a certificate issued by a national cybersecurity certification authority is not in principle recognised in other Member States. Companies thus may have to certify their ICT products, ICT services and ICT processes in several Member States where they operate [...], which thereby adds to their costs. Moreover, while new schemes are emerging, there seems to be no coherent and holistic approach to horizontal cybersecurity issues, for instance in the field of the IoT. Existing schemes

---

[124] Regulation (EU) 2019/881, Recital 2.

[125] Ibid.

[126] Regulation (EU) 2019/881, Recital 2.

[127] Regulation (EU) 2019/881, Recital 65.

[128] Durante (2021), pp. 29–30.

[129] Regulation (EU) 2019/881, Article 58.

[130] Regulation (EU) 2019/881, Article 60.

[131] Regulation (EU) 2019/881, Article 53.

[132] Chiara (2022a), pp. 120–121.

[133] Regulation (EU) 2019/881, Article 46(2).

[134] Kamara (2021), pp. 98–99; Spagnuelo et al. (2019); Stahl and Strausz (2017).

[135] See <https://www.sogis.eu/>.

> present significant shortcomings and differences in terms of product coverage, levels of assurance, substantive criteria and actual use, impeding mutual recognition mechanisms within the Union.[136]

Article 8 CSA arguably constitutes a direct interface between the two parts of the Regulation as ENISA is tasked to support and promote the development and implementation of EU policy on cybersecurity certification by preparing[137] a candidate scheme or reviewing[138] an existing European cybersecurity certification scheme for ICT products, services and processes (including, as previously clarified in Chap. 2, IoT systems[139])—following a request from the Commission[140] on the basis of the 'Union rolling work programme'[141] or from the European Cybersecurity Certification Group (ECCG),[142] even without referencing the rolling work programme,[143] the latter being however non-binding for the Agency.[144]

When preparing the scheme, in adherence to a formal, open, transparent and inclusive consultation process typical of the consensus-based standardisation process,[145] ENISA will consult all relevant stakeholders,[146] in particular, having regard to the opinion of the ECCG that assist and advise ENISA without binding force.[147] ENISA then transmits the candidate scheme to the Commission which may adopt it through an implementing act.[148] Once the implementing act is adopted, it produces a so-called 'standstill obligation', in a similar way to EU technical harmonisation,[149] since the national cybersecurity certification schemes with the same scope of the ECCS cease to produce effects.[150]

From a substantive legal viewpoint, the Regulation lays down objectives and minimum content of the cybersecurity certification schemes. Unsurprisingly, Article

[136] Regulation (EU) 2019/881, recital 67.

[137] Regulation (EU) 2019/881, article 8(1)(b).

[138] Regulation (EU) 2019/881, article 48.

[139] Hessel and Rebmann (2020), p. 32.

[140] Regulation (EU) 2019/881, article 48(1).

[141] Regulation (EU) 2019/881, article 47(1): EU Commission's yearly publication which identifies strategic priorities for future ECCS.

[142] Regulation (EU) 2019/881, article 62(2): the ECCG is composed of representatives of national cybersecurity certification authorities or other relevant national authorities.

[143] Regulation (EU) 2019/881, article 48(2).

[144] Regulation (EU) 2019/881, article 49(2).

[145] Blind (2016).

[146] Regulation (EU) 2019/881, article 49(3).

[147] Regulation (EU) 2019/881, articles 49(5), 49(6), 62(4).

[148] Regulation (EU) 2019/881, Article 49(7).

[149] Kamara (2021), p. 89.

[150] Regulation (EU) 2019/881, Article 57(1).

51 does not limit itself to cover classical computer and information security principles i.e., the CIA triad[151] and authentication,[152] but enriches the objectives of such schemes as to encompass further aspects of a holistic and more 'modern' interpretation of cybersecurity, such as: handling of vulnerabilities,[153] basic digital forensics principles,[154] disaster recovery,[155] security by design and by default,[156] and software & hardware updates.[157]

Article 54 instead contains a non-exhaustive list of elements that certification schemes must include: scope and object of the certification (including the categories of ICT products, services and processes covered), and how selected technical standards, evaluation methods and intended assurance levels ('basic', 'substantial' or 'high') correspond to the needs of the intended users of the scheme in question.[158]

Recourse to cybersecurity certification is voluntary. For they are voluntary private law instruments: the same happens in EU data protection law (Article 42(3) GDPR).[159] However, this general rule might encounter several exceptions. First, Union law, or Member State law—adopted in accordance with Union law—may provide for mandatory certification.[160] Furthermore, absent harmonised Union law, "Member States are able to adopt national technical regulations providing for mandatory certification under a European cybersecurity certification scheme in accordance with Directive (EU) 2015/1535 of the European Parliament and of the Council".[161]

The EU legislature did not rule out the scenario of imposing specific cybersecurity requirements *via* mandatory certification with a view to enhancing the overall level of cybersecurity in the Digital Single Market.[162] In this respect, the NIS2 Directive foresees the possibility for Member States to require essential and important entities to use certain ICT products, services and processes that are certified under specific European cybersecurity certification schemes adopted pursuant to Article 49 of Regulation (EU) 2019/881 (see Sect. 4.4).[163]

On a different note, Article 54(3) Cybersecurity Act can shed further light vis-à-vis the voluntary nature of cybersecurity certifications with respect to other

---

151 Regulation (EU) 2019/881, Article 51, letters (a) and (b).

152 Regulation (EU) 2019/881, Article 51, letter (c).

153 Regulation (EU) 2019/881, Article 51, letters (d) and (g).

154 Regulation (EU) 2019/881, Article 51, letters (e) and (f).

155 Regulation (EU) 2019/881, Article 51, letter (h).

156 Regulation (EU) 2019/881, Article 51, letter (i).

157 Regulation (EU) 2019/881, Article 51, letter (j).

158 Regulation (EU) 2019/881, Article 54(1); Recital 84.

159 Regulation (EU) 2016/679, Article 42(3): "the certification shall be voluntary and available via a process that is transparent".

160 Regulation (EU) 2019/881, Article 56(2); Recital 91.

161 Regulation (EU) 2019/881, Recital 91.

162 Regulation (EU) 2019/881, Recital 92.

163 Directive (EU) 2022/2555, Art. 24(1).

Union legislation. "Where a specific Union legal act so provides, a certificate or an EU statement of conformity issued under a European cybersecurity certification scheme may be used to demonstrate the presumption of conformity with requirements of that legal act".

This provision can thus be interpreted as an interface between *voluntary* Cybersecurity Act schemes and *mandatory* requirements under other Union legal acts.[164] Albeit voluntary, certification schemes may be used as a means to comply with mandatory requirements of other legal acts. As addressed in the next section, this would be the case especially with regard to EU product safety legislation.

Certification is offered in principle by private entities which, in order to issue EU cybersecurity certificates, must be accredited by national accreditation bodies.[165] However, in duly justified cases, a certification scheme may foresee that certificates resulting from said scheme are to be issued only by a public body, namely the national cybersecurity certification authority or another public body. Said public entities must be accredited.[166]

The risk-based approach[167] of the Cybersecurity Act is particularly reflected by foreseeing 'assurance levels' ('basic', 'substantial' or 'high') that would provide the corresponding rigour and depth of the evaluation of the level of risk associated with the intended use of the ICT product, service or process.[168] Indeed, the scalability and granularity of the cybersecurity certification mechanisms may be better appreciated by considering who can issue which type of certificate and under which conditions.

With regard to the 'basic' assurance level only, the Regulation allows manufacturers or providers of ICT products, services and processes that present a low risk—corresponding therefore to the lowest level—to perform a 'conformity self-assessment',[169] which must at least include a review of technical documentation.[170] This activity eventually results in an 'EU statement of conformity' demonstrating that an ECCS' requirements have been fulfilled.[171]

Conversely, a European cybersecurity certificate that refers either to the 'substantial' or 'high' assurance levels cannot be issued by the manufacturer. The conformity assessment bodies will issue certificates referring to 'basic' and 'substantial' levels.[172]

As regards the 'substantial' level, the evaluation activities must take into account the risk "carried out by actors with limited skills and resources" and shall include at least: (i) a review to demonstrate the absence of known vulnerabilities; and

164 Chiara (2022a), p. 122.

165 Regulation (EU) 2019/881, Article 60(1).

166 Regulation (EU) 2019/881, Article 56(5)(b); Article 60(2).

167 Mantelero et al. (2021).

168 Regulation (EU) 2019/881, Article 52(1); Recital 86.

169 Regulation (EU) 2019/881, Article 53(1).

170 Regulation (EU) 2019/881, Article 52(5).

171 Regulation (EU) 2019/881, Article 53(2).

172 Regulation (EU) 2019/881, Article 56(4).

(ii) testing.[173] Any subsequently detected vulnerabilities or irregularities that could hinder compliance with the requirements related to the scheme must be notified by the holder of the certificate to the authority or the conformity assessment body.[174]

This requirement is crucial since, paradoxically, certification—if obtained—may jeopardise its very own goals as a dynamic reality like cybersecurity could be falsely perceived as static. In other words, certification—if significant changes, such as subsequently discovered vulnerabilities, are not reported—"can make a product seem secure even if, after the trust mark is assigned, a serious security flaw is discovered".[175]

Depending on the type of update or patch, and in order to mitigate discovered vulnerabilities, cybersecurity re-certification of the component—or the whole system where the component is deployed—might be required. In turn, the cost of the re-certification process may constitute a hindrance to the regular production of updates and patches by manufacturers.[176] Thus, it has been estimated that the average cost of conformity assessment is in the range of €30.000–50.000 per company in a given year or €3.000–4.000 per product basis.[177] Moreover, in the absence of quantitative and qualitative criteria that would set a threshold for the "skills and resources" of third parties (or attackers), such a *relativist* approach can prove to be troublesome to apply in practice.

Lastly, where an ECCS requires a 'high' assurance level, the certificate under that scheme is to be issued by a national cybersecurity certification authority or by a conformity assessment body if: (a) the national authority approves the issuing by conformity assessment bodies for each individual certificate; or (b) the national authority relies on a general delegation for the task of issuing such certificates to a conformity assessment body.[178] 'High' assurance levels will be evaluated to minimise the risk of state-of-the-art attacks carried out by actors with significant skills and resources. Compared to the requisites of the 'substantial' assurance level, the evaluation activities in this stage must also include an assessment of security functionality resistance through penetration testing,[179] a cornerstone tool of cybersecurity.[180]

With regard to enforcement and supervision powers, national authorities can carry out investigations (audits) of and take measures against certification bodies, certificate holders and issuers of EU statements of conformity to verify their compliance with Regulation 2019/881.[181] More importantly, they can require immediate

[173] Regulation (EU) 2019/881, Article 52(6).

[174] Regulation (EU) 2019/881, Article 56(8).

[175] Denardis (2020), p. 119.

[176] Hernandez-Ramos et al. (2021), p. 101.

[177] European Commission (2014), p. 66.

[178] Regulation (EU) 2019/881, Article 56(6).

[179] Regulation (EU) 2019/881, Article 52(7).

[180] Bishop (2007).

[181] Regulation (EU) 2019/881, Article 58(8) letters (b) and (c).

cessation of infringements and impose penalties[182] according to the rules laid down by the Member States.[183] This decentralisation of an otherwise centralised legal framework may potentially lead, as noted by Kamara, "to a wide range of pecuniary penalties [and] undermine the guarantees to prevent forum-shopping offered by the common baseline rules".[184]

In conclusion, the EU cybersecurity certification legal framework, introduced by Regulation 2019/881, can arguably be seen as an important part of the Commission's ongoing programme in strengthen the Union's digital security. On the one hand, manufacturers, developers, vendors of ICT products, services and processes would rely on scalable and granular schemes to assess whether the specific security controls and measures of their technological solutions comply with specified security requirements. On the other hand, consumers and citizens will be offered information on the level of security of certified ICT assets in a transparent manner.

The investigation started with the question whether the Cybersecurity Act could eventually fill significant regulatory gaps and inconsistencies in the Union cybersecurity legal framework, in particular, regarding manufacturers and developers' lack of legal obligations vis-à-vis the cybersecurity of their technological solutions. This section demonstrated that looking at the Union cybersecurity certification framework as *purely* voluntary is not completely accurate. The Cybersecurity Act gives the EU and Member States the flexibility to impose certification schemes or legally binding standards (e.g., Article 24 NIS2 Directive, see Sect. 4.4).

Furthermore, it has been highlighted that other EU legal acts may foresee that a certificate (or an EU statement of conformity) adopted under the Cybersecurity Act can be used to demonstrate conformity with requirements of those legal acts. In this latter case, even if voluntary, certifications would be strictly linked with legally binding cybersecurity requirements.

Notwithstanding the negative externalities arising from the high costs and low incentives,[185] the ENISA conference on cybersecurity certification of 2–3 December 2021[186] stressed the key competitive advantage that comes with certification, as most of the customers and a significantly large part of the vendors of the supply chain look for certified products, services and processes, even if this costs them more.[187] In other words, market dynamics increasingly tend to make these private law instruments *de facto*, but not *de jure*, 'mandatory'.[188]

---

[182] Regulation (EU) 2019/881, Article 58(8)(f).

[183] Regulation (EU) 2019/881, Article 65.

[184] Kamara (2021), p. 98.

[185] Wavestone - CEPS - CARSA - ICF (2021), p. 72.

[186] https://www.enisa.europa.eu/news/enisa-news/going-full-throttle-on-cybersecurity-certification-and-market.

[187] Blythe et al. (2020).

[188] Chiara (2022a), p. 130.

4.2.1 The State of IoT Cybersecurity Certification and Standardisation

The European Commission started to tackle the debate around the governance of IoT in 2012 by holding a multi-stakeholder public consultation.[189] Most respondents claimed that IoT-specific legislation, with respect to cybersecurity and safety, was not necessary, opting for no governance at all out fearing that overregulation coupled with unnecessary compliance burdens could stifle a fast-growing ecosystem still in its infancy.[190]

Thus, there was a general consensus around the need for guidelines and standards, as a self-regulation governance approach was preferred. The initial pure self-regulatory policy option led to undesirable outcomes,[191] namely an EU Internal Market flooded with unsecure IoT devices. Whereas the previous section demonstrated which actions the EU institutions have taken to put matters right (i.e., the adoption of Regulation 2019/881), this section aims at casting light on the plethora of technical standards, both European and national, on which existing IoT cybersecurity labels and future certification schemes will be based.

Against the background of the IoT governance debate, some scholars argued that "we lack the proper technical standards that may enable multiple systems and different networks to communicate with each other, making full interoperability feasible".[192] Interestingly, the lack of interoperable solutions and upstream technical standards is echoed in Recital 66 of the Cybersecurity Act, warning that such gaps—coupled with missing practices and Union-wide mechanisms of certification—significantly affect the single market in the field of cybersecurity.[193]

The lack of interoperability is one of the factors negatively affecting IoT market uptake. As stressed by the EU Commission's 2019 Rolling Plan for ICT standardisation, after the adoption of the Cybersecurity Act, "[i]nteroperability between IoT networks operated by different companies along the value chain opens up opportunities to address EU policy objectives e.g., greater resource efficiency for a more circular economy, sustainable and responsible supply chains through transparency and traceability, and others".[194]

There is nevertheless an argument against the push for interoperability that deserves attention. Denardis notes that a certain degree of lack of interoperability could be at times beneficial in the IoT cybersecurity paradigm:

> Designing a medical monitoring device to communicate directly with a door lock is both unnecessary and undesirable, especially from a security standpoint. Having some inherent

[189] European Commission (2013); Weber (2013); Weber (2016).

[190] Weber and Studer (2016), p. 727.

[191] Floridi (2021).

[192] Pagallo et al. (2017), p. 74.

[193] Regulation (EU) 2019/881, recital 66.

[194] European Commission (2019), p. 25.

> lack of interoperability between different implementation settings, particularly by sector, assuming each environment itself develops sufficient stability and security, seems preferable to a wide-open plane of attack for cross-sector and cross-border security incursions.[195]

The argument made above may be better grasped through an example, namely the role Android played for smartphones. Before Android, there were many 'little islands' of non-interoperable phones (e.g., Nokia, Samsung, LG, etc.). Consequently, different apps had to be developed for each 'type of island'. With the advent of Android, most devices in the world (except Apple's) have become interoperable with each other.

On the one hand, this process has created a single point of failure, that is, an exploit for Android would endanger millions of devices. On the other hand, different sectors—medical devices and door locks—have different standards: to ensure interoperability in a single environment, it is necessary to have a higher standard that would link the sectorial standards at the lower level.

Beside the fact that security always plays a pivotal role in standardisation, sectorial fragmentation—while potentially representing a barrier to standardisation[196]—is crucial to uphold cybersecurity, as indeed highlighted, to a certain extent, by Denardis: "fragmentation by industry might be desirable so that [...] a lack of cross-industry interoperability can serve as a check on security problems".[197] A medical IoT device and a door lock might well interoperate in some way (even without any useful purpose), but they would still not be considered 'equal devices' when communicating because of the different (sectoral) standards, thus ensuring a desirable degree of security.

Nevertheless, in the 2021 Rolling Plan, the Commission noticed that "a large number of proprietary or semi-closed solutions to address specific problems have emerged, leading to non-interoperable concepts, based on different architectures and protocols. Consequently, the deployment of truly IoT applications i.e., where information of connectable "things" can be flexibly aggregated and scaled, has been limited to a set of "intranets of things — or goods".[198]

In this respect, it is worth recalling the IoT architecture taxonomy outlined in Chap. 2, as the strive for standards for these systems goes beyond the end devices—which are mostly constrained[199]—and involves communication networks, switching and routing systems, back-end analytics, applications, cloud services. Therefore, it extends to a plethora of different markets, business models and actors.

The Commission acknowledge on the other hand that one of the major achievements of the last few years has been the progressive strength of cooperation amongst

[195] Denardis (2020), p. 136.

[196] Ibid., p. 142.

[197] Ibid., p. 144.

[198] European Commission (2021a), p. 30.

[199] There are many standards and protocols for IoT constrained scenarios: CoAP, IPv6 over Bluetooth, LoRAWAN, DDS, DTLS, ZigBee, etc.

all actors in the field of IoT standardisation[200] to develop common technical standards, eschewing the path towards proprietary approaches. Against this backdrop, the question that arises is what the state of IoT standardisation in the specific area of security is.

At the end of 2018, ENISA conducted a preliminary analysis of the IoT-related landscape of security standards.[201] The model consists of mapping cybersecurity requirements to available standards, from European Standardisation Organisations (i.e., CEN, CENELEC and in particular ETSI TC Cyber), ISO/IEC JTC1 subcommittees including SC27 (IT Security Techniques) and SC41 (Internet of Things and related technologies) and ITU-T Series Y: "Global information infrastructure, internet protocol aspects and next-generation network". The multiple requirements identified by Annex I of the matrix are clustered around several classes. These are: 'security by design', 'privacy by design', 'organisational, people and process measures'.[202]

The Agency came to the conclusion that "there is no significant gap in standards to bring secure IoT to the market. This does not mean that the security of the IoT ecosystem as a whole has been addressed by means of standards. Elements of a holistic approach towards IoT security can be found in a series of standards, however, to achieve an overarching approach that protects the entire IoT ecosystem further work is needed".[203]

In other words, what is really lacking in IoT security standardisation is a *functional*—that is, sector and application (products, services or processes) specific, *flexible*, *holistic* combination of the technical requirements that already exist out there. As a consequence, it is possible "to deliver a device to the market that can authenticate its user, that can encrypt data it transmits, that can decrypt data it receives, that can deliver or verify the proof of integrity, but which will still be insecure".[204]

Amongst the many standards mapped out by ENISA, it is worth looking more closely at ETSI's Cybersecurity standard for Consumer IoT (ETSI EN 303 645) and ISO/IEC's IoT security and privacy (ISO/IEC CD 27402) standards. Indeed, they are mentioned by experts as a good basis for the development of harmonised standards for baseline cybersecurity of connected products.[205]

Whereas ISO/IEC 27402 (*Cybersecurity — IoT security and privacy — Device baseline requirements*) is currently under development,[206] in 2020 ETSI released a standard which specifies 13 cybersecurity baseline requirements for consumer IoT

[200] European Commission (2021a), p. 31.

[201] ENISA (2019b).

[202] Ibid., pp. 11–22.

[203] Ibid., p. 4.

[204] Ibid., p. 7.

[205] DIGITALEUROPE (2021a), p. 15.

[206] The standard proposal was approved in mid-June 2020. See <https://www.iso.org/standard/80136.html>.

devices, with specific considerations to constrained devices[207] (see Chap. 2), with the associated services being out of the scope.[208] The cybersecurity baseline requirements are:

(i) No universal default passwords: the passwords shall be unique per device and sufficiently randomized to reduce the risk of automated attacks (provisions 5.1–1,2). Moreover, authentication mechanisms shall use state-of-the-art cryptography (provision 5.1–3).
(ii) Implement a means to manage reports of vulnerabilities: the manufacturer shall render publicly available a vulnerability disclosure policy, including contact information for the reporting and information on timelines vis-à-vis the acknowledgment of receipt and status updates (provision 5.2–1). In this regard, the manufacturer should act on vulnerabilities in a timely manner without stopping the continuous monitoring (provisions 5.2–2,3).
(iii) Keep software update: all software components shall be securely updatable (provision 5.3–1) and the process will be simple (provision 5.3–3), automated (provision 5.3–4)—even if the update would involve dependencies on multiple actors along the supply chain and possibly separated from feature updates. The device should verify authenticity and integrity of software updates: in resource constrained paradigms, verification can be performed by a trusted device (provision 5.3–9). If a constrained device cannot have its software updated, it should be isolable (provision 5.3–15) and the manufacturer should publish the reasons for this, alongside the period and method of hardware's replacement provision (5.3–14). Finally, the manufacturer should inform users whether a security update is required, and how the risks have been mitigated (provision 5.3–11).
(iv) Securely store sensitive security parameters: security parameters like hard-coded unique identity shall be implemented in a way that resists tampering (provision 5.4–2).
(v) Communicate securely: device shall use best practice cryptography and state-of-the-art implementations to deliver network and security functionalities (provisions 5.5–1, 2).
(vi) Minimize exposed attack surfaces: the foundational 'principle of least privilege' shall be taken into the utmost account. As a consequence, software should run with the lowest possible number of privileges (provision 5.6–7), unused network and logical interfaces shall be disabled (provision 5.6–1) and, when in the initialized state, the former shall minimise the unauthenticated disclosure of security-relevant information (provision 5.6–2). If a debug interface is physically accessible, it shall be disabled in software (provision

[207] ETSI defines it as a "devices which has physical limitations in either the ability to process data, the ability to communicate data, the ability to store data or the ability to interact with the user, due to restrictions that arise from its intended use".
[208] ETSI (2020), p. 6.

5.6–4). Finally, the manufacturer should follow secure software development processes (provision 5.6–9).[209]

(vii) Ensure software integrity: software should be verified through secure boot mechanisms (provision 5.7–1) and if unauthorised change is detected, the device should alert the user and/or the administrator (provision 5.7–2).

(viii) Ensure that personal data is secure: this control upholds confidentiality of personal data, especially taking into account the ones transiting between a device and a service. Interestingly, ETSI provides for a definition of 'sensitive personal data' in "note 1" of the provision 5.8–2 which diverges to a certain extent from the GDPR approach: whereas the (exceptional) grounds for the processing of 'special categories of personal data',[210] that is, "sensitive data", laid down by Regulation (EU) 2016/679 are set in relationship to significant risks to the fundamental rights and freedoms,[211] ETSI conceives 'sensitive data' as data whose disclosure has a high potential to cause harm to the individual.

(ix) Make systems resilient to outages: *resilience by design*, that is, building devices taking into account the eventuality of power and network outages (provision 5.9–1): in case of a loss of network access the IoT device should remain operating (provision 5.9–2). Redundancy and mitigations against DDoS attacks should be included as well.

(x) Examine system telemetry data for security anomalies.

(xi) Make it easy for users to delete user data: user data shall be deleted from the device (provision 5.11–1) as well as from associated services (provision 5.11–2) in a simple manner. In this respect, users should be given clear instructions on how to do so (provision 5.11–3) and provided with confirmation about whether cancellation has been successful (provision 5.11–4).

(xii) Make installation and maintenance of devices easy: these steps should involve minimal decisions by the user (provision 5.12–1) and the manufacturer should provide users with sufficiently clear guidance on how to securely set up the device (provision 5.12–2) and how to check whether the previous step has been achieved (provision 5.12–3).

(xiii) Validate input data via user interfaces or transferred via APIs or between networks in services and devices (provision 5.13–1).[212]

In light of the above, it can be argued that numerous efforts have been made with respect to IoT security standardisation. In this respect, ENISA's mapping out of security standards applicable to IoT shows that "there is a gap in standards only

[209] ENISA (2019a).

[210] Regulation (EU) 2016/679, Article 9.

[211] Regulation (EU) 2016/679, Recital 51.

[212] ETSI (2020), pp. 13–24.

insofar as it is unclear what combination of standards, when applied to a product, service or system, will result in a recognisably secure IoT".[213]

However, it should be noted that technical experts agree that existing and soon-to-be-published standards, that is, ETSI TS 303645 and ISO/IEC 27402, would only cover roughly half (54%) of the technical requirements that can be used as harmonised standards based on current product legislation.[214]

Further work is therefore necessary in order to define baseline cybersecurity requirements for all IoT devices that would be referenced in harmonised standards under EU product legislation, which will be addressed subsequently in Sect. 4.3.

Based on the requirements of ETSI TS 303645, the Finnish Transport and Communications Agency (Traficom) has created a Cybersecurity Label, which is, a certification scheme for IoT devices or services.[215] The Finnish label extends ETSI's baseline cybersecurity requirements from 13 to 20 and prioritises them according the OWASP IoT threats list in order to encompass the most common security threats affecting the consumers of connected devices.[216]

From an operational viewpoint, the Finnish label shows how the relationship between certification (even though it has not been developed under the Cybersecurity Act framework) and standards upon which the former rely on works in practice. Following the Swedish lead, on 27 September 2022, the German Federal Office for Information Security (BSI) released an IT security label for IoT consumer devices, building on the EU cybersecurity standard for IoT consumer devices ETSI EN 303 645.[217]

Isolated national cybersecurity certification initiatives in the IoT sector (such as the Finnish and German IoT security labels) may even achieve their objectives and prove useful in the short term. They run the risk, however, of further fragmenting the EU cybersecurity certification landscape. The Cybersecurity Act, as shown in this section, aims to tackle the current fragmentation of the internal market with harmonised European Cybersecurity Certification Schemes.

Against this backdrop, the Rolling Plan of the EU Commission does not foresee a cybersecurity certification scheme directly addressing the IoT. Instead, the Commission focused on the need of harmonised technical standards for IoT security that are aligned with current information security relevant standards (i.e., ISO 27xxx) and the GDPR.[218] Moreover, EU standardisation bodies will be tasked to develop standards on the safety and cybersecurity for IoT consumer products under European Cybersecurity Act requests or sectorial legislation e.g., the NLF (see next section).[219]

---

[213] ENISA (2019b), p. 23.

[214] DIGITALEUROPE (2021a), p. 15.

[215] Finnish Transport and Communications Agency (2020).

[216] Ibid., p. 14.

[217] German Federal Office for Information Security (BSI) (2022).

[218] European Commission (2021a), p. 32.

[219] Ibid., p. 32.

Awaiting a possible candidate IoT cybersecurity scheme under the CSA,[220] three candidate schemes are currently being developed: the EU Cybersecurity Certification Scheme on Common Criteria (EUCC)[221]—which would replace national schemes operating under the SOG-IS MRA, and the two schemes on Cloud Services (EUCS)[222] and 5G.[223]

The EUCC, compared to the latter two, is more horizontal: "it may allow to improve the Internal Market conditions, and to enhance the level of security of ICT products dedicated to security (e.g., firewalls, encryption devices, gateways, electronic signature devices, means of identification such as passports, . . .) as well as of any ICT product embedding a security functionality (i.e., routers, smartphones, banking cards, medical devices, tachographs for lorries, . . .)".[224]

Eventually, on 31 January 2024 the Commission published on the Official Journal of the EU the implementing regulation setting out the first EU cybersecurity certification scheme, the EUCC.[225] The Common Criteria certification scheme applies to all ICT products (that is, hardware and software) and protection profiles (i.e., ICT process laying down security requirements for a specific category of ICT products).[226] The EUCC builds on the Mutual Recognition Agreement (MRA) of Information Technology Security Certificates of the SOG-IS using the Common Criteria. Accordingly, it is based on established international standard i.e., ISO/IEC 15408; ISO/IEC 18045, that is, the Common Criteria and Common Evaluation Methodology standards and uses Common Criteria's vulnerability assessment family (AVA_VAN). In terms of assessment procedures, with a view to strengthening trust,[227] this scheme does not foresee self-assessment; only third-party conformity assessment by ITSEF and certification bodies is allowed. Certification bodies shall then issue EUCC certificates at assurance level 'substantial' (AVA_VAN 1/2) and 'high' (AVA_VAN 3/4/5) only.[228]

Without dwelling on the procedure of the EUCC, it is worth noting that ICT products can undergo 'composite product certification', that is, the evaluation of an ICT product together with another underlying ICT product that has already received an EUCC certificate and on whose security functionality the composite ICT product

---

[220] ENISA Stakeholder Cybersecurity Certification Group (2021), pp. 10–13.

[221] ENISA (2021b, c).

[222] ENISA (2020b).

[223] See https://www.enisa.europa.eu/topics/standards/adhoc_wg_calls/ad-hoc-working-group-on-5g-cybersecurity-certification.

[224] ENISA (2021c), p. 11.

[225] European Commission, COMMISSION IMPLEMENTING REGULATION (EU) . . ./. . . of 31.1.2024 laying down rules for the application of Regulation (EU) 2019/881 of the European Parliament and of the Council as regards the adoption of the European Common Criteria-based cybersecurity certification scheme (EUCC), C(2024) 560 final.

[226] Ibid., Article 1.

[227] Ibid., recital 10.

[228] Ibid., Article 4(1).

depends.[229] Therefore, IoT manufacturers may consider certification for ICT products or services part of their IoT systems. This approach has been referred to as 'certification by composition': an IoT device may rely on certified components (e.g., firewalls) thanks to the EUCC and on a certified cloud service, thanks to the EUCS.[230]

In conclusion, a future candidate IoT security scheme should attempt to exploit synergies between existing labels and schemes. As Chap. 6 will later discuss vis-à-vis risk analysis frameworks, the need is to correctly position EU core values and principles in IoT standardisation taking into account existing global initiatives such as the ones of ISO/IEC.

4.3 EU Product Safety Legislation and IoT Cybersecurity

The entry into force of the so-called 'New Legislative Framework' (NLF) in 2008 reformed the EU model of governance of product safety. The NLF consists of Regulation (EC) 765/2008, setting out the requirements for accreditation and the market surveillance of products; Decision 768/2008 on a common framework for the marketing of products, which includes reference provisions to be incorporated whenever product legislation is revised; and, Regulation (EU) 2019/1020 on market surveillance and product compliance.

The New Legislative Framework updated the foundational principles of the 'New Approach', developed in the 80s as a legislative follow-up to the *Cassis de Dijon* seminal case,[231] in particular in terms of technical harmonisation in the context of EU products safety legislation.[232] The 'New Approach' model of governance pivoted around four core principles. First, legislative harmonisation should be limited to lay down the 'essential requirements' (ERs)—as opposed to overly detailed technical proscriptions that products placed on the EU market must meet in order to benefit from free movement within the EU.[233] Second, European Standardisation Organisations (ESOs) i.e., CEN, CENELEC and ETSI, shall be mandated by the Commission with the task of establishing specific technical standards—known as 'harmonised technical standards'—for products meeting the essential requirements set out in the legal acts.[234] Third, products manufactured in

---

[229] Ibid., Article 2(10).

[230] ECSO (2020), p. 15.

[231] Case 120/78, *Rewe-Zentral AG v Bundesmonopolverwaltung für Branntwein* (Cassis de Dijon) [1979] EU:C:1979:42.

[232] Hofmann (2016), p. 17.

[233] Gorywoda (2009), p. 163.

[234] In this respect, such delegation—either via contracts or not—raised a question of the constitutional legitimacy, in terms of the principles of access and transparency, of referencing (EU) harmonised technical standards or ISO standards in EU law without publishing their content in the Official Journal of the EU: see *ex multis* Gérardy (2021). Albeit extremely interesting, the

compliance with harmonised standards benefit from a presumption of conformity with the corresponding essential requirements of the applicable legislation. Fourth, the application of harmonised or other standards remains voluntary, and the manufacturer can always apply other technical specifications to meet the requirements.[235]

The NLF updated EU legislation with a more comprehensive and coherent regulatory framework in relation to market access (that is, notification process, accreditation, the conformity assessment procedures, CE marking) and market surveillance. The emphasis shifts from the traditional notion of 'placing on the market'—which focuses on the first time a product is made available on the EU market, to 'making a product available'[236]: the latter concept gives more importance to what happens after a product is first made available and facilitates the tracing back of a noncompliant product to the manufacturer.[237]

This approach is further complemented by putting in place a comprehensive policy on market surveillance, that is, Regulation (EC) no. 765/2008 and Regulation (EU) 2019/1020. "This has considerably changed the balance of EU legislative provisions from being fundamentally oriented at setting product related requirements to be met when products are placed on the market to an equal emphasis on enforcement aspects during the whole life-cycle of products".[238]

Against this background, most of the legal acts in the area of EU product safety legislation, and the related harmonised standards which specify the essential requirements thereof, were conceived before the advent of the IoT, when products were not connected and did not interact with each other or their environment.[239] Therefore, the EU Commission aimed at leveraging the EU product safety legal framework by including cybersecurity essential requirements in the revision process of different legislative pieces.[240] Thus, the Commission—at first—decided to tackle the problem of unsecure connected products from a sectorial viewpoint rather than introducing in EU law a horizontal legal act on connected products' cybersecurity anew.[241]

This section critically analyses the different EU legal acts regulating product safety to assess to what extent the cybersecurity of (IoT) products is considered. One

legal qualification of harmonised technical standards and the possibility of their undergoing judicial verification of their validity under EU law fall outside the scope of this work; see *inter alia,* Perotto (2020); Case C-613/14, *James Elliott Construction Limited c. Irish Asphalt Limited* [2016] ECLI: EU:C:2016:821.

[235]European Commission (2016), p. 8.

[236]On the difference between 'placing on the market' and 'making available on the market', see Decision No 768/2008/EC, Annex I, Article R1(1), (2) and Regulation (EC) No 765/2008, Article 2(1), (2).

[237]European Commission (2016), p. 10.

[238]Ibid., p. 10.

[239]Fosch-Villaronga and Mahler (2021).

[240]DIGITALEUROPE (2021a), p. 4.

[241]COMMISSION DELEGATED REGULATION (EU) 2022/30 of 29.10.2021 supplementing Directive 2014/53/EU of the European Parliament and of the Council with regard to the application of the essential requirements referred to in Article 3(3), points (d), (e) and (f), of that Directive, 5.

methodological caveat applies. Considerations on safety requirements generally involve the analysis of civil—or even criminal—liability regimes.[242] Nevertheless, liability issues fall outside the scope of this book.[243] Thus, this section delves into different legal acts of EU product legislation only to the extent that they incorporate cybersecurity essential requirements applicable to the IoT. Building on the theoretical premise of Sect. 3.2.4 (“*Degrees of Separation Between Cybersecurity and Safety in the IoT*”), this legal analysis casts light on how the EU co-legislator envisages the entanglement of the concepts of safety and cybersecurity with regard to the IoT devices.[244]

The first Directive under scrutiny is Directive 2014/53/EU on radio equipment which is particularly prominent in the context of the IoT ubiquitous connectivity. Regulation (EU) 2023/988 (General Product Safety Regulation) introduces a cybersecurity requirement that must be taken into account when assessing the safety of (connected) products, including therefore IoT. Moreover, Regulation (EU) 2017/745 (Medical Devices Regulation) is scrutinized as the first EU legal act in product safety legislation, having an impact on a specific IoT sector (i.e., e-Health), that incorporated cybersecurity requirements. Finally, Regulation (EU) 2023/1230 (Machinery Regulation), repealing Directive 46/2002/EC, is analysed for it lays down cybersecurity requirements for the design and construction of machinery products.

4.3.1 The Radio Equipment Directive, the Delegated Regulation 2022/30 and the IoT

Directive 2014/53/EU on radio equipment (RED)[245] establishes a legal framework for the making available of radio equipment on the EU market.[246] The RED aligned the former 1999/5/EC directive on radio and telecommunication terminal equipment with the New Legislative Framework.

In particular, an efficient traceability system pivoting on the identification of radio equipment is foreseen in the ‘EU declaration of conformity’[247]—issued by the manufacturer—in order to facilitate market surveillance authorities’ task of tracing economic operators (i.e., manufacturers, importers and distributors) who made non-compliant radio equipment available on the market.[248] Improved market

[242] European Commission Expert Group on Liability and New Technologies (2019).

[243] Chiara (2020b).

[244] Vedder (2019), pp. 14–15; Serpanos and Wolf (2018); Chiara (2021).

[245] Directive 2014/53/EU of the European Parliament and of the Council of 16 April 2014 on the harmonisation of the laws of the Member States relating to the making available on the market of radio equipment and repealing Directive 1999/5/EC Text with EEA relevance.

[246] Directive 2014/53/EU, Article 1(1).

[247] Directive 2014/53/EU, Annex IV.

[248] Directive 2014/53/EU, Recital 37.

surveillance is also testified by manufacturers' obligation to register radio equipment falling within categories affected by a low level of compliance with the essential requirements set out in Article 3 in a central system made available by the Commission before market placement.[249]

Article 3 sets out the 'essential requirements' (ER) radio equipment must respect. Among the nine ERs listed in Article 3(3), for the purpose of this work, it is worth focusing on Article 3(3)(d),[250] (e)[251] and (f),[252] namely the ERs that aim to address different elements of cybersecurity by ensuring network protection, safeguards for the protection of personal data and privacy, and, protection from fraud respectively. In this regard, it worth anticipating that Article 44 RED empowers the Commission to adopt delegated acts to specify which categories or classes of radio equipment are concerned by each ER of Article 3(3) RED.

As to the question whether IoT devices fall under the scope of the RED, Directive 2014/53 defines 'radio equipment' as an "electrical or electronic product, which intentionally emits and/or receives radio waves for the purpose of radio communication".[253] It follows that, if an IoT device communicate via radio-based protocols such as Bluetooth (indirect internet-connectivity) or Wi-Fi (direct internet-connectivity), it would be radio equipment within the meaning of Article 2(1) RED.[254] The Impact Assessment on the increased protection of internet-connected radio equipment and wearable radio equipment commissioned by the Commission from the *Centre for Strategy & Evaluation Services* came to the same conclusion.[255]

As radio equipment are increasingly connected to the internet (the number is estimated to rise to 7.43 billion in EU by 2030), concerns are mounting over the resilience and robustness of these devices—including machines, sensors and networks that make up the Internet of Things (IoT)—are sufficiently secure for they have to ensure that users' personal data and networks are protected, privacy is respected and frauds are avoided.[256]

In 2019, the Commission started a public consultation taking into account all the possible related aspects, "also in terms of the impacts for the society (e.g. consumers

[249] Directive 2014/53/EU, Article 5(1).

[250] Article 3(3)(d) mandates that radio equipment does not harm the network or its functioning nor misuse network resources, thereby causing an unacceptable degradation of service.

[251] Article 3(3)(e) prescribes that radio equipment incorporates safeguards to ensure that the personal data and privacy of the user and of the subscriber are protected.

[252] Article 3(3)(f) requires that radio equipment supports certain features ensuring protection from fraud.

[253] Directive 2014/53/EU, Article 2(1)(1).

[254] Hessel and Rebmann (2020), p. 34.

[255] Center for Strategy & Evaluation Services (2020), p. 13.

[256] Ibid., p. 14; Giovanni and Silva (2018), p. 4. See also <https://circabc.europa.eu/ui/group/43315f45-aaa7-44dc-9405-a86f639003fe/library/b4016779-5e33-4298-b64e-a2cce6f4dba2/details>; <https://circabc.europa.eu/ui/group/43315f45-aaa7-44dc-9405-a86f639003fe/library/ffef4de7-cbc0-4f78-968b-2b6b355d5aec/details>; OECD (2018).

and economic operators), the national Authorities, the common market access conditions and the implementation of, or synergies with, additional pieces of EU legislation, in particular those relating to (cyber)security, data protection and privacy".[257]

A study commissioned by the Commission highlighted several problems in this regard. To start off, the already existing pieces of EU legislation regulating privacy, data protection, frauds or networks security (i.e., GDPR, ePrivacy Directive, NIS Directive and Non-Cash Payment Directive) did not allow effective corrective measures to be taken in terms of withdrawing insecure connected products placed on the market. Under RED's legal framework, Member States competent authorities could not remove IoT products from the market if they failed to comply with relevant legislation (e.g., the GDPR, the e-Privacy Directive), without the adoption of a delegated act 'activating' relevant RED ERs.[258]

Furthermore, in the early stages of a product's design and engineering, if the manufacturer does not intend to process personal data, it would not be obliged then to follow, *inter alia*, security and data protection by design and by default principles.[259] It is very likely to have a scenario where an internet-connected radio equipment allegedly processing non-personal data would in fact collect, process and share personal data, in light of the broad definition of personal data ex Article 4(1) GDPR and relevant case-law.[260]

The Commission eventually adopted the Delegated Regulation (EU) 2022/30 on 29 October 2021,[261] with a view to specifying to which categories or classes of radio equipment the essential requirements set out in Article 3(3)(d), (e) and (f) RED apply.

As a result, the 'network-preservation' requirement of Article 3(3)(d) RED applies to radio equipment that are able to communicate *directly* and *indirectly*—i.e. via other equipment (e.g., Bluetooth and other similar protocols which may enable wireless data sharing with internet-connected equipment)—over the internet.[262]

As clarified by Recital 9 of the Delegated Act, the 'network security' requirement should be interpreted as broad as to encompass main cybersecurity threats,[263] such

[257] European Commission (2021b), p. 62.

[258] Center for Strategy & Evaluation Services (2020), p. 96.

[259] Ibid., 35.

[260] Case C-582/14 *Patrick Breyer v Bundesrepublik Deutschland* [2016] ECLI:EU:C:2016:779; Case C-434/16 *Peter Nowak v Data Protection Commissioner* [2017] ECLI:EU:C:2017:994.

[261] Commission Delegated Regulation (EU) 2022/30 of 29.10.2021 supplementing Directive 2014/53/EU of the European Parliament and of the Council with regard to the application of the essential requirements referred to in Article 3(3), points (d), (e) and (f), of that Directive.

[262] Delegated Regulation (EU) 2022/30, Article 1(1).

[263] Delegated Regulation (EU) 2022/30, recital 9: "an attacker may maliciously flood the internet network to prevent legitimate network traffic, disrupt the connections between two radio products, thus preventing access to a service, prevent a particular person from accessing a service".

as DDoS attacks.[264] The rationale behind such large understanding of the concept of "harm to network" is to be found in the increasingly complex and dynamic threat landscape (see Chap. 2).[265] As a result, Article 3(3)(d) RED would cover not only the 'expected' use of the network made by radio equipment but also the harmful consequences to the network arising from insufficient security.[266] "In other words, the delegated regulation would complement the framework established by the NIS Directive, ensuring that not only the networks *per se* are secure, but also that the connected radio equipment does not harm them".[267]

Instead, Article 3(3)(e) RED on privacy and data protection would apply not only to radio equipment capable of processing personal data and traffic or location data, but also to radio equipment designed or intended exclusively for childcare, toys (radio-equipment covered by Directive 2009/48/EC) and so-called 'wearables'.[268] The inclusion of 'toys' is not trivial: the seminal case of the '*Cayla* doll'[269] showed that competent authorities[270] encountered difficulties in removing the product from the market, notwithstanding security flaws and vulnerabilities had been exposed.[271]

Article 2 of the delegated act exclude medical and in-vitro devices from the scope of RED essential requirements scrutinised,[272] whilst motor vehicles, electronic road toll systems, equipment to control unmanned aircraft remotely as well as non-airborne specific radio equipment that may be installed on aircrafts are exempt from the requirements regarding the protection of personal data and protection against fraud.[273] Thus, Article 3(3)(d) RED against networks harm and misuse would still be applicable to such equipment.

All in all, the recently adopted delegated act brings the majority of IoT devices into the RED's scope, albeit radio equipment already on the market when the delegated regulation entered into force are not addressed. Even though the scope of the RED only covers wireless devices, thus not wired equipment, the adoption of the delegated act would indeed enhance and complement the existing standards of protection under EU cybersecurity and data protection legislation.

As a consequence, all manufacturers of internet-connected and wearable devices must therefore design and place on the market products embedding baseline cybersecurity and data protection requirements as a pre-condition for market access, even

---

[264] *Contra* see Banasinski and Rojszczak (2021), p. 7.

[265] ENISA (2019c).

[266] European Commission (2021b), pp. 12–17.

[267] Chiara (2022b), p. 106.

[268] Delegated Regulation (EU) 2022/30, Article 1(2).

[269] Mansfield-Devine (2017).

[270] Germany resorted to a longstanding legal act on espionage to remove the product on the market; See <https://www.bundesnetzagentur.de/SharedDocs/Pressemitteilungen/DE/2017/14012017_cayla.html?nn=690686>.

[271] European Commission (2021b), p. 27.

[272] Delegated Regulation (EU) 2022/30, Article 2(1).

[273] Delegated Regulation (EU) 2022/30, Article 2(2).

if they claim not to process personal data.[274] Related to that, competent authorities are granted powers to remove from the market products which are unsecure from a cybersecurity perspective and/or illegal from a privacy and data protection perspective because they are non-compliant with EU product safety legislation (i.e., RED and Delegated Act 2022/30).

Following the adoption of the delegated act, the European Commission has issued a standardisation request to the European Standardisation Organisations (ESOs). ESOs will have to prepare harmonised standards which may be used by manufacturers to demonstrate conformity with relevant ERs. The 2022 Union work programme for European standardisation set as goal the revision of EU standards supporting RED's cybersecurity requirements. This approach should be welcomed as there are already existing solutions which can be used. "For privacy, the "security by design" principle of the GDPR can already be addressed through specific standards. The same applies to the security of payments. For the protection of the network, there is already a pool of best practices and standards that stem from the implementation of the NIS Directive which can be taken as a benchmark and mirrored, where appropriate, into the design of equipment".[275]

Related to that, relevant stakeholders highlighted that the cybersecurity standardisation requests of the RED delegated act should be so open, that is, *performance-based* and *technology neutral*, that they can be reused in the context of future horizontal cybersecurity legislation, called for by the new cybersecurity strategy,[276] the Council,[277] the EDPS[278] and many private actors[279] (addressed later in Sect. 4.5).

4.3.2 The General Product Safety Regulation: Cybersecurity, Safety and the IoT

Regulation (EU) 2023/988 (General Product Safety Regulation, GPSR), which entered into force in June 2023 and repeals Directives 87/357/EEC and Directive 2001/95/EC (General Product Safety Directive, GPSD) from 13 December 2024,[280] sheds light on the Commission's approach with respect to introducing cybersecurity requirements in EU product safety legislation. Several scholars addressed the main legal challenges of the GPSD regime regarding safety and cybersecurity risks posed

[274] Center for Strategy & Evaluation Services (2020), p. 5.

[275] European Commission (2021b), pp. 52–53.

[276] European Commission and the High Representatitve of the Union for Foreign Affairs and Security Policy (2020), p. 9.

[277] Council of the European Union (2020), pp. 4–6.

[278] European Data Protection Supervisor (2021), p. 8.

[279] BDI, DIN and DKE (2021).

[280] Regulation (EU) 2023/988, Art. 50.

by connected devices.[281] However, the Proposal for a Regulation before, and the final text of the Regulation afterwards have not yet received great attention from the scholarly literature in terms of its impact in EU cybersecurity law.

As regards an explicit link with the 'IoT', AIOTI already expressed its view opposing a Regulation which would not be technology neutral: "mentioning and/or introducing provisions that are technology specific (AI, robotics, IoT) have no added value and would help to push the uptake of innovation due to legal uncertainty".[282] Whereas 'IoT' is not explicitly mentioned in the legal act, one of the normative novelties introduced by the Commission Proposal certainly was including the 'connectivity' element into the aspects to be taken into account to assess the safety of products.

In particular, Article 7(1)(b) and 7(1)(c) of the Commission Proposal placed the obligation to assess the effect on other products—and the one that other products might have on the product under scrutiny, where it is *reasonably foreseeable* that it will be used with other products, including the interconnection between them. In this respect, a compelling argument raised by DIGITALEUROPE would see as disproportionately wide "by reference to all products that may reasonably foreseeable be used with or connected to the product under assessment". It is recommended thus that these duties shall be limited to the impact assessment of products that are *intended* to be used together or connected.[283] Eventually, the final version of Article 6 did not transpose these nuances.

Against the background of including cybersecurity requirements in the legal act, DIGITALEUROPE and Orgalim explicitly opposed the approach proposed by the Commission, albeit from different angles. On the one hand, Orgalim consistently reiterates the necessity to address the issue of cybersecurity for connected products via horizontal harmonised legislation, rather than sectorial legislation, in particular, having regard to EU product safety legal frameworks.[284]

On the other hand, DIGITALEUROPE advises the Commission to delete letter (h) of Article 7 to avoid duplicative requirements under different pieces of Union legislation and inconsistencies. As regards the first issue, many cybersecurity requirements for products are also being dealt with under newly proposed instruments related to the Radio Equipment Directive (RED). The second, closely related, leverages the lack of agreed standards on what 'appropriate cybersecurity' entails and upon which economic operators can rely to comply with the legal obligation.[285]

On 10 December 2021, the EU Parliament Committee on the Internal Market and Consumer Protection published a draft report with significant amendments to the Commission's Proposal. The Rapporteur welcomed the adaptation of the product safety directive to the risks stemming from connected products, as well as the

---

[281] Fosch-Villaronga and Mahler (2021) pp. 7–8; Banasinski and Rojszczak (2021), pp. 6–7.

[282] AIOTI (2021).

[283] DIGITALEUROPE (2022a), p. 3.

[284] Orgalim (2021), p. 3; Orgalim (2020), pp. 4–6.

[285] DIGITALEUROPE (2022a), p. 3.

updated list criteria to evaluate their safety.[286] In the Parliament Draft, Article 7 paragraph 1 of the Commission proposal regarding the aspects for assessing whether a product is safe was moved to before Article 6 (presumption of conformity), thereby creating a new Article 5a. The rationale behind this regulatory choice is that the 'safety assessment' should precede the presumption of safety or, in NLF terms, presumption of conformity with (safety) essential requirements.

Notably, "these aspects are valid for all non-harmonised products regardless of whether the presumption of safety is applicable or not".[287] In this respect, it is worth noting the relevant change apported to the first half sentence of the Article 7(1) of the Commission proposal by Article 5a: the reference to the non-applicability of presumption of safety enshrined in Article 5 has been replaced with a much more coherent "when assessing whether a product is safe". As suggested by ANEC and BEUC, those criteria must be binding on economic operators and stakeholders (such as standardisation organisations, national market surveillance authorities, etc.) "for the whole life cycle of a product, from its design to its disposal", without unduly limiting their scope to a post market phase.[288]

Eventually, the final text of the GPSR aligns with the final Parliament draft report laying down a 'general safety requirement' (whereby economic operators must place on the market only safe products) at Article 5 and 'aspects for assessing the safety of products' at Article 6. Article 6(1)(g) specifically includes, "when required by the nature of the product, the appropriate cybersecurity features necessary to protect the product against external influences, including malicious third parties, where such an influence might have an impact on the safety of the product, including the possible loss of interconnection".

Compared to the Commission Proposal, the only addition is represented by the final snippet 'including the possible loss of interconnection', without however substantially changing the overall sense of the norm. Interestingly, with regard to the 'appropriate cybersecurity' standard, Article 6(1)(h) explicitly refers to external influences, opening traditional product safety mechanisms up to more holistic cybersecurity paradigms.

To move onto the issue of duplicative requirements, attention shall be paid to Recital 26: "specific cybersecurity risks affecting the safety of consumers as well as protocols and certifications can be dealt with by sectorial legislation. However, it should be ensured that, in cases where such sectoral legislation does not apply, the relevant economic operators and national authorities take into consideration risks linked to new technologies, when designing the products and assessing them

[286] European Parliament, Draft Report on the proposal for a regulation of the European Parliament and of the Council on general product safety, amending Regulation (EU) No 1025/2012 of the European Parliament and of the Council, and repealing Council Directive 87/357/EEC and Directive 2001/95/EC of the European Parliament and of the Council (COM(2021)0346 – C9-0245/2021 – 2021/0170(COD)), 96.

[287] Ibid., 37.

[288] ANEC and BEUC (2021), p. 5.

respectively, in order to ensure that changes introduced in the product do not jeopardise its safety".

Whereas the abovementioned stance adopted by Orgalim may be theoretically understandable, the approach endorsed by the Commission had taken a different turn as a policy option entailing a horizontal piece of legislation on cybersecurity for products with digital elements (read as: the Cyber Resilience Act) could not be as timely as one or more delegated acts under the RED.[289] Conversely, the position of DIGITALEUROPE deserves special attention.

Thus, the alleged risk of duplication is not well substantiated: the reference to the RED seems to suggest that the cybersecurity requirements of that legal act, coupled with the recently adopted delegated regulation, would comprehensively deal with the challenges posed by connected products. Notwithstanding the wide scope of the RED vis-à-vis connected products, it is ultimately a piece of legislation which covers solely the radio equipment sector.

Therefore, some connected products would fall outside the RED's scope, for example, wired connected devices. For this reason, such gaps might be covered by a revised GPSD in its role of 'safety net'.[290] In its function of *lex generalis*, the GPSR will apply to non-harmonised consumer products and to the harmonised consumer products for the aspects that are not covered by harmonised legislation,[291] as clarified by Recital 26 GPSR. In conclusion, rather than insisting on potential overlaps, it is worth looking at the extent to which convergences between the GPSR and RED (and its delegated act) can be exploited.

The second argument presented by DIGITALEUROPE is perhaps more convincing. On the one hand, upon mandate from the Commission, the European Standardisation Organisations (ESOs) shall develop harmonised standards to substantiate cybersecurity (essential) requirements in EU product legislation, providing manufacturers with the possibility (the reliance on harmonised standards being voluntary) of producing the presumption of conformity of products in accordance with harmonised standards.

This process will nonetheless require some time. Hence, in the short term, it is reasonable to expect manufacturers to rely on international standards (e.g., ISO/IEC) or in-house developed technical solutions. On the other hand, the lack of agreed standards on what 'appropriate cybersecurity' entails reveals a different piece of the jigsaw, namely the need for a clear, consistent definition of 'cybersecurity' in EU product safety legislation, as cybersecurity requirements are currently being included in several legislative proposals (i.e., the GPSR, the Machinery Regulation, the Artificial Intelligence Act and the delegated act under the Radio Equipment Directive—excluding the already applicable Medical Device Regulation).

The requirements vary from one legal act to the other: in some cases, the product in question must be able to "withstand, where appropriate to the circumstances and

[289] European Commission (2021b), pp. 5–6.

[290] European Commission (2021c), pp. 10–14.

[291] Ibid., 4.

the risks, the intended operating stresses and intended and unintended external influences, including reasonably foreseeable malicious attempts from third parties leading to a hazardous situation" (Annex III Section 1.2.1 of the Machinery Regulation), in others the cybersecurity features are defined as protection "against external influence" (Article 6(1)(h) General Product Safety Regulation) or as resilience "regarding errors, faults or inconsistencies that may occur within the system or the environment in which the system operates, in particular due to their interaction with natural persons or other systems; [and] against attempts by unauthorised third parties to alter their use, outputs or performance by exploiting system vulnerabilities" (Article 15(4); (5), Artificial Intelligence Act).

To ensure coherence between the different legal acts, one option could have been referring to the essential requirements in terms of cybersecurity provided for in the Medical Device Regulation (MDR),[292] as the MDR marked the beginning of incorporation of cybersecurity aspects within the safety essential requirements into EU product safety legislation. In particular, these requirements would have taken into account the core principles of information security risk management, therefore including minimum baseline requirements concerning IT security measures, such as protection against unauthorised access. It is worth noting however that the level of technical standardisation in terms of cybersecurity in the health sector is more mature than other market sectors, such as consumer device.[293]

Another viable option would have been modelling the GPSR cybersecurity requirement on the security objectives laid down in Article 51 of the Cybersecurity Act (see Sect. 4.2), such as protection against unauthorised access or disclosure of information, or protection against accidental or unauthorised lack of availability, verification of access and absence of vulnerabilities, or to follow the security by default principle and to securely update software and hardware.[294] The rationale behind this suggestion being the fact that these cybersecurity objectives are high-level and comprehensive in terms of assets protection coverage in products scenarios.

Moreover, the cybersecurity objectives of Article 51 have been compared with the identified requirements of several pieces of EU legislation by the project team that has been awarded the contract to carry out a "Study on the need of cybersecurity requirements for ICT products" (as addressed later in Sect. 4.5): the analysis has been based on the Cybersecurity Act as it is one of the most up-to-date and relevant

[292] Regulation (EU) 2017/745 of the European Parliament and of the Council of 5 April 2017 on medical devices, amending Directive 2001/83/EC, Regulation (EC) No 178/2002 and Regulation (EC) No 1223/2009 and repealing Council Directives 90/385/EEC and 93/42/EEC, Annex I, 14.2 (d).

[293] See for example the IEC technical standard on medical device software (EN 62304 2006) and ISO medical device risk management (EN 14971 2012) or ISO/IEC 80001 – Application of risk management for IT networks incorporating medical devices.

[294] Regulation (EU) 2019/881, Article 51.

pieces of EU legislation covering cybersecurity for ICT products on a broad spectrum.[295]

4.3.3 Cybersecurity Requirements in the Medical Devices Regulation

Regulation 2017/745 on medical devices (MDR) establishes a regulatory framework for the production, the placing on the market and putting into service of medical devices and their accessories on the EU market.[296] As mentioned in the previous section, the MDR is the first legal act within EU product safety legislation to incorporate cybersecurity requirements. That is the reason why RED Delegated Act left medical and in-vitro devices out of the scope of Art. 3(3)(d), (e), and (f) RED.

A medical device is whatever instrument, software or article *intended by the manufacturer* to be used, alone or in combination, for human beings for specific medical purposes (e.g., diagnosis, prevention, monitoring, prediction, prognosis, treatment or alleviation of disease, injury, disability, etc.).[297] In this respect, in *Snitem and Philips France,* the CJEU clarified that software, of which at least one of the functions makes it possible to use patient-specific data for medical purposes (such as detecting contraindications, drug interactions and excessive doses) is, in respect of that function, a medical device, even if such software does not act directly in or on the human body.[298] As a result, the Court seems to adopt a risk-based and case-by-case approach—coming close to the U.S. FDA system[299]—in order to qualify the software or device at stake as medical device: the *actual* function of the asset becomes as important as the intended use declared by the manufacturer.[300]

The Regulation mandates that, in order to be placed on the market and put into service in the Single Market, medical devices must meet the safety requirements set out in Annex I of the MDR.[301] In accordance with the principles of the NLF, manufacturers must undertake a conformity assessment before placing the product on the market,[302] involving clinical safety evaluations.[303]

---

[295] Wavestone - CEPS - CARSA - ICF (2021), p. 53.

[296] Regulation (EU) 2017/745, recital 2.

[297] Regulation (EU) 2017/745, Article 2(1), recital 19: "[w]hile software for general purposes, even when used in a healthcare setting, or software intended for life-style and well-being purposes is not a medical device".

[298] Case C-329/16 *Snitem and Philips France* [2018] ECLI:EU:C:2017:947.

[299] Quinn (2017), pp. 369–370.

[300] Gerybaite (2022), p. 8.

[301] Regulation (EU) 2017/745, Article 5(2).

[302] Regulation (EU) 2017/745, Article 52.

[303] Regulation (EU) 2017/745, Article 61.

Following a risk-based approach, manufacturers shall establish, document, implement and maintain a system for risk management (detailed in Annex I)[304] and a post-market surveillance system in a manner that is proportionate to the risk class and appropriate for the type of device.[305] Indeed, medical devices must be divided in certain classes according to the intended purpose of the devices and their inherent risks.[306] In other words, the classification of the device, as per Annex VIII MDR, "dictates the appropriate conformity assessment procedure: the higher the classification, the greater the level of assessment required by the notified bodies".[307]

Annex I of the Regulation, which sets out general safety and performance requirements, obliges manufacturers of medical devices to fulfil minimum requirements concerning hardware, IT networks characteristics and IT security measures, including protection against unauthorised access. Thus, devices shall be designed and manufactured to address and minimise "the risks associated with the possible negative interaction between software and the IT environment within which it operates and interacts".[308]

Most of the provisions are indeed dedicated to software. It should be developed and manufactured "in accordance with the state of the art taking into account the principles of development life cycle,[309] risk management, including information security, verification"[310] and the specific features of the mobile computing platform in combination with which it is used.[311] Another relevant cybersecurity ER addresses "minimum requirements concerning hardware, IT networks characteristics and IT security measures, including protection against unauthorised access, necessary to run the software as intended".[312]

In the context of the IoT, if the device is intended for use in combination with other devices or equipment the whole combination—including the connection system—shall be safe and shall not impair the specified performance of the devices.[313] In this scenario, the classification rules of the medical device and another (non-medical) device with which the former is intended to be used in combination shall apply separately to each of the devices, as "[a]ccessories are classified in their own right separately from the device with which they are used".[314]

To make things more complex, Article 1(3) MDR states that devices with both a medical and a non-medical intended purpose shall cumulatively fulfil the legal

---

304 Regulation (EU) 2017/745, Article 10(2).

305 Regulation (EU) 2017/745, Article 83.

306 Regulation (EU) 2017/745, Article 51(1).

307 Contardi (2019), p. 170.

308 MDR, Annex I, 14.2(d).

309 ENISA (2019a).

310 MDR, Annex I, 17.2.

311 MDR, Annex I, 17.3.

312 MDR, Annex I, 17.4.

313 MDR, Annex I, 14.1.

314 *Snitem and Philips France* (n 296), §10.

requirements applicable to devices with an intended medical purpose and those applicable to devices without an intended medical purpose.

Therefore, it may be the case that within an IoT ecosystem different requirements, in terms of cybersecurity, stemming from different legal frameworks (e.g., MDR and Machinery Directive[315]), apply (i) to different devices that may be manufactured by the same actor or (ii) cumulatively to the same device. With specific regard to the latter scenario, two different legal challenges arise, potentially leading to legal uncertainty.

The first aspect investigates how to exploit the potential synergies (or mechanisms of legal coordination and cooperation[316]) between cybersecurity requirements under different EU legal acts in the health sector. In this respect, the MDR addresses only manufacturers, while leaving other actors involved in the deployment of medical devices, such as hospitals and other care providers, off the hook.[317]

As seen in Sect. 4.1, these actors might nonetheless face cybersecurity responsibilities and duties under the NIS Directive, as OES; as such, they are required to manage the cybersecurity risks posed to the network and information systems—such as medical devices—which they use in their operations (Article 14(1) NIS). In other words, "obligations towards establishing information security of a specific integrated device effectively remain with the Health Delivery Organisation if it has mandated the integrator to connect a given medical device to the clinical/hospital IT network".[318]

As regards the issue of overlapping duties that would create legal uncertainty, if the cybersecurity requirements of the different legal acts that would cumulatively apply significantly diverge from one another—as seen in the previous section when discussing divergences in the content of cybersecurity requirements in product legislation, the standard of protection may differ.

Thus, the set of cybersecurity requirements of the MDR is more granular, scalable and detailed (including the security by design principle, security risk management, security capabilities or controls, risk assessment, minimum requirements, validation/verification and life-cycle considerations) when compared to the framework of the RED or the Machinery Regulation (next section). In terms of cybersecurity compliance, it can be argued that once the manufacturer fulfils the obligations laid down in the MDR, it should not incur in liability under the other legal regimes with respect to cybersecurity obligations.

Lastly, in order to comply with high-level requirements, manufacturers can use harmonised technical standards, the reference of which is published in the EU Official Journal, to provide a presumption of conformity with relevant legislation. However, on 26 June 2020, CEN and CENELEC rejected the Commission's

---

[315] Fosch-Villaronga and Mahler (2021), p. 8.

[316] Gerybaite (2022), pp. 10–12.

[317] Fosch-Villaronga and Mahler (2021), p. 7.

[318] Medical Device Coordination Group (2019), p. 12.

implementing decision M/565 requiring European Standardisation Organisations to standardise a series of existing regulations and new regulations to be drawn up as regards medical devices, in support of the Medical Devices Regulation MDR (EU) 2017/745 and the In Vitro Diagnostic Medical Devices Regulation IVDR (EU) 2017/746.[319]

Eventually, on 14 April 2021, the Commission filed a new standardisation request to ESOs whereby it requested a revision of existing harmonised standards in support of the MDR, including, in particular, EN ISO 14971:2019 on application of risk management to medical devices; EN 62304:2006+A1:2015 on (medical devices) software lifecycle processes; EN IEC 82304-1 Health Software Part 1: General requirements for Product Safety; EN ISO/IEC 80001-1 Application of Risk Management for IT Networks Incorporating Medical Devices[320]; EN 62366-1:2015 +AC:2015+AC:2016+A1:2020 Medical devices—Application of usability engineering to medical devices.

At the same time, the Commission also requested new harmonised standards to be drafted, the most relevant to cybersecurity being IEC/TR 60601-4-5 Medical Electrical Equipment—Part 4–5. Safety related technical security specifications for medical devices.[321] CEN and CENELEC will provide the Commission with the joint final report by 30 June 2024.[322]

4.3.4 *The Machinery Regulation and IoT Cybersecurity*

Given that the Machinery Directive (MD)[323] was outside the NLF, the Proposal for a Regulation on Machinery Products,[324] repealing the Directive, sought "to enhance the enforcement of the legal act through the alignment to the NLF".[325] Thus, the impact assessment accompanying the Proposal highlighted that most stakeholders largely supported the alignment of the Machinery Directive to the NLF, addressing *inter alia* shortcomings in the area of market surveillance—generally seen as insufficient and ineffective,[326] and conversion into a regulation.[327] In particular,

---

[319] European Commission (2020a).

[320] For further analysis, see Anderson and Williams (2018).

[321] European Commission (2021d), Article 1(1).

[322] Ibid., Article 3(3).

[323] Directive 2006/42/EC of the European Parliament and of the Council of 17 May 2006 on machinery.

[324] European Commission, "Proposal for a Regulation of the European Parliament and of the Council on machinery products" COM(2021) 202 final.

[325] Anglmayer (2021), p. 11.

[326] Ibid., p. 4.

[327] European Commission (2021e), p. 48.

the new Regulation would lay down cybersecurity requirements for the design and construction of machinery products.

The evaluation assessment of the Machinery Directive pointed out a number of regulatory gaps that should be addressed in the Directive revision. In particular, the assessment identified six problems: (i) insufficient coverage of new risks relating to emerging digital technologies; (ii) legal uncertainty due to a lack of clarity on the scope and definitions and possible safety gaps in traditional technologies; (iii) insufficient provisions for high-risk machines; (iv) monetary and environmental costs; (v) inconsistencies with other pieces of EU product-safety legislation; (vi) divergences in interpretation due to transposition.

This section will particularly elaborate on the first problem, as the revision process assumed that the Directive was not adequate as such, despite its technology-neutral design, to cope with the challenges arising from evolution of digital technologies, in particular, having regard to cybersecurity concerns.[328]

In terms of scope, the MD applied to all new machinery placed on the market for the first time, regardless of its origin i.e., whether manufactured within or outside the EU. The Parliamentary implementation appraisal of September 2021 claimed that the Directive's "scope of application is very broad, encompassing a vast array of machinery for industrial and private use, including construction machinery, lawnmowers, powered hand-tools, as well as certain modern machinery, including 3D printers, e-bikes, robots and drones".[329]

As a consequence, with specific regard to modern machinery, the Commission decided to significantly restrict the scope of the proposed Regulation. For instance, whereas e-bikes—and light vehicles more generally (such as electrically power-assisted cycles, hover boards, or self-balancing scooters)—would fall under the scope of the Directive,[330] they were excluded from the Commission's Proposal. Thus, following the suggestions made in the impact assessment,[331] Art 2(2) (e) explicitly excluded "vehicles which have as their only objective the transport of goods or persons by road, air, water or rail except for machinery mounted on those vehicles" from the Regulation's scope.

Moreover, having regard to drones, the relevant applicable law is the Commission Delegated Regulation (EU) 2019/945 on unmanned aircraft systems and on third-country operators of unmanned aircraft systems. Article 4(2) of that legal act states that "UAS (i.e., drones) that are not toys within the meaning of Directive 2009/48/EC shall comply with the relevant health and safety requirements set out in Directive 2006/42/EC [Machinery Directive, note of the author] only in relation to risks other

[328] Proposal for a Machinery Regulation, Recital 11.

[329] Anglmayer (2021), p. 2.

[330] Parliamentary question E-003051-19 to the Commission by Seán Kelly (PPE) (1 October 2019), <https://www.europarl.europa.eu/doceo/document/E-9-2019-003051_EN.html>.
Ms. Bieńkowska on behalf of the European Commission answered that "electric bicycles are already covered by the machinery Directive 2006/42/EC" <https://www.europarl.europa.eu/doceo/document/E-9-2019-003051-ASW_EN.html>.

[331] European Commission (2021e), p. 44.

than those linked to the safety of the UA flight". Therefore, the relevant essential requirements set out in the Machinery Directive apply to drones only insofar as they refer to aspects not related to the flight.

The Commission's proposal left out of scope many electrical and electronic (possibly connected) products, insofar as they fall within the scope of application of Directive 2014/35/EU or Directive 2014/53/EU: household appliances intended for domestic use; audio/video equipment, information technology equipment; office machinery; low-voltage switchgear and control gear; electric motors.[332] All in all, the proposed Regulation did not seem to cover a wide range of IoT devices.

Eventually, the Machinery Regulation (MR)[333] entered into force in July 2023 but will effectively repeal the Machinery Directive only from 14 January 2027. However, Article 54 MR provides that several parts of the Regulation will be applicable before January 2027.

In terms of scope, Article 2(2) MR maintains the approach of the Commission's proposal, by excluding manifold machinery applications—including the abovementioned electrical and electronic products. That being said, the scope of the MR is likely to be nevertheless broad given the provisions of Articles 2(1) and 3(1) MR, taken together.

The definition of 'machinery' falling in scope of the MR provided by Article 3(1)(a) includes "an assembly, fitted with or intended to be fitted with a drive system other than directly applied human or animal effort, consisting of linked parts or components, at least one of which moves, and which are joined together for a specific application".

Against the background of the inclusion of cybersecurity requirements, the aim of the Commission was to address those cybersecurity risks having an impact on safety, such as preserving machinery against malicious third-party attacks, without precluding the application of other Union legislation specifically addressing cybersecurity aspects to machinery products.[334]

Importantly, as regards the presumption of conformity of machinery products with the essential health and safety requirements set out in the Proposal, besides the typical NLF reference to harmonised standards, the MR foresees the possibility for manufacturers to refer to certificate or statement of conformity issued under a relevant cybersecurity scheme adopted pursuant to and in accordance with Article 54(3) of Regulation (EU) 2019/881.[335]

Annex III MR lays down the essential health and safety requirements relating to the design and construction of machinery products. In view of addressing the 'cybersecurity risk' with an impact on safety, the MR seemingly restricts—in

---

[332] Proposal for a Regulation on Machinery Products, Article 2(2)(m).

[333] Regulation (EU) 2023/1230 of the European Parliament and of the Council of 14 June 2023 on machinery and repealing Directive 2006/42/EC of the European Parliament and of the Council and Council Directive 73/361/EEC.

[334] Regulation (EU) 2023/1230, Recital 25.

[335] Regulation (EU) 2023/1230, Article 20(9); Recital 51.

Recitals 25 and 51—the scope of the new requirements to malicious third-party actions, thereby unduly moving away from more high-level and all-encompassing understandings of cybersecurity risks, enshrined for example in the Cybersecurity Act

Nevertheless, a closer look at the requirements under scrutiny, namely 1.1.9 and 1.2.1 of Annex III, reveals a more 'agnostic' perspective in terms of the sources of security threats. Thus, the requirement 1.1.9 explicitly addresses protection against *accidental* and intentional corruption. The incipit of the requirement is rather broad: "the machinery product shall be designed and constructed so that the connection to it of another device, via any feature of the connected device itself or via any remote device that communicates with the machinery product *does not lead to a hazardous situation* [emphasis added]". Hardware, software and data components that are critical for the machinery product's compliance with the relevant health and safety requirements must be adequately protected against not only intentional but accidental corruption as well.[336]

On the other hand, requirement 1.2.1 mandates that, following a risk-based approach, control systems shall withstand "the intended operating stresses and intended and *unintended* external influences, including malicious attempts from third parties to create a hazardous situation [emphasis added]". In conclusion, the reference to "malicious third-party attempts" made in the legal act shall be carefully assessed against the actual content of the essential requirements of Annex 4.III which broaden the scope of protection to accidental corruption, unintended external influence and hardware fault.

Against this background, as noted by CEN—CENELEC, one of the cornerstone principles of the New Legislative Framework is that harmonised legislation specifies essential requirements within the boundaries of a product's 'intended use' and 'reasonably foreseeable misuse'. "The 2016 edition of the Blue Guide clearly states in Section 2.7 that this consideration shall result from "lawful and readily predictable human behaviour". Hence intentional unlawful human behaviour should thus not fall under the "intended use" or "reasonably foreseeable misuse" under any NLF-legal acts, such as the proposed regulation. [. . .] Every kind of intentional violation (sabotage/spying) of a machine is de facto a criminal act".[337]

As a result, according to the European standardisation organisations, the new EHSR 1.1.9 and 1.2.1(a) are arguably in contradiction with the above-mentioned basic principle of the NLF as stated in the Blue Guide. Albeit from a different perspective, DIGITALEUROPE also criticises the reference to 'third parties' malicious attempts' of the proposal on the grounds that they would not be possible to foresee. "DIGITALEUROPE recommends that the Regulation only applies to those risks that are known when the equipment is placed on the market or put into service. State-of-the-art cyber security standards can be applied at the time the equipment is

[336] Regulation (EU) 2023/1230, Annex III, 1.1.9.

[337] CEN-CENELEC (2021), pp. 5–6.

placed on the market or put into service, but not beyond that point".[338] The EU legislature however took a different view, reflecting a more dynamic approach to cybersecurity, which might well be more challenging for economic operators.

4.3.5 *The Right Answer?*

Section 4.3 highlighted the European Commission's approach to the ever-growing number of unsecure IoT devices in the Single Market, which consisted in the revision of EU product safety legislation to include cybersecurity essential requirements. As already mentioned, EU product safety legal acts are traditionally focused on the design and manufacturing phases, for they are linked to the placing and making available of products on the market. Cybersecurity—and IoT security specifically—requires however dynamic risk management to be ensured throughout the entire life cycle of the devices.[339]

All in all, the inclusion of cybersecurity requirements in sectoral legislation has not been considered appropriate by many stakeholders, with EUROSMART being an exception.[340] DIGITALEUROPE,[341] Orgalim,[342] CEN—CENELEC,[343] Bundesverband der Deutschen Industrie (BDI)[344] and the European Economic and Social Committee (EESC)[345] argued that the Commission had embarked upon a path towards fragmented and contradictory legal requirements.

Albeit a vertical (or sectoral) approach vis-à-vis the problem of unsecure connected products may even deliver positive results in the short run, only horizontal legislation can address the problem at the core in the most efficient way.[346] The last section of this Chapter will elaborate extensively on this policy option.

Against this backdrop, the next section sheds light on how broader cybersecurity administrative, procedural and organisational requirements introduced by the revised NIS Directive (NIS2) may contribute to strengthening IoT cybersecurity when coupled with product-related requirements laid down in EU product legislation.[347]

---

[338] DIGITALEUROPE (2021b), p. 4.

[339] Ducuing (2019), p. 203.

[340] EUROSMART (2019).

[341] DIGITALEUROPE (2021b), pp. 7–8.

[342] Orgalim (2020).

[343] CEN-CENELEC (2021), p. 6.

[344] BDI (2021a).

[345] European Economic and Social Committee (2020).

[346] Wavestone - CEPS - CARSA - ICF (2021), pp. 256–257; Chiara (2022a).

[347] DIGITALEUROPE (2021a), p. 9.

4.4 The Revision of the NIS Directive: The NIS2 and the IoT

On 16 December 2020, the European Commission and the High Representative of the Union for Foreign Affairs and Security Policy presented the new European Cybersecurity Strategy,[348] a central element of a larger picture sketched by the European Digital Transition Plan,[349] the Recovery Plan[350] and the European Security Strategy of July 2020.[351]

The strategy defines three areas of EU action, for increased protection of citizens, businesses and institutions, through the deployment of regulatory, investment and policy instruments. These are: (1) resilience, technological sovereignty and leadership, (2) developing operational capabilities for prevention, deterrence and response, and (3) promoting a global and open cyberspace.

The Commission aimed at further improving the prevention, resilience and incident response capabilities of public and private entities, competent authorities, and the Union as a whole, in the field of cybersecurity. This ambitious objective led to two legislative proposals: the revision of the NIS Directive and a new Directive on Critical Entity Resilience.[352]

On 27 December 2022, Directive (EU) 2022/2555 (hereinafter, NIS2) was published in the Official Journal of the EU and entered into force on 16 January 2023.[353] The fast-paced action of the Commission in this sector underlines the increasing centrality of cybersecurity issues in the Union's political agenda.

The NIS2 seeks to revise the existing legal framework thereby addressing several weaknesses that prevented the NIS Directive from unlocking its full potential. The explanatory memorandum of the Proposal for the NIS2 acknowledged that the NIS Directive had contributed to improving cybersecurity capabilities at national level by requiring Member States to adopt national cybersecurity strategies and to appoint cybersecurity authorities. The NIS also had increased cooperation between Member States at Union level by setting up various fora facilitating the exchange of strategic and operational information.

Furthermore, the NIS Directive had improved the cyber resilience of public and private entities in seven specific sectors (energy, transport, banking, financial market infrastructures, healthcare, drinking water supply and distribution, and digital

348 European Commission and the High Representatitve of the Union for Foreign Affairs and Security Policy (2020).

349 See https://digital-strategy.ec.europa.eu/it.

350 See https://ec.europa.eu/info/strategy/recovery-plan-europe_en.

351 European Commission (2020b).

352 European Commission, *Proposal for a Directive of the European Parliament and the Council on the resilience of critical entities* COM(2020) 829 final.

353 On 27 December 2022, Directive (EU) 2022/2557 and Regulation (EU) 2022/2554, namely the directive on the resilience of critical entities and DORA regulation respectively, have also been published on the EU OJ.

infrastructures) and across the three digital services providers (online marketplaces, online search engines and cloud computing services) by requiring Member States to ensure that operators of essential services and digital service providers put in place cybersecurity requirements and report incidents.[354]

Nevertheless, the evaluation of the functioning of the NIS Directive highlighted six major areas of concern. First, the overly limited scope in terms of the sectors covered (due to the higher degree of IoT interconnectedness and the exclusion of sectors providing key services to the society). Second, the lack of clarity as regards the scope of OES and the national competence over DSP, resulting in fragmentation as certain types of entities have not been identified in all Member States. Third, the significant fragmentation among Member States when laying down security and incident reporting requirements for OESs, creating additional burden for companies operating in more than one Member State. Fourth, the ineffective supervision and enforcement regime, as Member States have been very reluctant to apply penalties. Fifth, the different level of progress among Member States in dealing with cybersecurity risks. Finally, the lack of information sharing between Member States.[355]

Therefore, the NIS2 has been structured with a view to addressing the abovementioned regulatory failures. In particular, the pillars of the NIS2 Directive are: (i) subject matter and scope; (ii) national cybersecurity frameworks; (iii) cooperation; (iv) cybersecurity risk management and reporting obligations; (v) jurisdiction and registration; (vi) information sharing; (vii) supervision and enforcement.[356]

Among the systemic and structural changes envisaged by the NIS2,[357] this section investigates whether and to what extent the NIS2 would ensure a higher standard of security for IoT devices by addressing the following legal challenges: (i) the broader scope of the NIS2, taking into particular account the inclusion of the 'manufacturing' sector; (ii) the vulnerability disclosure and handling procedures; and, (iii) new cybersecurity requirements for the supply chain.[358]

4.4.1 The Broader Scope of the NIS2

The explanatory memorandum to the EU Commission's NIS2 proposal highlighted that the "increased digitisation in recent years and a higher degree of interconnectedness" were considered as key factors contributing to the progressive inadequacy

354 European Commission, *Proposal for a DIRECTIVE OF THE EUROPEAN PARLIAMENT AND OF THE COUNCIL on measures for a high common level of cybersecurity across the Union, repealing Directive (EU) 2016/1148 COM(2020) 823 final*, 16 December 2020.

355 Ibid., p. 6.

356 Ibid., pp. 9–11.

357 Schmitz-Berndt (2021), Brighi and Chiara (2021), Sievers (2021), Biasin and Kamenjašević (2022).

358 Chiara (2022a).

of the NIS Directive's scope, which "no longer reflects all digitised sectors providing key services to the Union".[359] The IoT, implicitly evoked by the keyword 'interconnectedness', is in this regard one of the technological developments that prompted the EC to act.

Against this background, the NIS2 applies to public and private 'essential entities' (EEs) and 'important entities' (IEs),[360] thus replacing the NISD distinction between operators of essential services and digital services providers. In this respect, the broadening of the scope hinges on the level of criticality of the sector or of the type of service provided by the entity.

In a nutshell, the NIS2 adopts a cap-size rule to overcome Member States' divergences in terms of identifying the OESs falling in scope of the NIS legal framework. Entities that are medium-sized enterprises, or exceed such ceiling, and provide their services or carry out their activities within the Union operating in the sectors listed in Annex I and II fall in scope of the Directive. Annex I identifies eleven highly critical sectors: energy; transport; banking; financial market infrastructures; health; drinking water; waste water; digital infrastructure; ICT service management; public administration and space. Annex II instead groups other seven critical sectors: postal and courier services; waste management; manufacture, production and distribution of chemicals; food production, processing and distribution; manufacturing; digital providers and research.

In this respect, entities operating in Annex I sectors that exceed the ceiling of medium-sized enterprises are considered to be essential entities,[361] except for providers of public electronic communications networks or of publicly available electronic communications services which qualify as medium-sized enterprises.[362] Irrespective of their size, specific actors are deemed as essential entities, either because they provide specific services (qualified trust service providers, top-level domain name registries, DNS service providers) or due to their nature (central public administration entities, critical entities pursuant CER Directive). Important entities are connoted in the negative: entities of Annex I and II that do not qualify as essential entities, are important.[363]

The size-cap rule in general excludes small and micro enterprises. However, "Member States should also provide for certain small enterprises and microenterprises, as defined in Article 2(2) and (3) of that Annex, which fulfil specific criteria that indicate a key role for society, the economy or for particular sectors or types of service to fall within the scope of this Directive".[364] Accordingly,

---

[359] European Commission, *Proposal for a DIRECTIVE OF THE EUROPEAN PARLIAMENT AND OF THE COUNCIL on measures for a high common level of cybersecurity across the Union, repealing Directive (EU) 2016/1148 COM(2020) 823 final*, 16 December 2020, p. 6.

[360] Directive (EU) 2022/2555, Art. 2(1).

[361] Directive (EU) 2022/2555, Art. 3(1)(a).

[362] Directive (EU) 2022/2555, Art. 3(1)(c).

[363] Directive (EU) 2022/2555, Art. 3(2).

[364] Directive (EU) 2022/2555, Recital 7.

Art. 2(2) mandates that, regardless of the size, the NIS2 is nevertheless applicable if the entity fulfils certain requirements.[365]

Related to that, it is worth noting that Art. 7(2)(i) NIS2 mandates Member States to adopt, as part of the national cybersecurity strategy, policies with a view of "strengthening the cyber resilience and the cyber hygiene baseline of small and medium-sized enterprises, in particular those excluded from the scope of this Directive, by providing easily accessible guidance and assistance for their specific needs".

The rationale underlying the paradigm shift in terms of the scope of application of the Directive is to comprehensively cover sectors that are of "vital importance to key societal and economic activities",[366] and, as such, deserved to be praised. However, as highlighted by several stakeholders, the lack of granular and scalable risk-based obligations (e.g., business-to-business versus business-to-consumer models) may turn the NIS2 into "blanket legislation covering most ICT services without any real distinctions".[367]

With regard to the IoT, it is worth mentioning that Annex II lists entities operating in the manufacturing sector. The six 'manufacturing' sub-sectors (medical, computer, electronic, electrical, machinery, motor vehicles and transport equipment) are undoubtedly relevant to IoT market. Annex II of the NIS2 makes reference to the 'NACE Rev. 2 classification of economic activities' to further specify which types of undertakings fall within the sub-sectors under scrutiny.[368]

Recalling the outcomes of Sect. 4.1, connected devices part of the NIS of EEs and IEs would still be covered by the *rationae personae* scope of the NIS2. However, the NIS2 would not *directly* address the issue of unsecure IoT products and related services for it does not lay down product-related requirements, even if manufacturers and developers now fall within the scope of the NIS2 as IEs. Thus, sectoral product safety legislation already sets out cybersecurity requirements at product level.[369]

With the NIS2 maintaining a principle-based character, e.g. establishing procedural and 'organisational'[370] requirements, two regulatory novelties introduced by the revision of the NISD may intersect with product-related requirements. This might be the case with regard to: (i) vulnerabilities disclosure and handling procedures; (ii) supply chain cybersecurity requirements.

---

[365] For example, the entity is the sole provider in a Member State of a service which is essential for the maintenance of critical societal or economic activities (Art. 2(2)(b) NIS2).

[366] Directive (EU) 2022/2555, Recital 6.

[367] DIGITALEUROPE (2021b), p. 4; BDI (2021b), p. 7.

[368] For example, the manufacturing of computers and electronic products include inter alia consumer electronics, electronics components and communication equipment (NACE Rev. 2—Statistical classification of economic activites in the European Community, division 26, 69).

[369] DIGITALEUROPE (2021b), p. 6.

[370] DIGITALEUROPE (2021a), p. 9.

4.4.2 Vulnerabilities Handling and Disclosure

As seen in Chap. 3, the exchange of information on vulnerabilities is one main area of intersection between the public and private sector, as testified by the growing number of public-private partnership (PPPs) initiatives to strengthen cybersecurity.

In this respect, Article 12 NIS2 lays down a procedural framework for coordinated vulnerability disclosure. Each Member State has to designate a CSIRT as the coordinator of this process. The CSIRT will act as a trusted intermediary, where required facilitating the interaction between the reporting entity and the ICT service or product manufacturer or provider.[371] It is up to ENISA, instead, to develop and update a "European Vulnerability Register". The database shall contain information describing the vulnerability, the ICT products or services concerned, the severity of the vulnerability if exploited, the availability of relevant patches and, if not available, guidance to users of vulnerable products and services on how to mitigate the risks.[372] It is clear, therefore, how the intention of the EU legislature is to increasingly encourage an approach of close cooperation between private and public actors in the cybersecurity field.

Importantly, the original text proposed by the Commission has been amended by the Parliament in the sense of specifying that only those vulnerabilities for which a patch is available shall be listed in the vulnerability database.[373] Otherwise, this provision—which certainly does go in the direction of greater security—could create a paradoxical situation, where a vulnerability was published without any mitigation measures.

Albeit only in the recitals, the NIS2 affirms that "entities that develop or administer network and information systems should therefore establish appropriate procedures to handle vulnerabilities when they are discovered. Since vulnerabilities are often discovered and disclosed by third parties, the manufacturer or provider of ICT products or ICT services should also put in place the necessary procedures to receive vulnerability information from third parties".[374] Thus, Art. 21(2)(e) stipulates that entities shall take into account—as a baseline cybersecurity management measure (addressed in the next section)—the "security in network and information systems acquisition, development and maintenance, *including vulnerability handling and disclosure* [emphasis added]".

[371] Directive (EU) 2022/2555, Art. 12(1).

[372] Directive (EU) 2022/2555, Art. 12(2).

[373] European Parliament, REPORT on the proposal for a directive of the European Parliament and of the Council on measures for a high common level of cybersecurity across the Union, repealing Directive (EU) 2016/1148 (COM(2020)0823 – C9-0422/2020 – 2020/0359(COD)), Amendment 127 Proposal for a directive Article 6 – paragraph 2.

[374] Directive (EU) 2022/2555, Recital 58.

The Directive does not contain an 'obligation to patch' for manufacturers within a specific timeframe,[375] similar to what Directive (EU) 2019/771 has implemented with respect to sellers (but not manufacturers!).[376] For it would not be the proper legal instrument for implementing such an obligation, for the reasons discussed above. Rather, this might be better achieved by the incoming Cyber Resilience Act (addressed in Sect. 4.5).

If it is true that giving manufacturers more leeway in terms of vulnerability handling would come at a cost for consumers in terms of security, that has been welcomed by industry, as companies, when developing patches, "should not encounter additional outside pressure which could lead to a deterioration of the quality of the work".[377]

4.4.3 Supply Chain Cybersecurity Management Measures

Another legal challenge in terms of overlap with cybersecurity 'product requirements' is the cybersecurity management measure focusing on supply chain relationships. While adhering to a risk-based approach already envisioned by the NIS Directive,[378] the NIS2 introduces an appreciable element of novelty, that is, a list of minimum cybersecurity management measures to be taken indiscriminately by EEs and IEs to manage the risks posed to their network and information systems. These measures are:

(a) policies on risk analysis and information system security;
(b) incident handling;
(c) business continuity, such as backup management and disaster recovery, and crisis management;
(d) supply chain security, including security-related aspects concerning the relationships between each entity and its direct suppliers or service providers;
(e) security in network and information systems acquisition, development and maintenance, including vulnerability handling and disclosure;
(f) policies and procedures to assess the effectiveness of cybersecurity risk-management measures;
(g) basic cyber hygiene practices and cybersecurity training;

---

375 European Commission and the High Representatitve of the Union for Foreign Affairs and Security Policy (2020), p. 9.

376 See Art. 7(3) Directive (EU) 2019/771 (Sale of Goods Directive). Cfr. *inter alia* with: Janssen (2022); Wendehorst (2022). See also Dickmann (2022), pp. 4–5.

377 BDI (2021b), p. 6.

378 Directive (EU) 2022/2555, Art. 21(1): "Member States shall ensure that essential and important entities take appropriate and proportionate technical, operational and organisational measures to manage the risks posed to the security of network and information systems which those entities use for their operations or for the provision of their services, and to prevent or minimise the impact of incidents on recipients of their services and on other services".

(h) policies and procedures regarding the use of cryptography and, where appropriate, encryption;
(i) human resources security, access control policies and asset management;
(j) the use of multi-factor authentication or continuous authentication solutions, secured voice, video and text communications and secured emergency communication systems within the entity, where appropriate.[379]

These measures shall not only be based on a risk-based, but also on an all-hazard approach, that is, a holistic understanding of security that operates a Hegelian synthesis, so to speak, between digital and physical & environmental security. Thus, the physical and environmental protection of NIS from system failures, human error, malicious acts or natural phenomena is complementary and equally important for protection against digital threats.[380] This holistic conceptualisation of the notion of 'security', that is, to put cyber and physical security on an equal footing, signals from an epistemological perspective—as seen in Chap. 3—the increasing convergence of security, cybersecurity and safety in our digital societies.

In particular, for the purpose of this book, emphasis needs to be placed on the requirement to address the cybersecurity of the ICT supply chain, including security-related aspects concerning the relationships between each entity and its suppliers. The rationale underlying these high-level technical measures[381] must be found in an attempt to prevent incidents, where attackers disrupt the security of an entity's NIS by exploiting vulnerabilities contained in third party products and services.[382]

As reiterated in previous Chapters, the majority of IoT devices is comprised by a multitude of components from different hardware and software vendors, part of which could even be accounted for by small companies, including start-ups.[383] As a consequence, the attack surface is expanded globally.[384]

Importantly, when implementing risk management measures referred to Art. 21(2)(d), EEs and IEs "shall take into account the vulnerabilities specific to each supplier and service provider and the overall *quality of products* and cybersecurity practices of their suppliers and service providers [emphasis added]".[385] To assist entities in appropriately managing the cybersecurity risks related to supply chain, Article 22 NIS2 introduces coordinated supply chain risk assessments—which will take into account also non-technical risk factors (e.g., geopolitical)—thus mirroring

[379] Directive (EU) 2022/2555, Art. 21(2).

[380] Directive (EU) 2022/2555, recital 79.

[381] Interestingly, the Commission will adopt implementing acts (Art. 21(5) NIS2) to lay down the technical and the methodological specifications of the elements referred to in paragraph 2 of Art. 21 and to take account of new cyber threats, technological developments or sectorial specificities.

[382] Directive (EU) 2022/2555, Recital 43.

[383] See <https://www.startus-insights.com/innovators-guide/5-top-internet-of-things-startups-impacting-logistics-supply-chain/>; European Commission, "An SME Strategy for a sustainable and digital Europe" COM(2020) 103 final, 1.

[384] AIOTI (2021a), p. 3.

[385] Directive (EU) 2022/2555, Art. 21(3).

the approach of Recommendation (EU) 2019/534 on Cybersecurity of 5G networks.[386]

A combined reading of Art. 21(2)(d) and 21(3) NIS2 would *indirectly* lead to addressing products security. Entities will now be legally obliged to take into consideration, *inter alia*, the level of cybersecurity of suppliers' systems and products, hence "manufacturers will have strong incentives to enhance the security controls in their products".[387]

Moreover, to demonstrate compliance with certain requirements of Art. 21, the Commission foresees the possibility for Member States to require mandatory certification for ICT products, services and processes under specific ECCS adopted pursuant to Art. 49 CSA.[388] The Commission is empowered to adopt delegated acts (DA), specifying which categories of NIS entities shall be required to use certified ICT products, services and processes, or obtain a certificate and under which scheme.[389]

Contrary to the previous version of Art. 24(2) of the Commission Proposal, the official text explicitly states that, before the adoption of such delegated acts, the Commission shall carry out an impact assessment in accordance with Art. 56 CSA, with particular regard to paragraph 3.[390] Where no appropriate ECCS is available, the Commission may request ENISA to draft a candidate scheme.[391]

All in all, NIS2 supply chain provisions may prove to be burdensome for EEs and IEs as it is unclear how entities shall ensure that suppliers comply with relevant legal requirements.[392] This notwithstanding, the NIS2 considerably strengthens the level of cybersecurity in the Union and the IoT ecosystem would also benefit from the policy changes introduced by the revision of the NIS Directive. However, the manner in which the NIS2 legal framework will coordinate with the incoming Cyber Resilience Act, aiming at laying down cybersecurity product requirements, remains uncertain.

4.5 The Cyber Resilience Act

The Chapter has reviewed the EU legal frameworks addressing connected product cybersecurity, either directly or indirectly. The legislative gap analysis highlighted a fragmented regulatory landscape that does not specifically and comprehensively

---

[386] Commission Recommendation (EU) 2019/534 of 26 March 2019 Cybersecurity of 5G networks, OJ L 88, 29.03.2019, 42.

[387] Chiara (2022a), p. 13.

[388] Directive (EU) 2022/2555, Art. 24(1).

[389] Directive (EU) 2022/2555, Art. 24(2).

[390] DIGITALEUROPE (2022b), p. 3.

[391] Directive (EU) 2022/2555, Art. 24(3).

[392] BDI (2021b), p. 15; DIGITALEUROPE (2021b), p. 7.

tackle the problem of unsecure connected products. In December 2021, the Commission published a "Study on the need of cybersecurity requirements for ICT products" (hereinafter 'the Study') which aimed to explore the current state of cybersecurity in broad categories of ICT products as well as to identify the reasons for the lack of sufficient security.[393]

The study identified numerous problem drivers underlying the lack of appropriate security in products with digital elements (Problem 1), together with an insufficient understanding among users of the level of cybersecurity of ICT products (Problem 2).

From a regulatory perspective, the sectoral approach adopted by the Commission vis-à-vis the inclusion of cybersecurity essential requirements in product safety legislation is likely to create legal uncertainty for market operators for they have an additional compliance burden with possibly overlapping requirements stemming from different pieces of legislation.

From a market perspective, the failure to provide an optimal degree of cybersecurity has two main drivers i.e., information asymmetries and negative externalities.[394] On the one hand, consumers do not possess in general the necessary knowledge to assess digital products' cybersecurity and may not be willing to pay more for greater security; on the other hand, different models demonstrated that cybersecurity market is characterised by a sub-optimal level of investments.[395]

Against this backdrop, on 15 September 2022 the Commission—after announcing it on the 2021 State of the Union address—presented a "proposal for a regulation on horizontal cybersecurity requirements for products with digital elements, amending Regulation (EU) 2019/1020 (Cyber Resilience Act, CRA)". The main goal of the CRA is to provide a coherent legal framework with cybersecurity requirement for digital products.

The legal basis of this legislative initiative was identified once again in Art. 114 of the Treaty on the Functioning of the European Union (TFEU), whose objective is the establishment and functioning of the internal market by enhancing measures for the approximation of national rules. At the time of writing, the Cyber Resilience Act has not yet been published on the Official Journal of the EU: the legal analysis that follows is based on the final compromise text agreed by the Council of the European Union on 20 December 2023 following the political agreement reached by the co-legislators in the informal negotiations (trilogue meetings) on 30 November 2023 (Fig. 4.1).

[393] Wavestone - CEPS - CARSA - ICF (2021).

[394] Chiara (2022c), p. 256.

[395] Wavestone - CEPS - CARSA - ICF (2021), pp. 34–36.

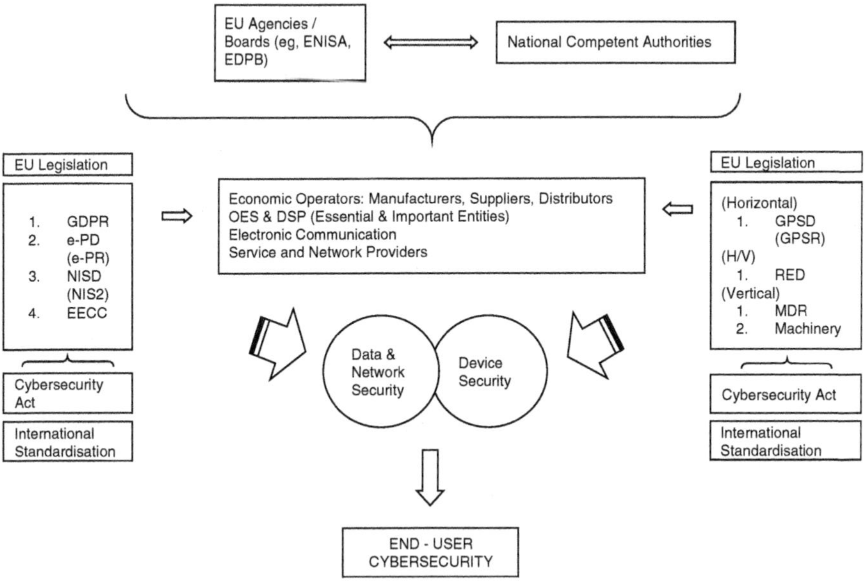

Fig. 4.1 EU cybersecurity regulatory landscape pre-CRA. Source: the author

4.5.1 The Scope of the CRA

The CRA applies "to products with digital elements made available on the market, whose intended purpose or reasonably foreseeable use includes a direct or indirect logical or physical data connection to a device or network".[396] Whereas the Commission's call for evidence for an impact assessment used to refer to 'digital products and ancillary services',[397] the Commission's proposal before and the final text after pivot on the concept of 'products with digital elements' i.e., "any software or hardware product and its remote data processing solutions, including software or hardware components to be placed on the market separately".[398]

The scope of the CRA is even broader than originally conceived by the Commission's call for evidence. The definition of 'products with digital elements' covers software as a separate product from hardware, as testified by the disjunctive use of the conjunction 'or'. The reading of recital 46 seems to confirm this line of reasoning for it explicitly envisages products with digital elements in the form of software. Vast legal literature, especially in the area of civil liability, debates on whether software should be considered as a product.[399] This, however, will not be part of the

[396] Cyber Resilience Act, Article 2(1).

[397] See <https://ec.europa.eu/info/law/better-regulation/have-your-say/initiatives/13410-Cyber-resilience-act-new-cybersecurity-rules-for-digital-products-and-ancillary-services_en>.

[398] Cyber Resilience Act, Article 3(1).

[399] Wagner (2022).

analysis. Instead, the extent to which the CRA covers software-as-a-product needs to be further explored.

The explanatory memorandum of the CRA explicitly acknowledges that "current EU legal framework does not address the cybersecurity of non-embedded software".[400] The chosen horizontal policy option intended to bring non-embedded software within its scope,[401] with the only exception of software-as-a-service (SaaS). Nevertheless, recitals 9 and 10 specify that the CRA may eventually also cover Software-as-a-Service (SaaS), i.e., cloud solutions, only if it constitutes "remote data processing solutions" *relating* to a product with digital elements. In other words, if software is designed and developed by or on behalf of the manufacturer of such product, and the absence of which would prevent such a product with digital elements from performing one of its functions, then it is considered a 'remote data processing solution' and it falls in scope of the CRA accordingly.

Therefore, the 'relationship' of the software with the product appears to be decisive to determine whether the CRA regime applies to SaaS. In this respect, the 'ancillary' perspective of the early stages of the Cyber Resilience Act is somewhat restored. Lastly, while the CRA proposal originally envisaged that free and open-source software (FOSS) would not fall within the scope of the CRA, in order not to hinder innovation or research,[402] the final text diverged. Thus, the CRA covers FOSS only to the extent (i) it is made available on the market; (ii) and supplied for distribution or used in the course of a commercial activity.[403] However, even though FOSS is not made available on the market but nonetheless intended for commercial activities, then the legal persons which provide support for the development of such solutions ('open-source software stewards') are subject to a light-touch and tailor-made regulatory regime (see Article 17a CRA).[404]

Moreover, the CRA would not apply to products already falling in scope of other Union legal acts, such as: Regulation (EU) 2017/745 (Medical Devices Regulation)[405]; Regulation (EU) 2017/746 (Regulation on in vitro diagnostic medical devices); Regulation (EU) 2019/2144 (Automotive type-approval general regulation)[406]; Directive 2014/90/EU (maritime equipment),[407] nor it does not apply to

[400] Explanatory Memorandum to the CRA proposal, p. 1.

[401] Ibid., p. 7.

[402] Cyber Resilience Act proposal, recital 10.

[403] Cyber Resilience Act, recital 10c.

[404] Cyber Resilience Act, recital 10d.

[405] Whereas the CRA does not cover medical devices, it would cover devices that gather and process health data not falling under the scope of the MDR. See Rak (2021), p. 483: "with reference to Article 2(1) of the MDR, the threshold between a 'medical' and 'non-medical' device is the "intended purpose": whether the device is intended to be used by the manufacturer, alone or in combination, for one of the listed "specific medical purposes". The recent rise of consumer (well-being, lifestyle) health devices has blurred the borderline between 'medical' and 'non-medical' devices".

[406] Cyber Resilience Act, Article 2(2).

[407] Cyber Resilience Act, Article 2(3a).

products with digital elements that have been certified in accordance with Regulation (EU) 2018/1139 (Common rules in civil aviation).[408] Other outright exclusions involve (i) spare parts to replace identical components in products with digital elements that are manufactured according to the same specifications as the components to be replace[409]; (ii) products with digital elements exclusively developed for national security, military purposes or specifically designed to process classified information.[410]

In line with the recent EU 'digital policies', the CRA adopts a risk-based approach,[411] which integrates the product safety approach. In relation to their level of cybersecurity risk, specific categories of products with digital elements can be classified as 'important' or 'critical'. The former are products that have the core functionality of a category that is listed either in class I[412] or class II[413] as set out in Annex III, where class II's products pose a greater cybersecurity risk. Whereas class I products either performs primarily functions critical to the cybersecurity of other products, networks or services or a function having a significant risk of adverse effects in terms of its intensity and ability to disrupt, control or cause damage to a large number of other products or to the health, security or safety of its users through direct manipulation, class II meet both of the aforementioned criteria.[414] Importantly, the Commission, through delegated acts, is empowered to amend Annex III by including new categories of products as well as moving a category from one class to the other. In this regard, the Commission takes into account several criteria such as the cybersecurity-related functionality, intended use in sensitive environments or of performing critical functions and the extent of an adverse impact.[415]

Conversely, the categories of 'critical' products, that are listed in Annex IIIa,[416] i) have a cybersecurity-related functionality; ii) perform a function which carries a significant risk of adverse effects in terms of its intensity and ability to disrupt, control or damage a large number of other products with digital elements through direct manipulation; and iii) are considered to be critical dependencies for NIS2 essential entities.[417]

[408] Cyber Resilience Act, Article 2(3).

[409] Cyber Resilience Act, Article 2(4a).

[410] Cyber Resilience Act, Article 2(5).

[411] De Gregorio and Dunn (2022).

[412] This class of products includes identity management systems and privileged access management software, password managers, network management systems, SIEM systems, smart home general purpose virtual assistants, smart home products with security functionalities, etc.

[413] This class of products includes hypervisors, firewalls, intrusion detection systems, tamper-resistant microprocessors and microcontrollers.

[414] Cyber Resilience Act, Article 6.

[415] Cyber Resilience Act, Article 6(2).

[416] These products are: hardware devices with security boxes; smart meter gateways; smartcards or similar devices.

[417] Cyber Resilience Act, Article 6a.

The different legal treatment between default, important and critical products with digital elements lies in the different conformity assessment procedure they have to comply with. Class II important products and critical products are subject to mandatory third-party conformity assessment; with regard to the latter category, the Commission may decide, having carried out an impact assessment, to subject these products, by means of a delegated act, to mandatory European cybersecurity certification. This option would create a scenario of mandatory certification –already foreseen by the Cybersecurity Act as addressed in Sect. 4.2.

4.5.2 Obligations for Economic Operators

With a view to ensuring effective cybersecurity along the entire supply chain (see in particular Sect. 2.3.4), the Cyber Resilience Act lays down a comprehensive and complex set of obligations addressing all the economic operators involved in the value-chain of the (many) products in scope. From manufacturers to distributors, importers and authorised representatives.

Traditionally, relationships between economic operators along the supply chain have primarily been contractual. The CRA designs a novel approach in EU cybersecurity law insofar as the law will now require manufacturers to exercise due diligence when integrating components (including FOSS) sourced from third parties in products with digital elements.[418] Importantly, during the trialogue negotiations, a provision was added to oblige manufacturers, whenever a vulnerability is found in a component (including open source) which is integrated in the product with digital elements, to (i) report the vulnerability to the entity manufacturing or maintaining the component, and address; (ii) to remediate the vulnerability and, notably (iii) to share the piece of software or hardware modification eventually developed to address said vulnerability.[419]

On a general level, three conditions apply for the placing on the market of products with digital elements:

(i) they shall be properly installed, maintained, used for their intended purpose and, where applicable, updated[420];
(ii) they shall be designed, developed and produced in accordance with the essential requirements laid down in Section 1 of Annex I[421];
(iii) the processes put in place by the manufacturer shall comply with the essential requirements set out in Section 2 of Annex I.[422]

---

[418] Cyber Resilience Act, Article 10(4).

[419] Cyber Resilience Act, Article 10(4)a.

[420] Cyber Resilience Act, Article 5, point (1).

[421] Art. 10(1); Art. 5, point (1) CRA Proposal.

[422] Cyber Resilience Act, Article 5, point (2).

The essential requirements set out in Section 1, Annex I relate to the properties of products with digital elements. *Inter alia*, products shall be designed, developed and produced to ensure an appropriate level of cybersecurity based on the risks; shall be delivered without any known exploitable vulnerabilities; shall be delivered with a secure by default configuration; shall ensure protection from unauthorised access by appropriate control mechanisms; shall protect the confidentiality of processed personal or other data by means of state-of-the-art encryption; etc.

The essential requirements in Section 2, Annex I instead focus on the processes put in place by manufactures, in particular, taking into account the handling of vulnerabilities. Therefore, manufacturers will: identify and document vulnerabilities and components contained in the product, including by drawing up a software bill of materials in a commonly used and machine-readable format covering at the very least the top-level dependencies of the product; address and remediate vulnerabilities without delay, including by providing security updates; apply effective and regular tests and reviews of the security of the product; publicly disclose information about fixed vulnerabilities, once a security update has been made available, etc.

With a view to complying with the obligation to place a product on the market in accordance with the essential requirements of Section 1, Annex I, manufacturers shall undertake an assessment of the cybersecurity risks related to a product category. The outcome of the risk assessment must be taken into account during the planning, design, development, production, delivery and maintenance phases of the product with digital elements[423] and must form part of the technical documentation (as per Art. 23 and Annex V).[424]

Related to that, the CRA mandates different documentation obligations with regard to relevant cybersecurity aspects of the product, such as handling vulnerabilities, information provided by third parties and the update of the risk assessment.[425] In this respect, Art. 23 specifies that the content of the technical documentation must be drawn up by the manufacturer before the product is placed on the market and must be kept at the disposal of the market surveillance authorities for 10 years after the product has been placed on the market.[426]

With regard to the cooperation duties with market authorities, manufacturers are also obliged to provide the authority with all the information necessary to demonstrate conformity with Annex I essential requirements and cooperate on any measurers taken to eliminate the cybersecurity risks posed by the product.[427] Moreover, they also have to inform the authority about the cessation of its operations with the consequence of not being able to comply with the obligations of the Regulation.[428]

[423] Cyber Resilience Act, Article 10(2).
[424] Cyber Resilience Act, Article 10(3).
[425] Cyber Resilience Act, Article 10(5).
[426] Cyber Resilience Act, Article 10(8).
[427] Cyber Resilience Act, Article 10(13).
[428] Cyber Resilience Act, Article 10(14).

Products with digital elements shall be marketed with the information and instructions (as per Annex II), in an electronic or physical form, in a clear, understandable, intelligible and legible language.[429] A copy of the EU declaration of conformity (or its simplified version) must be provided with the product as well.[430] To enable users to communicate in a direct fashion with them as well as to facilitate reporting on vulnerabilities, manufacturers have to designate a single point of contact.[431]

The CRA also foresees reporting obligations for manufacturers and adopts a *quasi*-centralised approach. In fact, manufacturers simultaneously notify, via a single reporting platform (Article 11b), to ENISA and the CSIRT designated as coordinator of any actively exploited vulnerability contained in the product and any severe incident having an impact on the security of the product.[432] From a procedural standpoint, the CRA mirrors the approach of the NIS2. Manufacturers have to submit (a) an early warning notification on an actively exploited vulnerability or on a severe incident without undue delay and in any event within 24 h after becoming aware of it; (b) a vulnerability or an incident notification, without undue delay and in any event within 72 h; (c) a final report no later than 14 days after a corrective or mitigating measure is available.[433] The CSIRT designated as coordinator may request manufacturers to provide an intermediate report on relevant status updates with regard to the notification submitted. Manufacturers also have to inform impacted users and where appropriate all users about the vulnerability or the sever incident as well as any corrective measures that users can deploy to mitigate the impact of the vulnerability or incident.[434]

The final version of the Cyber Resilience Act introduced a new actor, that is, open-source software (OSS) 'stewards'. OSS stewards are legal persons that, on a sustained basis, provide support for the development and ensure the viability of FOSS intended for commercial activities.[435] Accordingly, they are subject to a set of obligations which is nevertheless 'lighter' than the regime applicable to other economic operators. The 'light-touch approach' mainly consists in setting up and documenting in a verifiable manner a cybersecurity policy with a view to (i) developing a secure product, and (ii) handling effectively its vulnerabilities, including by fostering the voluntary reporting of vulnerabilities.[436] Reporting obligations as per Article 11 apply to OSS stewards only to a limited extent, e.g. if they are involved in the development of the products with digital elements.

[429] Cyber Resilience Act, Article 10(10).

[430] Cyber Resilience Act, Article 10(11).

[431] Cyber Resilience Act, Article 9c.

[432] Cyber Resilience Act, Article 11.

[433] Cyber Resilience Act, Article 11(2).

[434] Cyber Resilience Act, Article 11(8).

[435] Cyber Resilience Act, Article 3(18a).

[436] Cyber Resilience Act, Article 17a.

Lastly, Articles 12, 13 and 14 place obligations on the other economic operators in the supply chain beside manufacturers i.e., authorised representatives, importers and distributors. It shall be noted that if importers or distributors place a product on the market under their name or trademark or carry out a substantial modification of the product,[437] they will then be considered a manufacturer. Therefore, they will be subject to the obligations of the manufacturer set out in Articles 10 and 11(1), (2), (4) and (7).[438] Importantly, the same applies to any natural or legal person who substantially modifies the product.

4.5.3 *Essential Cybersecurity Requirements and Conformity Assessment*

As said, the CRA builds on the principles and procedures of the New Legislative Framework for product safety legislation. In particular, Article 18 regulates the presumption of conformity with the essential requirements of the regulation. As a general rule, products and processes in conformity with harmonised standards, or parts thereof, the references of which have been published in the Official Journal of the European Union, are presumed to be in conformity with the essential requirements of the Cyber Resilience Act. Alternatively, the above presumption of conformity applies also to EU statements of conformity or certificates issued under a European cybersecurity certification scheme adopted as per Regulation (EU) 2019/881 insofar as they cover those requirements. In this case, the Commission may specify through implementing acts the schemes that can be used to demonstrate conformity with the essential requirements of Annex I CRA and whether a cybersecurity certificate eliminates a manufacturer's obligation to carry out a third-party conformity assessment for the corresponding requirements.[439]

If harmonised standards are not available or if there are undue delays in the standardisation procedure or the Commission's request has not been accepted by the European Standardisation Organisations which are tasked to develop harmonised standards, the Commission can adopt 'common specifications' via implementing acts to demonstrate conformity with Annex I essential requirements.[440]

Manufacturers then prepare the EU declaration of conformity, stating that fulfilment of the applicable essential requirements set out in Annex I has been

[437] According to Article 3, point (31), 'substantial modification' "means a change to the product with digital elements following its placing on the market, which affects the compliance of the product with digital elements with the essential requirements set out in Section 1 of Annex I or results in a modification to the intended purpose for which the product with digital elements has been assessed".

[438] Cyber Resilience Act, Article 15.

[439] Cyber Resilience Act, Article 18(10).

[440] Cyber Resilience Act, Article 18(2).

demonstrated, in accordance with relevant documentation duties.[441] Annex IV contains the model structure of the EU declaration of conformity which must contain the elements specified in the relevant conformity assessment procedures set out in Annex VI[442] and shall be continuously updated.[443] If a product with digital elements is subject to more than one Union act requiring an EU declaration of conformity, it shall contain the identification of the Union acts concerned.[444]

As already mentioned in the previous section, the compliance of Class II important products with Annex I essential recruitments is limited to third-party assessment, that is, EU-type examination procedure (based on module B) followed by conformity to the EU-type based on internal production control (based on module C); conformity assessment based on full quality assurance (based on module H); or a EU cybersecurity certification scheme.[445] With regard to the categories of important products belonging to class I, manufacturers must adhere to said procedures only *if* they have not applied or *have only applied in part* harmonised standards, common specifications or European cybersecurity certification schemes; or where such harmonised standards, common specifications or European cybersecurity certification schemes do not exist.[446] Conversely, the conformity of critical products listed in Annex IIIa with the essential requirements has to be demonstrated by using European cybersecurity certification scheme. However, if such products do not fall in scope of delegated acts pursuant Article 6a(1) specifying which products of Annex IIIa are required to obtain a certificate—or if no delegated acts exist altogether, then manufacturers have to follow the assessment procedures applicable to Class II important products.[447]

The CE marking shall be affixed visibly, legibly and indelibly to the product before placing the product with digital elements on the market.[448] In this respect, economic operators shall follow the general NLF principles set out in Article 30 of Regulation (EC) No 765/2008.[449]

Finally, the CRA sets out the rules regulating the interactions with national conformity assessment bodies (notified bodies). Consistently with NLF principles, Member States must designate a notifying authority that will be responsible for

---

[441] Cyber Resilience Act, Article 20(1).

[442] These include: (a) the internal control procedure (based on module A of Decision 768/2008/EC); or (b) the EU-type examination procedure (based on module B) followed by conformity to EU-type based on internal production control (based on module C); or (c) conformity assessment based on full quality assurance (based on module H).

[443] Cyber Resilience Act, Article 20(2).

[444] Cyber Resilience Act, Article 20(3).

[445] Cyber Resilience Act, Article 24(3).

[446] Cyber Resilience Act, Article 24(2).

[447] Cyber Resilience Act, Article 24(3a)(b).

[448] Cyber Resilience Act, Article 22(1). For products with digital elements which are in the form of software, the CE marking shall be affixed either to the EU declaration of conformity referred to in Article 20 or on the website accompanying the software product.

[449] Cyber Resilience Act, Article 21.

setting up and carrying out the necessary procedures for the assessment and notification of conformity assessment bodies and monitoring of notified bodies.[450]

4.5.4 Enforcement Mechanisms: Market Surveillance

Member states must designate national market surveillance authorities (MSAs) to ensure the effective implementation of the CRA.[451] MSAs can be any existing or new authority, including competent authorities under the NIS2 and the Cybersecurity Act (CSA).[452] As an exception to the general rule, the MSAs designated for the purposes of the Artificial Intelligence Act (AIA) will be the authorities responsible for market surveillance activities required under the CRA for products with digital elements which are classified as high-risk AI systems according to the AIA.[453]

Against this backdrop, Eurosmart suggested to designate as MSAs the national cybersecurity certification authorities (NCCAs) under the Cybersecurity Act, as: (i) these public authorities already have the capability and necessary expertise in the cybersecurity field; (ii) NCCAs have been designated and have the relevant knowledge to supervise the NLF's Conformity Assessment Bodies.[454]

Beside the rules on market surveillance pursuant Regulation (EU) 2019/1020—which applies to the products with digital elements within the scope of the CRA,[455] as cybersecurity must be guaranteed throughout the entire lifecycle of products with digital elements, it has been deemed necessary "to extend the post-market surveillance activity to guarantee the security of product during the usage phase and when the products are removed from the market".[456]

Market surveillance authorities have to cooperate with: (i) other market surveillance authorities designated on the basis of other Union harmonisation legislation[457]; (ii) national cybersecurity certification authorities designated under the CSA[458]; and, (iii) as appropriate, with data protection authorities.[459] BEUC explicitly called for cooperation mechanisms between national authorities and consumer protection organisation "to create synergies towards a better market screening, raising awareness and prevent violations of CRA obligations".[460]

---

[450] Cyber Resilience Act, Article 26.

[451] Cyber Resilience Act, Article 41(2).

[452] Cyber Resilience Act, recital 55.

[453] Cyber Resilience Act, 41(10).

[454] Eurosmart (2022), pp. 9–10.

[455] Cyber Resilience Act, Article 41.

[456] Wavestone - CEPS - CARSA - ICF (2021), p. 196.

[457] Cyber Resilience Act, Article 41(4).

[458] Cyber Resilience Act, Article 41(3).

[459] Cyber Resilience Act, Article 41(5).

[460] BEUC (2022), p. 11.

In terms of the enforcement powers of MSAs vis-à-vis products with digital elements that pose cybersecurity risks, the Cyber Resilience Act distinguishes two different procedures i.e., at Member States and Union level. Where a national MSA has sufficient reason to consider that a product presents a cybersecurity risk (considering also non-technical risk factors), it carries out an evaluation of such product in respect of its compliance with all CRA's requirements.[461] If the MSA finds that the product under scrutiny does not comply with the requirements, there are three main enforcement scenarios: (i) the relevant economic operator can be required to take all appropriate corrective actions to bring the product with digital elements into compliance with those requirements; (ii) to withdraw it from the market; or (iii) to recall it. The Commission and other Member States shall be informed of the outcomes of this procedure if the non-compliance is not confined to the national territory of the inquiring MSA and also if provisional correction measures (e.g., MSAs can prohibit or restrict a product from being made available on national markets; the product can also be withdrawn or recalled) are taken.[462] Interestingly, Member States or the Commission may raise objections to such provisional measures taken by the MSA initiating the procedure within 3 months of receipt of the notification.[463] If objections are raised, then the Commission enters in consultation with the Member States and the economic operators involved with a view to evaluating the contested measure, which can either be considered justified or unjustified.[464]

Another circumstance may trigger MSAs enforcement powers. If, after the evaluation pursuant Art. 43, the MSA finds that although the product complies with the CRA, it nonetheless present a significant cybersecurity risk as well as a risk to: (a) the health and safety of persons; (b) compliance with Union or national obligations intended to protect fundamental rights; (c) the availability, authenticity, integrity or confidentiality of services offered using an electronic information system by NIS2 entities; (d) other aspects of public interest protection, then it requires the economic operator to take all appropriate measures.[465]

The procedure at EU level is triggered by the Commission where it has sufficient reason to consider that a product that presents a significant cybersecurity risk is non-compliant with CRA's essential requirements or it is compliant with the CRA but it nevertheless presents the four categories of non-cybersecurity related risks. In that case, the Commission has to inform MSAs and NIS2 authorities if drivers to the abovementioned significant cybersecurity risks are non-technical risk factors. The Commission carries out an evaluation of compliance only on three conditions: (i) circumstances justify an immediate intervention to preserve the good functioning of the internal market; (ii) there are sufficient reasons to consider that the product

[461] Cyber Resilience Act, Article 43(1).
[462] Cyber Resilience Act, Article 43(2).
[463] Cyber Resilience Act, Article 43(7).
[464] Cyber Resilience Act, Article 44.
[465] Cyber Resilience Act, Article 46(1).

remains non-compliant; (iii) no effective measures have been taken by relevant MSAs.[466] Accordingly, the Commission may adopt a corrective or restrictive measure through implementing acts at Union level, subject to consulting with the Member States concerned and relevant economic operators.[467]

The CRA also provides for a procedure where different MSAs carry out joint activities. These cooperative enforcement powers can be triggered by the Commission or ENISA, with the aim of ensuring cybersecurity and protection of consumers with respect to specific products with digital elements made available on the market.[468] These joint actions include so-called 'sweeps' i.e., simultaneous coordinated control actions of products, or products' categories, to check compliance with or to detect infringements to the CRA.[469] Sweeps are coordinated by the Commission, unless otherwise decided by the MSAs involved in the action.

In terms of sanctions, it is up to the Member States to set rules on effective, proportionate and dissuasive penalties applicable to infringements of the CRA. However, the discretion of Member States in setting up the framework on penalties is constrained by the Regulation. Firstly, non-compliance with the essential cybersecurity requirements of Annex I and the obligations set out in Articles 10 and 11 will be subject to administrative fines of up to 15 million EUR or, if the offender is an undertaking, up to 2.5% of its total worldwide annual turnover for the preceding financial year, whichever is higher.[470] Secondly, non-compliance with (i) obligations relating to economic operators other than manufacturers (Articles 12–17); (ii) rules relating to the conformity of the product with digital elements (Articles 20; 22; 23; 24; 24a); (iii) rules on notification of conformity assessment bodies (Articles 29; 31; 37; 38) and iv) with Article 42 will be subject to administrative fines of up to 10 million EUR or, if the offender is an undertaking, up to 2% of its total worldwide annual turnover.[471] Lastly, supply of incorrect, incomplete or misleading information to notified bodies and market surveillance authorities in reply to a request will be subject to administrative fines of up to 5 million EUR or, if the offender is an undertaking, up to 1% of its total worldwide annual turnover.[472] Member States must notify the Commission of the implemented rules and measures without undue delay.

To be effective in cybersecurity, market surveillance needs not only dissuasive sanctions,[473] but also necessary competences. "This is especially the case because of the important role that processes play in cybersecurity, going beyond the traditional product-based expertise of market surveillance authorities and the global nature of

[466] Cyber Resilience Act, Article 45(2).
[467] Cyber Resilience Act, Article 45(4).
[468] Cyber Resilience Act, Article 48.
[469] Cyber Resilience Act, Article 49.
[470] Cyber Resilience Act, Article 53(3).
[471] Cyber Resilience Act, Article 53(4).
[472] Cyber Resilience Act, Article 53(5).
[473] ANEC (2022), p. 6; Bitkom (2022), p. 4.

such processes and products".[474] To this end, it will be vital that MSAs enforcing the CRA are equipped with adequate resources.[475]

4.5.5 *Interplay with Other Union Policies*

The 'horizontal legislation' policy option as it has been presented in this section needs to be streamlined and aligned with the most recent initiatives undertaken by the Commission to close some gaps with regard to the cybersecurity of digital products, as addressed in this Chapter. In particular, the attention focuses on the RED Delegated Regulation 2022/30, the General Product Safety Regulation (GPSR), the Machinery Regulation (MR), the Medical Devices Regulation (MDR), the Cybersecurity Act and the NIS2.

4.5.5.1 Interplay Between the CRA and the General Product Safety Regulation

Article 7 of the CRA functions as an interface between the CRA and the General Product Safety Regulation which, as seen in Sect. 4.3.2, applies in its role of 'safety net' to non-harmonised products and to the harmonised consumer products for the aspects that are not covered by harmonised legislation. Art. 7 CRA reads as follows:

> By way of derogation from Article 2(1), third subparagraph, point (b), of Regulation (EU) 2023/988 Chapter III, Section 1, Chapters V and VII, and Chapters IX to XI of that Regulation shall apply to products with digital elements with respect to aspects and risks or categories of risks not covered by this Regulation where those products are not subject to specific safety requirements imposed by other Union harmonisation legislation as defined in Article 3, point (27) of Regulation (EU) 2023/988.

Recital 28 CRA, read in conjunction with the relevant articles of the GPSR, sheds light on the meaning of this provision. For it acknowledges that products covered by the CRA may pose safety risks that are not always cybersecurity-related but can be a consequence of security breaches. Such risks are already regulated by other EU legal acts within product safety *acquis*. It follows that if no other harmonised Union legislation is applicable, the GPSR legal framework would come into play, in accordance with its function of a 'safety net'. However, Article 2(1) GPSR states that where products are within the scope of Union product safety legislation, the rules laid down by the GPSR shall apply only to the aspects and risks not covered by those requirements, if those products are not subject to specific requirements imposed by other Union harmonisation legislation; in particular, Chapter III, Section 1, Chapters V and VII, Chapters IX to XI GPSR shall not apply.

---

[474] DIGITALEUROPE (2022c), p. 13.

[475] Schmitz-berndt and Chiara (2022), p. 14.

Therefore, the derogation found in Art. 7 CRA from the general rule mandated by Art. 2(1) GPSR finds its rationale in the targeted nature of the Cyber Resilience Act. Thus, the CRA only covers cybersecurity-related aspects without addressing more general health and safety requirements as the legal acts of EU product legislation. Consequently, extending the coverage of Chapter III, Section 1, Chapters V and VII, and Chapters IX to XI GPSR to products with digital elements with respect to safety risks not covered by the CRA should be seen in a fundamentally positive light.

4.5.5.2 Interplay Between the CRA and the Machinery Regulation

Similarly, the CRA proposal regulated the interface between the Cyber Resilience Act and the Machinery Regulation (Regulation (EU) 2023/1230). In particular, Art. 9 specifically fleshed out the interplay between the conformity assessments under the two pieces of legislation. Where machinery products are also products with digital elements within the meaning of the CRA and for which an EU declaration of conformity has been issued on the basis of the CRA, they will be deemed to be in conformity with the essential health and safety requirements set out in Annex III, Sections 1.1.9 and 1.2.1 to the Machinery Regulation, as addressed in Sect. 4.3.4.

However, the co-legislators erased that provision from the final version of the CRA. Some guidance can however be found in recitals. Contrary to what was envisaged in the CRA proposal, recital 30 CRA states that manufacturers should follow the applicable conformity assessment procedures set out in the CRA and in the MR respectively. Thus, the compliance with CRA's essential requirements might only 'facilitate' the compliance with MR essential requirements set out in Annex III, Sections 1.1.9 and 1.2.1 but it is up to the manufacturer to demonstrate how such synergy is eventually operationalised. In this regard, it will be crucial to promote consistency in the European standardisation work in terms of how the cybersecurity risks are to be covered by harmonised standards for the CRA and MR essential requirements respectively.

4.5.5.3 Interplay Between the CRA and the RED Delegated Act

The CRA explicitly acknowledges that the essential requirements set out in Annex 1 CRA include all the elements of the essential requirements referred to in Article 3(3) points (d), (e) and (f) of the RED.[476] Furthermore, CRA's essential requirements are also aligned "with the objectives of the requirements for specific harmonised standards included in the standardisation request" of the Commission to the European Standardisation Organisations to prove conformity with the RED's above-mentioned requirements.[477]

[476] Cyber Resilience Act, recital 15.

[477] Ibid.

Following this line of reasoning, it can be concluded that the so-called 'RED Delegated Act' (see Sect. 4.3.1) and the CRA would result in duplicative requirements. Thus, recital 15 CRA explicitly considers repealing or amending Delegated Regulation (EU) 2022/30 as a regulatory option on the Commission's table. In such case, the Commission and ESOs "should take into account the standardisation work carried out in the context of Commission Implementing Decision C(2022)5637 on a standardisation request for the RED Delegated Regulation 2022/30 in the preparation and development of harmonised standards to facilitate the implementation of this Regulation".[478] It is also worth noting that the final text of recital 15 explicitly calls on the Commission to provide guidance to manufacturers subject to the two aforementioned regulations to facilitate compliance during the transition period.

4.5.5.4 Interplay Between the CRA and the NIS2 Directive

Three main areas of interplay are considered in this section, mirroring the ones taken into account in the analysis of the NIS2. They regard: (i) the scope of the two legal acts; (ii) the rules regulating supply chain relationships; (iii) the reporting of incidents and vulnerabilities.

First, the NIS2 will complement the CRA by bringing into scope cloud computing services and cloud service models, such as Software-as-a-Service (SaaS), Platform-as-a-Service (PaaS) or Infrastructure-as-a-Service (IaaS).[479] Moreover, a criterion to be taken into account by the Commission when assessing the addition of new critical product categories to Annex IIIa is the existence of a critical dependence on such products by NIS2 essential entities.[480]

Second, the CRA will complement the NIS framework by ensuring the preconditions for strengthening supply chain cybersecurity.[481] Thus, complying with the supply chain cybersecurity requirements under Articles 21(2)(d), 21(3) and 22 of the NIS2 would be eased by the set of obligations introduced by the CRA: the latter will ensure that the digital products used by essential and important entities for the provision of their services are designed and manufactured according to state-of-the-art cybersecurity controls. Also, the dynamic and life-cycle approach of the CRA would guarantee that NIS2 entities have access to timely security updates for the products concerned.[482] Yet, the standard under the NIS2 might even be higher than of the CRA in terms of supply-chain cybersecurity measures. Thus, Member States can impose additional and stricter cybersecurity requirements for the use of ICT products by NIS2 entities than those laid down by the CRA to ensure a higher level

[478] Ibid.

[479] Cyber Resilience Act, recital 9a.

[480] Cyber Resilience Act, recital 27c; Article 6a(2)(a).

[481] Chiara (2022a), p. 12; Explanatory Memorandum to the CRA Proposal, p. 7.

[482] Cyber Resilience Act, recital 11.

of cybersecurity, in particular with regard to non-technical factors.[483] In this respect, Article 4a CRA allows Member States to impose restrictions on products with digital elements or suppliers of such products, that take account of non-technical factors.[484]

A third area of intersection consists of reporting duties. As seen above, manufacturers of products with digital elements primarily have reporting obligations in terms of actively exploited vulnerabilities and severe incidents that have impact on the security of the product (Art. 11 CRA). The *quasi*-centralised model of governance proposed by the Commission, which placed ENISA at the core of the notification system's procedural framework, was changed during the trilogue negotiations. A compromise was reached on a twin-track approach, whereby manufacturers simultaneously notify both to national CSIRTs and ENISA. This regulatory choice might increase procedural efficiency for a timely communication between relevant stakeholders, i.e. ENISA, the single point of contact of the Member States concerned (with respect to incidents to be notified under the NIS2), and the CSIRT designated for the purposes of coordinated vulnerability disclosure in accordance with Art. 12 of the NIS2 should not be a point of concern anymore. On the other hand, the final text introduced several exceptions that may limit the simultaneous access of both ENISA and other relevant CSIRTs to the notification, mainly based on (cyber)security related grounds to be justified by the CSIRT initially receiving the notification. In this regard, it will be crucial to ensure that the Commission's delegated act, specifying on the terms and conditions for when such grounds could be applied,[485] adopts a proportionate approach limiting therefore Member States' leeway in weighing more national security interests over the need to share relevant cybersecurity-related information.

4.5.5.5 Interplay Between the CRA and the Cybersecurity Act

The CRA aims to exploit synergies with the Cybersecurity Act mainly with regard to the conformity assessment procedure. Article 18(9) CRA lays down the interface between the two legal frameworks with a view to promoting the European cybersecurity certification schemes (ECCS) and facilitating the assessment of conformity of products with digital elements—if covered by an EU statement of conformity or certificate under a ECCS pursuant to Regulation (EU) 2019/881.

The Commission may specify the ECCSs that can be used for the presumption of conformity with CRA's essential requirements through the adoption of delegated acts; a cybersecurity certificate, at assurance level at least substantial, eliminates a manufacturer's obligation to carry out a third-party conformity assessment for the corresponding requirements.[486] The Commission is also empowered to adopt

[483] Cyber Resilience Act, recital 9b.

[484] See also recital 33g, Cyber Resilience Act.

[485] Cyber Resilience Act, recital 35c; Article 11b.

[486] Cyber Resilience Act, Article 18(10).

delegated acts to specify which products that have the core functionality of a category listed in Annex IIIa are required to obtain a certificate at assurance level at least substantial under a ECCS to demonstrate conformity with the essential requirements set out in the CRA.[487]

Finally, it is worth noting the seemingly benchmark role conferred to the CRA in respect to future ECCSs: "the need for new European cybersecurity certification schemes for products with digital elements should be assessed in the light of this Regulation. including when preparing the Union rolling work programme in line with Regulation (EU) 2019/881. Where there is a need for a new scheme covering products with digital elements, including in order to facilitate the compliance with this Regulation, the Commission may request ENISA to prepare candidate schemes in accordance with Article 48 of Regulation (EU) 2019/881. Such future European cybersecurity certification schemes covering products with digital elements should take into account the essential requirements and conformity assessment procedures as set out in this Regulation and facilitate compliance with this Regulation".[488]

4.6 Conclusion

This Chapter charted the different pieces of EU legislation in the field of cybersecurity to investigate the extent to which they tackle the specific security challenges raised by IoT connected devices. In other words, it investigated whether existing and proposed EU cybersecurity legal frameworks address the problem of unsecure digital connected devices.

The NIS Directive, the first EU legal instrument in the cybersecurity acquis, covers both governance (i.e., Member States obligations in terms of cybersecurity strategies, establishing CSIRTs, point of contacts, etc.), procedural and substantial cybersecurity aspects. In particular, it introduced anew in EU law cybersecurity incidents reporting and risk management measures for two categories of economic operators, i.e. operators of essential services and digital service providers. Albeit the Directive enhanced the overall level of security of key economic sectors within the Union, it did not target IoT products specifically, as shown in the legal analysis. Even the NIS2 Directive, which considerably strengthens the level of protection offered by the NIS Directive to the IoT ecosystem, would only cover the connected devices only insofar as they form part of the network and information systems of EE and IE.

Then, the analysis looked at the EU cybersecurity certification framework introduced by the Cybersecurity Act as a means to address the problem under scrutiny. By focusing in particular on the comprehensive security objectives for the EU cybersecurity schemes, laid down in Article 51, it might seem that this legal

[487] Cyber Resilience Act, Article 6a(1).

[488] Cyber Resilience Act, recital 39.

framework can cope with the lack of 'strong' cybersecurity of connected products in the Single Market. However, recourse to EU cybersecurity certification is voluntary. On the other hand, the legal analysis demonstrated that depicting the CSA framework as *purely* voluntary is inaccurate. Firstly, the CSA explicitly foresees the possibility of imposing specific cybersecurity requirements and making the certification thereof mandatory. Secondly, Member State or other Union law can provide for legally binding schemes, as testified by Article 24 NIS2 Directive. Finally, incentives towards certification may come from the market, as most of the customers and vendors along the supply chain look for certified products, services and processes, even at higher costs.

At the same time, the Commission—pressured by a surge in cyberattacks, both in terms of quality and quantity—took action by following a 'vertical' approach: it started with a systematic revision of EU product safety legislation with the view to including cybersecurity requirements. The investigation showed to what extent the RED, and in particular the Delegated Act activating Article 3(3)(d), (e), and (f), the MDR, the Regulation on General Product Safety and the Machinery Regulation address the above-mentioned regulatory failures.

This Chapter highlighted that while a vertical approach might be effective in the short run, only horizontal legislation will efficiently address the problem of the lack of legal obligations for the manufacturers of connected devices vis-à-vis the cybersecurity of their digital solutions at the core.

In this respect, the Cyber Resilience Act introduces a set of ex-ante and ex-post obligations impacting all the economic operators along the supply chain about the cybersecurity of their products with digital elements. Moreover, this policy option would address the second negative externality arising from the application of a theory of public good to the cybersecurity's dimension of robustness (Sect. 3.2.3): the costs of the failures will be borne by producers and will no longer fall on end users. The explanatory memorandum to the CRA proposal confirmed this line of reasoning stating that "any compliance costs for businesses would be outweighed by the benefits brought by a higher level of security of products with digital elements and ultimately an increase of users' trust in these products".[489]

With regard to the added costs in terms of compliance, in order not to overly burden economic operators, notified bodies should set conformity assessment fees proportional to the size of the undertaking. On the other hand, the horizontal policy option adopted would also bring significant benefits to the stakeholders involved: "for businesses, it would prevent divergent security rules for products with digital elements and decrease compliance costs for related cybersecurity legislation. It would reduce the number of cyber incidents, incident handling costs and reputational damage".[490] Pending the entry into application of the CRA, only time will tell if the economic and financial assessment of the Commission was accurate.

[489] Explanatory Memorandum to the CRA Proposal, p. 5.

[490] Legislative financial statement to the CRA Proposal, p. 69.

References

AIOTI (2021) AIOTI response to the public consultation on GPSD. https://aioti.eu/policy-and-strategies/

AIOTI (2021a) AIOTI Feedback to the Public Consultation on the Revised Draft NIS Directive (NIS2)

Anderson S, Williams T (2018) Cybersecurity and medical devices: are the ISO/IEC 80001-2-2 technical controls up to the challenge? Comput Stand Interf 56:134–143. https://doi.org/10.1016/J.CSI.2017.10.001

ANEC (2022) Response to EC Call for Evidence for an Impact Assessment on the Cyber Resilience Act (CRA) initiative

ANEC and BEUC (2021) Keeping Consumers Safe from Dangerous Products: How to make the General Product Safety Regulation a useful tool to ensure product safety

Anglmayer I (2021) Briefing implementation appraisal EPRS, Machinery Directive: Revision of Directive 2006/42/EC

Banasinski C, Rojszczak M (2021) Cybersecurity of consumer products against the background of the EU model of cyberspace protection. J Cybersecur 00:1–15. https://doi.org/10.1093/cybsec/tyab011

BDI (2021a) Position Paper on NIS 2-Directive

BDI (2021b) Position on ITRE-Amendments to NIS 2-Directive: German industry's position on the ITRE Committee's amendments to the Commission proposal for a Directive on measures for a high common level of cybersecurity across the Union, repealing Directive (EU) 2016/1148

BDI, DIN and DKE (2021) EU-wide Cybersecurity Requirements - Introduction of horizontal cybersecurity requirements based on the New Legislative Framework and bridge to the EU Cybersecurity Act. https://www.din.de/resource/blob/788018/f9708b36c89b2e527bcb1a66f523827a/2021-bdi-din-dke-position-cybersicherheit-europa-en-final-data.pdf

BEUC (2022) Cyber Resilience Act: Cybersecurity of Digital Products and Ancillary Services - BEUC response to public consultation

Biasin E, Kamenjašević E (2022) Cybersecurity of medical devices: new challenges arising from the AI Act and NIS 2 directive proposals. Int Cybersecurity Law Rev 3:163–180. https://doi.org/10.1365/S43439-022-00054-X

Bishop M (2007) About penetration testing. IEEE Secur Priv 5:84–87. https://doi.org/10.1109/MSP.2007.159

Bitkom (2022) Cyber Resilience Act (CRA)

Blind K (2016) The impact of standardisation and standards on innovation. In: Edler J, Cunningham P, Gök A, Shapira P (eds) Handbook of innovation policy impact. Edward Elgar Publishing Ltd., pp 423–449

Blythe JM, Johnson SD, Manning M (2020) What is security worth to consumers? Investigating willingness to pay for secure internet of things devices. Crime Sci 9:1–9. https://doi.org/10.1186/S40163-019-0110-3/FIGURES/3

Borghetti J-S (2019) How can artificial intelligence be defective? In: Lohsse S, Schulze R, Staudenmayer D (eds) Liability for artificial intelligence and the internet of things - Münster colloquia on EU law and the digital economy IV. Bloomsbury Publishing, pp 63–76

Borgogno O, Colangelo G (2021) SEPs licensing across the supply chain: an antitrust perspective. SSRN Electron J. https://doi.org/10.2139/SSRN.3766118

Brighi R, Chiara PG (2021) La cybersecurity come bene pubblico: alcune riflessioni normative a partire dai recenti sviluppi nel diritto dell'Unione Europea. Federalismiit 21:18–42

BSA (2020) The Software Alliance Comments on EU Commission's NIS Directive review. https://ec.europa.eu/info/law/better-regulation/have-your-say/initiatives/12475-Cybersecurity-review-of-EU-rules-on-the-security-of-network-and-information-systems/F543319_it

Burton C (2020) Article 33 notification of a personal data breach to the supervisory authority. In: Kuner C, Bygrave LA, Docksey C, Drechsler L (eds) The EU general data protection regulation (GDPR): a commentary. Oxford University Press, pp 640–653

Busch L (2011) Standards: recipe for reality. MIT Press
Calabresi G (1970) The cost of accidents - a legal and economic analysis. Yale University Press
CEN-CENELEC (2021) Response to the European Commission' s Public Consultation on the Draft Machinery Regulation. https://www.cencenelec.eu/media/PolicyOpinions/2021-07-07_cen-cenelecpositionondraftmachineryregulation.pdf
Center for Strategy & Evaluation Services (2020) Final Report: Impact Assessment on Increased Protection of Internet-Connected Radio Equipment and Wearable Radio Equipment
Chiara PG (2020a) Disentangling encryption from the personalization debate: on the advisability of endorsing the "relativist approach" underpinning the identifiability criterion. Univ Vienna Law Rev 4:168–188
Chiara PG (2020b) Sistemi intelligenti autonomi e responsabilità civile: stato dell'arte e prospettive nell'esperienza comunitaria. Dirit ed Econ dell'Impresa 1:105–128
Chiara PG (2021) The balance between security, privacy and data protection in IoT data sharing: a critique to traditional 'Security&Privacy' surveys. Eur Data Prot Law Rev 7:18–30. https://doi.org/10.21552/EDPL/2021/1/6
Chiara PG (2022a) The IoT and the new EU cybersecurity regulatory landscape. Int Rev Law Comput Technol 36:118–137. https://doi.org/10.1080/13600869.2022.2060468
Chiara PG (2022b) Commission delegated regulation (EU) 2022/30 supplementing Directive 2014/53/EU on radio equipment: strengthening cybersecurity, privacy and personal data protection of wireless devices. Eur Data Prot Law Rev 8:103–107. https://doi.org/10.21552/edpl/2022/1/15
Chiara PG (2022c) The cyber resilience act: the EU Commission's proposal for a horizontal regulation on cybersecurity for products with digital elements. Int Cybersecurity Law Rev 3: 255–272. https://doi.org/10.1365/S43439-022-00067-6
Chiara PG (2022d) Artificial intelligence, robots and torts: challenges and perspectives. Aracne, Roma
Contardi M (2019) Changes in the medical device's regulatory framework and its impact on the medical device's industry: from the medical device directives to the medical device regulations. Erasmus Law Rev 12:166–177. https://doi.org/10.5553/ELR.000139
Council of the European Union (2020) Council Conclusions on the cybersecurity of connected devices 13629/20
De Gregorio G, Dunn P (2022) The European risk-based approaches: connecting constitutional dots in the digital age. Common Mark Law Rev 59:473–500. https://doi.org/10.54648/COLA2022032
Denardis L (2020) The internet in everything - freedom and security in a world with no off switch, 1st edn. Yale University Press, New Haven & London
Dickmann R (2022) Vulnerability management as compliance requirement in product security regulation — a game changer for producers ' liability and consequential improvement of the level of security in the internet of things? Int Cybersecurity Law Rev. https://doi.org/10.1365/s43439-022-00064-9
DIGITALEUROPE (2021) Setting the standard: How to secure the Internet of Things
DIGITALEUROPE (2021a) Position paper on the new Machinery Regulation
DIGITALEUROPE (2021b) Position on the NIS2 Directive
DIGITALEUROPE (2022a) Comments on the proposed General Product Safety Regulation
DIGITALEUROPE (2022b) Reporting, mandatory certification and main establishment in final NIS2 trilogues
DIGITALEUROPE (2022c) Building blocks for a scalable Cyber Resilience Act
Ducuing C (2019) Towards an obligation to secure connected and automated vehicles "by design"? In: Security and law: legal and ethical aspects of public security, cyber security and critical infrastructure security. Intersentia, pp 183–214
Ducuing C (2021) Understanding the rule of prevalence in the NIS directive: C-ITS as a case study. Comput Law Secur Rev 40:105514. https://doi.org/10.1016/j.clsr.2020.105514

Durante M (2019) Safety and security in the digital age. Trust, algorithms, standards, and risks. In: Berkich D, D'Alfonso MV (eds) On the cognitive, ethical, and scientific dimensions of artificial intelligence. Springer Nature, pp 371–383

ECSO (2020) European Cyber Security Certification - Challenges ahead for the roll-out of the Cybersecurity

ENISA (2017a) Incident notification for DSPs in the context of the NIS Directive - A comprehensive guideline on how to implement incident notification for Digital Service Providers, in the context of the NIS Directive

ENISA (2017b) Baseline Security Recommendations for IoT in the context of Critical Information Infrastructures

ENISA (2019a) Good practices for security of IoT Secure Software Development Lifecycle

ENISA (2019b) IoT Security Standards Gap Analysis: Mapping of existing standards against requirements on security and privacy in the area of IoT

ENISA (2019c) Threat Landscape for 5G Networks

ENISA (2020a) Guidelines for Securing the Internet of Things - Secure supply chain for IoT

ENISA (2020b) EUCS, a candidate cybersecurity certification scheme for cloud services

ENISA (2021a) NIS Investments

ENISA (2021b) Public Consultation on the draft Candidate EUCC Scheme

ENISA (2021c) Candidate EUCC Scheme V1.1.1

ENISA Stakeholder Cybersecurity Certification Group (2021) Consultation Report on Draft URWP

ETSI (2020) EN 303 645 V2.1.1 - Cyber Security for Consumer Internet of Things: Baseline Requirements

European Commission (2013) Conclusions of the Internet of Things Public Consultation. https://ec.europa.eu/digital-single-market/en/news/conclusions-internet-things-public-consultation

European Commission (2014) COMMISSION STAFF WORKING DOCUMENT Part 1: Evaluation of the Internal Market Legislation for Industrial Products Accompanying the document: the Communication from the Commission to the European Parliament, the Council and the European Economic and Social Committee

European Commission (2016) The 'Blue Guide' on the implementation of EU products rules 2016 (2016/C 272/01). Off J Eur Union

European Commission (2017) State of the Union 2017 - Cybersecurity: EU Agency and Certification Framework

European Commission (2019) Rolling Plan for ICT Standardisation 2019

European Commission (2020) Communication from the Commission to the European Parliament, the Council, the European Economic and Social Committee and the Committee of the Regions An SME Strategy for a Sustainable and Digital Europe COM(2020) 103 Final

European Commission (2020a) COMMISSION IMPLEMENTING DECISION M/565 of 15.5.2020 on a standardisation request to the European Committee for Standardization and the European Committee for Electrotechnical Standardization as regards medical devices in support of Regulation (EU) 2017/745 of the European Parliament and of the Council and in vitro diagnostic medical devices in support of Regulation (EU) 2017/746 of the European Parliament and of the Council

European Commission (2020b) Communication from the Commission to the European Parliament, the European Council, the Council, the European Economic and Social Committee and the Committee of the Regions on the EU Security Union Strategy

European Commission (2021a) Rolling Plan for ICT standardisation 2021

European Commission (2021b) COMMISSION STAFF WORKING DOCUMENT IMPACT ASSESSMENT REPORT Accompanying the document Commission Delegated Regulation supplementing Directive 2014/53/EU of the European Parliament and of the Council with regard to the application of the essential requirements

European Commission (2021c) COMMISSION STAFF WORKING DOCUMENT IMPACT ASSESSMENT REPORT accompanying the document Proposal for a Regulation of the European Parliament and of the Council on general product safety, amending Regulation

(EU) No 1025/2012 of the European Parliament and of the Council, and repealing Council Directive 87/357/EEC and Directive 2001/95/EC of the European Parliament and of the Council" SWD(2021) 169 final

European Commission (2021d) COMMISSION IMPLEMENTING DECISION of 14.4.2021 on a standardisation request to the European Committee for Standardization and the European Committee for Electrotechnical Standardization as regards medical devices in support of Regulation (EU) 2017/745 of the European Parliament and of the Council and in vitro diagnostic medical devices in support of Regulation (EU) 2017/746 of the European Parliament and of the Council

European Commission (2021e) COMMISSION STAFF WORKING DOCUMENT IMPACT ASSESSMENT Accompanying the Proposal for a Regulation of the European Parliament and of the Council on machinery products' SWD(2021) 82 final

European Commission and the High Representatitve of the Union for Foreign Affairs and Security Policy (2020) Joint Communication to the European Parliament and the Council: The EU's Cybersecurity Strategy for the Digital Decade

European Commission and the High Representative of the Union for Foreign Affairs and Security Policy (2017) Joint Communication to the European Parliament and the Council Resilience, Deterrence and Defence: Building strong cybersecurity for the EU

European Commission Expert Group on Liability and New Technologies (2019) Liability for Artificial Intelligence and other emerging digital technologies

European Data Protection Supervisor (2021) Opinion 5/2021 on the Cybersecurity Strategy and the NIS 2.0 Directive

European Economic and Social Committee (2020) Revision of the Machinery Directive. https://www.eesc.europa.eu/en/our-work/opinions-information-reports/information-reports/revision-machinery-directive

European Parliament (2017) Resolution of 16 February 2017 with recommendations to the Commission on Civil Law Rules on Robotics

EUROSMART (2019) Revision of the Machinery Directive: Answer to the European Commission Public Consultation. https://www.eurosmart.com/revision-of-the-machinery-directive

Eurosmart (2022) Cyber Resilience Act (CRA) - new cybersecurity rules for digital products and ancillary services. https://www.eurosmart.com/cyber-resilience-act-cra-new-cybersecurity-rules-for-digital-products-and-ancillary-services/

Fairgrieve D, Howells G, Møgelvang-Hansen P et al (2017) Product liability directive. In: Machnikowski P (ed) European product liability: an analysis of the state of the art in the era of new technologies. Intersentia, pp 17–108

Finnish Transport and Communications Agency (2020) Finnish Cybersecurity Label. https://tietoturvamerkki.fi/sites/default/files/media/file/cybersecurity_label_presentation-280920.pdf

Floridi L (2021) The end of an era: from self-regulation to hard law for the digital industry. Philos Technol 34:619–622. https://doi.org/10.1007/S13347-021-00493-0

Fosch-Villaronga E, Mahler T (2021) Cybersecurity, safety and robots: strengthening the link between cybersecurity and safety in the context of care robots. Comput Law Secur Rev 41. https://doi.org/10.1016/J.CLSR.2021.105528

Fuster GG, Jasmontaite L (2020) Cybersecurity regulation in the European Union: the digital, the critical and fundamental rights. In: Christen M, Gordijn B, Loi M (eds) The ethics of cybersecurity. Springer, Cham, pp 97–115

Gerardy M (2021) Nemo censetur ignorare legem: the dilemma regarding the access to ISO standards referenced into EU law. In: REALaw.blog. https://realaw.blog/2021/11/23/nemo-censetur-ignorare-lege-the-dilemma-regarding-the-access-to-iso-standardsreferenced-into-eu-law-by-marie-gerardy/

German Federal Office for Information Security (BSI) (2022) IT security label for all 'smart consumer devices'. https://www.bsi.bund.de/SharedDocs/IT-Sicherheitskennzeichen/DE/Meldungen/Smarte-Verbrauchergeraete.html

Gerybaite A (2022) Exploring the regulatory interplay in health internet of everything: digital health technologies, data protection and cybersecurity. Forthcoming 1–18

Gijrath SJH (2021) (Re-)defining software defined networks under the European electronic communications code. Comput Law Secur Rev 40. https://doi.org/10.1016/J.CLSR.2020.105492

Giovanni C, Silva F (2018) Cybersecurity for connected products - ANEC BEUC Position Paper

Gorywoda L (2009) The new European legislative framework for the marketing of goods. Columbia J Eur Law 16:161–169

GSMA (2020) Consultation on the revision of the NIS Directive

Hadzovic S (2021) Internet of things from a regulatory point of view. In: 20th international symposium INFOTEH-JAHORINA (INFOTEH). Institute of Electrical and Electronics Engineers Inc., pp 1–4

Hernandez-Ramos JL, Matheu SN, Skarmeta A (2021) The challenges of software cybersecurity certification. IEEE Secur Priv 19:99–102. https://doi.org/10.1109/MSEC.2020.3037845

Hessel S, Rebmann A (2020) Regulation of internet-of-things cybersecurity in Europe and Germany as exemplified by devices for children. Int Cybersecurity Law Rev 1:27–37. https://doi.org/10.1365/S43439-020-00006-3

Hofmann HCH (2016) European regulatory union? The role of agencies and standards. In: Koutrakos P, Snell J (eds) Research handbook on the EU's internal market. Elgar Publishing, Cheltenham, pp 1–20

Janssen A (2022) The update obligation for smart products—time period for the update obligation and failure to install the update. In: Schulze R, Staudenmayer D (eds) Lohsse S. Nomos Verlag, Smart products: Münster Colloquia on EU law and the digital economy VI, pp 91–107

Kamara I (2021) Misaligned union laws? A comparative analysis of certification in the cybersecurity act and the general data protection regulation. In: Hallinan D, Leenes R, De Hert P (eds) Data protection and privacy: data protection and artificial intelligence. Hart Publishing

Klimas T (2008) The law of recitals in European Community legislation. ILSA J Int Comp Law 15: 61–94

Kohler C (2020) The EU cybersecurity act and European standards: an introduction to the role of European standardization. Int Cybersecurity Law Rev 1:7–12. https://doi.org/10.1365/S43439-020-00008-1

Mandalari AM, Roman K, Hamed H, Daniel JD, David C, (2020) "Towards Automatic Identification and Blocking of Non-Critical IoT Traffic Destinations" arXiv, available at: https://arxiv.org/abs/2003.07133

Mansfield-Devine S (2017) Weaponising the internet of things. Netw Secur 2017:13–19. https://doi.org/10.1016/S1353-4858(17)30104-6

Mantelero A, Vaciago G, Samantha Esposito M, Monte N (2021) The common EU approach to personal data and cybersecurity regulation. Int J Law Inf Technol 28:297–328. https://doi.org/10.1093/IJLIT/EAAA021

Markopoulou D, Papakonstantinou V, de Hert P (2019) The new EU cybersecurity framework: the NIS directive, ENISA's role and the general data protection regulation. Comput Law Secur Rev 35:105336. https://doi.org/10.1016/j.clsr.2019.06.007

Durante M (2021) *Computational power: the impact of ICT on law, society and knowledge.* Routledge

Medical Device Coordination Group (2019) Guidance on Cybersecurity in Medical Devices

Megas KN et al. (2021) Workshop Summary Report for "Building the Federal Profile for IoT Device Cybersecurity" Virtual Workshop NISTIR 8322

Miquel Martìn-Casals, "Causation and Scope of Liability in the Internet of Things (IoT)" (2019) in Sebastian Lohsse, Reiner Schulze, Dirk Staudenmayer (eds.) *Liability for Artificial Intelligence and the Internet of Things: Münster Colloquia on EU Law and the Digital Economy IV*, Nomos, pp. 201–228

NIS Cooperation Group (2020) Synergies in Cybersecurity Incident Reporting - CG Publication 04/20

OECD (2018) Consumer Product Safety in the Internet of Things

Orgalim (2020) Proposal for a horizontal legislation on cybersecurity for networkable products within the New Legislative Framework

Orgalim (2021) Orgalim position on the proposal for a General Product Safety Regulation

Pagallo U (2013) The laws of robots: crimes, contracts, and torts. Springer

Pagallo U, Durante M, Monteleone S (2017) What is new with the internet of things in privacy and data protection? Four legal challenges on sharing and control in IoT. In: Data protection and privacy: (in)visibilities and infrastructures. Springer, Cham, pp 59–78

Perotto G (2020) La standardizzazione europea nel settore dell'ICT nell'era dell'Internet of things: qualificazione giuridica e controllo di validità degli standard tecnici armonizzati. Dirit dell'economia 3:757–771

Quinn P (2017) The EU commission's risky choice for a non-risk based strategy on assessment of medical devices. Comput Law Secur Rev 33:361–370. https://doi.org/10.1016/J.CLSR.2017.03.019

Rak R (2021) Internet of healthcare: opportunities and legal challenges in internet of things-enabled telehealth ecosystems. 14th Int Conf Theory Pract Electron Gov 481–484. https://doi.org/10.1145/3494193

Sartor G, Omicini A (2016) The autonomy of technological systems and responsibilities for their use. In: Bhuta N, Beck S, Geiβ R et al (eds) Autonomous weapons systems: law, ethics, policy. Cambridge University Press, pp 39–74

Schmitz-Berndt S (2021) Cybersecurity is gaining momentum - NIS 2.0 is on its way. Eur Data Prot Law 7:580–586. https://doi.org/10.21552/edpl/2021/4/14

Schmitz-Berndt S, Anheier F (2021) Synergies in cybersecurity incident reporting—the NIS cooperation group publication 04/20 in context. Eur Data Prot Law Rev 7:101–107

Schmitz-berndt S, Chiara PG (2022) One step ahead: mapping the Italian and German cybersecurity laws against the proposal for a NIS2 directive. Int Cybersecurity Law Rev. https://doi.org/10.1365/s43439-022-00058-7

Schmitz-Berndt S, Cole M (2022) Towards an efficient and coherent regulatory framework on cybersecurity in the EU: the proposals for a NIS 2.0 directive and a cyber resilience act. Appl Cybersecurity Internet Gov 1:121–137. https://doi.org/10.5604/01.3001.0016.1323

Schmitz-Berndt S, Schiffner S (2021) Don't tell them now (or at all)–responsible disclosure of security incidents under NIS directive and GDPR. Int Rev Law Comput Technol 35:101–115. https://doi.org/10.1080/13600869.2021.1885103

Serpanos D, Wolf M (2018) Internet-of-things (IoT) systems - architectures, algorithms, methodologies. Springer International Publishing

Sievers T (2021) Proposal for a NIS directive 2.0: companies covered by the extended scope of application and their obligations. Int Cybersecurity Law Rev 2:223–231. https://doi.org/10.1365/S43439-021-00033-8

Stahl K, Strausz R (2017) Certification and market transparency. Rev Econ Stud 84:1842–1868

Sterk LAJ (2018) The hacker, product manufacturer, sensor manufacturer, software provider or infrastructure provider? Thesis LLM Law Technol Tilbg Law Sch

Tulibacka M (2016) Product liability law in transition: a central European perspective. Routledge

van Dam C (2013) European tort law, 2nd edn. Oxford University Press

Vedder A (2019) Safety, security and ethics. In: Vedder A, Schroers J, Ducuing C, Valcke P (eds) Security and law. Intersentia, pp 11–26

Wagner G (2022) Software as a product. In: Schulze R, Staudenmayer D (eds) Lohsse S. Nomos Verlag, Smart products: Münster Colloquia on EU law and the digital economy VI, pp 157–179

Wavestone - CEPS - CARSA - ICF (2021) Study on the Need of Cybersecurity Requirements for ICT Products - No. 2020-0715: Final Study Report, available at: https://cdn.ceps.eu/wpcontent/uploads/2022/01/VIGIE20200715_Cybersecurity-requirements-for-ICT-products.pdf

Weber RH (2013) Internet of things - governance quo vadis? Comput Law Secur Rev 29:341–347. https://doi.org/10.1016/j.clsr.2013.05.010

Weber RH (2016) Governance of the internet of things—from infancy to first attempts of implementation? Laws 5:28. https://doi.org/10.3390/LAWS5030028

Weber RH, Studer E (2016) Cybersecurity in the internet of things: legal aspects. Comput Law Secur Rev 32:715–728. https://doi.org/10.1016/j.clsr.2016.07.002

Weber RH (2017a) Liability in the internet of things. J Eur Consum Mark Law 6:207–212

Weber S (2017b) Coercion in cybersecurity: what public health models reveal. J Cybersecurity 3: 173–183. https://doi.org/10.1093/CYBSEC/TYX005

Wendehorst C (2022) The update obligation—how to make it work in the relationship between seller, producer, digital content or service provider and consumer. In: Lohsse S, Schulze R, Staudenmayer D (eds) Smart products: Münster Colloquia on EU law and the digital economy VI. Nomos Verlag, pp 63–89

Chapter 5
Privacy and Data Protection Challenges in IoT Data and Metadata Processing

5.1 The Interplay Between EU Privacy and Data Protection Legal Frameworks Concerning IoT Data and Metadata Processing

Navigating the *privacy* discourse surrounding the Internet of Things can be complex, for it is often the case of distinguishing issues relating to the right to privacy from ones relating to the right of data protection.[1] Indeed, the "technical literature"—understood as the research corpus that has not been shaped by legal scholars—usually refers to 'privacy' in a broad fashion, that is, to include *privacy-as-confidentiality* and *informational privacy* (see Chap. 3), with the latter including data protection related concerns, without operating an appropriate distinction.

In this respect, Konoudes and Kapitsaki performed a literature review with a view to identifying the state-of-the-art vis-à-vis IoT users' privacy protection. They analysed 84 scientific papers: whereas 58 had "privacy" in the title, only 6 of them referred to "personal data" or "data protection".[2] Unsurprisingly, all the contributions examined by the authors tackle several challenges brought about by the IoT in terms of applying GDPR[3] requirements. Albeit some may see this problematisation as a merely formalistic exercise, this trend, which arguably is due to an US-rooted reconstruction of privacy frameworks and values,[4] conceals deeper consequences, as

[1] For a functional definition of 'privacy', see Sect. 3.2.1.

[2] Kounoudes and Kapitsaki (2020).

[3] Regulation (EU) 2016/679 of the European Parliament and of the Council of 27 April 2016 on the protection of natural persons with regard to the processing of personal data and on the free movement of such data, and repealing Directive 95/46/EC (General Data Protection Regulation).

[4] van den Hoven et al. (2020): the European approach "conceptualises issues of informational privacy in terms of data protection", whilst US scholars in terms of privacy.

P. G. Chiara, *The Internet of Things and EU Law*, Issues in Privacy and Data Protection 67, https://doi.org/10.1007/978-3-031-67663-5_5

the incorrect framing of the problem will be reflected in a negative legacy at legal level.[5]

Against this background, without dwelling on privacy theories' taxonomies,[6] this section aims to highlight how structural IoT data and metadata harvesting, processing and sharing (see Chap. 2) trigger and challenge specific aspects of the relevant EU privacy and data protection legal frameworks i.e., the GDPR and ePrivacy laws,[7] to include the drafts of the ePrivacy Regulation as well,[8] proposed by the Commission in January 2017.[9]

As already stressed throughout this book, the ubiquitous data and metadata collection, processing and sharing among and though IoT systems implies a paradigm shift not only from a security viewpoint (Chaps. 3 and 4) but also from a privacy and personal data protection perspective. Even though the chapter's normative approach primarily explores the legal dimension, it is nevertheless worthwhile to give an account, albeit briefly, of some ethical implications arising from IoT data and metadata processing scenarios. Arguably, the main ethical concern is that the IoT has the potential to be a transnational private (but also public) 'surveillance' network.[10]

Networks and systems of sensors and actuators (e.g., cameras, microphones, other types of sensors capable of capturing other types of data, such as temperature) are not only deployed in every sector of the market but in our homes or even on our bodies (e.g, wearables) as well. IoT data processing scenarios (in terms of data collection) involve many different types of data. On a higher level, two categories can be distinguished, that is, product data and service data. The former broadly concerns product's characteristics, e.g. performance, that can be retrieved from the product by manufacturers/vendors and possibly users and third-parties (depending also on legal requirements). The latter category instead covers data generated during the provision of a service by the provider, including data recorded intentionally during the provision of the service and data resulting indirectly from the user's action and interaction (e.g., time of inaction).

This has two main consequences, which highlight the extent to which the IoT differs in terms of (privacy and data protection) impacts from other/previous digital

---

[5] Chiara (2021), p. 26.

[6] Koops et al. (2017), p. 483; Solove (2010).

[7] Directive 2002/58/EC of the European Parliament and of the Council of 12 July 2002 concerning the processing of personal data and the protection of privacy in the electronic communications sector (Directive on privacy and electronic communications).

[8] European Commission, Proposal for a Regulation of the European Parliament and of the Council concerning the respect for private life and the protection of personal data in electronic communications and repealing Directive 2002/58/EC (Regulation on Privacy and Electronic Communications) COM(2017) 10 final.

[9] Proposal for a Regulation of the European Parliament and of the Council concerning the respect for private life and the protection of personal data in electronic communications and repealing Directive 2002/58/EC (Regulation on Privacy and Electronic Communications, ePrivacy Regulation) COM/2017/010 final.

[10] Zuboff (2019); see Noto La Diega (2023), p. 236 and ff.

technologies. The 'intimacy veil' surrounding private homes and bodies, historically conceived "as the most sacred of private places",[11] is pierced by the IoT. For these connected devices capture—without our even noticing it—data about our habits, health, preferences of sort and send it to different parties (starting from manufacturers) into structured data flows, waiting for further processing and creation of profiles. Manufacturers and third-parties generate value not only from raw data but notably and foremost from aggregated data and the inferences that can be drawn from it. "A major challenge in the regulation of the IoT is that the addition of billions of sensors to the internet's network is allowing individual behaviour in the physical world to be 'as closely tracked as online activity'".[12]

Setting aside arguments suggesting a (re)alignment between privacy and data protection under the IoT paradigm,[13] this section scrutinises several legal challenges brought about by the IoT facing both the GDPR and ePrivacy laws: (i) lawfulness of IoT data and metadata processing, in particular, taking into account the effectiveness of relying on 'consent' as a legal basis; (ii) lack of control and information asymmetry, with due regard for the principle of transparency; (iii) information security risks, as opposed to device or network security, addressed in Chap. 4.

On a methodological note, the three above-mentioned issues were identified by the Article 29 Working Party in its 2014 'Opinion on the recent developments of the Internet of Things' (hereinafter, Opinion).[14] Drawing on the findings of that opinion, the analysis that follows aims to enrich the theoretical reflection by taking into account recent developments either at technological (e.g., innovative tracking techniques) or legislative (i.e., the ePrivacy Regulation Proposal) level. Some other risks identified by the Article 29 WP (i.e., profiling; limits of anonymisation; inferences derived from data) are seemingly left out of the discussion. However, given the fact that they can be considered different facets of the same problem, namely IoT data and metadata analysis, they will be dealt with in a unified and more comprehensive way by the remaining sections of this chapter.

It may be worth clarifying from the outset the difference between data and metadata. From an epistemological perspective, 'content data' present traits of subjective interpretation, whereas 'content metadata' are more meaningful and objective as they regard the time, the date, the source, the destination and the length fields of the communication.[15] In this respect, metadata set the context in which the content of the communication is formed and shared. Many scholars agree that a sharp separation in terms of the legal protection afforded to data and metadata, according to an outdated 'content—envelope' metaphor, would be detrimental in two respects.

[11] Noto La Diega (2023), pp. 235–236.

[12] Ibid., p. 256. See also Brown and Marsden (2013), p. 47.

[13] Pagallo et al. (2017), p. 59.

[14] Article 29 Data Protection Working Party (2014a).

[15] Palmirani and Martoni (2019), pp. 9–22.

First, there is no dispute that metadata can be as sensitive as content data.[16] Secondly, the boundaries between data and metadata, in network communication, are increasingly blurred.[17] A relativistic or contextual approach to distinguish between content and metadata considers the specific circumstances in which the information is formed or used: for example, a URL is at the same time a "delivery instruction", that is, metadata, and content since "essentially means sending a message saying "please send me back the page found at this URL"".[18]

On a more general level, the e-Privacy Directive—as amended by Directive 2009/136/EC[19]—seeks to harmonise national provisions to uphold fundamental rights and freedoms, in particular, the right to privacy (Art. 7 EU Charter of Fundamental Rights), intended in the sense of *confidentiality*, with respect to the specific electronic communication sector,[20] which may involve the processing of personal, non-personal data and data related to a legal person.[21]

Conversely, the GDPR protects the fundamental rights and freedoms of natural persons, and in particular their right to the protection of personal data,[22] horizontally, without restricting its scope to a particular (vertical) sector. As Poletti rightly noticed, "the IoT stands at the crossroads between these two coordinates, revealing that through the network of connected sensors, injuries to both rights can be generated; [. . .] it can be said that the IoT is now positioned in the middle between the GDPR, which does not properly fit this infrastructure, and Directive 2002/58/EC".[23]

The e-Privacy Regulation proposal aims to revise an outdated Directive, which is no longer coherent[24] and therefore fit for the increasing digitalised Single Market and, more generally, society and providing a level playing field for market players.[25]

---

[16] Joined Cases C-203/15 and C-698/15 *Tele2 Sverige AB v Post-och telestyrelsen and Secretary of State for the Home Department v Tom Watson and Others*, judgment of 21 December 2016 (Grand Chamber), ECLI:EU:C:2016:970, para. 99.

[17] Mitrou (2007), p. 422. See also See also Opinion of Advocate General Bobek, Case of 26 January 2017, *Rīgas satiksme*, C-13/16, ECLI:EU:C:2017:43, para. 95.

[18] Conley (2014), pp. 4–5.

[19] Directive 2009/136/EC of the European Parliament and of the Council of 25 November 2009 amending Directive 2002/22/EC on universal service and users' rights relating to electronic communications networks and services, Directive 2002/58/EC concerning the processing of personal data and the protection of privacy in the electronic communications sector and Regulation (EC) No 2006/2004 on cooperation between national authorities responsible for the enforcement of consumer protection laws [2009] GJ L 337/11.

[20] Art. 1(1) ePD.

[21] Art. 1(3) ePD.

[22] Art. 1(2) GDPR.

[23] Poletti (2022), p. 178.

[24] Etteldorf (2020), p. 568.

[25] European Commission, 'Explanatory Memorandum of the Proposal for the ePrivacy Regulation' (2017) 2; recital 6, ePrivacy Regulation proposal.

In the Proposal, the Commission broadened the material and territorial[26] scope of the previous Directive.

The e-Privacy Regulation proposal would apply to "the processing of electronic communications data carried out in connection with the provision and the use of electronic communications services and to information related to the terminal equipment of end-users" (Art. 2(1)), whereas the electronic communications services that are not publicly available would fall outside the scope (Art. 2(2)(c)).

It follows that the new e-privacy law would cover not only traditional telecom providers but also 'over-the-top' (OTT) players,[27] such as providers of voice over IP, text message and email services.[28] In this respect, both the Parliament[29] and Council[30] drafted legislative resolutions on the Commission's Proposal by amending Article 2 so to include the 'provision of publicly available directories' and the 'sending of direct marketing electronic communications'. In particular, the Parliament extended the scope of the Regulation to include information processed (not just stored) by end-users' terminal equipment and the placing on the market of software permitting electronic communications.

One significant source of friction between the co-legislators was whether the Regulation would apply to electronic communications data and metadata *stored* or, rather, only *in transit.* Whereas the Council explicitly supported the latter interpretation,[31] the Parliament amended Recital 15 by adopting an absolutist stance towards the prohibition of interception of communications, whether in transit or stored.[32]

Importantly, Recital 12 highlights the need to ensure full protection of the rights to privacy and confidentiality of machine-to-machine communications and Internet of Things services, unless IoT transmission is carried out via a private or closed network such as a closed factory network. However, the Commission Proposal did not further substantiate this recital in any article.

---

[26] Similar to the GDPR, the provisions of the ePrivacy Regulation would have an extraterritorial effect, as they would apply to the processing of electronic communications content, metadata and the information related to the terminal equipment of end-users in the Union (Art. 3).

[27] Body of European Regulators for Electronic Communication (2016).

[28] González et al. (2020), pp. 256–257.

[29] European Parliament, 'Report on the proposal for a regulation of the European Parliament and of the Council concerning the respect for private life and the protection of personal data in electronic communications and repealing Directive 2002/58/EC (Regulation on Privacy and Electronic Communications)' COM(2017) <https://www.europarl.europa.eu/doceo/document/A-8-2017-0324_EN.html>.

[30] Council of the European Union, 'Proposal for a Regulation of the European Parliament and of the Council concerning the respect for private life and the protection of personal data in electronic communications and repealing Directive 2002/58/EC (Regulation on Privacy and Electronic Communications)' (2021) <https://data.consilium.europa.eu/doc/document/ST-5008-2021-INIT/en/pdf>.

[31] Art. 2(2)(e) Council ePrivacy Proposal: [The Regulation does not apply to] electronic communications data processed after receipt by the end-user concerned.

[32] In the Parliament's reading, the new version of recital 15 states that "prohibition of interception of communications should apply *also* during their conveyance [emphasis added]".

Conversely, the Parliament amended the definition of 'electronic communications service' to include "a service consisting wholly or mainly in the conveyance of the signals, such as a transmission service used for the provision of a machine-to-machine service and for broadcasting, but excludes information conveyed as part of a broadcasting service to the public over an electronic communications network or service except to the extent that the information can be related to the identifiable end-user receiving the information; it also includes services which are not publicly available, but provide access to a publicly available electronic communications network".[33]

The words used by the Parliament to describe the M2M interaction, and the Internet of Things in general i.e., 'conveyance of the signals', echoes the phrasing of Art. 2(4)(c) of the European Electronic Communications Code.[34] While the Parliament[35] and some commentators highlight the risk of relying on another legal instrument when providing definitions,[36] the overall consistency effort between Union acts is positive as it ensures legal certainty and coherence.

The Article 29 Working Party, while welcoming the expansion of the scope to cover M2M interaction—"as such communications often contain information protected under privacy rights", argued, on the other hand, that "a narrow category of *pure* [emphasis added] machine-to-machine communication should be exempted if they have no impact on either privacy or the confidentiality of communications, such as for example the cases where such communication is performed in execution of a transmission protocol between network elements (e.g. servers, switches,) to inform each other on their status of activity".[37]

However, such an exception may lower the expectation of privacy of end-users as metadata analysis—even if the information at stake might be regarded as *purely* technical—can provide insights on terminals' states which, in turn, may lead to draw inferences on end-users' habits. Traffic data (i.e., metadata) generated, processed and shared by IoT devices through electronic communications networks and services, increasingly "involve personal data processing".[38] Section 5.3 will further address the risks of metadata analysis from a technical and legal integrated perspective.

Finally, as regards the relationship between the GDPR and the ePrivacy laws, Article 95 and recital 173 GDPR set the indisputable[39] *lex generalis* role of GDPR in EU data protection law. The ePrivacy Directive before, and possibly the Regulation

---

[33] Art. 4(3)(aa) Parliament ePrivacy Proposal.

[34] DIRECTIVE (EU) 2018/1972 of the European Parliament and of the Council of 11 December 2018 establishing the European Electronic Communications Code.

[35] Art. 4(3)(aa, ab, ac, ad, ae, af) Parliament ePrivacy Proposal.

[36] González et al. (2020), pp. 256–257. "The Parliament is of the idea that the ePrivacy Regulation should be a standalone instrument and contain its own provisions, not depending on the Electronic Communications Code. Therefore, the Parliament suggests that the definitions from the Code be incorporated in the Proposal, taking into account any adaptation needed".

[37] Article 29 Data Protection Working Party (2017), p. 28.

[38] EDPB (2019), p. 12.

[39] *Contra* see Zuiderveen Borgesius (2015).

afterwards, are *lex specialis* to the GDPR as they complement it with regard to the sector of electronic communications, insofar as those data processing operations involve personal data.[40]

In this respect, the EDPB explains that the aim of Art. 95 GDPR is "to avoid the imposition of unnecessary administrative burdens upon controllers who would otherwise be subject to similar but not quite identical administrative burdens".[41]

5.1.1 Lawfulness: The Challenges of 'Consent' in IoT Systems

Article 6(1) GDPR lays down the various legal grounds required by every processing involving personal data. At the same time, it substantiates the principle of 'lawful processing', enshrined in Art. 5 GDPR, and the provisions set forth by Art. 52-(1) Charter of Fundamental Rights of the European Union ('CFR') and Art. 8(2) European Convention of Human Rights ('ECHR') establishing the conditions under which fundamental rights may be limited. "The function of Article 6(1) GDPR, seen in relation to Article 52(1) CFR, is to specify in more detail what the terms 'objectives of general interest (recognised by the Union)' and 'necessity to protect the rights and freedoms of others' mean in the context of data protection".[42]

Among the six grounds laid down by Art. 6(1) for making the processing of personal data lawful, for which the GDPR does not set any ranking, consent usually has a role "as a potential substitute whenever there is no contractual context, no detailed legal rules about a fitting legal basis or the scope of 'legitimate interests of the controller or of a third party' is particularly difficult to assess".[43] For this reason, this sub-section dwells on the challenges that IoT systems pose to the notion of consent in EU privacy and data protection law.

Article 6(1)(a) GDPR provides for the lawfulness of the processing of personal data if the consent given by the data subject satisfies the conditions for valid consent in Art. 4(11), 7 and 8 GDPR. Consent must be freely given, specific, informed and unambiguous.[44] The cumulative nature of these criteria sets a high threshold to be met by data controllers.[45] In particular, Art. 7 GDPR, hinging on individual

[40] The CJEU has endorsed this broad understanding of the concept of personal data: it is not necessary that all the information allowing the identification of the individual must be in possession of one person (see Judgment of 19 October 2016, Patrick Breyer v Bundesrepublik Deutschland, C-582/14, paragraph 43).

[41] EDPB (2019), p. 15.

[42] Kotschy (2020), p. 326.

[43] Ibid., p. 329.

[44] Art. 4(11) GDPR.

[45] Bygrave and Tosoni (2020), p. 181.

autonomy "as expressed via the right to informational self-determination",[46] lays down the conditions regarding the exercising of valid consent.[47] In line with the principle of accountability laid down in Art. 5 GDPR, the responsibility to prove that valid consent—pursuant to the conditions laid down in Art. 7—was obtained from the data subject for a specific processing operation rest with the controller.

Importantly, Art. 7(3) mandates that controllers inform the data subject of the right to withdraw their consent at any time, before the consent is provided. Moreover, the consent shall be as easy to withdraw as to provide. "Where consent is obtained through use of a service-specific user interface (for example, via a website, an app, a log-on account, the interface of an IoT device or by e-mail), there is no doubt a data subject must be able to withdraw consent via the same electronic interface, as switching to another interface for the sole reason of withdrawing consent would require undue effort".[48]

Unsurprisingly, consent plays a prominent role in the ePrivacy Directive in relation to the confidentiality of communications. Thus, consent of the user or the subscriber is mentioned several times (e.g., Art. 5(3), 6, 9 and 13 ePD) as the only ground for the processing of their personal data. On the one hand, "the challenges that arise from the advancement of digital technologies, which the ePrivacy Directive aimed to tackle, justified the increased control of the user over the processing of his personal information and the protection of his privacy".[49] On the other hand, the role of consent in the ePrivacy Directive has created numerous conceptual and application difficulties, in particular, having regard to the provision of consent for the storing of and access to the information already stored in the terminal equipment of the user, namely 'cookies' (Art. 5(3) ePD).[50]

---

[46] Kosta (2013), p. 385.

[47] Kosta (2020), p. 350; the seminal Case C-673/17 *Planet 49 Gmbh v. Bundesverband der Verbraucherzentralen und Verbraucherverbände—Verbraucherzentrale Bundesverband e.V.* [2019] ECLI:EU:C:2019:801, and the Opinion delivered by the Advocate General Szpunar (ECLI:EU:C:2019:246). In particular, CJEU case *Planet49* may provide useful guidance vis-à-vis the interpretation of Article 7(4) as it concerns the assessment of whether consent may be *freely given* by means of 'pre-ticked' boxes. Moreover, the seminal case tackles the common practice of *bundling* consent to the processing of personal data to the provision of a service as part of a contract *even if the consent* (to the processing of personal data) *is not necessary for such execution*. Whereas Recital 43 GDPR suggests that such practices lead to a presumption that consent is not freely given, AG Szpunar interprets EU data protection law as meaning that "the prohibition on bundling is not absolute in nature" (para. 98). In the decision at issue, the AG concluded that consent to the processing of personal data is necessary for the conclusion of the contract i.e., participation in a prize game (para. 99). Despite this, the overturning of the presumption is "highly exceptional", see Article 29 Data Protection Working Party (2018), p. 9.

[48] Article 29 Data Protection Working Party (2018), p. 21.

[49] Kosta (2013), p. 390.

[50] Ibid., pp. 382–383. Art. 5(3) of the ePD, as modified by Directive 2009/136/EC, reads: "Member States shall ensure that the storing of information, or the gaining of access to information already stored, in the terminal equipment of a subscriber or user is only allowed on condition that the subscriber or user concerned has given his or her consent, having been provided with clear and comprehensive information, in accordance with Directive 95/46/EC, inter alia, about the purposes

The e-Privacy Directive defines consent, in Art. 2(f), by reference to the consent's definition enshrined in the Data Protection Directive, which has been repealed by Regulation (EU) 2016/679, that is, the GDPR. Therefore, this provision shall be read in conjunction with Art. 94 GDPR which stipulates that any reference to the repealed DPD shall be construed as references to the GDPR,[51] while Art. 95 GDPR prohibits the imposition of additional obligations in relation to processing governed by the e-PD. The Article 29 Working Party and several commentators evaluate this set of norms as to conclude that "the GDPR conditions for obtaining valid consent are applicable in situations falling within the scope of the e-Privacy Directive".[52]

However, according to Kosta, although the notion of consent should be understood in light of Article 4(11) GDPR, the specific requirements introduced in Article 7 GDPR should not apply in the electronic communications sector as they would create additional obligations, which would contradict the letter of Art. 95 GDPR. As a result, the reading of the two above-mentioned articles of the GDPR put the electronic communications operators in a quandary as to what standard to follow.[53] In 2019, the European Data Protection Board published an Opinion to clarify the interplay between the GDPR and the ePrivacy Directive where the processing triggers the material scope of both the legal instruments.[54]

In the Explanatory Memorandum to the Commission's Proposal for an ePrivacy Regulation, it is explicitly acknowledged that the "consent rule to protect the confidentiality of terminal equipment failed to reach its objectives as end-users face requests to accept tracking cookies without understanding their meaning and, in some cases, are even exposed to cookies being set without their consent".[55] Art. 9 of the Commission's Proposal is exclusively dedicated to 'consent' as the pivoting lawful grounds for the processing of electronic communications data. In particular, Art. 9(1) clarifies that not only the definition of but also the conditions for consent provided for under Art. 4(11) and 7 GDPR respectively apply.[56] This provision would arguably solve the conflict highlighted by Kosta.

Possibly the biggest point of contention in the trilogue negotiations between the European co-legislators pivoted around the broadening of the legal basis for the processing of electronic communications data so to include legitimate interest. Under the Croatian Presidency, the Council adopted a draft resolution that

---

of the processing. This shall not prevent any technical storage or access for the sole purpose of carrying out the transmission of a communication over an electronic communications network, or as strictly necessary in order for the provider of an information society service explicitly requested by the subscriber or user to provide the service".

[51] Art. 94 GDPR.

[52] Article 29 Data Protection Working Party (2018), p. 4; Bygrave and Tosoni (2020), p. 178.

[53] Kosta (2020), p. 348.

[54] EDPB (2019).

[55] European Commission, 'Explanatory Memorandum of the Proposal for the ePrivacy Regulation', p. 5.

[56] The Parliament draft version of the ePrivacy Regulation would remove the explicit reference to Articles 4(11) and 7 of the GDPR from the wording of Art. 9(1) ePR.

introduced the legitimate interest pursued by an electronic communications service or network provider and by a service provider as lawful grounds for the processing of electronic communication *metadata* (Art. 6b(1)(e); Recitals 17b and 17c) and to *use processing and storage capabilities of terminal equipment* or to *collect information* from an end-user's terminal equipment (Art. 8(1)(g); Recitals 21b and 21c) respectively. Eventually, the Council Proposal adopted in January 2021 under the German Presidency deleted those references, in line with the Opinion of the Article 29 Working Party.[57]

To tackle some of the inherent challenges stemming from the overvaluation of consent with regard to the use of information stored in and related to end-users' terminal equipment (including IoT devices), the EDPB suggested that the new Art. 4a of the Council Proposal on consent (former Art. 9 of the Commission Proposal) should "go further and oblige browsers and operating systems to put in place a user friendly and effective mechanism allowing controllers to obtain consent, in order to create a level playing field between all actors[.] Privacy settings should preserve the right to the protection of personal data and the integrity of terminals of users by default and should facilitate expressing and withdrawing consent in an easy, binding and enforceable manner against all parties".[58]

In this respect, Articles 9(2) and 10 of the Parliament draft seem to offer a higher threshold of protection, in line with the conclusions of the EDPB: the technical settings of a software placed on the market permitting electronic communications, through which the user may consent to the use of processing and storage capabilities, as well as the collection of information from end-users' terminal equipment (Art. 8(1)(b)), shall be binding for, and enforceable against any other party.[59] Moreover, the software's settings shall provide by design the option to prevent other parties from making use of the information under scrutiny and shall offer the option to opt out from cross-device tracking.[60] Lastly, the privacy settings shall be presented as to allow the end-user to take a fully informed decision and shall be easily accessible and modifiable during the use of the terminal equipment or software.[61]

However, the fast-evolving electronic communications sector and the increasing pervasiveness of online environments led to both an *under* and *over*-valuation of consent, as stressed by Kosta. On the one hand, "the lack of direct communication [between the data subject and the data controller] renders it even more difficult to ensure that the data subject has been duly informed before the provision of his consent and the provided consent is freely given, uninfluenced from any negative forces. The reliance on privacy policies in online transactions that are often used for construing the consent of the users is questionable. The example of privacy policies illustrates that the mere reliance on consent often constitutes *under*-valuation of

57 Article 29 Data Protection Working Party (2017), p. 7.

58 EDPB (2021), p. 3.

59 Art. 9(2) Parliament ePrivacy Proposal.

60 Art. 10(1) Parliament ePrivacy Proposal.

61 Art. 10(2) Parliament ePrivacy Proposal.

consent. The safeguarding of the privacy of the individuals should be complemented by a balance and proportionality test between the legitimate interest of the data controller that he wishes to serve via the obtaining of the user consent on the one hand and the privacy of the users on the other".[62]

On the other hand, "Art. 5(3) of the ePrivacy Directive seems to imply that the average user is able to understand the threats that are posed to his privacy by the installation and use of cookies and similar techniques and is able to make informed decisions on how to address them. However, the choice of the ePrivacy Directive to rely only on the consent of the data subject can be seen as an *over*-valuation of consent. The sole reliance on consent does not safeguard the protection of the privacy of the individual and should not be treated in itself as sufficient to legitimise all actions that infringe it. It should be complemented by a strict proportionality test in order to define the extent to which the providers can install cookies and collect information via them".[63] In this respect, consent appears in practice as the 'silver bullet' to *lawfully* circumvent otherwise illegitimate data processing.[64]

The above is all the more true in the field of IoT devices, where several legal expert commentators have already shed light on the *low-quality consent* that characterises the interaction between the users and their devices.[65] The typical hurdles of clicking/swiping and reading verbose and barely comprehensible privacy policies asking for consent are exacerbated by the inherent architectural complexity of IoT devices, bundling together almost invisible and always 'awake' sensors, actuators and networks (see Chap. 2).

"Even where formally having been given some form of a 'notice' and opportunity to 'consent' to general terms and conditions, individuals often find themselves inside a system designed to maximise the monetisation of personal data, which leaves no real choice or control to individuals".[66] Following this line of reasoning, Noto La Diega eventually comes to the conclusion that "consent can hardly be regarded as informed in most IoT scenarios, where users are unlikely to be aware of their Things' processing activities [...] This is also due to the fact that Things are ubiquitous and tend to disappear, while the relational black box makes it arduous to map the players involved in the data flows".[67]

To overcome or, at least, mitigate these deficiencies, organisational and technological tools may be designed to uphold individual privacy and data protection (e.g., Privacy Enhancing Technologies, PETs).[68] As regards the former, many IoT

---

[62] Kosta (2013), p. 391.

[63] Ibid., p. 393.

[64] Biega and Finck (2021), p. 52; Waldman (2021), p. 52.

[65] Pagallo et al. (2017), p. 64; Koolen (2021), p. 185.

[66] EDPS (2016), p. 5.

[67] Noto La Diega (2023), p. 242.

[68] ENISA (2017a); Bygrave and Schartum (2009); European Commission (2007). PETs have also been criticised by IT and legal scholars. For example, with regard to PETs' impacts on the principle of fairness, see Calvi et al. (2024).

resource-constrained devices present small screens, or none at all, with limited room for information: "a layered way of presenting information can be considered, where appropriate, to avoid excessive disturbance of user experience or product design".[69]

In terms of technological solutions, Koolen, among others, suggests a 'consent management platform' that would streamline the consent process in a IoT environment: "a dedicated software tool or an online page could be created where consumers can keep track of all smart devices that are present in their household, see information regarding privacy settings, and modify their consent vis-à-vis the collection of certain categories of personal data. It is imperative that such a digitally designed environment allows for ease of use".[70] The reading of the Parliament draft of the ePrivacy Regulation, in particular, having regard to Article 8, 9 and 10, in conjunction with the Statement of the EDPB, would indeed require the development of such solutions.

However, even if the data subject does not consent to some specific processing, the real lack of control over one's own information brought about by the IoT era precisely lies in those undertakings that are often still able to draw probabilistic inferences from other data collected from that same individual.[71] Moreover, from a legal perspective, a question that should be asked is why does the ePR refer so much to consent when consent has proven to be problematic for data subjects in the field of data protection[72]—as shown in this section.

This, in turn, brings us to the next legal challenge involving one core principle of EU data protection, that is, transparency. The obligation to provide the information related to the personal data processing in a transparent fashion is linked to consent in that there must always be information before there can be consent.[73] It is no coincidence that transparency mechanisms or tools (such as privacy icons) are often presented to substantiate the requirement of 'informed consent'.[74]

5.1.2 *Lack of Control and Information Asymmetry: IoT and Transparency*

Before engaging in the discussion on transparency in IoT from a European privacy and data protection perspective, a terminological point has to be made. The title used

---

[69] Article 29 Data Protection Working Party (2018), p. 14.

[70] Koolen (2021), p. 186.

[71] Ibid., p. 185.

[72] Jabłonowska and Michałowicz (2020).

[73] Opinion of Advocate General Szpunar in Case C-673/ 17, *Planet49 GmbH v Bundesverband der Verbraucherzentralen und Verbraucherverbände—Verbraucherzentrale Bundesverband e.V.*, delivered on 21 March 2019, ECLI:EU:C:2019:246, para. 112. See also Van Eecke and Haie (2019).

[74] Tamò-Larrieux (2018), p. 155.

for the present section, i.e. 'lack of control and information asymmetry' hinges on the first legal challenge identified by the Article 29 Working Party in the above-mentioned Opinion on the IoT. The Working Party puts forward the issue of users' control over their own data in terms of whether or not the collection and processing of their data has been made in a *transparent* manner or not.[75]

This, in turn, reflects systemic information asymmetry between users and IoT stakeholders (e.g., device manufacturers, APIs developers, generic third parties, and IoT data platforms, regardless of whether they qualify as data controllers),[76] as the former are often unaware of what data, for what purpose(s), and for how long is extracted by the latter: "in the absence of the possibility to effectively control how objects interact or to be able to define virtual boundaries by defining active or non-active zones for specific things, it will become extraordinarily difficult to control the generated flow of data".[77]

Even though transparency is an essential feature of ownership, this section avoids questions regarding the ownership of data generated by IoT devices,[78] debates on data ownership in the EU[79] and power asymmetries between data subjects and corporate data users.[80] Related to the issue of power imbalance between parties with asymmetric resources and control, this section will neither dwell too extensively on the problematic joint-controllership role of consumers/prosumers of domestic IoT devices and the legal uncertainties arising thereof.[81] This, in particular, is part of a broader coherence problem of EU data protection law—addressed in this Chapter albeit from other angles—that is, the fair allocation of appropriate responsibilities to the right actors under the current regime, by questioning on a contextual basis which role each of the parties taking part to the processing is *actually* playing, and which duties each actor should respect accordingly.

Against the background of market and information asymmetries between IoT manufacturers and IoT users, in 2023 the Data Act entered into force.[82] The Data Act is another pillar of the EU strategy for data[83] (February 2020), as it integrates and

---

[75] Article 29 Data Protection Working Party (2014a), p. 6.

[76] Tamò-Larrieux (2018), p. 63.

[77] Article 29 Data Protection Working Party (2014a), p. 6.

[78] Noto La Diega (2023), pp. 68–115. See also Janeček (2018); Farkas (2017); De Franceschi and Lehmann (2015); Wolfert et al. (2017); Drexl (2017).

[79] Malgieri (2016), p. 133; Purtova (2012); Purtova (2011); Van Erp (2017).

[80] Prainsack (2019).

[81] Chen et al. (2020).

[82] Regulation (EU) 2023/2854 of the European Parliament and of the Council of 13 December 2023 on harmonised rules on fair access to and use of data and amending Regulation (EU) 2017/2394 and Directive (EU) 2020/1828.

[83] European Commission, A European Strategy for Data COM(2020) 66 final.

complement the GDPR, the Open Data Directive[84] and the Data Governance Act.[85] The Data Act aims *inter alia* to give users access to data generated by them, which is often exclusively harvested by manufacturers; and to share such data with third parties to provide aftermarket or other data-driven innovative services.[86] Even though the Data Act falls outside the scope of this investigation, it is worth mentioning that the regulation's goal to unleashing the potential of information to be extracted from IoT data needs to be streamlined with the EU *acquis* in the field of personal data protection.[87]

'Lack of control and information asymmetry' might also implicate a wide debate on the notion of *group privacy* and *collective data protection.*[88] Although it does not form the subject of this Chapter, as IoT systems' personal data processing increasingly 'belongs to' clusters of individuals, this topic looms in the background. "Individuals are more often targeted as a member of a group, whereas they can even ignore being a part of that group on the basis of a set of ontological and epistemological predicates that cluster people into multiple categories".[89]

This leaves many issues open: how should we grasp the definition of group? What kind of right should the law grant a group? Pagallo et al. elaborate on the ECtHR seminal case in EU data retention field *Big Brother Watch and others v. UK* to assert the existence in EU law of "a procedural right to a judicial remedy against governments and states in the sphere of private life, i.e. on the basis of personal damage suffered by some individuals, such as the applicants and members of the group".[90] According to the authors, this view is reflected in the rationale underpinning Articles 80(1) and 80(2) GDPR: "[S]ince the data subject can be targeted and her privacy infringed due to her membership in a given (racial, ethnic, genetic, etc.) data group, it makes sense to grant such a group, or "anybody, organisation or association which aims to protect data subjects' rights and interests," a procedural right to a judicial remedy against the data controllers, processors or supervisory authorities".[91]

As seen in Chap. 3, European legal systems traditionally address, by proxy, data protection as *transparency,* whereas privacy is generally understood as a 'tool for *opacity*'.[92] The transparency principle is explained in Recital 39 GDPR[93] and

[84] Directive (EU) 2019/1024 of the European Parliament and of the Council of 20 June 2019 on open data and the re-use of public sector information.

[85] Regulation (EU) 2022/868 of the European Parliament and of the Council of 30 May 2022 on European data governance and amending Regulation (EU) 2018/1724 (Data Governance Act).

[86] Regulation (EU) 2023/2854, recital 5.

[87] EDPB-EDPS (2022); Graef and Husovec (2022); Kerber (2022).

[88] Mantelero (2017); Pagallo (2017a).

[89] Pagallo et al. (2017), p. 67.

[90] Ibid., p. 69.

[91] Ibid., p. 70.

[92] De Hert and Gutwirth (2006), p. 62; Pagallo et al. (2017), p. 62.

[93] Recital 39 GDPR: "It should be transparent to natural persons that personal data concerning them are collected, used, consulted or otherwise processed and to what extent the personal data are or will be processed. The principle of transparency requires that any information and communication

Recital 58 further illustrates its scope and relevance vis-à-vis increasing digitisation, where the IoT is only one element of a more complex picture.

On the one hand, *transparency* "requires that any information addressed to the public or to the data subject be concise, easily accessible and easy to understand, and that clear and plain language and, additionally, where appropriate, visualisation be used".[94] On the other hand, the Regulation acknowledges that "the proliferation of actors and the technological complexity of practice make it difficult for the data subject to know and understand whether, by whom and for what purpose personal data relating to him or her are being collected, such as in the case of online advertising".[95]

Furthermore, in a specific advertising context, that is, real-time bidding (RTB), some authors argue that core GDPR requirements including *inter alia* the transparency principle and informed consent are irreconcilable with the fundamental functioning of RTBs.[96]

Article 5(1)(a) GDPR states that personal data must be processed in a transparent manner in relation to the data subject, while Art. 12(1) mandates that the data controller has to take appropriate measures to provide any information to the data subject, either whether personal data are collected from the data subject or have not been obtained from him/her (Articles 13 and 14 GDPR respectively),[97] and any communication under Articles 15 to 22 and 34 relating to processing *in a concise, transparent, intelligible and easily accessible form, using clear and plain language*, in particular for any information addressed specifically to a child.

In that respect, the rationale of Art. 12 is to provide for procedural provisions—and not substantive rights—to inform and regulate the information flow between controllers and data subjects as regards the underlying personal data processing: data

---

relating to the processing of those personal data be easily accessible and easy to understand, and that clear and plain language be used".

[94] Recital 58 GDPR.

[95] Ibid.

[96] Veale et al. (2022), p. 19.

[97] De Terwangne (2020), p. 315: the author notes that certain aspects of Articles 12–14 are more connected to the fariness requirement.

subjects' substantive rights, notably the right of access to personal data,[98] "can serve their purpose only if supported by clear, proportionate and effective procedures".[99]

As mentioned earlier, the ePrivacy Directive applies to IoT devices insofar as they qualify as 'terminal equipment'.[100] Albeit the principle of transparency is not explicitly enshrined in the Directive as in the GDPR, Articles 5(3), 6(4) and 9 ePD add important provisions in terms of transparency obligations for undertakings in the field of IoT devices.

In particular, Art. 5(3) ePD mandates that in order to store or access information already stored in users' terminal equipment, providers must give users clear and comprehensive information about the purposes of the processing. Such disclosure is prodromal to consent.[101] Moreover, as regards the processing of metadata, Articles 6(4) and 9(1) ePD stipulate that providers must inform the users of the types of *traffic* and *location data* that are processed, of the duration of such processing and whether the (location) data will be transmitted to a third party, prior to obtaining the consent of users or subscribers.

When it comes to the Proposal for an ePrivacy Regulation, Art. 8—dealing with the protection of information stored in and related to end-users' terminal equipment – paragraph 2, letter b, mandates that "a clear and prominent notice is displayed informing of, at least, the modalities of the collection, its purpose, the person responsible for it and the other information required under Article 13 of Regulation (EU) 2016/679 where personal data are collected, as well as any measure the end-user of the terminal equipment can take to stop or minimise the collection".[102] Importantly, the information may be provided through *standardised icons* to give a meaningful account of the processing in a "easily visible, intelligible and clearly legible manner".[103]

---

[98] European courts have ruled on information and access rights in multiple cases. As regards the CJEU, see *inter alia* Case C-131/12, *Google Spain v Agencia Española de Protección de Datos (AEPD) and Mario Costeja González* [2014] ECLI:EU:C:2014:317; Joined Cases C-141/12 and C-372/12, *YS v Minister voor Immigratie, Integratie en Asiel and Minister voor Immigratie, Integratie en Asiel v M and S* [2014] ECLI:EU:C:2014:2081; Case C-486/ 12, *X* [2013] ECLI: EU:C:2013:836. As regards the ECtHR, it should be noted that the ECHR lacks a provision that define and regulates the exercise of access and information rights. However, the Court consistently implies that information and access rights are core components of Art. 8 ECHR and other fundamental rights. See, *ex multis,* ECtHR, 18 May 2010, (Application no 26839/ 05) *Kennedy v United Kingdom*; ECtHR, 25 September 2012, (Application no. 33783/ 09), *Godelli v Italy*; ECtHR, 4 December 2015, (Application no. 47143/ 06), *Roman Zakharov v Russia.*

[99] Polčák (2020), p. 401.

[100] Koolen (2021), p. 178.

[101] Art. 5(3) ePD: "[. . .] the subscriber or user concerned has given his or her consent, *having been provided* with clear and comprehensive information".

[102] Art. 8(2)(b) ePrivacy Regulation Proposal; recital 20 ePrivacy Regulation. This provision will be further addressed in Sect. 4.3.2 with regard to a possible lowering of the level of protection accorded by the GDPR.

[103] Art. 8(3) ePrivacy Regulation Proposal.

As regards the processing of electronic communications data, i.e. coupling together content and metadata, the Commission's Proposal does not explicitly lay down a transparency obligation: as seen in the previous section, providers of electronic communications services may process metadata, among the various legal grounds, if the end-users concerned have given their *consent* to the processing of their communications metadata for *one or more specified purposes,* provided that the purposes under scrutiny could not be achieved through anonymisation techniques.[104] Conversely, a transparency requirement can be tracked having regard to the information that undertakings shall provide to end-users for privacy settings and options: the software has to inform end-users about the privacy settings options and require the end-users' consent to a setting afterwards.[105]

Despite the existence of these instruments—while waiting the ePrivacy Regulation, IoT systems render a fully-fledged application of the principle of transparency rather challenging due to (i) architectural constraints; (ii) multiple and hardly traceable data flows; (iii) multiple actors involved in the processing.

To overcome these challenges, legal and technical literature have proposed to employ 'transparency tools'. These solutions typically combine technical measures with design features. Article 12(7) GDPR and Article 8(3) of the Commission's ePrivacy Regulation Proposal set forth a possibility for data controllers and service providers respectively to comply with their obligation to inform data subjects *via* 'standardised icons' that should help (and empower) the data subject in visualising the privacy setting from the outset of the data processing life cycle.

Icons, however, are just one of the "multiple additional options for how a controller can inform data subjects besides textual or spoken form. Thus, a controller can also use pictures or other forms of expression that are not standardised icons under Article 12(7) GDPR if these alternative means of expression provide for 'concise, transparent, intelligible and easily accessible' information".[106]

Thus, privacy certificates or labels (similarly to cybersecurity labels, see Sect. 4.2.1) address the need to verify that data controllers' processing operations comply with the relevant legal standards.[107] "Once verified, a product or service provider can post the certificate icon in order to publicly indicate that the company adheres to the standards of the certification authority".[108]

Push notifications are yet another fitting example suggested by scholars to present information in a clear and short fashion.[109] "If a consumer issued a voice command to his smart speaker, a notification could show up on his phone immediately

[104] Art. 6(2)(c) ePrivacy Regulation Proposal.

[105] Art. 10(2) ePrivacy Regulation Proposal.

[106] Polčák (2020), p. 410.

[107] Railean and Reinhardt (2018); Railean and Reinhardt (2021); van Diermen (2018); Shen and Vervier (2019).

[108] Tamò-Larrieux (2018), p. 137.

[109] Rosner and Kenneally (2018), pp. 16–19.

afterwards, reminding the user of the voice analysis process that takes place in the background".[110]

Against this backdrop, it should be investigated whether existing IoT architectures provide technological solutions in terms of transparency. In 2018, Janeček answered in negative.[111] Without dwelling on empirical research over existing market solutions too extensively, three case-studies from IoT industry-leading companies can nonetheless be considered.

Apple Inc. deployed important privacy features intended to help users make more informed decisions about their personal data. In particular, through a feature called the 'Privacy Nutrition Label', Apple requires every app—including its own—to provide users with a standardised, easy-to-view overview of the developer's data processing practices. The label give users key information about how an app uses their data—including whether the data is used to track them, linked to them, or not linked to them. Moreover, another feature, namely the 'App Tracking Transparency', "will require apps to get the user's permission before tracking their data across apps or websites owned by other companies. Under 'Settings', users will be able to see which apps have requested permission to track and make changes as they see fit".[112]

In 2021, Samsung also highlighted its commitment towards transparency in the context of smart devices' data processing. "Consumers, developers and partners are given the information needed to make decisions about how data is managed. The company offers users the option to review and manage their permissions from privacy setting on their Galaxy devices and Smart TVs and discloses Samsung's privacy policies through the Privacy Portal. Going forward, Samsung will collaborate with global security experts while continuing to release open-source security analysis tools to make its ecosystems more secure".[113]

Lastly, Xiaomi published an 'IoT users' privacy white paper', with the aim of casting light on the data protection practices of the company. In the white paper, Xiaomi breaks down data collections details and specific privacy & data protection features for six IoT products and three associated mobile applications with a view to enabling customers to develop a full understanding of how the company collect, use, and store data.[114]

In conclusion, transparency enhancing tools (TETs), deploying models such as 'privacy information management systems' (PIMS) or 'personal data management systems' (PDMS), may help in rebalancing the information asymmetry between

[110] Koolen (2021), p. 182.

[111] Janeček (2018), p. 1046.

[112] Apple, 'Data Privacy Day at Apple: Improving transparency and empowering users' (2021) Press release, available at < https://www.apple.com/hk/en/newsroom/2021/01/data-privacy-day-at-apple-improving-transparency-and-empowering-users/>.

[113] Samsung, 'Samsung Unveils Solutions for a New Era of Connected Experiences at SDC 21' (2021) Press release <https://news.samsung.com/us/samsung-sdc-2021-solutions-connected-experiences/>.

[114] Xiaomi, 'Xiaomi IoT Privacy White Paper' (2021) <https://trust.mi.com/>.

consumers (i.e., data subjects) and digital market companies by providing the former with actual means to deal with the processing of their personal data and, therefore, to fully exercise the rights granted by the GDPR.[115] As stated in the previous section, technical solutions such as user-friendly dashboards, which would display the information relevant to the data processing in a layered structure, also through the adoption of push notifications, would help to overcome inherent hurdles of the IoT ecosystem. These technical solutions would benefit both data subjects and digital providers.

On the other hand, counterarguments can be raised against a theory envisioning transparency as an effective means of mitigating power asymmetries between IoT organizations and individuals. Thus, critical literature has pointed out that transparency measures facilitate specific ways of disclosure (i.e., a company decides what to render 'transparent' and what not in light of its own interest), which, in turn, "always produce new types, forms, or levels of opacity".[116] Related to that, another problematic aspect vis-à-vis individual self-determination that is weaponised by transparency is the fact that GDPR transparency requirements simply operated on a 'formal' rather than 'substantial' level. In other words, companies might even render available legible information on the legitimacy of their processing practices, without however making any significant changes to those practices.[117]

Against this backdrop, the abovementioned technical and organisational means implementing the transparency principle (e.g., TETs), as opposed to 'simpler' and more standardised transparency practices (e.g., privacy notices or cookie banners) that have been criticised in terms of efficacy, have the potential to enhance awareness over complex data processing, including storage, transmission and profiling. More users' empowerment will be the main consequence. From being passive subjects in the 'data economy', users will have the chance to undertake a more proactive role in managing the data environment that surround and concern them. Market players, on the other hand, will benefit from a more meaningful compliance posture with the EU data protection legal framework.

5.1.3 *Lack of Adequate Security Controls: Eschewing the Scenario of an 'Internet of Insecure Things'*

The last legal challenge identified by the Article 29 Working Party hinges on the upward trend of information and network security risks raised, in particular, by resource-constrained devices. Section 2.2 already pointed out that many IoT devices may not have the computational power to run powerful and robust encryption algorithms.

[115] Bernes (2022), p. 200.

[116] Schade (2023), p. 481.

[117] Sanchez-Rola et al. (2019); Urban et al. (2018).

The Working Party explicitly states that "most of the sensors currently present on the market are not capable of establishing an encrypted link for communications since the computing requirements will have an impact on a device limited by low-powered batteries".[118] There is an urgent need therefore to develop security, privacy and data protection technical solutions for data at rest or in transit in constrained connected environments as well as secure mechanisms for horizontal handover.[119] In this respect, Sect. 2.2 shed light on the present discussion surrounding lightweight cryptographic standards and protocols for IoT resource-constrained devices.[120].

Art. 32 GDPR mandates that controllers and processors implement appropriate technical and organisational measures to ensure a level of security appropriate to the risk, taking into account the state of the art, the costs of implementation and the nature, scope, context and purposes of processing as well as the risk of varying likelihood and severity for the rights and freedoms of individuals. Importantly, encryption is explicitly listed in Art. 32 GDPR as a security (technical) measure that controllers and processors should implement 'as appropriate'.[121]

Albeit the deployment of encryption protocols is not *per se* mandatory, "Article 32 express a clear preference for them, making it likely that regulators will expect data controllers and processors to use them whenever possible".[122] In this respect, the CJEU on 14 December 2023 rendered a judgement *inter alia* on the interpretation of Art. 32.[123] The Court was asked by the Bulgarian Supreme Administrative Court five questions for a preliminary ruling seeking clarification on the conditions for awarding compensation for non-material damage in favour of a data subject whose personal data, held by a public agency, were unlawfully published on the internet as a result of a cyberattack. Thus, the person whose data were breached grounded the compensation claim on the mere fear of a possible misuse of such data in the future.

For the purpose of this book, however, this case is noteworthy for it is the first ruling of the CJEU specifically addressing GDPR's information security requirements laid down in Arts 32, 24 and 5(1)(f). In particular, the Court was expected to cast light on what the subject matter and scope of the judicial review of legality in the examination should be as to whether the technical and organisational measures implemented by the controller are appropriate pursuant to Article 32 of Regulation (EU) 2016/679.

---

[118] Article 29 Data Protection Working Party (2014a), p. 9.

[119] ENISA (2017b), p. 66; Shackelford (2020), pp. 71–72.

[120] Zeadally et al. (2021), pp. 6–7; Rizvi et al. (2020), p. 100240.

[121] Tamò-Larrieux (2018), p. 170: "Art. 32 relies on common terms from computer science, such as confidentiality, integrity, and availability, with which developers are familiar. Additionally, it broadens the scope of "security" by elaborating on pseudonymization or restoring availability and access after an incident. It thus provides broader guidance to data controllers while remaining technology- neutral".

[122] Burton (2020), p. 636.

[123] Case C-340/21 *VB v Natsionalna agentsia za prihodite*, ECLI:EU:C:2023:986.

On 27 April 2023, the AG Pitruzzella delivered its Opinion on the Case C-340/21 holding that the 'appropriateness' test of the technical and organisational measures must occur on a case-by-case basis taking into account the nature, scope, context and purposes of the processing as well as the likelihood and severity of the risks to the rights and freedoms of individuals.[124] In the preliminary observations, the AG highlights the correlation and complementarity between Arts. 32, 24, 5(2) and 5(1)(f) GDPR[125]—confirming the line of reasoning that will be outlined in Sect. 6.1.1.

In particular, the role of the accountability principle is reinforced in the context of choosing the appropriate technical and organisational cybersecurity measures.[126] Related to that, the AG tried to elaborate on the particularly problematic 'state-of-the-art' criterion: "the technological level of measures to be implemented is limited to what is reasonably possible at the time the measures are implemented: the suitability of the measure to prevent the risk must therefore be proportionate to the solutions that the state of the art in science, technique, technology and research offers at the time, also taking into account, as will be seen, the implementation costs".[127] Moreover, "measures may be 'appropriate' at a given time and, despite that, be circumvented by cybercriminals using highly sophisticated tools that are capable of breaching even security measures that are in accordance with the state of the art".[128]

Interestingly, in light of the 'costs of implementation' criterion, the AG stipulates that the assessment of cybersecurity measures' appropriateness "must be based on a balancing exercise between the interests of the data subject, which generally tend towards a higher level of protection, and the economic interests and technological capacity of the controller, which sometimes tend towards a lower level of protection".[129]

Finally, the last point that should be highlighted is the fact that a security breach as such does not necessarily constitute in itself proof of the inappropriateness of the technical and organisational cybersecurity measures adopted by the controller.[130]

Against this background, the Court held that national courts cannot infer from the occurrence of a data breach, being it an unauthorised disclosure of or access to personal data, that the cybersecurity measures implemented by the controller were not appropriate.[131] Thus, the Court endorses the conclusions of the AG: GDPR's obligations, including the ones related to technical and organisational (cybersecurity) measures, are obligations of means, rather than result. A data breach must not lead to conclude that the controller failed to comply with the legislation.

---

[124] Opinion of AG Pitruzzella delivered on 27 April 2023, Case C-340/21 *VB v Natsionalna agentsia za prihodite*, ECLI:EU:C:2023:353.

[125] Ibid., para. 20–25.

[126] Ibid., para. 23 and 31.

[127] Ibid., para. 32.

[128] Ibid., para. 33.

[129] Ibid., para. 36.

[130] Ibid., para. 37.

[131] Case C-340/21 *VB v Natsionalna agentsia za prihodite*, para. 39.

Secondly, with regard to the appropriateness test of the technical and organisational measures to be implemented by the controller, the Court held that cybersecurity measures as per Article 32 GDPR must be assessed by national courts in a concrete manner, "by taking into account the risks associated with the processing concerned and by assessing whether the nature, content and implementation of those measures are appropriate to those risks".[132] Again, the Court confirms the AG's stance, even though the latter shed more light on how to operationalise somewhat 'abstract' legal concepts and market-driven standards such as 'state-of-the-art'.

Finally, for the purpose of this chapter, the Court addressed the question whether the controller has the burden of proving that the cybersecurity measures it implemented are appropriate against the background of Article 32 GDPR. Not surprisingly, the Court held that the burden of proof lies with the controller, in line with the principle of accountability.[133] All in all, the value of this judgement rests in the acknowledgment of the fundamental importance of a strong cybersecurity culture in and for data protection, somewhat echoing an *infraethical* perspective (see Chap. 3).

We should now turn our attention to the ePrivacy legal framework. Whereas the ePrivacy Directive contains a specific provision on the 'security of processing'—as amended by Directive 2009/136/EC, the ePrivacy Regulation Proposal does not specifically address matters concerning the processing of personal data in order to ensure alignment with the GDPR which—as already mentioned—would be applicable as *lex generalis*.[134]

Thus, the revision of the ePD of 2009 added several paragraphs to Art. 4 specifying, on the one hand, the objectives of the (security) technical measures[135] and, on the other hand, notification duties for the provider of publicly available electronic communications services in the case of personal data breaches.

With a view to promoting a coherent framework, the proposed Regulation makes reference to Article 32 GDPR with regard to the protection of information stored in and related to end-users' terminal equipment.[136] Thus, the ePrivacy Regulation covers (network) security risks and provides for an obligation upon providers of electronic communications services to alert end-users in the event of a particular risk that may compromise the security of networks and services. In the Commission Proposal, Art. 17 postulates that providers of electronic communications services shall inform end-users of risks that may compromise the security of networks and

[132] Ibid., para. 47.

[133] Ibid., para. 57.

[134] European Commission, 'Explanatory Memorandum of the Proposal for the ePrivacy Regulation' (2017), p. 2.

[135] Ensuring the authentication principle, protecting personal data stored or transmitted against accidental or unlawful destruction, loss or alteration, and unauthorised or unlawful storage, processing, access or disclosure and ensuring the implementation of security policies.

[136] Art. 8(2) ePrivacy Regulation Proposal.

underlying services. If the risk cannot be mitigated by the measures to be taken by the provider, the latter shall inform end-users of any possible remedies. Whilst the Council deletes this provision from the Commission's draft, Parliament amends it heavily.

The first problematic aspect that needs to be considered is the likely overlap with the NISD and especially NIS2 notification duties, which may create duplicative requirements resulting therefore in legal uncertainty. The Parliament's amendment specifying that Art. 17 ePR should be without prejudice to the obligations provided for in Directive (EU) 2016/1148 is too vague; the EU co-legislators should, in that regard, ensure effective alignment with the NIS2 relevant provisions to strengthen legal coherence between the Union acts of the Digital Single Market.

Furthermore, it is explicitly stressed that providers shall ensure the confidentiality, integrity and protection against unauthorised access to the electronic communications data, either in transmission or stored, by means of "cryptographic methods including end-to-end encryption of the electronic communications data. When encryption of electronic communications data is used, decryption by anybody else than the user shall be prohibited".[137]

Importantly, the Parliament also warns Member States against the "weakening of the confidentiality and integrity of their networks and services or the terminal equipment, including the encryption methods used"[138] by imposing obligations on either electronic communications service providers or software manufacturers. The stance adopted by the European Parliament against the weakening of cryptographic methods (e.g., end-to-end encryption), will be assessed against the background of the so-called '*crypto-wars*' or 'encryption debate' which still animates the public debate.[139] Section 5.3 will shed further light on the policy debates regarding encryption.

Moreover, the Parliament draft places a second negative obligation on providers of electronic communications services, providers of information society services, and manufacturers of software permitting the retrieval and presentation of information on the internet: these entities must refrain from preventing users and subscribers from applying the best available techniques against intrusions and interceptions and to secure their networks, terminal equipment and electronic communications.[140]

All in all, it remains to be seen whether the Parliament's clear stand against the weakening of encryption has to prevail in the ePrivacy Regulation trilogue negotiations. Related to that, the next section will focus on cryptographic methods, from a multidisciplinary perspective, that is, technical and legal.

[137] Art. 17(1a) Parliament Proposal.

[138] Id.

[139] Koops and Kosta (2018); Ziccardi (2018).

[140] Art. 17(1b) Parliament ePrivacy Proposal.

5.2 The Role of Encryption Vis-à-Vis the Fundamental Rights to Privacy and Data Protection

This section hinges on the relationship between various cryptographic tools, having regard, but not limited to, encryption, and the traditional legal disciplines of privacy and data protection. Cryptographic techniques are crucial, as already explained throughout this book, to ensure adequate IoT security. Thus, a convergence of privacy, data protection and *cybersecurity*—to be understood broadly to cover information security (see Chap. 3)—is particularly striking when it comes to cryptographic technologies, for they aim to ensure data confidentiality both in transit and at rest.

Art. 32 GDPR lists encryption and pseudonymisation among the cybersecurity measures that the controller must take into account when deciding—in line with the accountability principle and the risk-based approach—which measures to implement according to the risks to data subjects' rights and freedoms posed by the specific processing scenario. Before assessing the relationship between encryption and pseudonymisation, it is necessary to address, from a technical perspective, the foundations of the two cybersecurity & data protection measures primarily envisaged by Art. 32.

In Sect. 5.2.1, the technical analysis sheds light on the rationale of encryption which substantially differs from hashing and pseudonymisation, albeit the latter is generally achieved by means of cryptography, and why this distinction matters when it comes to uphold the fundamental rights to privacy and data protection. Afterwards, the legal analysis casts light—in Sect. 5.2.2—on whether and to what extent state-of-the-art encryption protocols challenge the already blurred distinction between personal and non-personal data, underpinning the EU data protection legal framework. Finally, in Sect. 5.2.3 the discussion considers the often-overlooked impact of encryption on *privacy,* in terms of infringement of the fundamental right it aims to protect.

5.2.1 The Quest for Encryption, Beyond Pseudonymisation: A Technical Perspective

Since the ancient times, individuals have always had the need to masquerade information. In this respect, cryptographic techniques have always been a means to guarantee information security, with first examples of cryptography dating back to ancient Egypt and ancient Rome (e.g., the Caesar cipher).[141] Back to the present day, our increasingly data-driven society has exacerbated this need.[142] And IoT resource-

[141] Dooley (2018); Davies (1997).

[142] Hernandez-Ramos et al. (2020).

constrained devices require encryption protocols suited to their storage and computational power capabilities in order to secure the data flow.[143]

EU privacy and data protection laws primarily rely on encryption to ensure the fundamental rights to privacy and protection of personal data on the one hand and, on the other hand, the data/information security principle. The European Data Protection Supervisor claimed that encryption is "natural mean for data protection, and for personal data protection as well: GDPR, in this sense, is reflecting a natural state".[144]

The concept of 'encryption' may be misleading, or too broad. Therefore, a typology of cryptographic techniques is in order. To start off, computer science literature historically makes a first distinction between symmetric and asymmetric encryption.

Symmetric or private-key cryptography came first. Using mathematical operations, this technique aims to hide the actual content of a message, by making the information unintelligible to anyone without the cryptographic key.[145] In this respect, it is a two-way function: what is encrypted, *via* an algorithm called a "cipher", can be decrypted with the proper key. The *plain text* becomes *cyphertext* after the mathematical process. it follows that, without the cryptographic key, no one can theoretically see the content of the message i.e., the plain text. Block ciphers are the most widely spread symmetric encryption algorithms.[146]

Building on symmetric-key techniques, cryptographic hash functions are mostly adopted in symmetric-key setting.[147] They are commonly referred to as one-way functions, that is, irreversible processes with the goal of "scrambling variable-size plain text to produce a unique fixed-size message digest (i.e. the message output)".[148] The primary requirement is to be 'collision resistant', whereby collision means two inputs corresponding to the same plain text. In recent years, the most widely used hash function has been the Secure Hash Algorithm (SHA), developed by the federal US Agency NIST.

On a general level, symmetric encryption differs from asymmetric encryption for the latter hinges on the adoption of two separate keys, whereas the former only adopts one key.[149] This approach rests on the possibility of widely distributing one

---

[143] Rayes and Salam (2019), p. 211; Marwedel (2021), pp. 191–193; Serpanos and Wolf (2018), pp. 59–81; Pagallo et al. (2017).

[144] Wiewiórowski (2020).

[145] Schneier (1995), p. 21.

[146] Katz and Lindell (2015), p. 77; Stallings and Brown (2018), p. 55: "a block cipher processes the plaintext input in fixed-size blocks and produces a block of ciphertext of equal size for each plaintext block. The algorithm processes longer plaintext amounts as a series of fixed-size blocks. The most important symmetric algorithms, all of which are block ciphers, are the Data Encryption Standard (DES), triple DES, and the Advanced Encryption Standard (AES)".

[147] Katz and Lindell (2015), p. 153.

[148] EDPS and AEPD (2019), pp. 8–10.

[149] Stallings and Brown (2018), p. 67.

key, the public key, while the other, the secret key, must be kept secured.[150] In the classical example, Alice wants to send a message to Bob. Alice encrypts a message with Bob's public key; Bob then uses his private key to decrypt the resulting ciphertext.

An advanced asymmetric cryptographic scheme is represented by *homomorphic encryption*, which has been referred to as the 'Swiss army knife' of cryptography due to its extreme versatility.[151] Broadly speaking, it refers to those schemes that perform computation on encrypted data. "Secure multiparty computation epitomises the promise of cryptography, performing the seemingly impossible magic trick of processing data without having access to it".[152] "In addition to the usual encryption and decryption procedures, these schemes have an evaluation procedure that takes ciphertexts encrypting x and a description of a function f, and returns an "evaluated ciphertext" that can be decrypted to obtain the value $f(x)$".[153]

In terms of confidentiality properties, it is worth noting that the evaluated ciphertext does not reveal f even to the owner of the (secret) key. As addressed in the next section, homomorphic encryption may solve many open issues in terms of privacy preservation in IoT environments.[154]

Conversely, pseudonymisation is a data protection measure explicitly foreseen by the GDPR[155] with a view to *reducing* risks to data subjects.[156] It hinges on the replacement of one or more personal data identifiers with so-called pseudonyms, provided that the link between the pseudonyms and the initial identifiers are *adequately* protected.[157]

EU data protection law relies on pseudonymisation as a technical measure that can support data protection by design (Art. 25 GDPR) and the security of personal data processing (Art. 32 GDPR). Thus, pseudonymisation has been widely acknowledged as a 'privacy enhancing technology'[158]: not only does it masquerade data subjects' identities, but it can also contribute towards important data protection principles such as data minimisation and data accuracy as data controllers and/or processors process 'real' information (contrary to synthetic data) without having access to the identities of the data subjects to whom the information relates.

---

[150] Brooks (2014), p. 100.

[151] Barak and Brakerski (2012).

[152] Halevi (2017), p. 219.

[153] Ibid., p. 220.

[154] ENISA (2022a), p. 14; Heinz et al. (2021), p. 176.

[155] Art. 4(5) GDPR: "the processing of personal data in such a manner that the personal data can no longer be attributed to a specific data subject without the use of additional information, provided that such additional information is kept separately and is subject to technical and organisational measures to ensure that the personal data are not attributed to an identified or identifiable natural person".

[156] Recital 28 GDPR.

[157] ENISA (2018).

[158] ENISA (2015, 2022a).

Pseudonymised data are still personal data and thus falling in scope of the GDPR precisely because the re-identification risk is only *reduced* but not eliminated. Although such measure avoids direct identification, Recital 26 GDPR[159] explicitly points at the personal nature of such data.

In 2019, ENISA dedicated a report to shed light on the 'basic' pseudonymisation techniques that are applied. These are: counter; random number generator (RNG); hash function; message authentication code (MAC); symmetric encryption.[160] A report from 2021 further discusses more advanced techniques that can provide more sophisticated pseudonymisation solutions in real world scenarios, such as asymmetric encryption and homomorphic encryption, secure multiparty computation, zero-knowledge proof, secret sharing schemes and chaining mode.[161]

A key takeaway from ENISA's report is that a risk-based and case-by-case approach is needed with regard to the choice of the correct pseudonymisation technique to implement, reflecting the spirit of the GDPR. The best possible technique should be selected to properly address and mitigate the relevant privacy & data protection risks for a specific processing scenario.

From the above, it follows that the relation link between pseudonymisation and encryption might be built upon a 'speciality criterion', based on the different scope and rationale.[162] First, cryptographic techniques, such as encryption, are effectively used *as* pseudonymisation techniques, but not the other way round. In the same vein as ENISA, among the most adopted pseudonymisation techniques, the Article 29 Working Party listed symmetric encryption, such as block ciphers (AES algorithms), hash function (either with stored or deleted key) and so-called pepper[163] or salted hash.[164]

Second, the rationale underpinning encryption is to potentially protect any kind and any size of data or information, resulting therefore in a broader scope than pseudonymisation. Thus, different encryption protocols follow the entire data flow to address either data at rest (storage encryption) or data in motion (transmission encryption).[165] Conversely, the scope of pseudonymisation only considers the personal identifiers.

---

[159] Mourby et al. (2018), p. 225.

[160] ENISA (2019), pp. 21–26.

[161] ENISA (2021), pp. 14–26.

[162] Chiara (2020), p. 172.

[163] Stallings and Brown (2018), p. 983: in cryptography, a pepper is a "random [and secret value] that is concatenated with a password before applying the one-way encryption function used to protect passwords that are stored in the database of an access control system". It differs from salt, since the latter is not secret (merely unique) and can be stored alongside the hashed output; Grassi et al. (2017), sec. 5.1.1.2: NIST does not make any formal difference between salt and pepper, by referring to both as salt. The pepper value recommended is at least 32 bits: the US agency assures that if the pepper value is kept secret, brute-force attacks on the hashed memorised secrets are impractical.

[164] Article 29 Data Protection Working Party (2014b), pp. 20–21.

[165] NIST (2007).

Third, another variable of this analysis is predicated on the semantic value of the resulting text after these techniques have been implemented. Unlike encryption, data that have been pseudonymised still provide some degree of legible information. As a result, a third party may still be able to understand the underlying semantic structure.[166] Related to that, it is worth noting that the GDPR deems pseudonymisation as an appropriate safeguard for any processing for scientific, historical or statistical purposes.[167]

5.2.2 *State-of-the-Art Encryption and Pseudonymisation: Is It Always About Personal Data?*

The GDPR only applies to personal data. Non-personal data therefore falls outside its scope. The legal classification of data is therefore a crucial issue as it determines whether the data processing entity is subject to the various obligations imposed by the Regulation. Yet the binary construction of the European data protection regime still does not fully provide the legal certainty that market players desire.[168]

As already mentioned in the previous section, Recital 26 GDPR explicitly states that pseudonymised data are personal data,[169] whereas it does not take a stance on personal data that have undergone cryptographic techniques, such as encryption. Thus, this section aims to assess the extent to which the distinction between personal and non-personal data is 'dynamic', in particular, taking into account state-of-the-art security measures such as encryption and pseudonymisation.[170]

The notion of non-personal data in EU data protection law is not clearly defined. The European Regulation for the free flow of non-personal data (FFDR)[171] provides for a negative definition i.e., "data other than personal data as referred to in Article 4(1) of Regulation (EU) 2016/679".[172] Therefore, it is necessary to turn our attention at Art. 4(1) GDPR, which states that 'personal data' is "any information relating to an identified or identifiable natural person ('data subject')".

The legal test to assess the 'identifiability criterion' underlying the GDPR's dichotomous architecture, that is, between personal and non-personal data, pivots

---

[166] ENISA (2018), p. 17.

[167] Art. 89, recital 156 GDPR.

[168] Case C-345/17, *Sergejs Buivids v. Datu valsts inspekcija* [2019] ECLI:EU:C:2019:122; C-604/22, *IAB Europe v. Gegevensbeschermingsautoriteit* [2024] ECLI:EU:C:2024:214.

[169] Recital 26 GDPR: "Personal data which have undergone pseudonymisation, which could be attributed to a natural person by the use of additional information should be considered to be information on an identifiable natural person".

[170] Schiffner et al. (2018), p. 28.

[171] Regulation (EU) 2018/1807 of the European Parliament and of the Council of 14 November 2018 on a framework for the free flow of non-personal data in the European Union.

[172] Art. 3 FFDR.

on Recital 26 GDPR: "[...] To determine whether a natural person is *identifiable*, account should be taken of *all the means reasonably likely to be used*, such as singling out, either *by the controller or by another person* to identify the natural person *directly or indirectly*. To ascertain whether means are reasonably likely to be used to identify the natural person, account should be taken of all objective factors, such as the costs of and the amount of time required for identification, taking into consideration the available technology at the time of the processing and technological developments. The principles of data protection should therefore not apply to anonymous information, namely information which does not relate to an identified or identifiable natural person or to personal data rendered anonymous in such a manner that the data subject is not or no longer identifiable [emphasis added]".

As a preliminary remark, it should be noted that non-personal data can be divided in two over-arching categories: data that have never been personal, i.e. not relating to an identified or identifiable person, or data that have been personal but were subsequently anonymised. Accordingly, it is possible to look at the categorization of data, i.e. whether personal or non-personal, from a *static* and a *dynamic* perspective. In particular, the latter takes into account "what kind of status modification data can have due to its lifecycle".[173]

Against this background, Recital 26 GDPR sets out the test to be performed to assess how different data processing techniques affect the binary distinction between personal and non-personal data. However, some tenets of Recital 26 created a state of uncertainty as to the interpretation to be given to core tenets of the test; it resulted in diverging views between supervisory authorities and legal scholars.

To establish the identifiability of a person, it is necessary to consider all the means that the controller or any third party may reasonably use to identify that natural person, either directly or indirectly. In order to ascertain the reasonable likelihood of using the means to identify the natural person, all objective factors should be considered, including the costs and time required for identification, taking into account both the technologies available at the time of processing and technological developments.

The test set out in Recital 26 of the GDPR essentially embraces a *dynamic* risk-based approach to determining whether the data is personal or not. Where there is a reasonable risk of identification, the data should be treated as personal data. Where, on the other hand, the risk is negligible, the data may be processed as non-personal data, even if identification cannot be excluded with absolute certainty.[174]

This contextual risk-based understanding of the test, and therefore of the Regulation, has met with resistance, especially in the so-called 'absolutist' stance[175] adopted by the Article 29 Working Party, which has been followed by some supervisory authorities, such as the French[176] and Irish Data Protection

[173] Podda and Palmirani (2021), p. 271.

[174] Finck and Pallas (2020), pp. 11–36.

[175] Kuner (2007), p. 92.

[176] Podda and Vigna (2021), p. 109; CNIL (2020).

Authorities.[177] This interpretation takes into account all the possibilities and occasions on which anyone would be able to identify the data subject. Whereas the GDPR only foresees the possibility of identifying ('singling out') individuals, the Working Party goes beyond the legal standard, for it adds to the re-identification test the criteria of (i) *linkability* of information relating to the individual in different datasets; and (ii) *inference* i.e., the possibility of deducing, with significant probability, the value of an attribute from the values of a set of other attributes.[178]

As a result, "even theoretical chances of combining data so that the individual is identifiable are included".[179] Seemingly developing its own 'zero-risk test', the Working Party seeks to equate anonymisation with erasure in terms of reversibility.[180] However, the flourishing literature on the non-absolute and *dynamic* character of anonymisation[181]—due to technical advancements—makes it difficult to defend the Working Party's interpretation.

By following the 'zero-risk test', we could not rely on widely used anonymisation techniques (such as k-anonymity or differential privacy[182]), since these do not—in absolute terms—exclude the risk of re-identification.[183] It follows that any information would always remain within the scope of the GDPR, making data protection law 'the law of everything'.[184] Therefore, when it comes to assessing cryptographic techniques, according to the absolute approach, if *anyone* is *theoretically* able to decrypt the dataset, then "the operations of the controller or processor using this encrypted data are subject to data protection legislation, even if they don't possess the key for decryption".[185]

Another interpretation of Recital 26, the so-called relativist reading, considers only the efforts that data controllers have to put in order to identify an individual, without entering the murky field of mere theoretical possibilities.[186] Several authors[187] and the UK Data Protection Authority, the Information Commissioner's Office (ICO), have argued that data resulting from anonymisation operations by

---

[177] Data Protection Commission (2019).

[178] Article 29 Data Protection Working Party (2014b), p. 3.

[179] Spindler and Schmechel (2016), p. 165.

[180] Article 29 Data Protection Working Party (2014b), p. 6.

[181] Ohm (2009); Sweeney (2000); Narayanan and Shmatikov (2008).

[182] Pagallo (2017b), p. 37. The author states that Apple mastered such techniques in order to process health data for statistical purposes, to which the GDPR's regime does not apply. In particular, having regard to the anonymisation process for statistical purposes, see EDPS (2017a, b); Graef et al. (2020), p. 613: "even when organisations are only in possession of aggregate statistical data and the initial identifiers have been destroyed, such data might still be considered personal depending upon whether it has been subjected to anonymisation techniques, and whether the latter are considered adequate".

[183] ENISA (2022a), pp. 10–13; Gellert (2018).

[184] Purtova (2018); Gellert (2021).

[185] Spindler and Schmechel (2016), p. 165.

[186] Ibid., p. 166.

[187] Esayas (2015).

means of cryptographic techniques should not be considered personal if two requirements are met: the cryptographic method must be robust and up-to-date and the controller is not in possession of the decryption key, nor is there any reasonable possibility for them to obtain the key.[188]

In particular, the ICO did not seemingly change its view from the 2012 guidance. In the draft report on anonymisation and pseudonymisation of 2021—to be published in 2022 after a public consultation—the DPA explicitly confirms the 'relativist' approach by stating that "the same information can be personal data to one organisation, but anonymous information in the hands of another organisation. Its status depends greatly on its circumstances, both from your perspective and in the context of its disclosure".[189]

Besides the potential applications in the field of cloud computing,[190] when applied to cryptography, this approach would lead to interesting results.[191] If the cryptographic method adopted is suited to the data processing at stake and up-to-date and the data controller is either not in possession of the decryption key or has no reasonable chances of obtaining the key, then the data which result from that processing should not be considered as personal data.[192]

Interestingly, the Working Party arguably shared this line of reasoning in the 2007 'Opinion on the concept of personal data': if appropriate technical measures such as irreversible hashing have been put in place, "even if identification of certain data subjects may take place despite all those protocols and measures (due to unforeseeable circumstances such as accidental matching of qualities of the data subject that reveal his/her identity), the information processed by the original controller may not be considered to relate to identified or identifiable individuals taking account of all the means likely reasonably to be used by the controller or by any other person".[193] The conflict between the two Opinions of the Working Party 29 is real, and all bear witness to the complexity of the arguments at stake.

However, the most convincing position is the one based on the risk approach, which inspired the Regulation and has been confirmed by the CJEU, which seems to have distanced itself from the *YS*[194] jurisprudence.[195] In the seminal *Breyer* case,[196] the CJEU confirmed the risk-based approach as the Court carried out an evaluation

---

[188] Information Commissioner's Office (2012), p. 66.

[189] Information Commissioner's Office (2021), p. 9.

[190] Kuan Hon et al. (2011).

[191] Chiara (2020).

[192] Esayas (2015), pp. 8–9; Lundevall-unger and Tranvik (2011).

[193] Article 29 Data Protection Working Party (2007), p. 20.

[194] Joined Cases C-141/12 and C-372/12, *YS v Minister voor Immigratie, Integratie en Asiel and Minister voor Immigratie, Integratie en Asiel v M and S* [2014] ECLI:EU:C:2014:2081. In essence, the Court in YS stated that if the information under scrutiny cannot be corrected and accessed then it cannot be considered as personal data.

[195] Zanfir-Fortuna (2018), p. 17.

[196] Case C-582/14 *Patrick Breyer v Bundesrepublik Deutschland* [2016] ECLI:EU:C:2016:779.

on the actual risk of identification.[197] The judges of Luxembourg considered the dynamic IP address of Mr. Breyer as personal data even if the additional data necessary for identification of the subject were not held by German authorities i.e., the data controller in said scenario, but by the internet service provider, therefore, a third party.[198] This ruling *prima facie* exclude a *pure* relativist approach, as "there is no requirement that all the information enabling the identification of the data subject must be in the hands of one person".[199]

Against this backdrop, the General Court of the European Union (EGC) delivered on 26 April 2023 a ground-breaking judgment in the *SRB v EDPS* case.[200] The General Court held that pseudonymised data sent to a recipient should not be considered personal data if the receiving party does not have the actual means to re-identify the individuals concerned from the data in question. Importantly, the General Court builds its reasoning on the *Breyer* case adopting *prima facie* a pure relativist approach towards the re-identification conundrum.

According to the Court, the EDPS should have ascertained whether the party receiving the pseudonymous data from SRB had legal means available (i.e., 'means reasonable likely to be used') to re-identify the individuals to whom the pseudonyms referred to.[201] Instead, according to the Court, the EDPS merely considered whether re-identification was possible from the SRB's perspective and not from the perspective of the recipient of the pseudonymised data.[202]

Thus, the General Court held that the 're-identifcation test' must be carried out from the perspective of the recipient of the data,[203] regardless of the possibility that another party may have to re-identify data subjects (e.g., the sender of the pseudonymised data having access to the database with the original identifiers). Accordingly, this line of reasoning explicitly advocates for a pure relativist approach. It should be noted nonetheless that the EDPS will most likely appeal this ruling before the Court of Justice of the European Union.

All in all, if there is a reasonable likelihood that certain data, even if subjected to irreversible encryption operations to achieve anonymisation (e.g., salted/peppered

---

[197] Zuiderveen Borgesius (2017).

[198] Case C-582/14, para. 49.

[199] Ibid., para. 43; see also Article 29 Data Protection Working Party (2013), p. 31: "a very significant grey area, where a data controller may believe a dataset is anonymised, but a motivated third party will still be able to identify at least some of the individuals from the information released".

[200] General Court of the European Union, Case T-557/20, *SRB v EDPS*, ECLI:EU:T:2023:219. The dispute relates to Regulation (EU) 2018/1725 on the protection of natural persons with regard to the processing of personal data by the Union institutions, bodies, offices and agencies and on the free movement of such data. However, given that the definition of personal data under Art. 3(1) of Regulation (EU) 2018/1725 is identical to the GDPR's one, the judgment might also shed light on how to interpret the GDPR.

[201] Ibid., para. 104.

[202] Ibid., para. 103.

[203] Ibid., para. 97.

hash function), can be (re-)linked to the natural person they originally referred to, they must be qualified as personal data. On the other hand, if de-identification has been sufficiently robust that identification is no longer reasonably likely, that data must be considered as non-personal.[204]

To this end, determining the resources (e.g., in terms of time and money) that are needed for a successful re-identification is key to effectively adhere to the GDPR notion of 'risk'. For instance, Finck and Pallas calculated the time and energy costs that are 'reasonably likely' to be spent to carry out a successful reidentification (through brute-force attack) on cryptographic hash functions, such as SHA-3.[205] They conclude that the adoption of SHA-3, with an appropriate pepper length (such as 32 bits), "would lead to more than 140 years with 10,000 current GPUs",[206] an effort that cannot possibly be deemed as 'reasonably likely'.

As a consequence, that data should fall outside the GDPR's scope: "if data can be matched to a natural person with reasonable likelihood, it qualifies as personal data and falls within the GDPR's scope of application. If de-personalisation has been sufficiently strong so that identification is no longer reasonably likely, this is non-personal data and accordingly falls outside the Regulation's scope of application".[207] The EDPS and AEPD (Spanish Agency for Data Protection) reached the same conclusion, even if with a more cautious approach.[208]

In conclusion, a sound technical risk assessment—pivoting on solid technical assumptions based on actual calculations—is needed to ascertain the extent to which re-identification is reasonably likely. Such thorough and justifiable assessment would *inter alia* meaningfully implement the principle of accountability.

5.2.3 Encryption's Inherent Conflict, Amidst Inbuilt Vulnerabilities and Innovative Methods to Uphold Fundamental Rights

The previous section expressly acknowledged encryption as natural means of data protection and information security. Nevertheless, the inherent dependency on allegedly trusted third parties for key management and certification creates (new) vulnerabilities—in addition to the ones that the very same technologies scrutinised

[204]EDPS and AEPD (2019).

[205]Dworkin (2015), section V: this standard will "[p]rovide resilience against future advances in hash function analysis, because they rely on fundamentally different design principles. In addition to design diversity, the hash functions in this Standard provide some complementary implementation and performance characteristics to those in FIPS 180-4".

[206]Finck and Pallas (2020), p. 26.

[207]Ibid., p. 34.

[208]EDPS and AEPD (2019), pp. 17–18.

aim to mitigate—that necessitate "further digital security technologies to detect fraudulent third parties or attacks against trusted platforms".[209]

This section, building on the outcomes of the previous legal analysis, dwells on different state-of-the-art cryptographic protocols with a view to addressing (i) the legal classification of data being processed by these cryptosystems; and, (ii) trust and privacy—understood by proxy as confidentiality—issues in the specific context of (resource-constrained) IoT devices.

The first cryptosystem under investigation is (secure) multi-party computation (SMPC). An SMPC allows many parties to collectively evaluate an aggregate function on the data they all—separately—provided, and learn the output of the function, without revealing and learning anything beyond their own inputs and outputs to any other party.[210]

SMPC can be achieved through *threshold* and *somewhat* homomorphic encryption. The former method allows a secret value to be revealed to any set of at least x parties, while revealing no information about that value to any set smaller than x. One party will be able to decrypt if it knows at least x out of the many decryption keys (n). "Computation on homomorphic encryptions can be performed by the n parties holding the decryption keys for the cryptosystem".[211]

The difference between homomorphic encryption is that the latter only supports a finite number of sequential calculations.[212] Similarly, SMPC can be based on *Shamir's secret sharing*[213] scheme, which "allows a value to be shared among n parties so that certain coalitions of them can recover it from their shares, and certain other, smaller coalitions obtain no information about that value from their shares. Most frequently, there is a threshold t, so that all the coalitions with a size of at least t can find the value, and no coalition smaller than t gets any information".[214]

Polymorphic encryption is yet another cryptosystem that is worth analysing.[215] The Polymorphic Encryption and Pseudonymisation (PEP) model, designed by Verheul, Jacobs, Meijer, Hildebrandt and de Ruiter, is a novel approach to sensitive personal data management, in the health care sector. In particular, it provides for the necessary security and privacy & data protection infrastructure for big data analytics where there are multiple sources of personal data,[216] like in IoT scenarios.

The starting point is that traditional encryption is quite rigid, as there is only 'one key' to decipher the encrypted information. The PEP approach hinges on encrypting 'at the source', that is, directly after the generation of personal data; decisions about who can decrypt are therefore postponed. Personal data transfer and storage at cloud

[209] Hildebrandt (2019), p. 262.

[210] Laud et al. (2015), p. 1.

[211] Ibid., p. 13.

[212] Ibid., p. 15.

[213] Shamir (1979).

[214] Laud et al. (2015), p. 10.

[215] Chiara (2020).

[216] Verheul (2016).

facilities is secure and the cloud provider cannot gain access to the encrypted data for it does not hold the keys.

The data subject is placed at the centre of the processing, as they play a crucial role in deciding who can decrypt such data, according to a proactive approach towards data protection similar to the one seen with transparency enhancing tools. The chosen party (e.g., a doctor, a medical researcher, etc.) will be provided with a unique private key, generated from the user's private master key *x,* which is securely stored at a trusted Key Server.

An intermediary, the 'tweaker', then grants access to the chosen parties by *re-keying* the encrypted data with the public master key *x* without knowing *x,* and thus working blindly. It cannot access the information it is giving access to.[217] The Tweaker is "a central converter who exclusively knows how to turn the wheel on a polymorphic lock so that keys of specific parties fit".[218] The Tweaker also assigns *local* pseudonyms. Each data subject will have a different pseudonym at different parties, since "[t]hese parties could somehow lose their data, or even maliciously combine data with others. If different parties use different pseudonyms for the same patient, it is in principle not possible to combine the data, at least not on the basis of identifiers".[219]

Using this innovative approach, a lightweight cryptosystem based on polymorphic encryption has been proposed to secure both hardware and the data flow associated with IoT resource-constrained devices. The implementation of a cryptosystem as flexible as the polymorphic encryption—which is resistant to the most common attacks—at the hardware level would ensure better security and performance than the software implementation.[220]

There may be reasons to consider the data resulting from computations performed by complex cryptosystems, such as the above mentioned, as non-personal data. Some argue that in specific scenarios, such as the healthcare-domain, "multi-party computation has the potential to fulfil the requirements for computational anonymity by creating anonymised data in a way that does not allow the data subjects to be identified with means reasonably likely to be used".[221]

Others, in turn, analysed the possible outcomes in terms of personal or non-personal data by applying the relative and absolute approaches (in Recital 26 GDPR) to several SMPC use-cases.[222] The range of results contemplated by the authors is not binary i.e., personal or non-personal data, and thus application or non-application of the GDPR, but they also include the outcome 'SMPC as a data protection by design measure' as they consider scenarios where SMPC effectively

[217] Ibid., p. 8.

[218] Ibid., p. 7.

[219] Ibid., p. 11.

[220] Dutta et al. (2020), p. 6.

[221] Spindler and Horváth (2019), p. 63; Spindler and Schmechel (2016), p. 176.

[222] Helminger and Rechberger (2022).

minimises personal data output. Yet, in the latter case, the information resulting from the SMPC would still be personal data.

However, to assess whether the output data of a cryptosystem is personal or not, a sound technical (i.e., calculation) risk assessment must be carried out to ascertain the extent to which re-identification of previously de-identified personal data, using state-of-the-art anonymisation techniques, is reasonably likely, as seen in the previous section.[223] "Saying cryptosystems such as these do not legally process personal data will usually be a shaky argument".[224]

On a different note, the case of polymorphic encryption in particular might be seen as a compelling argument for claiming that digital security technologies, such as encryption, are paradoxically not neutral vis-à-vis fundamental rights as they generate new digital security risks. Thus, cryptosystems rely on "trusted third parties for key management and certification [:] to the extent that trust is intransitive and does not scale, this implies that encryption generates new vulnerabilities that require further DSTs to detect fraudulent third parties or attacks against trusted platforms".[225]

It follows that the higher the number of keys, the higher the risk. In polymorphic encryption, the number of keys for the polymorphic 'locks' of the parties granted to decrypt and process the personal data by the user is potentially unlimited.[226] If the trusted Key Server (that holds the master private key) and the Tweaker (that holds the key factors for re-keying and therefore decrypting) collude, the system fails.[227]

On the one hand, one has to acknowledge the ineradicable dependency relationship between risk and trust: where there is trust, there is always a degree of risk.[228] On the other hand, organisational and technical measures can be adopted to reduce the risk of collusion. Besides organisational measures such as data and physical access control, entry logs, availability control and cybersecurity and data protection educational trainings, contractual arrangements or non-disclosure agreements between the parties aiming at avoiding re-identification are often included in any legal framework for the anonymisation of personal data.

To further lower the risk of potential collusions, technical means might be adopted for data fragmentation, such as 'secret sharing' security protocols.[229] Trust in the system would increase accordingly. A secret sharing scheme is highly flexible: combined with other cryptographic techniques such as SMPC, it may be applied to personal data sets after the acquisition and prior to the analysis (at cloud level, say) phases by dividing personal data into unintelligible and random 'shares'

---

[223] Chiara (2020), p. 183.

[224] Veale (2019).

[225] Hildebrandt (2019), p. 262.

[226] Verheul et al. (2016), p. 7.

[227] Verheul and Jacobs (2017), p. 170.

[228] Durante (2019), p. 380.

[229] Katz and Lindell (2015), pp. 501–507.

that will end up in different servers, enabling multi-party computation on those 'shares'.[230]

Such complex cryptographic architectures aim to give the data subject (the patient, in the health care domain) "total control over the generation and management of the decryption keys without relying on a trusted authority"[231] and thus are particularly suitable for cloud environments.

However, there is no silver bullet for information and network security. Risk is the unavoidable flip side of trusting (or relying on) technical means such as cryptosystems. In particular, the next section explores several privacy-invasive scenarios vis-à-vis IoT metadata analysis, even if the communication is encrypted, and introduces the applicable legal framework under EU law.

5.3 Privacy Risks Despite Encryption: IoT Metadata Analysis and the EU Privacy and Data Protection Legal Frameworks

Notwithstanding the lightweight—in case of resource-constrained devices—or 'stronger' encryption protocols that may be adopted to secure (IoT) device communication, serious privacy threats can nevertheless materialise. In fact, an adversary can draw inferences related to user activity by relying on some properties of metadata accompanying the encrypted data. Encrypted traffic analysis, i.e., metadata analysis, is definitely a 'hot topic' in the search for IoT users' privacy security.[232]

Against the background of the last three legal challenges identified by the Article 29 Working Party in its Opinion on the IoT,[233] Sect. 5.3.1 casts light on state-of-the-art attacks and eavesdropping techniques on encrypted traffic that enable granular profiling and surveillance in terms of habits and behavioural patterns. Section 5.3.2 addresses the main legal instruments under EU privacy and data protection law that can be adopted to tackle the challenges seen in the previous section.

[230] Ismail et al. (2020); Spindler, Horváth (2019), pp. 48–56.

[231] Ismail et al. (2020), p. 250.

[232] Rayes and Salam (2019), p. 235.

[233] Article 29 Data Protection Working Party (2014a), pp. 7–8. The challenges are: (i) inferences derived from data and repurposing of original processing; (ii) intrusive bringing out of behaviour patterns and profiling; and, (iii) limitations on the possibility to remain anonymous when using services.

5.3.1 *Device and User Identification: An Overview of Fingerprinting and Inferencing Techniques*

As consistently emphasised throughout this work, in the dawn age of IoT's hyper-connection, data reuse and data mining, it will become increasingly arduous to discern whether data or metadata "does and does not and will likely not impact" individuals' fundamental rights,[234] amid increasingly easier way to single out an individual on very few data points.[235]

Despite the adoption of transport layer encryption, the cybersecurity measure *par excellence* in the field of data protection and information security,[236] IoT traffic metadata (which is not encrypted) is enough for a motivated threat actor to infer from network traffic either users' activities or devices states and possibly obtain sensitive information.[237] The concept of 'fingerprinting' refers to the possibility of creating data records which map certain properties of the encrypted data observed to the corresponding files, website or device: "given a corresponding data base of finger-prints, it is possible to find a match in the database of fingerprints and thus perform file or website identification even on encrypted traffic".[238]

File and website fingerprinting can be subsumed under the broad category of network metadata analysis. Website fingerprinting aims at identifying which website, or part thereof, a user is browsing, by looking only at the user's encrypted traffic.[239] However, for the purpose of this section, 'files fingerprinting' and 'device identification'—especially in the context of smart environments—are the categories that most deserve our attention.

File fingerprinting, through the adoption of machine learning algorithms (such as decision trees and random forests),[240] allows for the detection of known data, even in real-time, in encrypted communication channels with high accuracy.[241] In the context of IoT-surveillance, AI algorithms (e.g., random forest classification model) have proven to be useful in the analysis of encrypted video content. Based on the statistical characteristics of encrypted traffic, a ML model can classify the user behaviour underlying the surveillance video traffic, provided that the traffic patterns of cloud monitoring cameras differ significantly when users do different activities on their monitoring screens.[242]

---

[234] Graef et al. (2018), p. 2.

[235] EDPS (2018), p. 3.

[236] See Sect. 4.2.

[237] Apthorpe et al. (2019); Acar et al. (2020); Ren et al. (2019).

[238] ENISA (2020), p. 27.

[239] Panchenko et al. (2016); Sirinam et al. (2018).

[240] Casarin et al. (2021).

[241] Böttinger et al. (2015), pp. 633–638.

[242] Wang et al. (2019).

Device identification could even shed more light on the sensitivity of IoT metadata. Through sniffing techniques, an eavesdropper can observe the traffic rate, network protocols, source and destination addresses, packets sizes and header metadata[243] of the network traffic.[244] As was the case with the other types of fingerprinting, the monitoring of the network traffic is functional to feeding machine learning algorithms[245] that extract different device features (e.g., timing, sensor state, device state, controller state, controller location) from the encrypted traffic, enabling the accurate identification of the interactions that caused the network traffic.[246] In other words, "an eavesdropper can reliably learn a user's interactions with a device across a wide range of categories, opening the potential for profiling and other privacy-invasive techniques".[247]

After device identification, *via* fingerprinting, a motivated tech-savvy adversary may infer valuable information, such as the timing of user activities from changes in traffic rates, correlated to device state changes. "Most user interactions with IoT devices occur at discrete time points or over short periods surrounded by extended periods of no interaction. For example, turning on a lightbulb, falling asleep, querying a personal assistant, and measuring blood pressure do not occur continuously".[248]

Moreover, the observer could infer sensitive information about the states, the actions, the types of smart devices and sensors as well the related user activities.[249] "The limited-purpose nature of most IoT devices makes this possible. Users interact with traditional computing devices, such as PCs and smartphones, for a variety of purposes, making it difficult to associate any particular change in network traffic rate with a specific activity. In comparison, once an attacker has identified the identity of a particular IoT device, it is often trivial to associate specific traffic rate changes with user activities".[250]

Unlike web browsing, IoT devices generally communicate with few servers, mainly operated by manufacturers, and only one, non-overlapping flow of network traffic is usually needed to perform activity inference. "Additionally, many devices queried individual domains that uniquely identify the device or manufacturer without requiring the use of a set-based fingerprint. This ability to fingerprint based on destination IP addresses is specific to the IoT setting".[251]

---

[243] Data packets communicated (transport layer) from the IoT system to the server are sent with so-called timestamps, i.e., the time and date of the action delivered by the device: in case of aggregated timestamps, one can retrieve timing patterns.

[244] Apthorpe et al. (2017).

[245] Such as decision trees, random forests and naïve bayes.

[246] Acar et al. (2020).

[247] Ren et al. (2019), pp. 276–277.

[248] Apthorpe (2020), pp. 192–193.

[249] Takbiri et al. (2019).

[250] Apthorpe (2020), p. 193.

[251] Ibid., p. 194.

In real world scenarios, machine learning models, such as the ones described above, if trained on a small set of devices, would not work on a large set of unknown IoT devices. A solution has been proposed to keep the model updated with local data and perform regular neural network-based models retraining at the edge, rather than at the cloud server level.[252]

It follows that IoT devices can be identified based on their network behaviour, using resources available on devices themselves (i.e., at the edge of the network). In other words, the accurate and automated inference of the category of a newly connected IoT device to a network, albeit complex, is feasible.

Conventional technical solutions to the identified problem are hardly applicable to IoT scenarios. Protecting metadata with cryptographic means, claimed elsewhere as a possible mitigation against Internet service providers' privacy invasive activities,[253] would require too much computational power for devices that are mostly constrained. Accordingly, most of IoT devices are not suited to deploying anonymous communication systems like The Onion Router (TOR) which are highly demanding in terms of processing and storage capacity. Similarly, firewalls and virtual private networks (VPN) may severely impact device functionality due to an increase in data usage while still allowing activity inference in certain scenarios.[254]

As a consequence, there is a need for innovative 'lightweight' privacy preserving methods. At a higher level of abstraction, proposed solutions aim to protect IoT traffic rate metadata by obfuscating the (real) user activities with (false) generated traffic patterns.[255] The vast majority of currently available IoT devices is vulnerable to the inference attacks on privacy described in this section.

Without significant changes, in terms of privacy protection techniques to be adopted by manufacturers, this issue will also remain for new classes of IoT devices that are expected to flood our market. On the other hand, adopting proposed privacy-preserving solutions is equivalent to placing a relevant burden on manufacturers' side. Without the right incentives, either at regulatory or market level, IoT manufacturers will likely not develop and deploy such solutions.

5.3.2 'Private Surveillance': EU Legal Frameworks Applicable to IoT Metadata Analysis

The previous section gave an overview of how and to what extent data inference and re-identification could heavily impact individuals' rights to privacy and data protection, potentially leading—in the era of hyper-connection of every-day life objects—"to humiliation or even threat to life due to the disclosure of confidential

[252] Kolcun et al. (2021).

[253] Schulz and van Hoboken (2016), pp. 22–23.

[254] Apthorpe (2020), p. 187.

[255] Ibid., pp. 204–218; Acar et al. (2020), pp. 11–12; Takbiri et al. (2019).

information".[256] Even when state-of-the-art technical safeguards for data security are deployed, like means of encryption, metadata still retain considerable privacy and data protection implications.

The 2022 ENISA annual report on cybersecurity research & innovation highlights the increasing interest of private and public agents in the surveillance of citizens as a major and cross-sectoral concern. Bolstered by IoT hyperconnectivity, eavesdropping of communications data and metadata could become a major threat, compromising the privacy and protection of users' data.[257] Without dwelling at length on the legal challenges surrounding 'State surveillance', as an analysis on public and criminal law would exceed the scope of this section, a brief note on the subject is required in order to grasp the extent of the legal debate on metadata processing.

From the seminal *Digital Rights Ireland* case,[258] which invalidated the contested Data Retention Directive[259] and *Tele2*[260] judgments to the more recent *Privacy International*[261] and *La Quadrature du Net*[262] cases, the CJEU consistently condemned the *general* and *indiscriminate* retention of metadata to fight serious crime and for national security purposes without appropriate procedural limitations and guarantees according to the proportionality principle.

Thus, the CJEU, similarly to the ECtHR,[263] makes it clear that the objectives of protecting national security may legitimise indiscriminate surveillance programmes for as long as necessary to neutralise a *foreseeable* and *concrete* threat to the integrity of the state.[264] Otherwise, the fight against 'mere' serious crime would only justify measures whose scope is delimited by objective criteria (e.g., geographical, subjective), which must highlight a link between the (meta)data collected and the objectives pursued.[265]

---

[256] ENISA (2015), p. 13.

[257] ENISA (2022b), p. 14.

[258] CJEU, Joined Cases C-293/12 and C-594/12, *Digital Rights Ireland Ltd v Minister for Communications, Marine and Natural Resources and Others and Kärntner Landesregierung and Others*, ECLI:EU:C:2014:238.

[259] Directive 2006/24/EC of the European Parliament and of the Council of 15 March 2006 on the retention of data generated or processed in connection with the provision of publicly available electronic communications services or of public communications networks and amending Directive 2002/58/EC.

[260] *Tele2* (n 13).

[261] Case C-623/17, *Privacy International v Secretary of State for Foreign and Commonwealth Affairs and Others*, ECLI:EU:C:2020:790.

[262] CJEU, Joined Cases C-511/18, C-512/18 and C-520/18, *La Quadrature du Net and Others v Premier ministre and Others*, ECLI:EU:C:2020:791.

[263] ECtHR, 25 May 2021, (Application no. 58170/13, 62,322/14 and 24,960/15), *Big Brother Watch and Others v. United Kingdom*. However, there is a divergence between the two Courts regarding bulk surveillance. *Ex multis* see Tzanou and Karyda (2022); Van Der Sloot (2021).

[264] *La Quadrature du Net* (n 251) §§ 136–137.

[265] ibid. §§ 143–148; *Privacy International* (n 250) § 75.

In its caselaw, the CJEU acknowledges that metadata taken as a whole, can afford "very precise conclusions to be drawn concerning the private lives of the persons whose data has been retained, such as everyday habits, permanent or temporary places of residence, daily or other movements, the activities carried out, the social relationships of those persons and the social environments frequented by them".[266] In other words, metadata analysis may lead to granular profiles of the individuals concerned by such activity, as seen from a technical viewpoint in the previous section.

Leaving aside the issues pertaining to Art. 15(1) of the ePD, in terms of the balancing exercises between protecting fundamental rights and Member States' security needs, the ePD lays down in Art. 5(1) the principle of the confidentiality of communication and related traffic data. National legislation must thus prohibit the listening, tapping, storage or any other ways of surveillance of communications and related traffic data without the consent of the users concerned.[267]

Importantly, after the 2009 revision of the ePD, the storing of information or the gaining of access to information already stored in the terminal equipment of a user is allowed if the user has given his or her consent,[268] unless the technical storage or access is deemed necessary for (i) the transmission of a communication over a network; (ii) the provision of a service explicitly requested by the user.[269]

Device fingerprinting, as described in the previous section, would *prima facie* fall outside the scope of the so-called 'cookies provision' enshrined in Art. 5(3). Accordingly, online services would not need users' consent to perform such metadata processing for the purposes of tracking or building profiles for providing analytics.

However, already in 2014, the Article 29 Working Party addressed the relationship between Art. 5(3) and device fingerprinting. Having acknowledged a substantial difference from 'cookies', in that device fingerprinting operates covertly, therefore exacerbating privacy and data protection risks, the WP concluded that those "device fingerprints which are generated *through the gaining of access to, or the storing of, information on the user's terminal device* must first obtain the valid consent of the user [emphasis added]".[270]

On the one hand, by bringing into scope the most common use-cases of device fingerprinting at that time, the extensive interpretation of the WP strengthens the standard of protection afforded by the principle of confidentiality of communications as provided for by Art. 5 ePD. On the other hand, AI-powered network analysis of communications metadata—as addressed in the previous section—would not require *per se* the 'gaining of access to, or the storing of, information on the user's terminal device'. It follows that such activities may not be covered by Art. 5(3) ePD.

[266] *Tele2* (n 13) §99.

[267] Art. 5(1) ePD.

[268] Which shall be in accordance with the relevant GDPR provisions.

[269] Art. 5(3) ePD.

[270] Article 29 Data Protection Working Party (2014c).

The Italian Data Protection Authority implicitly confirmed this interpretation: "the controller uses a reading technique [i.e., device fingerprinting] that *does not require the storage of information within the user's device*, as it only envisages observing the configurations applying to that specific user and making him or her identifiable; the outcome is ultimately a 'profile' that remains in the controller's sole possession, to which the data subject obviously has no free and direct access and of which the data subject might actually be totally unaware [emphasis added]".[271]

Even if Art. 5(3) would not apply, fingerprinting techniques are likely to fall nonetheless under the scope of the GDPR, to the extent that passive network analysis process data—alone or in combination with others—that may lead to the identification of users.[272] To be lawful, such processing would require a legal basis under Art. 6 GDPR, which may be consent—which, in turn, would be required if Art. 5(3) applied.

Recourse to the GDPR as *lex generalis* should not, however, divert attention away from this regulatory gap in the EU ePrivacy framework, as the GDPR was not meant to address specifically electronic communication networks or communications data—notably including metadata—as such.

In this respect, the focus should now shift towards the relevant provisions of the proposed ePrivacy Regulation. While Art. 5 lays down the general prohibition for anyone to interfere with electronic communications data (including, therefore, metadata) other than the end-users concerned,[273] except when permitted by the ePR (e.g., Art. 6, see Sect. 5.1), an entire article is devoted to the protection of end-users' terminal equipment information.

Art. 8(1) ePR reads: "the use of processing and storage capabilities of terminal equipment and the *collection of information from end-users' terminal equipment, including about its software and hardware,* other than by the end-user concerned shall be prohibited [emphasis added]".[274] The broad formulation of the new provision differs significantly from its predecessor: the 'storing/gaining access' standard of the ePD would be enhanced by a more comprehensive 'collection of information from terminal equipment'. It follows that passive information sniffing activities relating to the usage of such terminal equipment in electronic communications networks would fall under the scope of Art. 8 and therefore would only be allowed with the end-users' consent.

---

[271] Garante per la Protezione dei Dati Personali (2021), p. 21.

[272] See Art. 4(1); recital 26 GDPR. This would be for example the case of indirectly identifiable MAC addresses of devices.

[273] EDPB (2021), p. 2: "[T]his right to confidentiality must be applied to every electronic communication, regardless of the means by which they are sent, at rest and in transit, from the sender to the receiver, and must also protect the integrity of every user's terminal equipment".

[274] Art. 8(1) ePR.

This interpretation, implicitly confirmed by the Article 29 Working Party[275] and explicitly by the EDPS[276] Opinion on the ePR, is underpinned by Recital 20 ePR which directly addresses the problem: "[. . .] Information related to the end-user's device may also be collected remotely for the purpose of identification and tracking, using techniques such as the so-called 'device fingerprinting', often without the knowledge of the end-user, and may seriously intrude upon the privacy of these end-users. Techniques that surreptitiously monitor the actions of end-users, for example by tracking their activities online or the location of their terminal equipment, or subvert the operation of the end-users' terminal equipment pose a serious threat to the privacy of end-users. Therefore, any such interference with the end-user's terminal equipment should be allowed only with the end-user's consent and for specific and transparent purposes".[277]

Against this background, the second paragraph of Art. 8 further substantiates the general prohibition of collecting information *emitted by terminal equipment* for the purposes of connecting to another device or to network equipment but introduces two exceptions. The general ban can in fact be derogated where the collection is carried out in order to 'establish a connection'.[278] The second and perhaps more problematic exception would only require the display of a "clear and prominent notice [. . .] informing of, at least, the modalities of the collection, its purpose, the person responsible for it and the other information required under Article 13 of Regulation (EU) 2016/679 where personal data are collected, as well as any measure the end-user if the terminal equipment can take to stop or minimize the collection".[279]

As noticed by the Article 29 WP and the European Supervisor, Art. 8(2)(b) seems to suggest that information related to the terminal equipment may be collected "to track the physical movements of individuals (such as "Wi-Fi-tracking" or "Bluetooth-tracking") without the consent of the individual concerned",[280] with a mere 'notice' being sufficient. Yet, this exception clashes with the rationale of Recital 20, which strongly states that such activities "may seriously intrude upon the privacy of these end-users".[281]

Alongside the 'transparency' requirement, the European legislator should consider introducing an obligation for the parties performing surveillance practices to obtain users' consent, as suggested interestingly by both the Council[282] and the Parliament[283] in their drafts. As noted by the A29 WP, "only in a limited number of

[275] Article 29 Data Protection Working Party (2017), p. 9.

[276] EPDS (2017a), p. 28.

[277] Recital 20 ePR.

[278] Art. 8(2)(a) ePR.

[279] Art. 8(2)(b) ePR.

[280] Article 29 Data Protection Working Party (2017), p. 11; EPDS (2017a), p. 29.

[281] Recital 20 ePR.

[282] Art. 8(2)(b) EU Council ePrivacy Draft.

[283] Art. 8(2)(b) EU Parliament ePrivacy Draft, amendment 34.

circumstances might data controllers be allowed to process the information emitted by the terminal equipment for the purposes of tracking their physical movements without the consent of the individual concerned".[284]

However, as already highlighted in Sect. 5.1.1, recurring continuously to consent as a panacea proves to be fallacious in our hyper-digital world. Individuals' fundamental rights to privacy and data protection are constantly and systematically infringed online. To make things worse, consent may even turn into the 'trojan horse' of users' tracking practices, such as first-party ID leaking and browser fingerprinting, which are increasingly deployed online regardless of whether users have consented or rejected 'cookies' in relevant banners.[285] In conclusion, in the words of former European Data Protection Supervisor Giovanni Buttarelli, there is an urgent need for a new ePrivacy law.[286] Years later, this plea is still valid, as this section has tried to show.

5.4 Conclusion

This Chapter charted out different privacy & data protection legal challenges brought about by structural IoT data and metadata collection and processing. Drawing on the findings of the Article 29 Working Party's Opinion on IoT, the analysis contributes to the 'IoT privacy debate' by taking into account recent developments from both a technological and regulatory standpoint.

The first legal challenge concerned the realignment of the traditional matters of privacy and data protection that can be observed under IoT data and metadata sharing, and how this structural sharing challenges the two different regimes of the ePrivacy Directive and the GDPR. The first section thus assessed whether relevant provisions of the GDPR, ePrivacy Directive and notably the proposed ePrivacy Regulation are up to the task of coping with the challenges raised by IoT to the traditional notions of consent, transparency and information security.

In the same vein as Chap. 4, the investigation concluded that there is a missing piece in the EU privacy & data protection regulatory jigsaw, namely the long-awaited ePrivacy Regulation. However, while the ePrivacy Regulation is much needed to offer end-users a higher standard of protection, alone it will still not be enough. Thus, organisational and technological tools (e.g., privacy enhancing technologies, transparency enhancing technologies, privacy preserving technologies, etc.) must be designed and deployed to complement the legal protection offered by EU law to individual privacy and data protection.

The second legal challenge hinged on the relationship between various cryptographic technical tools and the traditional legal disciplines of privacy and data

---

[284] Article 29 Data Protection Working Party (2017), p. 12.

[285] Papadogiannakis et al. (2021).

[286] https://edps.europa.eu/press-publications/press-news/blog/urgent-case-new-eprivacy-law_en.

protection. The analysis shed light on the rationale and technical aspects of encryption, which substantially differs from hashing and pseudonymisation, and why taking this distinction matters when it comes to data protection. Afterwards, the legal investigation cast light on whether and to what extent state-of-the-art encryption protocols challenge the broad concept of personal data underlying the EU data protection legal framework. It concluded that a sound technical risk assessment—pivoting on solid technical assumptions based on actual calculations—is needed to ascertain the extent to which re-identification is reasonably likely.

All in all, encrypted computation—if performed at the edge—increasingly leads large firms holding technological infrastructure claiming that they do not process personal data, eschewing therefore GDPR's application. Whereas such technical solutions are intended to protect mainly confidentiality, EU data protection law is about many more normative (ethical and legal) principles and rights. The pivoting of EU data protection's material scope on the binary distinction between 'personal' and 'non personal' data risks, especially in the context of cryptographic solutions, to somewhat defy EU Commission's goal of rebalancing power in the digital data-driven age.

Finally, the discussion considered the often-overlooked impact of cryptosystems (such as, secure multi-party computation and polymorphic encryption) on *privacy,* as their reliance on third-parties for key management and certifications generates new vulnerabilities. To mitigate the risks of internal (i.e., collusion) and external attacks, the analysis mapped out several organisational and technical measures. On the one hand, contractual arrangements (e.g., non-disclosure agreements), data and physical access control, entry logs, availability control and cybersecurity & data protection educational training have been proposed. On the other hand, to lower the risk of potential collusions between trusted parties, technical means for data fragmentation, such as 'secret sharing' security protocols, have been considered.

Notwithstanding the lightweight—in the case of resource-constrained devices—or 'strong' encryption protocols that may be adopted to secure (IoT) device communication, serious privacy concerns nevertheless arise as an adversary can draw inferences related to user activity by relying on some properties of metadata accompanying the encrypted data.

Against this background, the last legal challenge, that is, IoT metadata analysis, cast light on state-of-the-art attacks and eavesdropping techniques on encrypted traffic enabling granular profiling and surveillance. After a more technical overview, the investigation addressed the relevant provisions of the ePrivacy Directive and the proposed ePrivacy Regulation that can tackle the above-mentioned challenge, in particular, having regard to device fingerprinting.

The main takeaway is that the much-needed and long-awaited ePrivacy Regulation would strengthen and enhance users' privacy protection vis-à-vis passive network analysis compared to the existing legal framework, as laid down in Art. 5(3) of the Directive, which may not cover AI-powered network analysis on communications metadata.

Despite this, the broad formulation of Art. 8 of the Regulation proposal, which would cover 'sniffing' passive network activities, needs to be streamlined in order to avoid derogations from the principle of obtaining users' consent for companies performing surveillance practices even if clear and prominent notices are displayed to inform the users where data are collected.

References

Acar A, Fereidooni H, Abera T et al (2020) Peek-a-boo: I see your smart home activities, even encrypted! WiSec 2020. In: Proceedings of the 13th ACM Conference on Security and Privacy in Wireless and Mobile Networks, pp 207–218. https://doi.org/10.1145/3395351.3399421

Apthorpe N (2020) Network privacy and user protection in the internet of things. Princeton University

Apthorpe N, Reisman D, Feamster N (2017) A smart home is no castle: privacy vulnerabilities of encrypted IoT Traffic. arXiv

Apthorpe N, Huang DY, Reisman D et al (2019) Keeping the smart home private with smart(er) IoT traffic shaping. Proc Priv Enhancing Technol 3:128–148. https://doi.org/10.2478/popets-2019-0040

Article 29 Data Protection Working Party (2007) Opinion 04/2007 on the concept of personal data

Article 29 Data Protection Working Party (2013) Opinion 03/2013 on Purpose Limitation

Article 29 Data Protection Working Party (2014a) Opinion 8/2014 on the Recent Developments on the Internet of Things

Article 29 Data Protection Working Party (2014b) Opinion 05/2014 on Anonymisation Techniques

Article 29 Data Protection Working Party (2014c) Opinion 9/2014 on the application of Directive 2002/58/EC to device fingerprinting

Article 29 Data Protection Working Party (2017) Opinion 01/2017 on the Proposed Regulation for the ePrivacy Regulation (2002/58/EC)

Article 29 Data Protection Working Party (2018) Guidelines on Consent under Regulation 2016/679

Barak B, Brakerski Z (2012) The Swiss Army Knife of Cryptography. In: Wind. Theory - A Res. Blog. https://windowsontheory.org/2012/05/01/the-swiss-army-knife-of-cryptography/

Bernes A (2022) Enhancing transparency of data processing and data Subject's rights through technical tools: the PIMS and PDS solution. In: Senigaglia R, Irti C, Bernes A (eds) Privacy and data protection in software services. Springer Nature, pp 197–208

Biega AJ, Finck M (2021) Reviving purpose limitation and data minimisation in data-driven systems. Technol Regul 44–61. https://doi.org/10.26116/techreg.2021.004

Body of European Regulators for Electronic Communication (2016) Report on Ott Services. https://www.berec.europa.eu/en/document-categories/berec/reports/berec-report-on-ott-services

Böttinger K, Schuster D, Eckert C (2015) Detecting fingerprinted data in TLS traffic. In: ASIACCS 2015 - Proceedings of the 10th ACM Symposium on Information, Computer and Communications Security. Association for Computing Machinery, pp. 633–638

Brooks RR (2014) Introduction to computer and network security: navigating shades of Gray, 1st Editio edn. Chapman and Hall/CRC Routledge

Brown I, Marsden CT (2013) Regulating code: good governance and better regulation in the information age. The MIT Press

Burton C (2020) Article 32 security of processing. In: Bygrave AL, Docksey C, Drechsler L (eds) Kuner C. Oxford University Press, The EU general data protection regulation (GDPR): a commentary, pp 630–639

Bygrave LA, Schartum DW (2009) Consent, proportionality and collective power. In: Reinventing data protection? Springer, Netherlands, pp 157–173

Bygrave LA, Tosoni L (2020) Article 4(11). Consent. In: Kuner C, Bygrave LA, Docksey C, Drechsler L (eds) The EU general data protection regulation (GDPR). Oxford University Press

Calvi A, Malgieri G, Kotzinos D (2024) The unfair side of privacy enhancing technologies: addressing the trade-offs between PETs and fairness. In: FAccT '24: The 2024 ACM Conference on Fairness, Accountability, and Transparency
Casarin R, Facchinetti A, Sorice D, Tonellato S (2021) Decision trees and random forests. In: Zoynul Abedin M, Hassan MK, Hajek P, Mohi Uddin M (eds) The essentials of machine learning in finance and accounting, 1st edn. Routledge, Taylor and Francis Inc, pp 7–36
Chen J, Edwards L, Urquhart L, McAuley D (2020) Who is responsible for data processing in smart homes? Reconsidering joint controllership and the household exemption. Int Data Priv Law 10: 279–293. https://doi.org/10.1093/idpl/ipaa011
Chiara PG (2020) Disentangling encryption from the personalization debate: on the advisability of endorsing the "relativist approach" underpinning the identifiability criterion. Univ Vienna Law Rev 4:168–188
Chiara PG (2021) The balance between security, privacy and data protection in IoT data sharing: a critique to traditional 'Security&Privacy' surveys. Eur Data Prot Law Rev 7:18–30. https://doi.org/10.21552/EDPL/2021/1/6
CNIL (2020) L'anonymisation de données personnelles
Conley C (2014) Metadata: Piecing together a privacy solution. https://www.aclunc.org/publications/metadata-piecing-together-privacy-solution
Data Protection Commission (2019) Guidance on Anonymisation and Pseudonymisation
Davies D (1997) A brief history of cryptography. Inf Secur Tech Rep 2:14–17. https://doi.org/10.1016/S1363-4127(97)81323-4
De Franceschi A, Lehmann M (2015) Data as tradeable commodity and new measures for their protection. Ital Law J 1:51–72
De Hert P, Gutwirth S (2006) Privacy, data protection and law enforcement. Opacity of the individual and transparency of the power. In: Claes E, Duff A, Gutwirth S (eds) Privacy and the criminal law. Intersentia
De Terwangne C (2020) Article 5. Principle relating to processing of personal data. In: Kuner C, Bygrave LA, Docksey C, Drechsler L (eds) The EU general data protection regulation (GDPR): a commentary. Oxford University Press, pp 309–320
Dooley JF (2018) History of cryptography and cryptanalysis: codes, ciphers, and their algorithms. Springer, Cham
Drexl J (2017) Designing competitive markets for industrial data - between propertisation and access. JIPITEC 8:257–292
Durante M (2019) Safety and security in the digital age. Trust, algorithms, standards, and risks. In: Berkich D, D'Alfonso MV (eds) On the cognitive, ethical, and scientific dimensions of artificial intelligence. Springer Nature, pp 371–383
Dutta IK, Ghosh B, Carlson AH, Bayoumi M (2020) Lightweight polymorphic encryption for the data associated with constrained internet of things devices. In: 2020 IEEE 6th World Forum on Internet of Things (WF-IoT). IEEE, pp 1–6
Dworkin MJ (2015) SHA-3 Standard: Permutation-Based Hash and Extendable-Output Functions. https://nvlpubs.nist.gov/nistpubs/FIPS/NIST.FIPS.202.pdf
EDPB (2019) Opinion 5/2019 on the interplay between the ePrivacy Directive and the GDPR, in particular regarding the competence, tasks and powers of data protection authorities
EDPB (2021) Statement 03/2021 on the ePrivacy Regulation
EDPB-EDPS (2022) Joint Opinion 2/2022 on the Proposal of the European Parliament and of the Council on Harmonised Rules on Fair Access to and Use of Data (Data Act). https://edpb.europa.eu/system/files/2022-05/edpb-edps_joint_opinion_22022_on_data_act_proposal_en.pdf
EDPS (2016) Opinion 9/2016 EDPS Opinion on Personal Information Management Systems: Towards more user empowerment in managing and processing personal data
EDPS (2017a) Opinion on Safeguards and Derogations under Article 89 GDPR in the Context of a Proposal for a Regulation on Integrated Farm Statistics

EDPS (2017b) Opinion on the Proposal for a Regulation on Privacy and Electronic Communications (ePrivacy Regulation)

EDPS (2018) EDPS Comments on a framework for the free-flow of non-personal data in the EU

EDPS and AEPD (2019) Introduction to the Hash Function as a Personal Data Pseudonymisation Technique

ENISA (2015) Privacy by design in big data: An overview of privacy enhancing technologies in the era of big data analytics

ENISA (2017a) A tool on Privacy Enhancing Technologies (PETs) knowledge management and maturity assessment

ENISA (2017b) Ad-hoc & sensor networking for M2M Communications Threat Landscape and Good Practice Guide

ENISA (2018) Recommendations on shaping technology according to GDPR provisions: An overview on data pseudonymisation

ENISA (2019) Pseudonymisation techniques and best practices: Recommendations on shaping technology according to data protection and privacy provisions

ENISA (2020) Encrypted Traffic Analysis: Use Cases & Security Challenges

ENISA (2021) Data Pseudonymisation Techniques: Advanced Techniques & Use Cases. Technical analysis of cybersecurity measures in data protection and privacy

ENISA (2022a) Data Protection Engineering: From Theory to Practice

ENISA (2022b) Research and Innovation Brief: Annual Report on Cybersecurity Research and Innovation

Esayas SY (2015) The role of anonymisation and pseudonymisation under the EU data privacy rules : beyond the 'all or nothing' approach. Eur J Law Technol 6:1–28

Etteldorf C (2020) A new wind in the sails of the EU Eprivacy-regulation or hot air only? On an updated input from the council of the EU under german presidency. Eur Data Prot Law Rev 6: 567–573. https://doi.org/10.21552/edpl/2020/4/13

European Commission (2007) Communication from the Commission to the European Parliament and the Council on Promoting Data Protection by Privacy Enhancing Technologies (PETs) COM(2007) 228 final

Farkas TJ (2017) Data created by the internet of things: the new gold without ownership? Rev La Prop Inmater 23:5–17. https://doi.org/10.18601/16571959.N23.01

Finck M, Pallas F (2020) They who must not be identified — distinguishing personal from non-personal data under the GDPR. Int Data Priv Law 10:11–36

Garante per la Protezione dei Dati Personali (2021) Guidelines on the use of cookies and other tracking tools

Gellert R (2018) Understanding the notion of risk in the general data protection regulation. Comput Law Secur Rev 34:279–288. https://doi.org/10.1016/J.CLSR.2017.12.003

Gellert R (2021) Personal data's ever-expanding scope in smart environments and possible path (s) for regulating emerging digital technologies. Int Data Priv Law 11:196–208. https://doi.org/10.1093/idpl/ipaa023/6071468

González EG et al (2020) The proposed ePrivacy regulation: the Commission's and the Parliament's drafts at a crossroads? In: Hallinan D, Leenes R, Gutwirth S, de Hert P (eds) Data protection and privacy: data protection and democracy. Hart Publishing, Bruxelles

Graef I, Husovec M (2022) Seven Things to Improve in the Data Act. SSRN Electron J

Graef I, Gellert R, Purtova N, Husovec M (2018) Feedback to the Commission's Proposal on a Framework for the Free Flow of Non-Personal Data. SSRN Electron J. https://doi.org/10.2139/ssrn.3106791

Graef I, Gellert R, Husovec M (2020) Towards a holistic regulatory approach for the European data economy: why the illusive notion of non-personal data is counterproductive to data innovation. Eur Law Rev 44:605–621. https://doi.org/10.2139/ssrn.3256189

Grassi PA et al. (2017) Digital Identities Guidelines. NIST Special Publication 800-63B

Halevi S (2017) Homomorphic encryption. In: Lindell Y (ed) Tutorials on the foundations of cryptography. Springer International Publishing

Heinz C, Wall N, Wansh AH, Grimm C (2021) Privacy, GDPR, and homomorphic encryption. In: Zivkovic C, Guan Y, Grimm C (eds) IoT platforms, use cases, privacy, and business models: with hands-on examples based on the VICINITY platform. Springer Nature, Cham

Helminger L, Rechberger C (2022) Multi-party computation in the GDPR. In: Privacy Symposium 2022 - Data Protection Law International Convergence and Compliance with Innovative Technologies (DPLICIT)

Hernandez-Ramos JL, Geneiatakis D, Kounelis I et al (2020) Toward a data-driven society: a technological perspective on the development of cybersecurity and data-protection policies. IEEE Secur Priv 18:28–38. https://doi.org/10.1109/MSEC.2019.2939728

Hildebrandt M (2019) Digital security and human rights: a plea for counter-infringement measures. In: Susi M (ed) Human rights, digital society and the law, 1st edn. Routledge, London

Information Commissioner's Office (2012) Anonymisation: managing data protection risk code of practice

Information Commissioner's Office (2021) Introduction to anonymisation

Ismail T, Touati H, Hajlaoui N, Hamdi H (2020) Hybrid and secure E-health data sharing architecture in multi-clouds environment. In: ICOST 2020: the impact of digital technologies on public health in developed and developing countries. Springer, Cham, pp 249–258

Jabłonowska A, Michałowicz A (2020) Planet49: pre-ticked checkboxes are not sufficient to convey User's consent to the storage of cookies. Eur Data Prot Law Rev 6:137–142. https://doi.org/10.21552/edpl/2020/1/19

Janeček V (2018) Ownership of personal data in the internet of things. Comput Law Secur Rev 34:1039–1052. https://doi.org/10.1016/J.CLSR.2018.04.007

Katz J, Lindell Y (2015) Introduction to modern cryptography. CRC Press Taylor & Francis Group

Kerber W (2022) Governance of IoT data: why the EU data act will not fulfill its objectives. SSRN Electron J. doi:https://doi.org/10.2139/SSRN.4080436

Kolcun R, Popescu DA, Safronov V, et al. (2021) Revisiting IoT device identification. In: Network Traffic Measurement and Analysis Conference (TMA). p 9

Koolen C (2021) Transparency and consent in data-driven smart environments. Eur Data Prot Law Rev 7:174–189. https://doi.org/10.21552/EDPL/2021/2/7

Koops BJ, Kosta E (2018) Looking for some light through the lens of "cryptowar" history: policy options for law enforcement authorities against "going dark". Comput Law Secur Rev 34:890–900. https://doi.org/10.1016/J.CLSR.2018.06.003

Koops BJ, Clayton Newell B, Timan T et al (2017) A typology of privacy. Univ Pennsylvania J Int Law 38:483–575

Kosta E (2013) Consent in European data protection law. Martinus Nijhoff Publishers, Leiden

Kosta E (2020) Article 7 conditions for consent. In: Kuner C, Bygrave LA, Docksey C, Drechsler L (eds) The EU general data protection regulation (GDPR): a commentary. Oxford University Press

Kotschy W (2020) Article 6 lawfulness of processing. In: Kuner C, Bygrave LA, Docksey C, Drechsler L (eds) The EU general data protection regulation (GDPR). Oxford University Press

Kounoudes AD, Kapitsaki GM (2020) A mapping of IoT user-centric privacy preserving approaches to the GDPR. Internet of Things 11. https://doi.org/10.1016/J.IOT.2020.100179

Kuan Hon W, Millard C, Walden I (2011) The problem of 'personal data' in cloud computing: what information is regulated?—the cloud of unknowing. Int Data Priv Law 1:211–228

Kuner C (2007) European data protection law: corporate compliance and regulation. Oxford University Press

Laud P, Pankova A, Kamm L, Veeningen M (2015) Basic constructions of secure multiparty computation. In: Laud P, Kamm L (eds) Application of secure multiparty computation. IOS Press, Amsterdam

Lundevall-unger P, Tranvik T (2011) IP addresses—just a number? Int J Law Inf Technol 19:53–73. https://doi.org/10.1093/IJLIT/EAQ013

Malgieri G (2016) Property and (intellectual) ownership of consumers' information: a new taxonomy for personal data. Priv Ger 4:133–150

Mantelero A (2017) From group privacy to collective privacy: towards a new dimension of privacy and data protection in the big data era. In: Taylor L, Floridi L, van der Sloot B (eds) Group privacy. Springer, pp 139–158

Marwedel P (2021) Embedded system design: embedded systems foundations of_cyber-physical systems, and the_internet of_things, fourth. Springer

Mitrou L (2007) Communications data retention: a Pandora's box for rights and liberties? In: Acquisti A, Gritzalis S, Lambrinoudakis C, Di Vimercati S (eds) Digital privacy: theory, technologies, and practices. Auerbach Publications, New York, pp 409–433

Mourby M, Mackey E, Elliot M et al (2018) Are 'pseudonymised' data always personal data? Implications of the GDPR for administrative data research in the UK. Comput Law Secur Rev 34:222–233. https://doi.org/10.1016/j.clsr.2018.01.002

Narayanan A, Shmatikov V (2008) Robust de-anonymization of large sparse datasets. In: Proceedings - IEEE Symposium on Security and Privacy. pp 111–125

NIST (2007) Guide to storage encryption technologies for end user devices: recommendations of the National Institute of Standards and Technology

Noto La Diega G (2023) Internet of things and the law: legal strategies for consumer-centric smart technologies. Routledge, Taylor and Francis Inc., Abingdon, Oxon

Ohm P (2009) Broken promises of privacy: responding to the surprising failure of anonymization. UCLA Law Rev 57:1701

Pagallo U (2017a) The group, the private, and the individual: a new level of data protection? In: Taylor L, Floridi L, van der Sloot B (eds) Group privacy. Springer, pp 159–173

Pagallo U (2017b) The legal challenges of big data: putting secondary rules first in the field of EU data protection. Eur Data Prot Law Rev 3:36–46

Pagallo U, Durante M, Monteleone S (2017) What is new with the internet of things in privacy and data protection? Four legal challenges on sharing and control in IoT. In: Data protection and privacy: (in)visibilities and infrastructures. Springer, Cham, pp 59–78

Palmirani M, Martoni M (2019) Big data, governance dei dati e nuove vulnerabilità. Not Polit 35:9–22

Panchenko A, Lanze F, Zinnen A et al (2016) Website Fingerprinting at Internet Scale. In: NDSS

Papadogiannakis E, Kourtellis N, Papadopoulos P, Markatos EP (2021) User tracking in the post-cookie era: how websites bypass GDPR consent to track users. In: Proceedings ofthe Web Conference 2021 (WWW'21), April 19–23, 2021, Ljubljana, Slovenia. ACM, New York, NY, USA, pp 2130–2141

Podda E, Palmirani M (2021) Inferring the meaning of non-personal, anonymized, and anonymous data. In: Rodrìguez-Doncel V, Palmirani M, Araszkiewicz M et al (eds) AI approaches to the complexity of legal systems XI-XII. AICOL AICOL XAILA 2020 2018 2020. Springer International Publishing, Cham, pp 269–282

Podda E, Vigna F (2021) Anonymization between minimization and erasure: the perspectives of French and Italian data protection authorities. In: Kö A, Francesconi E, Kotsis G et al (eds) Electronic government and the information systems perspective: 10th international conference, EGOVIS 2021. Springer International Publishing, pp 103–114

Polčák R (2020) Article 12. Transparent information, communication and modalities for the exercise of the rights of the data subject. In: Kuner C, Bygrave LA, Docksey C, Drechsler L (eds) The EU general data protection regulation (GDPR): a commentary. Oxford University Press, pp 398–411

Poletti D (2022) IoT and privacy. In: Senigaglia R, Irti C, Bernes A (eds) Privacy and data protection in software services. Springer, pp 175–185

Prainsack B (2019) Logged out: ownership, exclusion and public value in the digital data and information commons. Big Data Soc 6. https://doi.org/10.1177/2053951719829773

Purtova N (2011) Property in personal data: second life of an old idea in the age of cloud computing, chain informatization, and ambient intelligence. In: Gutwirth S, Poullet Y, De Hert P, Leenes R (eds) Computers, privacy and data protection: an element of choice. Springer, Dordrecht, pp 39–64

Purtova N (2012) Property rights in personal data: a European perspective. Wolters Kluwer Law International

Purtova N (2018) The law of everything. Broad concept of personal data and future of EU data protection law. Law Innov Technol 10:40–81. https://doi.org/10.1080/17579961.2018.1452176

Railean A, Reinhardt D (2018) Let there be lite: design and evaluation of a label for IoT transparency enhancement. In: MobileHCI 2018 - Beyond Mobile: The Next 20 Years - 20th International Conference on Human-Computer Interaction with Mobile Devices and Services, Conference Proceedings Adjunct. pp 103–110

Railean A, Reinhardt D (2021) OnLITE: on-line label for IoT transparency enhancement. In: Asplund M, Nadjm-Tehrani S (eds) Secure IT systems - 25th Nordic conference (NordSec 2020). Springer International Publishing, pp 229–245

Rayes A, Salam S (2019) Internet of things from hype to reality. Springer

Ren J, Mandalari AM, Dubois DJ et al (2019) Information exposure from consumer IoT devices: A multidimensional, network-informed measurement approach. Proc ACM SIGCOMM Internet Measurement Conference IMC 267–279. https://doi.org/10.1145/3355369.3355577

Rizvi S et al (2020) Threat model for securing internet of things (IoT) network at device-level. Internet Things 11:100240. https://doi.org/10.1016/J.IOT.2020.100240

Rosner G, Kenneally E (2018) Privacy and the internet of things: emerging frameworks for policy and design. In: Berkeley Center for Long-Term Cybersecurity (CLTC) White Paper Series

Sanchez-Rola I, Dell'Amico M, Kotzias P, Balzarotti D, Bilge L, Vervier PA, Santos I (2019) Can I opt out yet? GDPR and the global illusion of cookie control. In: Proceedings of the 2019 ACM Asia conference on computer and communications security: 340–51. ACM, New York

Schade F (2023) Dark sides of data transparency: organized immaturity after GDPR? Bus Ethics Q 33:3

Schiffner S, Berendt B, Siil T et al (2018) Towards a roadmap for privacy technologies and the general data protection regulation: a transatlantic initiative. In: Medina M, Mitrakas A, Rannenberg K et al (eds) Annual privacy forum 2018: privacy technologies and policy. Springer, Cham, pp 24–42

Schneier B (1995) Applied cryptography: protocols, algorithms, and source code in C. Wiley Inc.

Schulz W, van Hoboken J (2016) Human rights and encryption. UNESCO Ser Internet Free

Serpanos D, Wolf M (2018) Internet-of-things (IoT) systems - architectures, algorithms, methodologies. Springer International Publishing

Shackelford SJ (2020) The internet of things, what everyone needs to know. Oxford University Press

Shamir A (1979) How to share a secret. Commun ACM 22:612–613. https://doi.org/10.1145/359168.359176

Shen Y, Vervier PA (2019) IoT security and privacy labels. In: Naldi M, Italiano GF, Rannenberg K et al (eds) Privacy technologies and policy, 7th annual privacy forum. Springer, Cham, pp 136–147

Sirinam P, Imani M, Juarez M, Wright M (2018) Deep fingerprinting: undermining website fingerprinting defenses with deep learning. In: Proceedings of the 2018 ACM SIGSAC Conference on Computer and Communications Security. ACM, New York, pp 1928–1943

Solove DJ (2010) Understanding privacy. Harvard University Press

Spindler G, Horváth AZ (2019) SODA Project: D3.5 Use-case specific legal aspects

Spindler G, Schmechel P (2016) Personal data and encryption in the European general data protection regulation. J Intellect Prop Inf Technol E-Commerce Law 7:163–177

Stallings W, Brown L (2018) Computer security: principles and practice, 4th edn. Pearson

Sweeney L (2000) Simple demographics often identify people uniquely. Carnegie Mellon University, Data Privacy Working Paper 3

Takbiri N, Houmansadr A, Goeckel DL, Pishro-Nik H (2019) Matching anonymized and obfuscated time series to users' profiles. IEEE Trans Inf Theory 65:724–741. https://doi.org/10.1109/TIT.2018.2873134

Tamò-Larrieux A (2018) Designing for privacy and its legal framework: data protection by design and default for the internet of things. Springer

Tzanou M, Karyda S (2022) Privacy international and quadrature du net: one step forward two steps Back in the data retention saga? Eur Public Law 28:123–154. https://doi.org/10.54648/euro2022007

Urban T, Tatang D, Degeling M, Holz T & Pohlmann N (2018) The unwanted sharing economy: an analysis of cookie syncing and user transparency under GDPR. arxiv.org/abs/1811.08660

van den Hoven J et al (2020) Privacy and information technology. In: Zalta EN (ed) Stanford Encyclopedia of philosophy. Stanford University Press

van Der Sloot B (2021) Big brother watch and others v. the United Kingdom & centrum för rättvisa v. Sweden: does the grand chamber set back the clock in mass surveillance cases? Eur Data Prot Law Rev 7:319–326. https://doi.org/10.21552/EDPL/2021/2/24

van Diermen R (2018) The internet of things: a privacy label for IoT products in a consumer market. Leiden University. https://openaccess.leidenuniv.nl/handle/1887/64571

Van Eecke P, Haie AG (2019) Advocate general opinion on the Planet49 case: some clarifications on the consent requirements with regard to cookies. Eur Data Prot Law Rev 5:434–437. https://doi.org/10.21552/edpl/2019/3/20

Van Erp S (2017) Ownership of data: the numerus clausus of legal objects. Prop Rights Conf J 6: 235–257

Veale M (2019) Knowing without seeing: informational power, cryptosystems and the law. University College London

Veale M, Nouwens M, Teixeira Santos C (2022) Impossible asks: can the transparency and consent framework ever authorise real-time bidding after the Belgian DPA decision? Technol Regul 2022:12–22. https://doi.org/10.26116/techreg.2022.002

Verheul E (2016) Polymorphic Encryption and Pseudonymisation for Personalised Healthcare. https://pep.cs.ru.nl/

Verheul E, Jacobs B (2017) Polymorphic encryption and pseudonymisation. NAW 5:168–172

Waldman AE (2021) Industry unbound: the inside story of privacy, data, and corporate power. Cambridge University Press

Wang J, Cao Z, Kang C, Xiong G (2019) User behavior classification in encrypted cloud camera traffic. In: In: 2019 IEEE global communications conference, GLOBECOM 2019 - proceedings. Institute of Electrical and Electronics Engineers Inc., pp 1–6

Wiewiórowski W (2020) Keynote: Data protection needs encryption. EDPS, 1st Online IPEN Work

Wolfert S, Ge L, Verdouw C, Bogaardt MJ (2017) Big data in smart farming—a review. Agric Syst 153:69–80. https://doi.org/10.1016/J.AGSY.2017.01.023

Zanfir-Fortuna G (2018) Personal data for joint controllers and exam scripts. Int J Data Prot Off Priv Off Priv Couns 2:12–18

Zeadally S et al (2021) Cryptographic technologies and protocol standards for internet of things. Internet of Things 14:. https://doi.org/10.1016/J.IOT.2019.100075

Ziccardi G (2018) The GDPR and the LIBE study on the use of hacking tools by law enforcement agencies. Ital Law J 4

Zuboff S (2019) The age of surveillance capitalism: the fight for a human future at the new frontier of power. PublicAffairs

Zuiderveen Borgesius F (2015) Personal data processing for behavioural targeting: which legal basis? Int Data Priv Law 5:163–176

Zuiderveen Borgesius F (2017) The Breyer case of the court of justice of the European Union: IP addresses and the personal data definition. Eur Data Prot Law Rev 3:130–137. https://doi.org/10.21552/edpl/2017/1/21

Chapter 6
Holistic Risk Analysis for IoT

6.1 Risk Assessment in EU Data Protection and Cybersecurity: Similarities and Divergences

6.1.1 The Data Protection Impact Assessment 'Risk to Rights' Approach

Risk management has always been an essential element of data protection regulations.[1] With the emergence of new technologies and the increasing complexity of data processing scenarios, the EU legislature introduced new specific risk management provisions to modernise the EU data protection legal framework, notably Articles 35 and 36 GDPR. "This has shifted the focus of data protection regulation away from the legitimacy of data processing and the data subject's self-determination to the controllers' accountability and risk management".[2]

In particular, the principle of accountability (Art. 5(2) GDPR) reflects the GDPR co-regulative model of governance, according with which data controllers shall be able to prove compliance with the principles relating to personal data processing enshrined in Art. 5(1).[3] Art. 24 and 25(1)[4] further substantiate the nature and scope of such improved responsibility of controllers.

---

[1] Gellert (2016).

[2] Mantelero (2019), p. 8.

[3] Pagallo et al. (2019), p. 9.

[4] Art. 25 enucleates the principles of data protection by design and by default. The former is embodied in Art. 25(1) which requires data controllers to integrate the necessary safeguards—by means of organisational and technical measures—into the processing, both at the time of the determination of the means for processing and at the time of the processing itself, in order to meet the principles and requirements of this Regulation and protect the rights of data subjects. 'Data Protection by default' is instead substantiated by Art. 25(2) as controllers must implement appropriate technical and organisational measures for ensuring that, by default, only personal data which

P. G. Chiara, *The Internet of Things and EU Law*, Issues in Privacy and Data Protection 67, https://doi.org/10.1007/978-3-031-67663-5_6

As seen in Sect. 5.1.3 in the analysis of the Opinion of the AG Pitruzzella, to effectively comply with the GDPR, controllers have to take organisational and technical measures to meet the requirements of the law, taking into account, *inter alia,*[5] the risks of varying likelihood and severity to the rights and freedoms of the individuals concerned. "The risk-based approach to data protection lies in the use of this notion of risk so as to enable controllers to implement abstract legal norms in an appropriate and effective manner".[6]

Provided that the normative architecture of the GDPR is structured around the notion of risk, the question that now should be asked is what kind of *risk* does the GDPR address. In this regard, Gellert argues that the GDPR is about 'compliance risk': following a traditional understanding of risk being composed of an event and its consequences, the GDPR would envisage the lack of compliance as the 'event', whereas the 'consequence' arising from the event would be the risks to the data subjects' rights and freedoms.[7] In other words, the lower the compliance the higher the consequences upon the data subjects' rights.

Against this backdrop, Art. 35 GDPR provides for the obligation to carry out data protection impact assessments (DPIAs), a risk management iterative process to be performed by the controller prior to processing which is likely to result in a "high risk to the rights and freedoms of natural persons".[8] In a similar vein to Art. 24(1) and 25(1),[9] the DPIA shall be regarded as the culmination of the accountability principle rooted in the risk-based approach,[10] i.e. the inherent risk of a specific processing of personal data determines the degree of expected compliance.

The controller—after having received advice from the data protection officer (DPO)[11]—has to evaluate whether a particular type of processing may entail a 'high risk to the rights and freedoms' "by taking into account the nature, scope, context and purposes of the processing",[12] particularly if it makes use of new technologies. The processor might only be involved in assisting the controller in carrying out a DPIA *via* contractual means and if it performs all or part of the processing.[13]

The reference to 'rights and freedoms' deserves careful attention. Even if the GDPR impact assessment hinges on data protection, as we are reminded by the

are necessary for each specific purpose of the processing are processed. See *ex multis* Bincoletto (2021).

[5] Articles 24 and 25(1) make reference to the state-of-the-art, the cost of implementation and the nature, scope, context and purposes of processing.

[6] Quelle (2018), p. 503.

[7] Gellert (2018).

[8] Art. 35(1) GDPR.

[9] Kosta (2020), pp. 669–670.

[10] Christofi et al. (2021), p. 6. See also recital 84 GDPR.

[11] Art. 35(2); 39(1)(c) GDPR.

[12] Art. 35(1) GDPR.

[13] Art. 28(3)(f) GDPR.

heading of Art. 35, the risks that ought to be considered by the controller's assessment should not only concern privacy and data protection rights but all the fundamental rights that may be impacted by the processing under scrutiny.[14] Section 6.1.3 will further elaborate on this often-neglected point when Art. 35 is operationalised, as DPIA models offered by the DPAs fail to offer a comprehensive account of risks to a broader set of rights than privacy and data protection.

The GDPR enucleates only three specific cases of 'risk-to-rights' processing operations. The non-exhaustive list[15] of Art. 35(3) contains:

1. Systematic and extensive evaluation of personal aspects relating to natural persons which is based on automated processing, including profiling, and on which decisions are based that produce legal effects concerning the natural person or similarly significantly affect the natural person, the effect of which potentially exclusion or discrimination;
2. Processing on a large scale of special categories of data or personal information relating to criminal convictions and offences;
3. Large-scale extension of systematic monitoring of publicly accessible areas.

Beside these cases, in the event where it is not clear whether a DPIA is required, the WP29 guidelines recommend performing the assessment nonetheless "as a DPIA is a useful tool to help controllers comply with data protection law".[16]

On the other hand, Art. 35 contains several exemptions to such 'rule of thumb'. A DPIA is not required where (i) a processing is not likely to result in high risk[17]; (ii) a data protection authority (DPA) establishes that a particular processing would not require a DPIA[18]; (iii) where the legal basis of a processing is to be found in Art. 6(1)(c) or Art. 6(1)(e) GDPR and the relevant legal acts regulate such processing and a DPIA has already been carried out as part of a general assessment in the context of the adoption of the legal basis.[19]

Recital 75 GDPR sheds light on several aspects of the DPIA. In particular, it significantly contributes to clarifying the meaning as well as the scope of 'risk to rights and freedoms'. It identifies six criteria to assess the risk, of varying likelihood and severity, for the rights and freedoms of natural persons that may result from personal data processing which could lead to physical, material or non-material damage.[20] In other words, "it contains several risk criteria pertaining to the consequences [of the event i.,e., type of processing operation]"[21]:

---

[14] Hallinan and Martin (2020), Kosta (2020), p. 671; Mantelero (2019), p. 8.

[15] As the words 'in particular' of Art. 35(3) indicate.

[16] Article 29 Data Protection Working Party (2017), p. 8.

[17] Following the line of reasoning of Art. 35(1) GDPR.

[18] Art. 35(5) GDPR.

[19] Art. 35(10) GDPR.

[20] Mantelero (2019), p. 9.

[21] Gellert (2018), p. 286.

1. The potential harm for natural persons resulting from the personal data processing (e.g., discrimination, identity theft or fraud, financial loss, damage to reputation, loss of confidentiality of personal data protected by professional secrecy, unauthorised reversal of pseudonymisation, or any other significant economic or social disadvantage);
2. The deprivation of data subjects' rights and freedoms or control over their personal data;
3. The nature of the data that has been processed (sensitive data);
4. The creation or use of personal profiles;
5. The particular conditions of vulnerable data subject, in particular of children;
6. The scale of the personal data processing (involving a large amount of personal data with an impact on a large number of data subjects).

A key challenge of every DPIA, and arguably of every risk analysis, is deciding which risks to consider, how to weight them and how to assess their likelihood and severity. From a first reading of Recital 75, risks to individuals might be framed in two broad categories[22]: (i) material harms (i.e., physical threat or injury, financial or economic loss, unlawful discrimination, identity theft, loss of confidentiality, accidental/unlawful destruction, alteration, unauthorised disclosure or access, unauthorised reversal of pseudonymisation, breach of professional secrecy and other significant economic or social disadvantage); (ii) non-material harms (i.e., damage to reputation or goodwill, individuals deprived of rights and freedoms, or prevented from exercising control over their data; etc.).

However, Article 29 WP has made it explicitly clear that "the risks-based approach goes beyond a narrow 'harm-based-approach' that concentrates only on damage and should take into consideration every potential as well as actual adverse effect, assessed on a very wide scale ranging from an impact on the person concerned by the processing in question to a general societal impact (e.g., loss of social trust)".[23]

Therefore, to provide a more concrete set of processing operations that require a DPIA due to their inherent high risk, Article 29 WP put forward nine criteria in its 2017 guidelines:

(i) evaluation or scoring, including profiling and predicting;
(ii) automated decision-making with legal or similar significant effect;
(iii) systematic monitoring;
(iv) sensitive data or data of a highly personal nature;
(v) data processed on a large scale;
(vi) matching or combining datasets;
(vii) data concerning vulnerable data subjects;
(viii) innovative use or application of new technological or organisational solutions;

[22] Centre for Information Policy Leadership (2016), p. 16.
[23] Article 29 Data Protection Working Party (2014), p. 4.

(ix) when the processing in itself "prevents data subjects from exercising a right or using a service or a contract".[24]

Finally, in terms of the actual content of a DPIA, the GDPR contains a non-exhaustive minimum list of elements that such assessment must contain. These are: (i) a systematic description of the processing and its purposes; (ii) an assessment of the necessity and proportionality of the processing operations in relation to the purposes; (iii) an assessment of the risks to individuals' rights and freedoms; (iv) the measures envisaged to mitigate the risks.[25]

If the technical and organisational measures *ex* Art. 35(7)(d) GDPR cannot adequately mitigate the high risk, then the controller shall consult the competent supervisory authority prior to processing,[26] providing *inter alia* the full DPIA.[27] The guidelines of the Working Party clarified that 'prior consultation' with the DPA must occur where "the identified risks cannot be sufficiently addressed by the data controller (i.e., the residual risks remain high) that the data controller must consult the supervisory authority".[28]

Importantly, as the risk management process is not a 'static' assessment, DPIAs should not be seen as a one-time task.[29] Hence, DPIAs should be periodically reviewed and re-assessed "whenever circumstances arise that significantly affect the severity and likelihood of risks or introduce new ones".[30] The Article 29 WP guidelines do not mention definite time periods; the choice is left up to the controller as part of its general accountability obligations.[31]

The last paragraph of Art. 35 GDPR mandates that, when performing the assessment, controllers shall seek the views of data subjects (or their representatives, such as associations) on the intended processing, without prejudice to trade secrets, commercially sensitive information or the security of processing operations. Some authors have characterised similar regulatory measures aiming to increase civil society's influence as well as engagement in digital governance as 'multistakeholderism'. Accordingly, "multistakeholderism sees collective consultation and participation as grounds for legitimacy".[32] Article 29 WP considers that data subjects' views could be gathered through several means, depending on the context (e.g., surveys, questionnaires, etc.) but if the controller deems it not appropriate to carry out this step, it can avoid doing so as long as it documents its justification (consistently with the accountability principle).

---

[24] Article 29 Data Protection Working Party (2017), pp. 9–11.

[25] Art. 35(7) GDPR.

[26] Art. 36(1); recital 84 GDPR.

[27] Art. 36(3) GDPR.

[28] Article 29 Data Protection Working Party (2017), p. 18.

[29] Kosta (2020), p. 675.

[30] Mantelero (2019), p. 18; Art. 35(11) GDPR.

[31] Article 29 Data Protection Working Party (2017), p. 14.

[32] See Griffin (2023), p. 48.

Finally, albeit the GDPR does not require the DPIA to be published, the Article 29 WP notes how publishing the outcomes of the DPIA can benefit all the parties concerned by the processing.[33] On the one hand, publicity may foster data subjects' (and society in general) trust[34] as they would develop a better understanding of (i) the functioning of digital technologies processing their personal data; (ii) the risk implications, in particular, in terms of their fundamental rights and liberties. On the other hand, the decision to publish the DPIA might be leveraged by data controllers as a means to implement accountability and transparency principles. On a different level, transparent DPIAs might even lead to foster an informed public debate on the different normative (ethical, legal and social) implications of emerging digital technologies.

In the context of IoT, a preliminary reflection should revolve around the question of whether IoT data processing always require a DPIA. Thus, the Working Party mentions IoT only once, in its eighth criterion: "Internet of Things applications could have a significant impact one individuals' daily lives and privacy; and, therefore, require a DPIA".[35] It falls short however of a more in-depth analysis of the extent to which IoT systems are likely to pose a high risk and to which rights and freedoms. Against this backdrop, the Spanish DPA (AEPD) elaborated on the main IoT risks to privacy and data protection by building on the previous Article 29 Working Party Opinion on IoT (see Chap. 5).[36] All in all, the AEPD adds little to the six-year-prior analysis of the A29 Working Party and, more importantly, misses the opportunity to clarify the 'risks to rights and freedoms' standard of GDPR in the IoT domain to the detriment of controllers who lack the necessary guidance to integrate a rights-based approach into DPIA methodologies.

---

[33] Article 29 Data Protection Working Party (2017), p. 18; Tamò-Larrieux (2018), pp. 188–89; Kosta (2020), p. 675.

[34] The objective of enhancing public trust in digital technologies permeates nearly every area of EU action: cybersecurity (Cybersecurity Act, recital 2); data economy (Data Governance Act, recital 3); artificial intelligence (Artificial Intelligence Act, recital 1); online services (Digital Services Act, recital 3); etc.

[35] Article 29 Data Protection Working Party (2017), p. 10.

[36] AEPD (2020a). These risks are: (i) the invasive disclosure of profiles and behaviour patterns, potentially leading to surveillance; (ii) lack of control and information asymmetry, potentially impeding data subjects to correctly exercise their data protection rights; (iii) lack of transparency, linked to the fact that certain classic methods for obtaining consent are not easily applicable for some types IoT devices, may, in fact, render impossible to obtain valid consent or seriously affect the validity of other legal grounds; (iv) the capture of personal or sensitive data of individuals which may find themselves nearby some IoT system, even if they have no intention or idea of interacting with it; (v) asymmetries in the compliance level of each actor, as multiple parties participate in a IoT system with different degrees of responsibility (controllership, joint-controllership or in the role of data processor); (vi) lack of appropriate security measures at any layer level, either due to the limitations of the devices themselves, or for deficiencies in the application of data protection principles from design (e.g., non-encrypted communications, passwords by defect, etc.); (vii) limitations to the possibilities to remain anonymous as soon as this service is used, not to mention the risk of re-identification.

The manufacturers of IoT products, although not required by the GDPR if they are not data controllers, may also carry out a DPIA. This exercise may prove to be particularly useful wherever a technological solution is likely to be used by different controllers deploying the products or applications: "of course, the data controller deploying the product remains obliged to carry out its own DPIA with regard to the specific implementation, but this can be informed by a DPIA prepared by the product provider, if appropriate".[37] As noted by Kosta, "the product provider's DPIA and sharing of information occur at the provider's discretion, unless the provider is a controller or is a processor subject to contractual obligations pursuant to Article 28(3)(f) GDPR".[38]

Before looking at the core of the 'risk to rights' requirement of Art. 35 (Sect. 6.1.3)—which will serve as a basis for the critical analysis of existing IoT DPIA methodologies, the next section focusses on specific risk management standards to spot both points of contact and differences with the GDPR risk management model enshrined in Art. 35.

6.1.2 Information Security Risk Management Frameworks

The GDPR does not rely on any specific standards, nor does it adopt a detailed risk management method to comply with the requirement of Art. 35. Mantelero rightly observes that this approach deserves credit. "First, standardisation processes are often opaque, not open to broad stakeholder participation and influenced by the power of the industrial entities involved. Second, existing information management standards are mainly focused on security, underestimating the other aspects of the impact of data use".[39] In particular, this section aims to cast light on the latter aspect, that is, the rationale, the value and scope underpinning international information security risk management standards to highlight the main differences with the GDPR 'risk-to-rights' approach. To this end, the analysis briefly charts out the main characteristics of known and widely adopted standards, such as relevant ISO technical standards.[40]

Information security and EU data protection law i.e., the GDPR, have different rationales, although they do share some objectives. As said in Chap. 3, information security traditionally has the goal of protecting information, through the implementation of an applicable set of controls, selected through the chosen risk management process, with a focus on the organisation.[41] Thus, the information security risk is

[37] Article 29 Data Protection Working Party (2017), p. 8.

[38] Kosta (2020), pp. 672–673.

[39] Mantelero (2019), p. 11.

[40] For a general overview on ISO governance and functioning, see: Hatto (2010).

[41] ISO/IEC 27000:2018, p. 12.

associated with the eventuality of threats exploiting the vulnerabilities of an information asset, thereby causing harm to an organisation.[42]

The well-known CIA triad (confidentiality, integrity and availability), which had long been central to the field of computer security, has been further expanded to include other principles such as non-repudiation, authenticity, accountability and auditability.[43] Conversely, the risk management process introduced by the GDPR is a tool for managing risks to the rights of the data subjects, and thus takes their perspective.[44]

Before delving into information security risk management standards, a classificatory remark is due, for ISO's broad body of standards has its own semantic and conceptual background. Legal and technical scholarships do not always take into account the different nuances between the intertwined concepts of risk management, risk analysis and risk assessment. For example, Gellert affirms that "risk analysis is composed of two steps: risk assessment and risk management. Risk assessment measures the level of risk (in terms of likelihood and severity), while the point of risk management is to decide whether or not to take the risk".[45]

On the other hand, ISO 31000 standard charts out the complex relationship between these concepts starting from an overarching understanding of risk management being the "coordinated activities to direct and control an organisation with regard to risk",[46] involving "the systematic application of policies, procedures and practices to the activities of communicating and consulting, establishing the context and assessing, treating, monitoring, reviewing, recording and reporting risk".[47]

Instead, risk assessment is defined as "the overall process of risk identification, risk analysis and risk evaluation: [it] should be conducted systematically, iteratively and collaboratively, drawing on the knowledge and views of stakeholders".[48]

Finally, the goal of risk analysis is to develop an understanding of the nature, the characteristics and level of risk: "[it] provides an input to risk evaluation, to decisions on whether risk needs to be treated and how, and on the most appropriate risk treatment strategy and methods. [...] Risk analysis should consider factors such as: the likelihood of events and consequences; the nature and magnitude of

---

[42] Although the ubiquitous IoT interconnection renders the metaphor of a 'security perimeter' rather anachronistic, it can still prove to be useful in highlighting the key concepts of information security. The vulnerability (at the design, implementation, operation or management level) can be conceived as a weakness of one or more segments of the perimeter that can leave the allegedly protected system exposed to an attack. On the other hand, a 'threat' is represented by an accidental or deliberate action, which can lead to the violation of defined security objectives.

[43] Nieles et al. (2017).

[44] Article 29 Data Protection Working Party (2017), p. 17.

[45] Gellert (2018), p. 280.

[46] ISO 31000:2018, p. 1.

[47] Ibid., p. 8.

[48] Ibid., p. 11.

consequences; complexity and connectivity; time-related factors and volatility; the effectiveness of existing controls; sensitivity and confidence levels.".[49]

Therefore, in the view of the International Standardisation Organisation, risk analysis is part of the broader risk assessment which, in turn, is a component of the risk management process. In this respect, this book will rely on ISO's taxonomy.

The ISO 27xxx group of standards is intended to help organisations in keeping informational assets secure. The most known standard of the ISO 27xxx series is ISO/IEC 27001. It provides requirements for establishing, implementing, maintaining and continually improving an information security (ISMS). Although the previous Plan–Do–Check–Act model (P-D-C-A)[50] of ISO/IEC 27000 has been formally abandoned by the 2017 version of ISO/IEC 27001, the well-established PDCA approach still proves to be effective in practice.[51] In 2022, ISO released the updated version of the 27,001 standard (approved by CEN as European standard in July 2023), superseding the 2017 version.

The 'plan' phase deals with issues like defining the scope of the ISMS, defining the roles within the organisation and how the ISMS will be managed. This part includes the definition of the risk assessment approach to identify and evaluate information security risks;[52] the evaluation of the various options for risk treatment; the selection of the controls to be implemented for each risk;[53] the drafting of a statement of applicability (SoA) and a risk treatment plan.

The 'do' phase concerns the implementation of the planned procedures for the risk treatment plan and technical controls. The 'check' step instead consists of monitoring, reviewing, testing and auditing. Finally, the 'act' phase refers to the

---

[49] Ibid., p. 12.

[50] Tamò-Larrieux (2018), p. 173: "developers and engineers should continually improve and optimize systems by planning for security, integrating security measures, checking whether said mea- sures are working according to the plan, and acting if necessary".

[51] Watkins (2013), p. 21.

[52] The value of each asset is estimated according to the three information security attributes (i.e., confidentiality, integrity and availability) and assessed via the traditional "risk = likelihood X impact" relationship. Every organization sets its own risk-acceptance threshold, above which a decision has to be taken as to what to do about each of them (e.g., controls, accepting the risk, transferring the risk to via insurance, etc).

[53] ISO lists 114 different controls within 14 categories; the list is nonetheless non-exclusive, as specific sector requirements could go beyond the generic ones. Watkins (2013), at p. 32 groups these controls under six categories: (i) information security organisation, structure and human resources (organisation's commitment, security roles and objectives relating to information security); (ii) assets, access control and classification (assets are classified to a defined labelling scheme, and the classification will indicate the level of protection required); (iii) physical access and environmental issues (perimeters around secure areas should be defined in all three dimensions); (iv) networks and IT (capacity planning, new developments testing, back-ups and so on); (v) incidents (the need to regularly test the business continuity plans in order to learn from the experience and improve the plans ahead of any security breach); (vi) compliance and internal audit (legal compliance).

process of ongoing review, further testing and improvement implementation, if necessary.[54]

With the GDPR progressively setting a 'gold standard' in data protection across the world,[55] ISO seized the opportunity to enter the EU privacy standards & certification market: ISO/IEC 27701 and ISO/IEC 29134 are perhaps the two most prominent examples. Whereas the former is an extension of ISO 27001 providing for GDPR compliance support, the latter has been designed *inter alia* as a means to demonstrate compliance with the obligation to conduct a DPIA.

In particular, the standard ISO 27701:2019 complements the ISMS contained in ISO/IEC 27001 in that it gives guidance to set up a 'Privacy Information Management System' (PIMS) with a view to providing GDPR compliance. In other words, the ISMS requirements of ISO/IEC 27001 would, as an additional step, address the "protection of privacy as potentially affected by the processing of Personal Identifiable Information".[56]

The ISO/IEC 29134 standard sheds light on how to undertake a privacy impact assessment (PIA). Notably, ISO acknowledges the PIA as part of organisations' overall information security risk management (ISMS) effort.[57] The standard frames the PIA process in 5 subsequential steps: (i) identification of the information flow, as regards personal data (personal identifiable information "PII", according to the ISO methodology); (ii) analysis of the use-case's implications; (iii) determination of the relevant privacy safeguarding requirements; (iv) assessment of the privacy risks; (v) preparation for risks' mitigation. The risk is evaluated by the organisation performing the PIA by determining the likelihood and the impact, either adopting a qualitative, semi-quantitative or quantitative method, or a combination of these, depending on the circumstances".[58]

A twofold, conceptual and structural, misalignment between ISO and the GDPR frameworks can be observed from the outset.

From a conceptual standpoint, ISO standards' approach is inevitably narrower than the broader scope of the GDPR. Firstly, the ISO framework is rooted in information security and thereby promotes a hierarchy that subordinates data protection to information security.[59] Accordingly, ISO acknowledges the protection of privacy (including, selected aspects of EU data protection) as an additional requirement of information security.

Whereas ISO puts information security on top of the value chain, the GDPR, as already stressed in this book, conceives information security or, more precisely,

---

[54] Clader (2013), pp. 45–46.

[55] Albrecht (2016); Mantelero (2021).

[56] Lachaud (2020), p. 198.

[57] ISO/IEC 29134:2020, *Information technology. Security techniques. Guidelines for privacy impact assessment* (2020), vi.

[58] Ibid., p. 18.

[59] Lachaud (2020), p. 204.

integrity and confidentiality,[60] as only one of the principles relating to processing of personal data (see Art. 5(1) GDPR).[61] Recalling the outcomes of Chap. 3, specific dimensions of information security (i.e., technical measures) are crucial for safeguarding fundamental rights (notably, Articles 7 and 8 of the Charter) and freedoms of natural persons, without information security being a fundamental right in itself.[62]

ISO's approach is difficult to reconcile with the rights-based rationale of EU data protection law, for it aims to safeguard "*fundamental rights and freedoms* of natural persons and in particular their right to the protection of personal data [emphasis added]",[63] not only privacy. This perspective is maintained in Art. 35, which sets out an obligation to assess the risks to rights and freedoms, not only privacy and data protection.

Conversely, ISO 29134 considers the losses of confidentiality, integrity and availability as the first factors to be taken into account when assessing privacy risks, excluding other rights from the scope of the assessment. Yet, in the attempt to bridge the gap with the GDPR's approach, the standard details other aspects that ought to be considered by the risk assessment, such as the "insufficient information concerning the purpose for processing the PII [personally identifiable information] (lack of transparency)", the unjustified retention of PII, or the failure "to consider the rights of the PII principal (loss of the right of access)".[64] Moreover, the standard explicitly suggests organisations to "examine separately privacy risks from a PII principal's point of view and privacy risks from the organisation's point of view".[65]

The latter point leads us to a second consideration pertaining to the conceptual misalignment between ISO and the GDPR, that is, whose interests the impact assessment takes into account. Whereas ISO's ISMS (and, accordingly, the PIA) is preoccupied with the organisation, the GDPR aims to protect individuals i.e., data subjects, rather than organisations i.e., data controllers.[66] This is once again explained by the fact that ISO 29134 solidly anchors to ISO's framework: ISO is "[s]tepping slightly out its comfort zone when trying to address fundamental rights issues while continuing to use essentially its old toolbox".[67]

A further discrepancy between the two frameworks is given by the different terminology. As seen above, ISO privacy standards refer to 'personally identifiable information' (PII) instead of personal data; the 'PII principal' instead of data subject; 'privacy controls' instead of technical and organisational measures; and, of course,

---

[60] Art. 5(1)(f) GDPR: "including protection against unauthorised or unlawful processing and against accidental loss, destruction or damage, using appropriate technical or organisational measures".

[61] De Terwangne (2020).

[62] Papakonstantinou (2022).

[63] Art. 1(2) GDPR.

[64] ISO/IEC 29134:2020 (n 55), p. 16.

[65] Ibid., p. 8.

[66] Christofi et al. (2021), p. 12.

[67] Christofi et al. (2021), p. 17.

'privacy' also to encompass data protection. This conceptual divergence may eventually create confusion for data controllers using ISO's privacy standards with a view to complying with the GDPR.[68]

Finally, ISO attempts to *quantify* risks to privacy. However, it is very hard, if not ultimately impossible, to numerically determine the value scale of fundamental rights.[69] Fundamental rights resist easy quantification mainly due to their inherently subjective interpretation which require interpretative reasoning and normative judgment.[70] As a result, "neither the severity of damage nor the likelihood of its occurrence can be meaningfully quantified".[71] Christofi et al. clearly explain this:

> One may be able to quantify a system's vulnerabilities, the likelihood of external attacks and certain consequences of a data breach, e.g. as regards the number of individuals affected and the sensitivity of the personal information at stake. It is much more difficult – if not impossible – to quantify potential harms on 'rights and freedoms', which are of course intangible. Moreover, in the pursue of quantification, ISO's approach (strictly) focuses on possible consequences for the individual data subjects, lacking a collective dimension.[72]

In this respect, the next section will shed light on possible avenues for quantifying risk thresholds in DPIAs.

Furthermore, the risk assessment in the GDPR goes beyond the ISO's narrower 'harm-based' approach. As clarified by the Article 29 WP, "risk-based approach goes beyond a narrow "harm-based-approach" that concentrates only on damage and should take into consideration every potential as well as actual adverse effect, assessed on a very wide scale ranging from an impact on the person concerned by the processing in question to a general societal impact (e.g. loss of social trust)".[73] Indeed, the potential harms that a DPIA should be preoccupied with are not limited to ISO privacy-related risks (e.g. illegitimate use of personal information, data security), "but also include other prejudices, mainly concerning discriminatory or invasive forms of data processing".[74]

On the other hand, it should be acknowledged that ISO 29134, when articulating users' harms, refers to "physical, financial, reputational harm, embarrassment and invasion of domestic life [and, further,] different types of privacy such as bodily privacy, location and space privacy, behavioural privacy, privacy of communications, privacy of data and image, privacy of thoughts and feelings and privacy of associations".[75] As noted by Christofi et al., this list of harms, while focusing solely on privacy, rather broadens the scope of privacy ('privacy of thoughts and feelings and privacy of associations') "to the instrumental role that privacy plays with respect

---

68 Lachaud (2020), p. 202.

69 Sampaio (2019), p. 2863.

70 Alexy (2003).

71 Friedewald et al. (2022), p. 432.

72 Christofi et al. (2021), p. 14.

73 Article 29 Data Protection Working Party (2014), p. 4.

74 Mantelero (2019), p. 21.

75 ISO/IEC 29134, Clause 6.3.1.

to other rights and freedoms of individuals".[76] Such phrasing can arguably be seen as yet another attempt of ISO to fill the gap with the broader GDPR's rights-based approach.

Yet, data controllers would find easier to "articulate a number of more measurable 'harms' concerning data security breaches"[77] when faced with the operationalisation of the high-level 'risk-to-fundamental-rights' legal standard set by Art. 35 GDPR.

To make things more complex, Annex 2 of the Guidelines of Article 29 WP Guidelines on DPIA lays down the criteria that data controllers should look up to assess whether or not a DPIA is comprehensive enough to be compliant with the GDPR legal standard.

However, when it comes to the assessment of the risks to the rights and freedoms of data subjects (step 3), the Guidelines unduly restrict the scope on data security,[78] not only with regard to the events leading to the risk[79] but also with regard to the risks itself: "origin, nature, particularity and severity of the risks are appreciated (cf. Recital 84) or, more specifically, for each risk (*illegitimate access, undesired modification, and disappearance of data*) from the perspective of the data subjects [emphasis added]".[80] This is confusing at best.

Moreover, in Annex 1 the Guidelines explicitly call on ISO/IEC 29134 as an "international standard [that] will provide guidelines for methodologies used for carrying out a DPIA". Without dwelling on the delicate and critical issue of delegation of regulatory power to a private body,[81] against the background of the misalignment between ISO 29134 and the GDPR's 'risk-to-fundamental-rights' approach, Christofi et al. note that there is no evidence that Article 29 WP performed a diligent analysis. According to the authors, the endorsement of the ISO standard would amount to a 'blank cheque'.[82]

All in all, "ISO/IEC 29134 should be designed and used for what it can really provide rather than be subtly re-branded as a DPIA methodology".[83] The value of international standards, such as ISO 27701 and ISO 29134, lies in showing possible

---

[76] Christofi et al. (2021), p. 13.

[77] Quelle (2018), pp. 505–506.

[78] Ibid., p. 506.

[79] Article 29 Data Protection Working Party (2017), p. 22: "potential impacts to the rights and freedoms of data subjects are identified in case of events including illegitimate access, undesired modification and disappearance of data" [emphasis added].

[80] Id.

[81] This is part of a broader problem concerning the position of EU authorities on the legal status of standards (see CJEU C-613/14 James Elliott Construction ECLI:EU:C:2016:821). In turn, this generates problems in data protection law (as seen, uptake of ISO based DPIA could weaken the level of protection offered by the GDPR), competition law (the use of conformity assessment processes may conflict with EU competition law when they contribute to exclude competitors from the market and/or when they distort the conditions of access to the market at the expenses of certain competitors, see Daskalova and Heldeweg (2019) and constitutional law (see Gérardy (2021)).

[82] Christofi et al. (2021), p. 18.

[83] Christofi et al. (2021), p. 17.

ways to comply with relevant requirements. For example, the informative Annex D of ISO 27701 outlines an indicative map illustrating which provisions of the standard can provide compliance with which articles of the GDPR (in particular, Articles 5–49, except for Article 43).[84] The data protection requirements identified regard, *inter alia*: management of personal data breach; identification of a legal basis for processing personal data (specifying how to obtain and record consent); privacy (data protection) impact assessment; relationship with data processors; joint controllership; obligations to data subjects (herein called PII principals) and privacy by design and by default.[85]

In a scenario where data protection authorities (DPAs) have not yet provided controllers with the proper guidance on how to meaningfully operationalise the challenging rights-based approach at the core of the DPIA into methodologies, it is understandable that data controllers rely on such standards that, at least on paper, can help them demonstrate compliance.

While Sects. 6.2.1 and 6.2.2 will investigate a specific DPIA methodology (for IoT devices) developed by the French DPA more closely, the next section further investigates avenues to substantiate GDPR's 'risk-to-fundamental-rights' standard into DPIA methodologies.

Lastly, it is worth mentioning that ISO/IEC are working to establish IoT *cybersecurity&privacy* guidance. The international standard (ISO/IEC) 27402, *Cybersecurity—IoT security and privacy—Device baseline requirements* is currently under development: the proposal was approved in mid-June 2020.[86]

6.1.3 Towards a Holistic, Fundamental Rights-Based DPIA

In light of the above, this section aims to provide a theoretical framework for meaningfully integrating a comprehensive fundamental rights assessment in a generic, that is, not sector- or case-specific, DPIA model. This would provide useful benchmarks for a DPIA designed specifically for IoT devices later addressed in the following sections.

The concept of 'rights and freedoms' in Art. 35(7)(c) should be read as a reference to *all* fundamental rights and freedoms, as convincingly put by Hallinan and Martin. Among the three arguments made by the authors to substantiate their thesis,[87] the most significant is perhaps considering the DPIA's risk assessment process in light of

[84] ISO/IEC 27701:2019, *Security techniques — Extension to ISO/IEC 27001 and ISO/IEC 27002 for privacy information management — Requirements and guidelines*, p. 67.

[85] Ibid., pp. 33–51.

[86] See https://www.iso.org/standard/80136.html.

[87] These are: (i) a consideration of the DPIA risk assessment process in light of other substantive provisions in the GDPR, such as the fairness principle (Clifford and Ausloos (2018)); and, (ii) a consideration of the DPIA risk assessment process in light of the phenomena it seeks to regulate.

the overarching goal of the GDPR enshrined in Article 1(2), stating the Regulation's objective, that is, to protect 'the *fundamental rights and freedoms of natural persons* and in particular their right to the protection of personal data [emphasis added]'.[88] "In this statement, there is no indication that the concept of fundamental rights and freedoms should be understood to deviate from the [full catalogue of EU fundamental rights framework]".[89]

Indeed, Article 29 WP points out in the DPIA Guidelines that "the reference to "the rights and freedoms" of data subjects primarily concerns the rights to data protection and privacy but may also involve other fundamental rights such as freedom of speech, freedom of thought, freedom of movement, prohibition of discrimination, right to liberty, conscience and religion".[90] However, as noted in the previous section, the examples of risks made by the Guidelines solely focuses on information security.

If the attention is devoted to DPIA models currently made available by supervisory authorities to provide guidance to data controllers, then it can be observed that generally the risk assessment phase does not encompass the full breadth of Art. 35(7)(c). Thus, the traditional European data protection's procedural approach has led DPAs to design risk assessment models (PIA, i.e. Privacy Impact Assessment, under the Data Protection Directive) that are primarily centered on the processing, task allocation, data quality, and data security, leaving aside the nature of safeguarded interests: "despite specific references in the GDPR to the safeguarding of rights and freedoms in general as well as to societal issues, the new assessment models do nothing to pay greater attention to the societal consequences than the existing PIAs".[91]

For example, Friedewald et al. evaluate and compare DPIA methodologies from various authorities (i.e., French, British, German and Dutch) to design and test a

---

[88] Durante (2021), p. 130: "Art. 1(2) GDPR conveys a conception of law as a means to affirm and protect a human person in some fundamental respect, that is, with regard to what is situated at the foundation of the construction of personality".

[89] Hallinan and Martin (2020), p. 183. Hallinan and Martin convincingly contend that the European fundamental rights framework can fulfil the criteria they previously identified for a legitimate normative reference point in (data protection) risk assessment. Thus, EU fundamental rights framework (i) represents a normatively ideal state of being; (ii) has a relationship with the phenomenon (i.e., the processing of personal data) which poses the harm to be evaluated in the risk assessment process; (iii) the nature and likelihood of impacts is uncertain from the outset, that is, in between neither known nor unknowable.

[90] Article 29 Data Protection Working Party (2017), p. 6.

[91] Mantelero (2022), p. 23. The author rightly points out that "whereas the driving values behind data security and data management are technology-based (e.g. integrity of data) and can therefore be generalised across varying social contexts, the situation with regard to social and ethical values is different. These are necessarily context-based and differ from one community to another, making it hard to pinpoint the benchmark to adopt for this kind of risk assessment". Cfr. with Tamò-Larrieux (2018), p. 189: the author highlights that the alingment of DPIA models towards risk management shifts the focus from transparency to security when considering the technical mechanisms for data protection.

DPIA process generic enough to be used in all possible application areas.[92] However, in the DPIA execution phase, and more specifically in the risk identification step, they only identify 'privacy risks' although they had previously acknowledged that the focus of the execution phase should focus on the assessment of risks to the rights and freedoms of data subjects pursuant to Art. 35 (7)(c) GDPR.[93]

Against this background, after having examined the Article 29 WP guidelines for a DPIA in the previous section, the ENISA methodology may provide useful insights on the extent to which the guidance from EU authorities, notably the EU cybersecurity agency, holistically considers rights and freedoms without flattening the assessment on a pure information security risk-management approach.

In its report 'Handbook on Security of Personal Data Processing', ENISA presents an approach to evaluate risk that can be adopted "in all cases where risk assessment is envisaged under the Regulation (e.g. Data Protection Impact Assessment)".[94] It has four consequential steps: (i) definition of the processing operation and its context; (ii) understanding and evaluating impact; (iii) definition of possible threats and evaluation of their likelihood; (iv) evaluation of risk.

The first step aims to define the processing operations and its context. For the purpose of this work, it is worth dwelling more extensively on the second step, that is, understanding and evaluation of the impact. Importantly, ENISA clarifies from the outset that at this stage the data controller must specifically assess "the impact on the fundamental rights and freedoms of the individuals, resulting from the possible loss of security [i.e., confidentiality, integrity and availability] of the personal data".[95] Moreover, the handbook provides a short but effective informative description of examples for each of the four levels of impact considered (low, medium, high, very high).

The impacts on the 'rights and freedoms of natural persons' span from minor (such as time spent re-entering information, irritations) and significant (e.g., extra costs, denial of access to business services, fear, lack of understanding, stress) inconveniences to significant (e.g., misappropriation of funds, blacklisting by financial institutions, property damage, loss of employment) or irreversible (inability to work, long-term psychological or physical ailments, death) consequences.[96]

It is clear therefore that the risks contemplated by ENISA does not pertain solely to 'privacy' or information security but rather they encompass a much broader set of rights and freedoms. Moreover, ENISA also acknowledges that risk assessment is a qualitative process, as a quantitative analysis is not well suited,[97] and a number of factors must be considered by the data controller.

92 Friedewald et al. (2022).

93 Ibid., p. 430.

94 ENISA (2017), p. 6.

95 Ibid., p. 10.

96 Ibid., p. 11.

97 Danish Institute for Human Rights (2020), p. 98; Friedewald et al. (2022), p. 432.

Consistently, in the online tool for the security of personal data processing, the EU cybersecurity agency maintains the distinction between security risk assessment and DPIA: “while the former is a critical part of the latter, a DPIA takes into account several other parameters that are related to the processing of personal data and go beyond security”.[98]

The third step defines the possible threats related to the *overall* processing’s environment and assesses their likelihood (threat occurrence probability), whereas the fourth step consists of the final evaluation of risk, according to the evaluation of likelihood and impact.

Data protection impact assessment models, especially in data-driven privacy-intensive systems such as the IoT, should be broader in scope so that the full catalogue of EU fundamental rights and freedoms is appropriately contextualised and assessed in a specific use case scenario. A sector-specific approach shall focus on the rights and values potentially impacted in the case under scrutiny rather than the technology itself (AI, IoT, etc.). Depending on the application domain (e.g., domotics, healthcare, industry, etc.), different sets of rights, freedoms and values are at stake. It follows that sectoral (that is, not generic) assessment models should be concerned with the context and the values that assume relevance in a given context.

Bearing this in mind, the second part of this Chapter hinges on a DPIA model for the IoT. In particular, it aims to provide a structured methodology which would effectively and comprehensively implement the requirement of Art. 35, in particular, with a view to assessing risks to rights and freedoms arising in IoT environments. The methodology builds on the CNIL DPIA methodology for IoT devices: accordingly, it is horizontal for IoT systems rather than sector specific. On the other hand, it is worth keeping in mind that the proposed DPIA methodology is not merely a technological assessment but a methodology that should assist sector-specific IoT DPIA in conducting rights-based and values-oriented assessments.

6.2 Holistic Risk Analysis Methodology for IoT

6.2.1 The CNIL DPIA Methodology for IoT Devices

This section presents the methodology developed by the French Data Protection Authority (CNIL), which was the first DPA to publish in 2018 guidelines for conducting a DPIA in the specific context of IoT devices, taking as a case-study a fictional connected toy (thus comprising not only the device i.e., the toy, but also a mobile app and an online service).[99]

The guidelines are based upon the CNIL’s DPIA methodology which, in turn, is made up of three documents, publicly accessible from the agency website: the PIA

[98] See https://www.enisa.europa.eu/risk-level-tool.

[99] CNIL (2018a).

methodology[100]; the PIA templates[101]; and the PIA knowledge bases.[102] The first charts out the approach, the second contains elements that could be used in formalising the analysis and the third one provides a knowledge base, or rather a catalogue of controls to comply with legal requirements and to manage risks, with examples.

The model consists of four phases: (i) study of the context; (ii) study of the fundamental principles; (iii) study of data security risks; (iv) validation of the DPIA. Importantly, the CNIL DPIA methodology guidelines state that the CNIL model covers all the criteria of the WP29 guidelines[103] i.e., (i) a systematic description of the processing (Art. 35(7)(a) GDPR); (ii) assessment of necessity and proportionality (Art. 35(7)(b) GDPR); (iii) management of risks to the rights and freedoms of data subjects (Art. 35(7)(c) GDPR); (iv) involvement of the interested parties (Art. 35(7)(d) GDPR).[104]

The first phase of the DPIA aims to provide a clear overview of the personal data processing operations. Firstly, the model suggests presenting the IoT device scrutinised (a connected toy, in the CNIL example), its nature, scope, context, purposes and stakes. In terms of the data processing, the preliminary step is to identify the data controller and processors, if any. Afterward, sector-specific (either voluntary or mandatory) standards applicable to the processing at stake must be listed, including the approved codes of conduct (art. 40 GDPR) and certifications (art. 42 GDPR). Processing can then be defined and described in detail. The data controller has to take into account three different layers of complexity. They regard: (i) the data processed (which categories of personal data are involved; who the recipients are; the persons with access thereto; the duration of the storage); (ii) the life cycle of data processing (how the product works, with a diagram of data flows and a description of the processes carried out); (iii) data supporting assets (IT systems on which the data rely and other supporting assets).

The second phase of the DPIA interestingly targets manufacturers of IoT devices first. Thus, the core objective of this step is to "build the system that ensures compliance with privacy principles".[105] Behind this lies a presumption that the manufacturer is usually the data controller of the IoT data processing. In particular, the CNIL suggests explaining and justifying the technical choices and the controls selected in the design phase vis-à-vis compliance with GDPR fundamental principles and legal requirements. This analysis comprises two progressive assessments: (i) assessment of the controls guaranteeing the proportionality and necessity of the processing; (ii) assessment of controls protecting data subjects' rights.

---

[100] CNIL (2018c).

[101] CNIL (2018d).

[102] CNIL (2018b).

[103] CNIL (2018c), p. 11.

[104] Article 29 Data Protection Working Party (2017), p. 22.

[105] CNIL (2018a), p. 6.

The former breaks down the processing operations with a view to checking compliance with the GDPR principles envisaged by Art. 5(1). In particular, the data controller shall: (i) set out the purposes of the processing and justify their legitimacy[106]; (ii) identify a suitable legal basis for the processing to comply with the lawfulness criteria as per Art. 6 GDPR; (iii) minimise the personal data that will be processed to what is strictly necessary for the purposes for which they are processed[107]; (iv) set out the data quality compliance controls[108]; (v) define a storage duration for each type of data justified by the legal requirements.[109]

The latter casts the light on the controls protecting data subjects' rights. In particular, the data controller shall: (i) describe how controls for the right to information are implemented on the device, mobile app and personal account, pursuant to Articles 12, 13 and 14 GDPR[110]; (ii) demonstrate that the data subject has consented (where applicable) and provide the data subject with the possibility to easily withdraw his/her consent at any time, pursuant to Articles 7 and 8 GDPR[111]; (iii) ensure users' right of access to all personal data concerning them and to data portability, pursuant to Articles 15 and 20 GDPR[112]; (iv) ensure the rights to rectification and erasure, pursuant to Articles 16 and 17 GDPR[113]; (v) ensure the right to restriction of processing (either concerning the different purposes or the entire operation) and right to object, pursuant to Articles 18 and 21 GDPR[114]; (vi) identify any data processors in the processing contract, by detailing the contractual terms of their relationship with the data controller pursuant to Articles 28 GDPR[115]; (vii) set out the geographic storage location of the device, mobile

[106] Art. 5(1)(b) GDPR.

[107] Art. 5(1)(c) GDPR.

[108] Art. 5.1(d) GDPR.

[109] Art. 5.1(e) GDPR.

[110] Here, technical controls may include the easy display of terms & conditions; clauses specific to the device; thorough presentation of the personal data collected; legible presentation of the purposes of transmission to third parties, etc.

[111] Here, technical controls may include express consent during activation, segmented consent *per* data categories, express consent prior to sharing data with other users, obtaining parents' consent for minors under 13 years of age, etc.

[112] As regards technical controls enforcing the right of access, specific controls might include the possibility of accessing all the user's personal data, via the common interfaces or the possibility of securely consulting the traces of use associated with the user; as regards the right to data portability, the possibility of retrieving, in an easily reusable format, personal data provided by the user, so as to transfer them to another service.

[113] Here, technical controls may include the possibility of rectifying personal data; possibility of erasing personal data; indication of the personal data that will nevertheless be stored, etc.

[114] Here technical controls may include the existence of 'Privacy' settings; an invitation to change the default settings; possibility to access the 'Privacy' settings when activating and after activating the device; existence of a parental control system for children under 13 years of age, etc.

[115] The aspects to be included in the agreement shall cover: duration, scope, purpose, documented processing instructions, prior authorisation where a processor is engaged, prompt notification of any data breach, etc.

app and personal account data in the cloud, that is, comply with the obligations concerning the transfer of personal data outside the European Union, pursuant to Articles 44 to 50 GDPR and applicable case-law.[116]

The third phase of the DPIA focuses on the risks posed to data security, with a specific reference to Article 32 GDPR. This phase is once again divided into two sequential assessments: the assessment of existing or planned (security) controls and a traditional information security risk assessment bearing on potential *privacy* breaches.

The assessment of security controls, generally performed by the person in charge of data security aspects, is threefold, for it identifies: (i) controls specifically aimed at the data being processed: encryption,[117] anonymisation,[118] data partitioning,[119] logical access control,[120] traceability,[121] archiving,[122] integrity monitoring and paper document security; (ii) general security controls regarding the system in which the processing is carried out: operating security,[123] backups, hardware security, network security,[124] physical access control, monitoring, maintenance, website security, protecting against non-human sources of risks; (iii) organisational controls (governance): organization,[125] policy, project management, personnel management, risk management,[126] management of incidents and breaches, relations with third parties, supervision.

The risk assessment then takes into account three feared events that can potentially lead to privacy breaches, all pertaining to the field of information security and, more specifically the 'CIA triad': illegitimate access (breach of personal data confidentiality); unwanted change (breach of data integrity); disappearance (breach of data availability).

---

[116] The CJEU, with the seminal *Schrems II* ruling (Case C-311/18 *Facebook Irland and Schrems* [2020] EU:C:2020:559), has once again invalidated the Commission's adequacy decision (so-called Privacy Shield) on transfers of personal data to the US.

[117] The CNIL suggests describing the encryption means for data at rest and data in transit implemented in the processing, as well as the procedure for managing encryption keys.

[118] The CNIL suggests indicating whether anonymisation mechanisms are implemented, which ones and for what purpose.

[119] Whether it is planned, and how, or not.

[120] The CNIL suggests indicating the specification of the implemented authentication means and password criteria.

[121] Whether events are logged and for how long.

[122] The CNIL suggests describing the archiving management processes.

[123] Description of how software updates and security patches are implemented.

[124] Description of the type of network on which the processing is carried out and specification of which firewall system, intrusion detection systems or other active or passive devices are in charge of ensuring network security.

[125] Whether the roles and responsibilities for data protection and cybersecurity are defined.

[126] Whether the privacy risks posed by new processing on data subjects are assessed, whether or not it is systematic and, if applicable, according to which method.

Importantly, for each breach data controllers have to consider the main risk sources, the main threats, the main potential impacts, the principal controls mitigating the risk, and finally the severity and likelihood. In accordance with traditional information security risk assessment models, the level of risk is estimated, rather than quantified, by determining its severity (i.e., the potential impact) and likelihood (i.e., the possibility of a risk occurring).

Afterwards, data controllers have to assess whether the controls in place (or planned) adequately mitigate the risk. If any additional control may prove necessary, it will be indicated. Finally, once the additional controls have been implemented, the residual risk will be determined by determining the severity and likelihood in view of such additional controls.

The last phase of the DPIA, consisting of the model's validation, is divided into two steps: preparation of the material required for validation and the formal validation. The former serves a twofold purpose: presenting the findings of the DPIA (i.e., visual presentation of the controls as *per* phase 2 and 3, mapping the risks—initial and residual, if any—depending on their severity and likelihood, drafting an action plan to implement the additional controls) and documenting the consideration of stakeholders (i.e., advice of the DPO, pursuant to Article 35(2) GDPR and the view of data subjects or their representatives, pursuant to Article 35(9) GDPR). The latter consists of deciding whether the selected controls, residual risks and action plan are acceptable, with justifications, in view of the previously identified stakes and views of the stakeholders: the DPIA can be validated, conditional on improvement or refused.

6.2.2 A Critical Analysis of the CNIL Model: Consistency with the Holistic 'Risk-to-Rights' Approach

In light of the first part of the Chapter, this section provides a critical discussion regarding the CNIL DPIA methodology for IoT devices. Different layers of complexity are under scrutiny. They regard: (i) whether and to which extent the methodology integrates a rights-based assessment; (ii) how the CNIL methodology strikes a balance between, on the one hand, information security and, on the other, the more-encompassing concept of cybersecurity (see Chap. 3); (iii) the extent to which the CNIL model can be adapted to encompass other devices within the IoT domain.

6.2.2.1 The 'Rights-Based' Test

By operationalising the DPIA as a compliance check of both GDPR and IT requirements, the CNIL methodological approach has become the most popular.[127] Sion et al. carried out a comprehensive state-of-the-art review of existing approaches and tools to support DPIA, which range from simple template and questionnaire-based approaches to dedicated modelling frameworks.[128] These models are taken from national Data Protection Authorities guidelines (in particular, French, German and Dutch), available commercial tools and specific literature on privacy and security requirements engineering. According to the indicators used as proxies by the authors in their analysis,[129] the CNIL approach was considered as the most comprehensive, outscoring the German and Dutch approaches with regard to model's completeness and soundness as well as identification of legal compliance issues.[130]

With specific regard to the identification of compliance issues, the approach adopted by CNIL has also been referred to as 'compliance assessment': "this approach suggests a DPIA risk assessment need only take the concrete principles outlined in the GDPR – such as those in Articles 5 (b)-(f), 6-8, 12-18, 20, 21, 28 and 44-49 – as a normative reference point. An assessment of risks to the concrete principles in the GDPR should certainly be included as part of the DPIA risk assessment process. However, a consideration of risks to these concrete data protection principles alone does not equate to a consideration of risks to all rights and freedoms".[131]

This is therefore the focal point of the first legal challenge raised by CNIL methodology, i.e., to what extent the DPIA methodology for IoT devices integrates a comprehensive assessment of the risks to the rights and freedoms of data subjects. Admittedly, the other criteria of the WP29 guidelines are convincingly covered by the French model. In this regard, the title of the third phase of the DPIA, i.e., the 'study of data security risks',[132] is rather eloquent.

On the one hand, the analysis of information security controls in the CNIL model comes after the implementation of the controls on the proportionality and necessity of the processing—which, incidentally, do not address Art. 5(1)(a) GDPR, and especially cornerstone data protection principles such as fairness and

[127] Friedewald et al. (2022), pp. 425–26.

[128] Sion et al. (2020).

[129] DPIA methodology support; coverage of A29WP concepts; support for soundness criteria; support for legal criteria; tool support; document generation and model management.

[130] Sion et al. (2020), pp. 8–9.

[131] Hallinan and Martin (2020), p. 184.

[132] CNIL (2018a), p. 22.

transparency[133]—and the controls protecting data subject's rights.[134] It follows that, in the CNIL's view, specific information security measures facilitate data protection goals, in particular, the lawfulness of the processing.

This approach recalls the *infraethical* perspective (Chap. 3): a 'good' design of cybersecurity measures that is oriented towards facilitating the occurrence of what is morally good, the protection of personal data and the safeguarding of rights and freedoms of individuals.[135] Using the words of the Spanish Data Protection Authority (AEPD), "the technical and organisational measures needed to ensure the confidentiality, integrity and availability of information must be aimed at implementing data protection principles to guarantee the rights and freedoms of individuals in a State governed by the rule of law, even beyond a potential breach of the rule of law".[136]

On the other hand, by focusing only on data security risks as feared events for the assessment, the CNIL DPIA reveals itself as "merely a data security methodology".[137] To make things worse, the second step of the third phase advises data controllers "to determine the potential impacts on data subjects' privacy", unduly restricting the scope of the DPIA to a 'privacy impact assessment (PIA)'.

In so doing, the CNIL methodology fails to take into consideration the full breadth of the GDPR's requirements for a DPIA, with particular regard to the obligation of assessing the 'risks to the rights and freedoms of natural persons' as per Art. 35(7)(c).

IoT personal data processing may thus impact individuals in many ways, going beyond 'more established' risks to the rights to privacy and data protection. Beyond the rights and freedoms already mentioned in the Article 29 WP Guidelines (i.e., freedom of expression and information (Art. 11 of the EU Charter of Fundamental Rights), freedom of movement (Art. 45 EU Charter), freedom of thought, conscience and religion (Art. 11 EU Charter), right to liberty and security (Art. 6 EU Charter) and prohibition to discriminate (Art. 21 EU Charter)),[138] the negative consequences suffered by individuals brought about by IoT data processing—e.g., from fear and stress to more significant impacts such as, misappropriation of funds, blacklisting by

[133] Related to that, it might be interesting to explore the option of 'non-processing' in those instances where the lawfulness of data processing might be very hard to reach in practical terms.

[134] In the phrasing of the CNIL, this subset of controls is generally carried on by the prime contractor (which can be a delegate, representative or processor) and then assessed by the person in charge of data security: i.e., the chief information security officer (CISO) or the DPO themselves. It is evident that a sort of holistic approach is already in place: the cyber or information security controls weighing specifically on the data being processed are assessed, by the CISO, in order to better understand the privacy risk. Against this background, there are attempts to integrate the CNIL DPIA with the EBIOS risk manager, the method for assessing and treating digital cybersecurity risks published by National Cybersecurity Agency of France (ANSSI).

[135] Chiara (2021), p. 30.

[136] AEPD (2020b).

[137] Gellert (2018), p. 283.

[138] Article 29 Data Protection Working Party (2017), p. 6.

financial institutions, property damage, loss of employment or inability to work, long-term psychological or physical ailments and death—can be mapped out to other rights and freedoms from the catalogue of EU fundamental rights' framework.

Let us take as an example the fictional connected toy analysed by the CNIL. Article 3 of the Charter protects the integrity of a person's body, both mental and physical[139]: interferences with this right consist of the causation of injuries, pain, or other bodily and mental harm.[140] The IoT, for it is a cyber-physical intermediating system, brings about risk factors that potentially result in a spectrum of harms, from mental damage to physical injury.[141] A DPIA methodology for a connected toy has to assess impacts to Art. 3 of the Charter.

Moreover, given the interaction between the connected toy and young users, who can be influenced by the device's value-laden content, either crafted by the manufacturer or dangerously continuously re-shaped by an embedded AI system, other fundamental rights further impacted can be the freedom of thought (Art. 10 CFR[142]) and the right to education, in particular, the right of parents to guarantee the education and teaching of their children in conformity with their religious, philosophical and pedagogical convictions (Art. 14 CFR[143]).

However, by mirroring the approach of pre-GDPR 'PIAs', CNIL's risk assessment is more preoccupied with a *technical* understanding of privacy, adhering to an information security's tradition. It can be concluded that the CNIL falls short of meaningfully integrating a rights-based assessment in its DPIA methodology.

However, the GDPR requirement of Art. 35(7)(c) is not actually met by other risk assessment models proposed for IoT systems either. To name one, ANASTACIA H2020 project developed a 'Dynamic Security and Privacy Seal' to address the constant discovery of vulnerabilities in IoT components, combining security and privacy standards and real time monitoring and online testing. The 'Seal' aims to provide a quantitative and qualitative run-time evaluation of privacy risks and security levels, which can be easily understood and controlled by the final users.[144]

The project deliverable D2.3 explored relevant privacy risks: ANASTACIA identified seven risks to the rights and liberties of individuals taking place at the IoT network level. They regard: (i) unauthorised access/disclosure of personal data (loss of confidentiality); (ii) unauthorised modification of personal data (loss of integrity); (iii) unauthorized or inappropriate linking of personal data (potential for data re-identification); (iv) unauthorized removal or deletion of personal data (loss of

---

[139] Conversely, the ECtHR envisages the protection of physical and mental integrity under the right to private life (Art. 8 ECHR). See ECtHR, *X and Y v the Netherlands*, CE:ECHR:1985:0326JUD000897880, para 22; ECtHR, *Stubbings and others v UK*, CE:ECHR:1996:1022JUD002208393, para 61.

[140] Lock (2019a).

[141] Denardis (2020), p. 224.

[142] Lock (2019b).

[143] Lock (2019c).

[144] ANASTACIA Project, "Advanced Networked Agents for Security and Trust Assessment in CPS/IOT Architectures".

availability); (v) excessive collection or retention of personal data (loss of operational control); (vi) lacking protection of traffic information and location data; (vii) impairment of data subject's rights.[145]

It is true that ANASTACIA project managed to go beyond traditional information security risks to the CIA triad (i.e., points i), ii) and iv)). The introduction of data re-identification risk, loss of operational control and impairment of data subject's rights is an attempt to meaningfully assess risks to individuals' rights and freedoms. A closer look, however, reveals that the reference to the impairment of data subject's rights, which seemingly assure compliance with the challenging high standard of the GDPR, is nothing more than an open, final clause. Indeed, ANASTACIA does not specify what this risk amounts to, for it only addresses the underlying threats, i.e. Dos and DDoS attacks (see Chap. 2).[146]

6.2.2.2 Adequacy of the Cybersecurity Risks' Coverage

The second challenge hinges on whether cybersecurity risks are adequately assessed by the CNIL DPIA. As stated, the third phase focuses on 'data security risks', with the feared events being illegitimate access, unwanted change and disappearance of personal data, covering the notorious 'CIA' triad (confidentiality, integrity and availability) of information security.

The question to be asked is whether in 'IoT scenarios', that is, environments with connected devices interacting with other systems and individuals, the feared events that ought to be considered by the risk assessment should be limited to the CIA triad or rather extend to other cybersecurity principles as seen in previous Chapters. In particular, Art. 51 of the Cybersecurity Act sets a comprehensive and high-level set of security objectives within the context of a broad and general notion of cybersecurity that goes beyond information security, to include device and network security. This provision can be taken as a benchmark irrespective of the fact that it was originally conceived for the purpose of certification schemes.[147] The security objectives laid down by Art. 51 CSA are:

(a) to protect stored, transmitted or otherwise processed data against accidental or unauthorised storage, processing, access or disclosure during the entire life cycle of the ICT product, ICT service or ICT process;
(b) to protect stored, transmitted or otherwise processed data against accidental or unauthorised destruction, loss or alteration or lack of availability during the entire life cycle of the ICT product, ICT service or ICT process;

[145] Quesada Rodriguez et al. (2018), pp. 52–60.

[146] Ibid., p. 57.

[147] Wavestone - CEPS - CARSA - ICF (2021), p. 166: "Art. 51 was taken as a reference as it represents one of the most up-to-date piece of legislation concerning cybersecurity and providing a comprehensive set of requirements for products and services".

(c) that authorised persons, programmes or machines are able only to access the data, services or functions to which their access rights refer;
(d) to identify and document known dependencies and vulnerabilities;
(e) to record which data, services or functions have been accessed, used or otherwise processed, at what times and by whom;
(f) to make it possible to check which data, services or functions have been accessed, used or otherwise processed, at what times and by whom;
(g) to verify that ICT products, ICT services and ICT processes do not contain known vulnerabilities;
(h) to restore the availability and access to data, services and functions in a timely manner in the event of a physical or technical incident;
(i) that ICT products, ICT services and ICT processes are secure by default and by design;
(j) that ICT products, ICT services and ICT processes are provided with up-to-date software and hardware that do not contain publicly known vulnerabilities, and are provided with mechanisms for secure updates.

Whereas illegitimate access is covered by letter a) and c) of Art. 51, letter b) aims to avoid the unwanted change and disappearance of data. The remaining objectives can be mainly linked to security controls, already foreseen by CNIL methodology. In particular, letters e) and f) are covered by logical access control and traceability requirements under Sect. 3.1.1 of the CNIL's DPIA methodology. Moreover, letter h) and j) deal respectively with backups and updates controls that are listed in Sect. 3.1.2 of the CNIL's DPIA methodology. If the 'security by design and by default' objective outlined in letter i) is too high-level to be considered a security control or an operationalisable objective, letters d) and g) are preoccupied with the issues of vulnerabilities.

If it is true that, on the one hand, identifying and managing systems' vulnerabilities can be considered a technical control, on the other hand, the possible exploitation of known vulnerabilities may indeed represent a feared event with a potential impact on individuals' rights and freedoms. However, the feared event 'exploitation of vulnerabilities' would be preliminary to the ones identified by the CNIL (i.e., illegitimate access, unwanted change and disappearance of data), for it operates at a different level, i.e., at system level.

Moreover, following an all-encompassing interpretation of the CIA triad (see Chap. 3), the three security risks contemplated by the CNIL methodology would also take into account the security principles of authenticity, accountability, non-repudiation and reliability, therefore not limiting their scope to confidentiality, integrity and availability. An unwanted change of data is a breach of integrity, guarding against improper data modification and would therefore ensure *non-repudiation* and *authenticity*. On the other hand, the disappearance of data is a breach of availability, which aims to ensure *reliable* access to and use of data.[148]

[148] NIST (2015), pp. 42–43.

All in all, the analysis of Art. 51 CSA showed that the CNIL methodology is flexible enough to cover the security objectives laid out in the Cybersecurity Act, thanks to both the various cybersecurity technical controls and a broader understanding of traditional information security risks.

6.2.2.3 The IoT 'Generalisation Test'

Finally, the last issue under consideration is the extent to which the CNIL methodology can be successfully transposed to and implemented in every IoT scenario. When mapping the data flow in the first phase of the DPIA, the CNIL 'only' considers a simplified IoT interaction-model wherein machine-to-machine (M2M) communication is neglected.

Instead, in the fictional IoT device (the connected toy), the CNIL appears to be more preoccupied with human-to-machine communication (e.g., the child interacting with the connected toy, the parents monitoring the related data, etc.) and machine-to-manufacturer communication (e.g., data, recorded via sensors on the IoT device, are transferred to the mobile app, directly via the device or through the cloud servers, data analysis algorithms in the cloud generate the response data on the basis of previous dialogues and the interests detected and produce statistics on use and advertising targeting).[149]

The lack of reference to the machine-to-machine (M2M) communication is a weakness of the methodology, for it is a core feature of IoT systems bearing on security and privacy. On the one hand, it is a legitimate choice to design a connected product without the possibility of interacting with other devices; on the other hand, a DPIA methodology for IoT devices should also take this concern into consideration.

6.2.3 A Rights-Based Data Protection Impact Assessment Methodology for IoT Devices

The last section of the Chapter aims to offer a DPIA methodology for a connected IoT device that integrates a comprehensive assessment of the rights and freedoms impacted in a fictional IoT scenario. To this end, the proposed DPIA methodology builds not only on the legal analysis on DPIAs of this chapter, but also on Chap. 2 (insofar as the IoT technical architecture and threat landscape is concerned) and Chap. 3 (insofar as a theoretical framework for cybersecurity is concerned).

The proposed DPIA methodology is based on the guidance of Article 29 WP, ENISA and, in particular, the CNIL's DPIA for IoT devices, bearing in mind the lessons learned from the previous section. For the sake of ensuring consistency with

[149] CNIL (2018c), pp.4–5.

the CNIL methodology, the examples made to contextualise this methodology refer to a connected toy.

As seen above, the fair balance effort performed by supervisory authorities, EU agencies and private parties provides for a remarkable knowledge base which can be easily integrated into the CNIL methodology to better assess the risk to rights in such complex scenarios. Provided that the CNIL methodology satisfactorily operationalises the first two criteria of the WP29 guidelines on DPIAs, the model presented here can be almost completely superposed on Phases 1, 2 and 4 of the CNIL methodology. 'Almost', because the first step of the DPIA model here proposed makes some room for M2M communication in the functional description of the processing operation and main functionalities of the device under scrutiny.

A particular emphasis is placed on the third criterion of the WP29 guidelines, which corresponds to phase 3 of the CNIL methodology, as it has not satisfactorily been addressed by the CNIL. The model presented in this section enhances the CNIL's methodology insofar as the assessment of the impact on the rights is concerned, by implementing the methodology proposed by Mantelero. In particular, the proposed DPIA methodology relies on Mantelero's model with regard to (i) the identification of the variables of the relevant risk dimensions (i.e., severity and likelihood) to contextualise more meaningfully risk's components; and, (ii) a method to 'quantify' impacts on the aforementioned variables.

Related to that, the severity of the envisaged impacts is the combination of the gravity of the prejudice in the exercising of the rights and freedoms, and the effort to overcome said consequences. On the other hand, the likelihood is estimated by considering the probability of a risk occurring and exposure, that is, the potential number of people at risk. Mantelero suggests assessing the expected impact using a four-step ordinal scale from 1 to 4, where 1 corresponds to low; 2 to medium; 3 to high; 4 to very high. Then, the two variables shall be combined using a cardinal scale to obtain the overall level of the two risk dimensions (i.e., severity and likelihood): 1–2 corresponds to low; 3–6 to medium; 8–9 to high; 12–16 to very high.[150]

In turn, Mantelero's methodology can be integrated by the ENISA methodology (Sect. 6.1.3) to the extent that the latter can provide benchmarks to assess the variables of the risk components. With regard to the *effort to overcome the prejudice* variable, 'low' will refer to minor inconveniences (e.g., irritation; time-waste); 'medium' will refer to significant inconveniences (e.g., extra costs; fear; stress); 'high' will refer to significant consequences (e.g., property damage; physical injuries); 'very high' will refer to irreversible consequences (e.g., long-term psychological or physical ailments, death). The *gravity* variable predicates on the seriousness of the prejudice encountered by individuals in the exercise of their rights and freedoms. If 'low' (i.e., minor inconveniences in the exercise of rights) and 'very high' (i.e., irreversible consequences) can be quite straightforward, it might be hard to distinguish between 'medium' and 'high'.

[150] Mantelero (2022), pp. 54–57.

It is up to who performs the risk assessment to assign values to the expected prejudice in light of the context, that is, by taking into account the characteristics of the data processing scenario under scrutiny, the application scenario, the categories of individuals potentially impacted, etc. This assessment shall be carried out by a (multidisciplinary) team with expertise in the fundamental rights framework (e.g., the Charter of Fundamental Rights of the European Union, relevant case-law of the Court of Justice of the European Union and possibly relevant legal doctrine) for it requires interpretative reasoning and normative judgments.

Regarding the *probability* variable, 'low' will refer to very improbable chances that the prejudice can materialise; 'medium' will refer to the possibility that the prejudice can actually materialise; 'high' will refer to a high probability that the prejudice materialises; 'very high' will refer to situations where the risk is very likely to materialise. With respect to the *exposure* variable, 'low' will refer to situations where only few of the identified individuals will be affected; 'medium' will refer to scenarios where a part of the identified individuals will be affected; 'high' will refer to scenarios where the majority identified individuals will be affected; 'very high' will refer to scenarios where almost every, if not every identified individual will be affected. In a similar vein to the assessment of the *severity* dimension, the assessment of the *probability* and *exposure* variables shall be carried out by experts and needs to be contextual, that is, based on available historical data that can be translated to the situation at hand.

In line with the outcomes of Sect. 6.2.2.1, the assessment will go beyond the risks to privacy as addressed by the CNIL model, to explore the wider range of consequences on different rights and freedoms triggered by the IoT (a connected toy, in our—and CNIL's example) personal data processing, therefore ensuring full compliance to the requirement enshrined in Art. 35(7)(c) GDPR. For instance, a DPIA for a connected toy should also take into account an assessment of the risks to the right of parents to ensure the education and teaching of their children in conformity with their religious, philosophical and pedagogical convictions (Art. 14 CFR) and to the right to the integrity of the person (Art. 3 CFR), as previously discussed in Sect. 6.2.2.1.

6.2.3.1 Step 1. Setting the Context

General Information

1.1 Product Description

The description of the IoT device shall cast light on all the IoT components relevant to data processing as addressed in Chap. 2: from the device layer, including sensors and actuators (e.g., microphones, cameras, buttons, etc.), to the network and application layers (e.g., Wi-Fi connectivity, mobile app or online services, etc.).

1.2 Processing Purposes
The purposes of the processing must be detailed: e.g., interacting with the child, enabling the child to browse the internet and communicate with other users, etc.

1.3 Data Controller(s) and Data Processor(s)
Data controllers and processors must be determined. For example, the manufacturer of the IoT device will be a data controller; data processors may be firms hosting and providing various services (e.g., device interactivity, data analysis, advertising, etc.).

Focus on Personal Data Processing

1.4 Personal Data Processing
The type of personal data processed (e.g., information about users, data entered in third-party app, data collected by the device, data provided by the device as a result of the interaction with the user based on life habits, advertising, etc.) and the categories of such data (e.g., common data, data relating to a minor, sensitive data according to Art. 9 GDPR, etc.); the recipients (e.g., controllers and processors); and the persons authorised to process said data.

1.5 Data Supporting Assets
List of the hardware and software components on which data rely.

1.6 Lifecycle of Data and Processes
For the sake of clarity, it is preferable to present the processes carried out *via* a diagram of data flows. This shall be complemented by a detailed description of the processing activities performed and how the product generally works, i.e., whether only human-to-machine interaction is foreseen or also machine-to-machine interaction, whether the data stay in the device for computation, or whether they are sent to cloud servers *via* a mobile app, whether a degree of AI is embedded in the system, etc.

6.2.3.2 Step 2. Assessment of the Necessity and Proportionality of the Processing

Assessment of the Necessity and Proportionality of the Processing

2.1 Purposes
The purposes of each data processing operation must be explained and justified (e.g., third-party sharing, profiling, provision of primary service, etc.), according to Art. 5(1)(b) GDPR.

2.2 Legal Basis
A suitable legal basis (Art. 6, 9 GDPR) shall be chosen for each processing operation. As noticed by the CNIL model, "there can be several types of bases for a processing operation: for example, a contract associated with the purchase of a

product for using it for its primary purpose and consent for its secondary purposes (improving the service, marketing, etc.) which will be obtained when the product is activated".[151]

Moreover, if consent has been chosen as legal basis for the processing, in the context of a connected toy—where information society services may be offered directly to a child under 16 years of age, consent shall be given by the holder of parental responsibility over the child (Art. 8(1) GDPR).

2.3 Data Minimisation
Firstly, the amount of personal data that will be processed shall be limited to what is strictly necessary for the purposes of the processing (Art. 5(1)(c) GDPR). Secondly, technical and organisational measures can be adopted to further minimise the sensitivity of the processing (e.g., pseudonymisation, randomisation, etc.).

2.4 Data Quality
Data must be accurate and kept up to date (Art. 5(1)(d) GDPR).

2.5 Storage Limitation
For each type of data, a storage limitation period, and also an erasure mechanism must be set (Art. 5(1)(e) GDPR).

Assessment of the Measures Guaranteeing Data Subjects' Rights

2.6 Information for the Data Subjects
Measures to provide information to users (or their parents, if applicable), as provided for in Articles 12, 13 and 14 GDPR. These measures include the presentation, at the moment of activation and thereafter, of legible and easy-to-understand terms and conditions; a detailed and easy-to-understand description of the processing purposes and data flows; a detailed presentation of the data collected, inferred, processed and transmitted (e.g., to third parties), etc. In this regard, see in particular Sect. 5.1.2.

2.7 Measures on Consent
If the processing is based on consent, measures to ensure compliance with consent requirements must be in place (Articles 7 and 8 GDPR). These may include: granular and specific consent *per* data category or processing type; presentation in an intelligible and easy-to-understand language adapted to the target user (particularly for children); parents' consent for minors under the age of 13 years, consent can be withdrawn easily and at any time. Against the background of technical solutions to facilitate consent in IoT systems, see Sect. 5.1.1.

2.8 Rights of Access and to Data Portability
Measures to implement the rights of access (Art. 15 GDPR) and to data portability (Art. 20 GDPR) on the device. These may include the possibility of accessing (and

[151] CNIL (2018a), p. 9.

downloading) all the users' personal data and retrieving, in an easily reusable format, personal data provided by the user.

2.9 Right to Rectification and to Erasure
Measures to implement the rights to rectification (Art. 16 GDPR) and erasure (Art. 17 GDPR) on the device. These may include easily understandable information about how to erase data, also remotely in the event that the device is lost.

2.10 Right to Object and to Restriction of Processing
Measures to implement the rights to object (Art. 18 GDPR) and to restriction of processing (Art. 21 GDPR) on the device. These may include a notification to change the default privacy settings when activating the device; a parental control system for children; the possibility of deactivating some of the device's features; compliance with legal requirements and DPA guidelines related to tracking technologies, such as cookies.

2.11 Geo-Localisation of the Processing
Several legal arrangements must be implemented, depending on the country where the personal data are stored i.e., whether outside the EU or not.

6.2.3.3 Step 3. Assessment of the Risks to Rights and Freedoms of Data Subjects

Risk Assessment

3.1 Risk to the Right to Privacy and Protection of Personal Data (Articles 7 and 8 CFR)[152]

(i) *determine the risk sources*: e.g., rogue neighbour; hackers; negligent or rogue user/family member/friend; AI-processed/predetermined sentences at the base of the interaction between the toy and the user.
(ii) *determine the main threats*: e.g., illegitimate access to personal data; unwanted change of personal data; disappearance of personal data; intrusion of the toy into the user's private sphere.
(iii) *determine the potential impacts*: e.g., profiling; targeted advertising; identity theft; loss of history and personal service settings; provision of unexpected content—including sensitive personal data—by the user when interacting with the toy; surveillance.

Taking into account the above, the *severity* (i.e., the first risk component) can be assessed. To this end, it shall be estimated (i) the gravity of the prejudice to the right assessed; and (ii) the effort to overcome it and to reverse the negative impacts. The *likelihood* shall be assessed in the same way. Taking into account the above

[152] For the purpose of this analysis, these two distinct rights will be assessed together.

information, the experts performing the evaluation shall estimate (i) the probability of the risk occurring; and (ii) the exposure.

Finally, the initial assessment determines the risk index, namely the *overall impact* for the specific right/liberty considered by combining the two risk components (severity and the likelihood):

low-low= low;
low-medium= medium; low-high=medium; low-very high=medium;
medium-high= high; medium-very high= high;
high-very high= very high; very high-very high= very high.

3.2 Risk to the Right to the Integrity of the Person (Art. 3 CFR)

(i) *determine the risk sources*: e.g., hackers; rogue neighbours; malfunctions; AI embedded in the IoT product (if any) and learning abilities.
(ii) *determine the main threats*: e.g., unexpected and hazardous behaviour of the IoT product.
(iii) *determine the potential impacts*: e.g., physical harm (depending on the actual size and characteristics of the toy); physiological harm.

Taking into account the above, the *severity* (i.e., the first risk component) can be assessed. To this end, it shall be estimated (i) the gravity of the prejudice to the right assessed; and (ii) the effort to overcome it and to reverse the negative impacts. The *likelihood* shall be assessed in the same way. Taking into account the above information, the experts performing the evaluation shall estimate (i) the probability of the risk occurring; and (ii) the exposure.

Finally, the initial assessment determines the risk index, namely the *overall impact* for the specific right/liberty considered by combining the two risk components (severity and the likelihood):

low-low= low;
low-medium= medium; low-high=medium; low-very high=medium;
medium-high= high; medium-very high= high;
high-very high= very high; very high-very high= very high.

3.3 Risk to the Right to Education (Art. 14 CFR)

(i) *determine the risk sources*: e.g., manufacturer's choices in terms of the content underlying the interaction between the IoT product—child; AI embedded in the IoT product (if any) and learning abilities.

(ii) *determine the main threats*: e.g., transmission of value-oriented content to the user interacting with the connected toy; unwanted and unsolicited influences on the child.
(iii) *determine the potential impacts*: e.g., limitation to parents' right to ensure moral and religious education of their children in accordance with their religious, philosophical and pedagogical convictions.

Taking into account the above, the *severity* (i.e., the first risk component) can be assessed. To this end, it shall be estimated (i) the gravity of the prejudice to the right assessed; and (ii) the effort to overcome it and to reverse the negative impacts. The *likelihood* shall be assessed in the same way. Taking into account the above information, the experts performing the evaluation shall estimate (i) the probability of the risk occurring; and (ii) the exposure.

Finally, the initial assessment determines the risk index, namely the *overall impact* for the specific right/liberty considered by combining the two risk components (severity and the likelihood):

low-low= low;
low-medium= medium; low-high=medium; low-very high=medium;
medium-high= high; medium-very high= high;
high-very high= very high; very high-very high= very high.

Assessment of Technical and Organisational Mitigation Measures and Re-Assessment for Each Identified Risk

3.4 Technical Measures Regarding the Personal Data Being Processed
To mitigate the risks found, detail here the technical security measures implemented in the processing of personal data adopted: e.g., end-to-end encryption; pseudonymisation; anonymisation; access control; two-factors authentication; etc.[153]

3.5 Technical Measures Regarding the System Where the Processing Is Carried Out
To mitigate the risks found, detail here the technical security measures implemented in the system adopted: e.g., hardware authentication; access logging; storage duration; backups; operating security; etc.[154]

[153] ENISA (2017): see Annex A.

[154] Id.

3.6 Organisational Measures
Detail here the organisational mitigation measures adopted: e.g., closed set of communication input for the connected product; possibility to access, verify and modify the pre-installed phrases at the basis of the communication between the connected toy and the user (the child); possibility to deactivate sensing/monitoring features of the device; excluding interaction with other IoT devices; etc.

3.7 Re-assessment
In light of the mitigation measures adopted, the risk assessment shall be performed again to determine the final impact on the rights and freedoms of natural persons brought about by the personal data processing performed by the connected product scrutinised.

6.2.3.4 Step 4. Involvement of Stakeholders

Preparation of the Documentation for Validation

4.1 Consolidate the DPIA's findings through a visual presentation of each step.

4.2 Document the consideration of stakeholders, in particular, the advice of the person in charge of 'data protection' aspects (Art. 35(2) GDPR) and the view of data subjects or their representatives (Art. 35(9) GDPR).

Formal Validation

4.3 Taking into account the selected measures, the residual risks and the considerations of stakeholders, the DPIA may be: (a) validated; (b) conditionally validated on improvement; (c) refused.

6.3 Conclusion

This Chapter dwelt on the GDPR's requirement to carry out a data protection impact assessment (DPIA). In particular, it broke down Art. 35 GDPR into all its components, stressing the centrality of the requirement to manage 'the risks to the rights and freedoms of data subjects' (Art. 35(7)(c) GDPR).

Existing DPIA models, even those provided by data protection authorities, tend to limit the scope of this obligation to an assessment of the impact on the right to privacy alone, without departing from the 'pre-GDPR approach' of privacy impact assessments (PIAs) that used to focus on data quality and security. This approach is arguably more aligned with traditional information security risk assessments, such as the ISO group of 'privacy standards'. The latter nonetheless differs in scope and rationale from the legal standard set by the GDPR.

Hence, the analysis demonstrated that a more meaningful interpretation of the Regulation should go beyond upholding only the right to privacy and the protection of personal data, to encompass, in line with Article 1(2) GDPR, the full catalogue of the EU fundamental rights framework.

Against this backdrop, this chapter presented an original DPIA methodology for connected devices (IoT). It builds on the CNIL model which fell short of implementing the requirement of assessing the impact of risks to 'the rights and freedoms of data subjects'. The last section of this Chapter presented a holistic 'rights-based' DPIA methodology for an IoT device, with the underlying hope of providing useful guidelines for technology development and improved compliance with GDPR requirements, too often interpreted as a 'ticking-the-box' exercise, in line with a more consolidated information security tradition.

The main contribution of this chapter is indeed represented by a DPIA methodology including the assessment of the impact on different rights and freedoms that have been deemed to be relevant to the specific nature of the given application i.e., a connected toy—to ensure continuity with the CNIL methodology. The model is intended to provide help and guidance to assessors by (i) breaking down single high-level requirements into more concrete subsequent steps to achieve meaningful GDPR-compliance; (ii) providing a flexible methodology to assess the 'risk to rights' standard of Art. 35(7)(c) GDPR; (iii) listing, by means of examples, several fundamental rights that may be impacted by an IoT device to be deployed in a given scenario (e.g., a connected toy).

Some might argue that this methodology represents an additional burden for economic operators involved in the IoT and AI industry. Considering the full catalogue of fundamental rights and freedoms enshrined in EU primary law would, according to this view, set the threshold too high. Moreover, the line of reasoning behind a broad interpretation of Art. 35(7)(c) GDPR can to some extent contribute to 'distort' the rationale of data protection law, which inevitably becomes '*the law of everything*': "complying with and enforcing such a law in a meaningful way is impossible, and something – enforcement or compliance – will have to give".[155]

However, it can be argued that applying the requirement of Art. 35 GDPR to the letter would not be disproportionate for manufacturers-as-data controllers vis-à-vis the risks they bring to society and the profits they make out of it, building on the long-standing tradition of law and economics theories.[156] Furthermore, the adoption of these types of holistic methodologies presents data controllers with an opportunity in the form of competitive advantage compared to competitors that do not operationalise and specify high-level and vague GDPR requirements, such as Art. 35(7)(c).[157]

155 Purtova (2018), p. 77.

156 Cooter (1991), p. 11.

157 Mantelero (2022), p. 32; Fuster et al. (2022).

All in all, lacking more adequate and comprehensive legal instruments, data protection law has inevitably taken on a somewhat uncomfortable protective role for the entire catalogue of fundamental rights in tackling the normative (legal, ethical and societal) challenges brought about by the 'digital revolution'. In a way, Article 8 of the Charter of the Fundamental Rights have become from 2018 onwards a *super* fundamental right. Against this backdrop, more fine-tuned legal tools aiming at safeguarding fundamental rights in the digital economy & society recently introduced in the EU, such as the Fundamental rights impact assessment (Art. 27, Artificial Intelligence Act) and the Systemic risk assessment (Art. 34, Digital Services Act), could have the effect, among others, of 'scaling down' the scope of the right to data protection.

References

AEPD (2020a) IoT (I): what is IoT and which risks does it entail

AEPD (2020b) Data protection and security. Prensa y Comun

Albrecht JP (2016) How the GDPR will change the world. Eur Data Prot Law Rev 2:287–290

Alexy R (2003) Constitutional rights, balancing, and rationality. Ratio Juris 16:2

Article 29 Data Protection Working Party (2014) Statement on the Role of a Risk-Based Approach in Data Protection Legal Frameworks

Article 29 Data Protection Working Party (2017) Guidelines on Data Protection Impact Assessment (DPIA) and Determining Whether Processing Is "Likely to Result in a High Risk" for the Purposes of Regulation 2016/679

Bincoletto G (2021) Data protection by design in the E-health care sector, Luxembourg legal St. . . . Nomos

Centre for Information Policy Leadership (2016) Risk, high risk, risk assessments and data protection impact assessments under the GDPR

Chiara PG (2021) The balance between security, privacy and data protection in IoT data sharing: a critique to traditional 'Security&Privacy' surveys. Eur Data Prot Law Rev 7:18–30. https://doi.org/10.21552/EDPL/2021/1/6

Christofi A, Dewitte P, Ducuing C, Valcke P (2021) Erosion by standardisation: is ISO/IEC 29134: 2017 on privacy impact assessment up to (GDPR) standard? In: Research anthology on privatizing and securing data. IGI Global, pp 1790–1817

Clader A (2013) Nine steps to success: an ISO27001:2013 implementation overview, Second. IT Governance Publishing

Clifford D, Ausloos J (2018) Data protection and the role of fairness. Yearb Eur Law 37:130–187. https://doi.org/10.1093/yel/yey004

CNIL (2018a) PIA: Application to IoT Devices

CNIL (2018b) Privacy Impact Assessment (PIA) Knowledge Bases

CNIL (2018c) Privacy Impact Assessment (PIA) Methodology

CNIL (2018d) Privacy Impact Assessment (PIA) Templates

Cooter RD (1991) Economic theories of legal liability. J Econ Perspect 5:11–30

Danish Institute for Human Rights (2020) Human rights impact assessment: guidance and toolbox

Daskalova VI, Heldeweg MA (2019) Challenges for responsible certification in institutional context: the case of competition law enforcement in markets with certification. In: Rott P (ed) Certification – trust, accountability, liability. Springer, Cham

De Terwangne C (2020) Article 5. Principles relating to processing of personal data. In: Kuner C, Bygrave LA, Docksey C (eds) The EU general data protection regulation (GDPR). Oxford University Press, pp 309–320
Denardis L (2020) The internet in everything - freedom and security in a world with no off switch, 1st edn. Yale University Press, New Haven
Durante M (2021) Computational power: the impact of ICT on law, society and knowledge. Routledge
ENISA (2017) Handbook on security of personal data processing
Friedewald M, Schiering I, Martin N, Hallinan D (2022) Data protection impact assessments in practice: experiences from case studies. In: ESORICS 2021: computer security. ESORICS 2021 international workshops. Springer International Publishing, pp 424–443
Fuster GG, Van Brakel R, De Hert P (2022) Co-regulation and competitive advantage in the GDPR: data protection certification mechanisms, codes of conduct and data protection-by-design. In: González Fuster G, van Brakel R, De Hert P (eds) Research handbook on privacy and data protection law: values, norms and global politics. Edward Elgar Publishing, pp 402–432
Gellert R (2016) We have always managed risks in data protection law: understanding the similarities and differences between the rights-based and the risk-based approaches to data protection. Eur Data Prot Law Rev 2:481–492
Gellert R (2018) Understanding the notion of risk in the general data protection regulation. Comput Law Secur Rev 34:279–288. https://doi.org/10.1016/J.CLSR.2017.12.003
Gérardy M (2021) Nemo Censetur Ignorare Legem: the dilemma regarding the access to ISO standards referenced into EU law. REALawblog. https://realaw.blog/2021/11/23/nemo-censetur-ignorare-lege-the-dilemma-regarding-the-access-to-iso-standards-referenced-into-eu-law-by-marie-gerardy/>
Griffin R (2023) Public and private power in social media governance: multistakeholderism, the rule of law and democratic accountability. Transnatl Leg Theory 14:1
Hallinan D, Martin N (2020) Fundamental rights, the normative keystone of DPIA. Eur Data Prot Law Rev 6:178–193. https://doi.org/10.21552/edpl/2020/2/6
Hatto P (2010) Standards and standardization handbook. http://www.nanostair.eu-vri.eu/filehandler.ashx?file=12450
Kosta E (2020) Article 35 data protection impact assessment. In: Kuner C, Bygrave LA, Docksey C, Drechsler L (eds) The EU general data protection regulation (GDPR): a commentary. Oxford University Press, pp 665–680
Lachaud E (2020) ISO/IEC 27701 standard: threats and opportunities for GDPR certification. Eur Data Prot Law Rev 6:194–210. https://doi.org/10.21552/EDPL/2020/2/7
Lock T (2019a) Article 3 CFR: right to the integrity of the person. In: Kellerbauer M, Klamert M, Tomkin J (eds) The EU treaties and the charter of fundamental rights. Oxford University Press, New York, pp 2103–2104
Lock T (2019b) Article 10 CFR: freedom of thought, conscience and religion. In: Kellerbauer M, Klamert M, Tomkin J (eds) The EU treaties and the charter of fundamental rights. Oxford University Press, pp 2129–2131
Lock T (2019c) Article 14 CFR: right to education. In: Kellerbauer M, Klamert M, Tomkin J (eds) The EU treaties and the charter of fundamental rights. Oxford University Press, pp 2142–2144
Mantelero A (2019) Comment to articles 35 and 36. In: Cole MD, Boehm F (eds) *GDPR commentary*. Edward Elgar Publishing, Forthcoming, available at: https://papers.ssrn.com/sol3/papers.cfm?abstract_id=3362747
Mantelero A (2021) The future of data protection: gold standard vs. global standard. Comput Law Secur Rev 40:105500. https://doi.org/10.1016/J.CLSR.2020.105500
Mantelero A (2022) Beyond data: human rights, ethical and social impact assessment in AI. Springer
Nieles M et al (2017) An introduction to information security. NIST Special Publication 800-12

NIST (2015) NISTIR 8074 - Supplemental Information for the Interagency Report on Strategic U.S. Government Engagement in International Standardization to Achieve U.S. Objectives for Cybersecurity

Pagallo U, Casanovas P, Madelin R (2019) The middle-out approach: assessing models of legal governance in data protection, artificial intelligence, and the web of data. Theory Pract Legis 7: 1–25. https://doi.org/10.1080/20508840.2019.1664543

Papakonstantinou V (2022) Cybersecurity as praxis and as a state: the EU law path towards acknowledgement of a new right to cybersecurity? Comput Law Secur Rev 44. https://doi.org/10.1016/J.CLSR.2022.105653

Purtova N (2018) The law of everything. Broad concept of personal data and future of EU data protection law. Law Innov Technol 10:40–81. https://doi.org/10.1080/17579961.2018.1452176

Quelle C (2018) Enhancing compliance under the general data protection regulation: the risky upshot of the accountability- and risk-based approach. Eur J Risk Regul 9:502–526. https://doi.org/10.1017/err.2018.47

Quesada Rodriguez A et al. (2018) D2.3 ANASTACIA: Privacy Risk Modelling and Contingency Initial Report

Sampaio JS (2019) Proportionality: measuring impacts on fundamental rights. In: Seller M, Kriste S (eds) Encyclopedia of the philosophy of law and social philosophy. Springer

Sion L et al (2020) DPMF: a Modeling framework for data protection by design. Int J Concept Model 15:1–53. https://doi.org/10.18417/emisa.15.10

Tamò-Larrieux A (2018) Designing for privacy and its legal framework: data protection by design and default for the internet of things. Springer

Watkins SG (2013) An Introduction to Information Security and ISO27001:2013, A Pocket Guide, Second. IT Governance Publishing

Wavestone - CEPS - CARSA - ICF (2021) Study on the Need of Cybersecurity Requirements for ICT Products - No. 2020-0715: Final Study Report

Chapter 7
The Path Ahead

This work started with several open questions. To begin with, efforts towards a shared definition of 'Internet of Things' are still on-going. Also, from a theoretical and definitional standpoint, further reflections are still needed to map out the exact boundaries of the concepts of cybersecurity, safety and privacy—and the underlying relationships between them—in light of the ubiquitous IoT.

Having regard to cybersecurity and safety in particular, given that 'EU cybersecurity law' is still in its infancy, enforceable cybersecurity rules need to be strengthened. Against the background of the fast-evolving European cybersecurity regulatory framework—including the revision of the NIS Directive and several pieces of product safety legislation and the proposal for a Cyber Resilience Act (CRA), coherence within the EU cybersecurity *acquis* shall be ensured, especially in view of isolated moves forwarded by Member States to respond to the fast-paced digital threat landscape.[1]

On the other hand, EU privacy and data protection laws should also be (re-) assessed to investigate whether they are (still) up to the challenges brought about by the structural data and metadata processing of highly hyper-connected environments. While awaiting the adoption of the CRA, a common EU-wide approach to address cybersecurity risks in IoT is still missing. Related to that, existing data protection risk assessment models do not encompass the full breadth and depth of the standard set by the GDPR, in particular, taking into account the requirement to assess the risks to the rights and freedoms of data subjects enshrined in Art. 35(7)(c) GDPR.

The added value of this book lies in the critical analysis of the values underpinning the EU legal frameworks on *security and privacy*, against the backdrop of the IoT paradigm shift blurring the boundaries between the digital and the physical dimensions. By introducing the current technical landscape (Chap. 2) and exploring the interwoven dimension of cybersecurity and privacy (Chap. 3), the book aimed to (i) bridge the communication gap between technical and legal communities;

[1] Schmitz-Berndt and Cole (2022).

P. G. Chiara, *The Internet of Things and EU Law*, Issues in Privacy and Data Protection 67, https://doi.org/10.1007/978-3-031-67663-5_7

(ii) address the relevant regulatory gaps in EU 'security and privacy' legal frameworks vis-à-vis the challenges brought about by the IoT; (iii) design a holistic risk assessment methodology that brings together traditional information security frameworks and the GDPR rights-based approach.

With this in mind, Chap. 2 provided a working definition and architecture taxonomy of the 'Internet of Things' and 'resource-constrained devices', coupled with a threat landscape where specific attacks are linked to specific layers of the IoT architecture taxonomy. Chapter 3 laid down the theoretical foundations for an interdisciplinary approach and a holistic vision of cybersecurity, safety and privacy justified by the 'IoT revolution' through the so-called *infraethical* perspective. Cybersecurity, conceived as an *instrumental* value, can *facilitate* or *hinder* the enjoyment of fundamental values, such as fundamental rights and personal safety, depending on how different types of cybersecurity policies and technical controls have been designed and set up.

Chapter 4 investigated whether and to what extent the fast-evolving European cybersecurity regulatory framework addresses the security challenges brought about by the IoT by allocating legal responsibilities to the right parties. The critical analysis of the EU cybersecurity *acquis,* which does not target IoT products specifically and comprehensively, culminated with an overview of the CRA. This horizontal legislation on cybersecurity for products with digital elements, building on the principles and structures of the NLF, is the last piece of the jigsaw, ensuring coherence in the EU legal frameworks regulating (connected) products cybersecurity.

Chapters 5 and 6, on the other hand, focused on 'privacy' understood by proxy to include EU data protection. In particular, Chap. 5 addressed three legal challenges brought about by the ubiquitous IoT data and metadata processing to EU privacy and data protection legal frameworks i.e., the ePrivacy Directive and the GDPR. In the same vein as Chap. 4, the critical analysis came to the conclusion that European privacy laws are incomplete without a reform of the ePrivacy Directive.

Chapter 6 cast light on the risk management tool enshrined in EU data protection law, or rather, the Data Protection Impact Assessment (DPIA). After concluding that existing DPIA models (even those designed specifically for IoT devices) are too narrowly focused on assessing only risks to the right to privacy—without fulfilling the requirement to manage 'the risks to the rights and freedoms', an original DPIA methodology for connected devices was proposed, building on the CNIL model.

Related to that, the above reading of Article 35—in conjunction with Art. 1(2) GDPR—exposes the other face of EU data protection law. In the absence of more suitable legal tools, the GDPR has inevitably taken on the somewhat uncomfortable role of fundamental rights' 'protector' in tackling the normative (legal, ethical and societal) issues of the 'digital revolution'. In this regard, the AI Act's Fundamental Rights Impact Assessment[2] can be seen as a more comprehensive legal answer to the challenges in terms of fundamental rights raised by digital technologies

[2]Mantelero (2024).

(in particular artificial intelligence) that *inter alia* would properly set data protection in place in the broader context of EU fundamental rights.

Whereas legal research at the intersection of the IoT and privacy & data protection has been flourishing in the recent years,[3] future research should continue to explore technical and organisational measures with a view to strengthening individuals' cybersecurity and upholding the rights to privacy and data protection vis-à-vis an increasingly connected and 'decentralised' society.

More specifically, future legal research should continue developing the theoretical foundations underlying the search for autonomy of 'EU cybersecurity law', which has been significantly shaped by the EU Commission since 2013 with the first EU Cybersecurity Strategy. This book (in particular, Chap. 4) critically analysed whether recent developments in this policy area contribute to ensure a coherent legal framework thereby closing relevant regulatory gaps as well as addressing market failures.

Thus, the model of governance of EU cybersecurity evolved from organisational and technical legislation to a more comprehensive multi-level and multi-stakeholder regulatory approach. Hence, the cybersecurity field in EU law is a privileged means to study the increasingly frequent adoption of hybrid governance strategies and regulatory approaches in 'EU digital law'.[4] As shown, those approaches are not mutually exclusive.

On the one hand, with regard to product (safety &) security, several pieces of sectoral legislation (vertical approach) have been revised to include specifically cybersecurity essential requirements. At the same time, the Commission proposed in 2022 the Cyber Resilience Act introducing horizontal cybersecurity rules for products with digital elements. On the other hand, traditional product safety regulatory approaches (i.e., the NLF) have been hybridized with rights-based approaches. This is the case of the CRA insofar as products with digital elements—even if compliant with the Regulation—pose a risk to fundamental rights.[5] Similarly, the AI Act creates a synthesis between the product-safety approach (e.g., products' requirements; reliance on harmonised technical standards; conformity assessment procedures) and rights-based approach (e.g., risk management systems that providers of high-risk AI system have to put in place shall identify and analyse known and foreseeable risks that such systems can pose to fundamental rights; fundamental rights impact assessment; etc.).[6]

Another governance trend that can be observed in the development of EU cybersecurity law is the institutionalisation of the adoption of 'all-hazard' approaches. The implications are twofold. Cybersecurity technical, organisational and procedural measures not only aim to cover traditional digital information

[3]Noto La Diega (2023), p. 274. See also Ioannidou and Sklavos (2021), Urquhart et al. (2019), Tanczer et al. (2017), Siegel (2020), Wachter (2018).

[4]Bygrave (2024), p. 10.

[5]Cyber Resilience Act, recital 58, 59; Article 45.

[6]Evas (2024), p. 100.

security threats: they shall also take into account the physical environment in which network and information systems are located with a view to ensuring a 'holistic' protection.[7] Against the background of the relationship between the physical security and cybersecurity, it is not surprising that the EU legislator envisaged the NIS2 Directive and the CER Directive, which lays down measures to achieve physical resilience of critical entities, to be implemented in a coherent and complementary manner.[8]

The second implication concerns the inclusion of non-technical factors as part of cybersecurity risk management measures. In the context of the NIS2, potential non-technical risk factors[9] are taken into account in the coordinated risk assessments of critical supply-chain risks carried out by the (NIS) Cooperation Group.[10] The same factors are also relevant in the context of the CRA enforcement. Thus, when determining the significance of a cybersecurity risk within the meaning of the CRA, "the Commission and the market surveillance authorities should also consider non-technical risk factors, in particular those established as a result of Union level coordinated security risk assessments of critical supply chains in accordance with Article 22 of Directive (EU) 2022/2555".[11]

The 2020 Cybersecurity Strategy advocates for and promotes structured exchanges and cooperation between stakeholders, including the private sector, academia and civil society.[12] Within the scope of cybersecurity as a shared responsibility (see Chap. 3), the public sector enacted, on the one hand, legal frameworks to facilitate the development of standards and certification (Cybersecurity Act) and, on the other hand, legislation to enhance the level of security vis-à-vis entities that are essential to the functioning of our societies (NIS2 Directive) and economic operators involved in the manufacturing of products (Cyber Resilience Act). At the same time, "the private sector bears the responsibility of designing robust systems, developing and improving methods to foster robustness of the services and products that they offer, and collaborating with the public sector for the controlling and testing mechanisms".[13] In this regard, traditional top-down governance models prove not to be effective in a scenario where internet's infrastructure is mostly privately owned and digital services are often offered by private providers.[14] Arguably, one of the reasons for the 'success' achieved by the GDPR was definitely its reliance on co-regulative

---

[7] Directive (EU) 2555/2022, recital 79; Article 21(2).

[8] Directive (EU) 2555/2022, recital 30; Directive (EU) 2557/2022, recital 9, 13, 24; Article 1(2).

[9] Directive (EU) 2555/2022, recital 90: these risk factors include "undue influence by a third country on suppliers and service providers, in particular in the case of alternative models of governance, include concealed vulnerabilities or backdoors and potential systemic supply disruptions, in particular in the case of technological lock-in or provider dependency".

[10] Directive (EU) 2555/2022, Article 22.

[11] Cyber Resilience Act, recital 33g; Article 43(1a).

[12] European Commission and the High Representatitve of the Union for Foreign Affairs and Security Policy (2020), p. 23.

[13] Taddeo (2019), p. 351.

[14] European Commission (2013), p. 2; Council of the European Union (2024), p. 5.

mechanisms.[15] Security measures and processes once left exclusively to the public sector are increasingly dependent on private mechanisms.

Related to that, a further governance trend that can be observed in general in EU digital policies pertains to the increasing use of flexible, risk-based 'abstract' legal standards such as 'appropriate and proportionate technical and organisational measures' (TOMs)[16] and 'state of the art'. The latter being a particularly blurred market-driven dynamic concept[17]: "use of this phrase necessitates regular revisiting of security practices in light of changing extra-legal perceptions as to which technical and organisational standards provide optimal security".[18]

On 17 October 2022, Member States approved Council conclusions with a view to strengthening the security of ICT supply chains.[19] Against the background of future highly likely supply chain cyberattacks (see Chap. 2), the Council acknowledges the need to maximise and streamline the use of existing EU instruments and approaches to achieve these objectives as well as the need to continually adapt to the changing cyber threat landscape by introducing additional suitable measures and mechanisms.[20]

Beside the need to align existing and forthcoming supply chain cybersecurity requirements under different legislative instruments (i.e., Cybersecurity Act, NIS2 and Cyber Resilience Act), as addressed in Chap. 4, particular emphasis is placed on public procurement: the Commission is invited by the Council to develop methodological guidelines in order to encourage the contracting authorities to place appropriate focus on the cybersecurity practices of tenderers and their subcontractors, and assess or revise—if needed—relevant public procurement legislation.[21]

Drawing on the lessons from the consequences of strategic dependencies of the EU single market on foreign-country resources, from fossil fuels to rare earths (the latter in particular urged EU action in the form of an European Chips Act[22] and an European Critical Raw Materials Act[23]), as well as from the impacts of the disruptions in supply chains during the COVID-19 pandemic, efforts shall be made to

[15] Pagallo et al. (2019).

[16] See Regulation (EU) 2016/679, Arts. 24(1), 25(1), 32; Directive 2002/58/EC, Art. 4; Directive (EU) 2555/2022, Art. 21; Directive (EU) 2018/1972, Art. 40; Directive (EU) 2557/2022, Art. 13; Regulation (EU) 2554/2022, Arts. 6(8); 9; 11; 16; 24 [no explicit mention to 'technical and organisational measures'].

[17] Porcedda (2023), pp. 146 and ff.

[18] Bygrave (2024), p. 10.

[19] Council of the European Union (2022).

[20] Ibid., p. 6.

[21] Ibid., p. 7.

[22] Regulation (EU) 2023/1781 of the European Parliament and of the Council of 13 September 2023 establishing a framework of measures for strengthening Europe's semiconductor ecosystem and amending Regulation (EU) 2021/694 (Chips Act).

[23] Regulation (EU) 2024/1252 of the European Parliament and of the Council of 11 April 2024 establishing a framework for ensuring a secure and sustainable supply of critical raw materials and amending Regulations (EU) No 168/2013, (EU) 2018/858, (EU) 2018/1724 and (EU) 2019/1020.

avoid unwanted strategic external dependencies in relation to ICT products and services which, eventually, form part of the IoT.

Moreover, the 2020 Cybersecurity Strategy, and the legislative initiatives that followed, more boldly highlighted how the EU intends to regulate cybersecurity across the Digital Single Market. Cybersecurity however is not included as a policy field in the EU Treaties.[24] And the predominant use of Art. 114 TFUE as a legal basis for the EU legal acts on cybersecurity testifies the absence of an autonomous legal ground.[25] The EU Commission has thus progressively built on the market rationale its competence to legislate in this field.[26] Thus, the EU does not have *per se* an explicit competence to enact legislation in the cybersecurity field pursuant to the principle of conferral as spelled out in Art. 5 TFUE.[27]

Against this background, several scholars have started to debate on the possibility of acknowledging a new fundamental right to cybersecurity in EU law[28] with a view to upholding individuals' expectation to enjoy a secure digital life and, subordinately, granting EU secondary legislation an autonomous legal basis, thereby following a similar path of EU data protection law.[29] Yet, since fundamental rights do not establish competences,[30] a Treaty modification however intricate this might be,[31] appears therefore necessary to protect cybersecurity on the highest level, notwithstanding any allegedly 'parent right'[32] in the off-line sphere, and to give EU mandate to regulate a field which is progressively at odds with the only internal market legal basis.

In particular, taking into account the seminal article by Papakonstantinou—who first attempted to formally lay down a theoretical framework to introduce such new right in EU law, this book contributed to the on-going discussion from a twofold perspective.

Without dwelling on the distinction between *cybersecurity-as-praxis* and *cybersecurity-as-a-state*, used by Papakonstantinou as proxies for developing a doctrine for the establishment of this new fundamental right, here it is enough to map out relevant takeaways from this book to some corollaries of the legal challenges raised by the theory for a right to cybersecurity.

In particular, the first challenge hinges on the relationship between *cybersecurity* and *security*, notably, whether the former could be subsumed under the latter. This leads to one of the crucial issues of this theory, that is, whether an amendment to the

[24] Odermatt (2018), p. 359.

[25] Brandão and Camisão (2022).

[26] Schmitz-Berndt and Cole (2022).

[27] Schütze (2015).

[28] Papakonstantinou (2022), Chiara (2024). On a comparative note see: Shackelford (2019), Kilovaty (2020).

[29] Fuster (2014), p. 166; van der Sloot (2017), pp. 12–19.

[30] Treaty on European Union, Article 6(1); see also Lock (2019), p. 82.

[31] Jakab and Kirchmair (2022), p. 11; Closa (2018).

[32] Dror-Shpoliansky and Shany (2021), p. 1256.

existing general right to security,[33] or an extensive interpretation thereby extending its traditional application to the digital sphere,[34] would not be enough to encompass the legal challenges that a right to cybersecurity aims to solve. The second legal challenge entails the actual legal measures that would implement a new right to cybersecurity.

Having regard to the first challenge, Papakonstantinou concludes that the concept of cybersecurity and security differ, "because security includes real-world circumstances, protecting against real-world threats, while cybersecurity refers to the digital realm, protecting from cyber threats".[35] More interesting is what follows. "The two set of threats do not necessarily coincide. While a time may well be imagined that the real and the digital converge, until such time cybersecurity and security, although sharing the same linguistic root and interpretational difficulties, should be treated as two different concepts and rights, each to be assessed by its own merit".[36]

In this regard, Chap. 3 attempted to shed some light on this entanglement. IoT hyper-interconnectedness has been conceived throughout this book as a game-changer. Cybersecurity, security and safety are intertwined more than ever before, as the IoT ultimately blurs the boundaries between the *digital* and the *physical* dimensions. As seen, our hyperconnected world faces risks and threats not only affecting the network and information systems underlying digital markets & society. There is more at stake. Cyberattacks could also infringe individuals' fundamental rights, impair physical safety[37] and have critical consequences for a society as a whole (e.g., large-scale incidents to critical infrastructure).

Against the conclusion that the 'general right to security' would be enough to encompass also such issues, it can be argued on the other hand that the above-mentioned paradigm shift (brought about *inter alia* by the IoT) would rather call for introducing a new right to cybersecurity in new EU law, provided that "an extensive interpretation of Art. 6 CFR on security to include cybersecurity, from a strictly legal standpoint, seems not a viable path".[38] By moving on the analysis of the normative (i.e., legal, ethical and societal, see Chap. 3) and technical challenges (e.g., in terms of threats, see Chap. 2) facing cybersecurity and security, it would be clear that the legal means traditionally adopted in the physical dimension to safeguard the

[33] EU Charter of Fundamental Rights, Article 6: "everyone has the right to liberty and security of person".

[34] Thereby aligning with the so-called 'normative equivalence paradigm' which predicates that traditional rights can sufficiently cope with the challenges brought about by the digital sphere: Cocito and De Hert (2023), La Rue (2011), Dror-Shpoliansky and Shany (2021), p. 1252.

[35] Papakonstantinou (2022), p. 7.

[36] Ibid., pp. 7–8.

[37] 'Internet of Medical Things' (IoMT) is a prominent example of how cybersecurity is progressively taking into account safety considerations as cybersecurity technologies must ensure the integrity of life against cyber (or digital) attacks.

[38] Chiara (2024), p. 3. "The rights in Article 6 EU CFR "are the rights guaranteed by Article 5 of the ECHR [. . .] and they have the same scope". And art. 5 ECHR—as consistently interpreted by the ECtHR—cannot at present stage be interpreted to include cybersecurity".

interests' protected by 'security' do not translate in the digital sphere. EU secondary law confirms this line of reasoning. Chapter 4 highlighted how the recent legislative developments in the field of cybersecurity separate the issues pertaining to physical and cyber- security.[39]

Thc second legal challenge hinges on examining whether existing and proposed legislation grants remedies to individuals if EU cybersecurity law's addressees infringe the legal duties they shall comply with. Without dwelling on the subject-matter, scope, recipients and addresses of such a new right too extensively, for it exceeds the scope of this Chapter, a brief discussion of the actual content of this right is any case necessary and preliminary to how such a new right could be implemented.

I argued elsewhere that the European Declaration on Digital Rights and Principles for the Digital Decade (hereinafter, the Declaration),[40] in particular, taking into account the 16th principle concerning a 'protected, safe and secure digital environment'[41] could be used as a source of inspiration for shaping this new fundamental right.[42] But there are some caveats. First, recipients of a new right to cybersecurity shall be individuals, whereas the 16th principle extends to businesses and public institutions that are potentially affected by cybersecurity risks as well. Second, a new right to cybersecurity shall not *directly* cover the technological assets used by individuals nor it should serve another right (e.g., the fundamental right to privacy: 'privacy-protective'). Rather, it should leave to secondary law how to implement a right for individuals to enjoy a 'secure digital life' through appropriate and proportionate regulatory measures. Third, a new right to cybersecurity shall only guarantee security by design and by default goals, hence cybersecurity-as-robustness, whereas other public goods pertaining (or intersecting with) to the cybersecurity domain as well, such as national security, shall not be covered by such a new right.

Related to that, Chap. 3 clearly shows that both the NIS Directive (and the NIS2 likewise) and the Cybersecurity Act do not afford any rights to individuals, for they are primarily based on a 'market rationale' and thus not on directly protecting natural persons. Moreover, the Cyber Resilience Act is also based on Art. 114 TFEU. Like

[39] As mentioned above, Directive (EU) 2022/2557 (CER) concerns the resilience of critical entities in terms of physical security. Therefore, it does not cover cybersecurity, as it is already adequately addressed by Directive (EU) 2022/2555 (NIS2). At the same time, the CER Directive acknowledges the importance of cybersecurity for the resilience of critical entities and the complementary relationship between physical security and cybersecurity (Recitals 9 and 24 CER).

[40] Joint Declaration of the European Parliament, the Council and the European Commission, European Declaration on Digital Rights and Principles for the Digital Decade (2023/C 23/01).

[41] "Everyone should have access to digital technologies, products and services that are by design safe, secure, and privacy-protective, resulting in a high level of confidentiality, integrity, availability and authenticity of the information processed".

[42] Chiara (2024).

other legal instruments in EU cybersecurity legislation, the CRA does not provide any remedies to individuals.[43]

All in all, the policy benchmarks particularising the principle seems comprehensive enough in terms of the challenges that a right to cybersecurity will face. Thus, the Declaration lists three political commitments accompanying the 16th principle: "a) taking further measures to promote the traceability of products and make sure only products which are safe and compliant with EU legislation are offered on the Digital Single Market [emphasis added]; b) protecting the interests of people, businesses and public institutions against cybersecurity risks and cybercrime including data breaches and identity theft or manipulation. This includes cybersecurity requirements for connected products placed on the single market [emphasis added]; c) countering and holding accountable those that seek to undermine, within the EU, security online and the integrity of the digital environment or that promote violence and hatred through digital means".

Having regard to the first and second commitments in particular, a new right to cybersecurity can already be implemented—insofar as product (cyber)security is concerned—by the incoming Cyber Resilience Act. On the other hand, insofar as services' cybersecurity is concerned, Directive (EU) 2022/2555 (NIS2) regulates the vast majority of digital services offered in the EU.

From a law-making perspective, the right to cybersecurity may be introduced in the Cyber Resilience Act and/or in the NIS2 *via* targeted amendments. Another option would be amending (again[44]) the Cybersecurity Act.[45] "It is not necessary first for a new right to be spelled out in the Treaties, in order for secondary legislation to further detail its particulars. As personal data protection has demonstrated, a Directive (or, a Regulation, for example the EU Cybersecurity Act) could well grant to Europeans rights and obligations akin to a right, before a right per se finds its way into the Treaties".[46]

This book showed that the increasingly 'physical', or analogical, relevance of the digital threat landscape, driven *inter alia* by the IoT, calls for action as individuals' legitimate expectation to enjoy a 'secure digital life' is not *expressively* and *comprehensively* safeguarded by any EU fundamental right. Furthermore, recent policy initiatives clearly reveal that cybersecurity pose normative challenges (legal, ethical and societal) going far beyond market-related obstacles.

A new fundamental right to cybersecurity would best protect individuals' (on-) life. Moreover, a Treaty revision with a view to safeguarding cybersecurity at the

[43] BEUC (2022), p. 12. Without this, consumers that have suffered damage caused by the infringements of relevant CRA cybersecurity obligations by economic operators would have to resort to national torts and product liability legal frameworks e.g., the Italian consumer code, see Vecchi and Turra (2020).

[44] European Commission (2023).

[45] Papakonstantinou (2022), p. 13.

[46] Ibid., p. 13.

highest level in EU law, drawing lessons from data protection law,[47] would guide the fast-growing regulatory landscape and support the emergence of the new policy field of EU cybersecurity law. Although introducing a new fundamental right in EU law is not straightforward, this Chapter tried to illustrate how the EU has already taken steps in this direction.

References

BEUC (2022) Cyber Resilience Act: Cybersecurity of Digital Products and Ancillary Services - BEUC response to public consultation. https://www.beuc.eu/sites/default/files/publications/beuc-x-2022-051_cyber_resilience_act_public_consultation_beuc_position_paper.pdf

Brandão AP, Camisão I (2022) Playing the market card: the commission's strategy to shape EU cybersecurity policy. J Common Mark Stud 60:1335

Bygrave LA (2024) The emergence of EU cybersecurity law: a tale of lemons, angst, turf, surf and grey boxes. University of Oslo Faculty of Law Legal Studies Research Paper Series No. 2024-04. https://papers.ssrn.com/sol3/papers.cfm?abstract_id=4714393

Chiara (2024) Towards a right to cybersecurity in EU law? The challenges ahead. Comput Law Secur Rev 53:105961

Closa C (2018) The politics of ratification of EU treaties. Routledge

Cocito C, De Hert P (2023) The transformative nature of the EU declaration on digital rights and principles: replacing the old paradigm (normative equivalency of rights). Comput Law Secur Rev 50:3

Council of the European Union (2024) Council Conclusions on the Future of Cybersecurity: implement and protect together. 9252/24. https://data.consilium.europa.eu/doc/document/ST-10133-2024-INIT/en/pdf

Dror-Shpoliansky D, Shany Y (2021) It's the end of the (offline) world as we know it: from human rights to digital human rights-a proposed typology. Eur J Int Law 32:1249

European Commission (2023) Proposal for a REGULATION OF THE EUROPEAN PARLIAMENT AND OF THE COUNCIL amending Regulation (EU) 2019/881 as regards managed security services. COM(2023) 208

European Commission and the High Representatitve of the Union for Foreign Affairs and Security Policy (2020) Joint Communication to the European Parliament and the Council: The EU's Cybersecurity Strategy for the Digital Decade. JOIN(2020) 18 final

Evas T (2024) The EU artificial intelligence act: advancing innovation for trustworthy AI. AIRe - J AI Law Regulat 1:1

Fuster GG (2014) The emergence of personal data protection as a fundamental right of the EU. Springer International Publishing

Ioannidou I, Sklavos N (2021) On general data protection Regulation vulnerabilities and privacy issues, for wearable devices and fitness tracking applications. Cryptography 5:29

Jakab A, Kirchmair L (2022) Two ways of completing the European fundamental rights union: amendment to vs. reinterpretation of article 51 of the EU charter of fundamental rights. Cambridge Yearb Eur Leg Stud 23:1

Kilovaty I (2020) An extraterritorial human right to cybersecurity. Notre Dame J Int Comp Law 10: 35

La Rue F (2011) Report of the Special Rapporteur on the promotion and protection of the right to freedom of opinion and expression. A/HRC/17/27

[47] van der Sloot (2017), p. 11.

Lock T (2019) Article 6 TEU. In: Kellerbauer M, Klamert M, Tomkin J (eds) The EU treaties and the charter of fundamental rights: a commentary. Oxford Academic
Mantelero A (2024) The Fundamental Rights Impact Assessment (FRIA) in the AI Act: roots, legal obligations and key elements for a model template. SSRN. https://papers.ssrn.com/sol3/papers.cfm?abstract_id=4782126
Noto la Diega G (2023) Internet of things and the law: legal strategies for consumer-centric smart technologies. Routledge, Taylor and Francis Inc., Oxon
Odermatt J (2018) The European Union as a cybersecurity actor. In: Blockmans S, Koutrakos P (eds) Research handbook on EU common foreign and security policy. Edward Elgar Publishing
Pagallo U et al (2019) The middle-out approach: assessing models of legal governance in data protection, artificial intelligence, and the web of data. Theory Pract Legisl 7:1
Papakonstantinou V (2022) Cybersecurity as praxis and as a state: the EU law path towards acknowledgement of a new right to cybersecurity? Comput Law Secur Rev 44:105653
Porcedda MG (2023) Cybersecurity, privacy and data protection in EU law. A law, policy and technology analysis. Hart Publishing
Schmitz-Berndt S, Cole MD (2022) Towards an efficient and coherent regulatory framework on cybersecurity in the EU: the proposals for a NIS 2.0 directive and a cyber resilience act. Appl Cybersecurity Inter Gov 1:1
Schütze R (2015) EU competences: existence and exercise. In: Chalmers D, Arnull A (eds) The Oxford handbook of European Union law. Oxford Academic
Shackelford S (2019) Should cybersecurity be a human right? Exploring the 'shared responsibility' of cyber peace. Stanf J Int Law 55:2
Siegel J (2020) When the internet of things flounders: looking into GDPR-Esque security standards for IoT devices in the United States from the consumers' perspective. J High Technol Law 20:1
Taddeo M, (2019) "Is Cybersecurity a Public Good?" Minds and Machines, Vol. 29, pp. 349–354
Tanczer L et al (2017) IoT and its implications for informed consent - PETRAS IoT hub, STEaPP. UCL, London. https://discovery.ucl.ac.uk/id/eprint/10050101/1/IoTandConsent_PM_Workshop_Report-11Comp.pdf
Urquhart L et al (2019) Demonstrably doing accountability in the internet of things. Int J Law Inform Technol 27:1
van der Sloot B (2017) Legal fundamentalism: is data protection really a fundamental right? In: Leenes R et al (eds) Data protection and privacy: (in)visibilities and infrastructures. Springer
Vecchi D, Turra M (2020) Italy. In: Varner C, Kitchens M (eds) The product Regulation and liability review. Law Business Research Ltd, London
Wachter S (2018) Normative challenges of identification in the internet of things: privacy, profiling, discrimination, and the GDPR. Comput Law Secur Rev 34:3